THE MERTON ANNUAL

Studies in Culture, Spirituality, and Social Concerns

Volume 20	2007

Edited by

Victor A. Kramer

Book Reviews Coordinated by

Glenn Crider

THE MERTON ANNUAL
Studies in Culture, Spirituality, and Social Concerns

THE MERTON ANNUAL publishes articles about Thomas Merton and about related matters of major concern to his life and work. Its purpose is to enhance Merton's reputation as a writer and monk, to continue to develop his message for our times, and to provide a regular outlet for substantial Merton-related scholarship. *THE MERTON ANNUAL* includes as regular features reviews, review-essays, a bibliographic survey, interviews, and first appearances of unpublished, or obscurely published Merton materials, photographs, and art. Essays about related literary and spiritual matters will also be considered. Manuscripts and books for review may be sent to the editor.

EDITOR

Victor A. Kramer
University Catholic Center for Emory
1753 North Decatur Road
Atlanta GA 30307
Email: victorak@bellsouth.net

PRODUCTION MANAGER

Glenn Crider
University Catholic Center for Emory
1753 North Decatur Road
Atlanta GA 30307
Email: wcrider@emory.edu

Grateful acknowledgement is expressed to The Merton Legacy Trust for permission to print the manuscript edited by Br. Daniel Carrere, O.C.S.O., "Prayer and Identity." Cover artwork is a drawing by Thomas Merton. Used with permission of the Merton Legacy Trust and the Thomas Merton Center at Bellarmine University.

PUBLISHED BY:
Fons Vitae
49 Mockingbird Valley Drive
Louisville KY 40207
502.897.3641
Email: Fonsvitaeky@aol.com
http://www.fonsvitae.com

SPONSORED BY:
International Thomas Merton Society
Thomas Merton Center
Bellarmine University
2001 Newburg Road
Louisville KY 40205
502.452.8187 or 8177
Email: merton@bellarmine.edu
http://www.merton.org/ITMS/

Further details about membership and subscribing to *The Merton Seasonal* and *The Merton Annual* are available at http://www.merton.org/ITMS/membership.htm or by contacting the Thomas Merton Center at the above address.

For members of the International Thomas Merton Society, available for $15.00, plus shipping and handling. Individual copies are available through bookstores and direclty from the publisher for $19.95. Institutions $39.95. *Copyright*: All rights reserved.

Library of Congress Control Number: 2008922429

ISBN 1-891785-14-1

The Merton Annual

Volume 20	2007

Book Reviews

To Pray Contemplatively is to Work Mysteriously toward the Center

Victor A. Kramer

I

Prayer deals with a variety of experience which science can never easily touch, for science always deals with some type of reductionism which allows it to communicate with itself on its own terms. Mature prayer and ultimately contemplative prayer confronts the knowledge of unknowability and in a surrender to the mystery of the gift of a universe given in myriads of changing ways celebrates this in wonder and awe. Yet we must come to learn this almost intuitively. This is a Truth which the prophets of old, the Church in its wisdom, and our best poets (and I would include Thomas Merton) sense and reveal over and over. As E. Glenn Hinson makes clear in his article, included in this book, the contemplative tradition makes us ready for prayer.

In a way praying might best be compared to the slow perfection of the marriage relationship. In prayer, especially as younger persons, we begin with simple requests and desires. As we mature we learn that the possibilities for praying will change as our needs, desires, hopes, frustrations, ambitions, disappointments, strengths, and challenges change. Our "longing for God" remains always at the core while the actions in which we are involved differ. Nonetheless everything done by any seeker toward unification with God is done because of a fundamental, unshakeable and universal search for wholeness.

As we approach the topic of prayer and its centrality within the thinking and living of Thomas Merton, a somewhat surprising link comes to mind and takes my thought back to many years of teaching World Literature, especially to sophomores in required classes. In those classes we would begin with familiar readings from the Old Testament and then go on to Homer's *The Odyssey*. What followed then was a study of myriads of examples of epic and lyric expressions about wanderers, aware perhaps of their calls from God, while frequently these literary figures were only able to hear a call from gods, or God, somewhat vaguely. For my students, however, the love of life and place always seemed to take on special meaning.

Homer's Odysseus never doubts his enduring love for his Penélopê and the structure of this epic story, circle-by-circle moving back to Ithaka, brings the hero home. His sense of quest and honor, his seeking of home and household (a symbol, I am sure, of Western man's wandering away from wholeness) is at the center of this ur-story and this motif remains fundamental for so much of our Western literature. In Wendell Berry's essay "The Body and the Earth," he stresses that our present individualistic disruption and separation from what *only* will make us whole has roots in our cultural disrespect for the land and thus suggests our need for place, and above all need for home. In moving testimony to the faithfulness of Odysseus, Berry demonstrates how the notion of Homer's narrative inevitably brings that wandering husband home:

> ... Odysseus's journey from the cave of Kalypso to the bed of Penélopê, has revealed a structure that is at once geographical and moral. This structure may be graphed as a series of diminishing circles centered on one of the posts of the marriage bed. Odysseus makes his way from the periphery toward that center. ...Odysseus makes his way across a succession of boundaries, enclosed and enclosing, with the concentricity of a blossom around its pistil, a human pattern resembling a pattern of nature. He comes to his island, to his own lands, to his town, to this household and house, to his bedroom, to his bed. As he moves toward this center he moves also through a series of recognitions, tests of identity and devotion. By these, his homecoming becomes at the same time a restoration of order.[1]

Berry's insights can, I think, be used analogously to approach what Merton, systematically, yet inevitably and intuitively, figured out and pondered about humankind's need for wilderness, and simultaneously, our longing for order and for honest prayer which again and again slowly reunites us with our Creator.

Berry's point about Odysseus is that in the renewal of the marriage of Ulysses and Penélopê the restoration of order in Odysseus' kingdom is also advanced. Odysseus's marriage, therefore, was not just some legal arrangement. Rather it is the very confirmation of the essential bond between husband and wife, their immediate community and also all the resources of life which made them one with their culture and indeed their hidden Creator. In this return of Odysseus we see, says Berry, "a complete marriage and a complex fidelity" (p. 122). That seeking of wholeness, I now see, is similar to what all must seek in prayer.

Something similar to this type of total dedication and conviction must also inform the breast of all persons who truly seek God by means of prayer. There is a center, a wholeness, a place where unity is sought, and which must be honored. Thus, when Terrence Kardong goes back, within the essay included here, to examine Benedict's *Rule* and the section in the *Rule* about the Oratory, we see that place, the most sacred place reserved for the action of monks with God (alone and in community) was crucial fifteen-hundred years ago and by implication this must still be so today.

II

All the articles included in the section of commissioned essays about prayer stress the fact of humankind's longing for union with God. Some of the scholars who have been asked to address this issue deal with aspects of this quest by using Merton's life, meditations, poetry, and friendships to examine the fundamental reality of the continuing need for prayer of all persons—something which, especially in this complex "scientific age" of which we are part, can so easily be forgotten or, if not forgotten, can be processed into abstractions.

The article, included here, by Richard Hauser reveals both his love of his Ignatian training as a Jesuit and the mystery of how Hauser came to appreciate prayer because of his study of modern psychology and Thomas Merton, an appreciation to which he came by quite another route than the Ignatian Exercises. Concretized, brought *home* to the particulars of his own life, Hauser says—after years of searching—he prayed and then he was able to understand Ignatius far better too.

Merton ultimately saw his fundamental monastic job as prayer. In a set of related 1960 journal entries he comments on the two elements St. Benedict held as most integral to the successful fulfillment of the monastic vocation, balancing a concern with self and another equally important concern with community in the widest sense:

December 13, ...

Work. To be a solitary and not an individualist. Not concerned with mere perfecting of my own life. This, as Marxists see, is an indecent luxury (because there is so much illusion in it). My solitude belongs to society and to God. Are these just works? Solitude for its special work, deepening of thought and awareness. The struggle against alienation. The danger of a solitude that is the worst alienation. *Not* a matter of holding the community at arm's length. Important that I continue to be Novice Master for the time being (and he [the Abbot] wants me to anyway). But I think at night of St. Mary of Carmel [the new retreat-conference building]. I go to sleep thinking of the quiet hermitage and wishing I were there in bed (there is no bed) in the silent woods where the owl cries. "Self-love" they would say.

It is simply time that I must pray intently for the needs of the whole world and not be concerned with other, seemingly "more effective" forms of action. For me prayer comes first, the other forms of action follow, if they have their place. And they no doubt do to some extent. Prayer (yesterday Mass) for Latin America, for all of America, for this Hemisphere—sorrow for the dolts, for the idiot civilization that is going down to ruin and dragging everything with it.[2]

This dual entry clarifies with its seriousness, yet with a humor also, the absolute centrality of prayer and the sense of home in Merton's spiritual life. He both longed for extreme solitude, and realized he had to have more connections with the whole world. Merton's solitude is, therefore, not selfishness, but was to be sought in the hope that because of prayerful solitude the special work of his life would be fulfilled. Merton might then, paradoxically, be delivered from both alienation and separation.

In solitude, properly cultivated, Merton realized he might be given a deepening of understanding. For this to come about and for this not to be a selfish act, he immediately notes, he must pray intently not for himself, but for the "needs of the whole world." Such a constant juggling act, perhaps the central process of prayer, it seems to me, is like the process of individuation in Jung's terms.

That process of "individuation" has to be a life-long journey. It is to some degree conscious (but usually less so), a quest which allows any motivated person to move toward a fuller, more "complex" understanding of the way conscious and unconscious factors, emotional and rational actions and reactions, may be being integrated and thus allowing that person to function (or not) at various stages of life while doing so within a "complexity" of self which is that unique person's inheritance and home. Prayer must also work this way. It is not a formula for a solitary or a way to stress individualism. It is a way of finding one's home.

All persons develop qualities which remain special *only* to that individual. Those qualities, both conscious and unconscious awareness of tendencies toward *anima* and *animus*, and all the tensions generated by their presence are apparently constantly blending with still other developing psychic characteristics which often at earlier stages of life remain submerged, or even hidden. In addition, the power of the "Collective Unconscious" (in which *all* persons also share) is as well a factor which can help or hinder any individual's drive toward clearer manifestations of his or her personal "individuation." Understanding the interaction of these many forces can assist an individual to account for, and to adjust to the rhythm of life's stages.

Is such a process of "individuation," then, as William Johnston describes in his recent autobiography *Mystical Journey*, the need to embrace the nothingness (which is all) which St. John of the Cross describes? Is this what we must learn to do in prayer? Is this what is revealed in the larger rhythm of Merton's learning to pray? Is it necessary for the developing individual to become more aware of the *all* (and the archetypal patterns of birth into death for all) by "letting go" of dwelling upon a consciousness of self which is always what can only be experienced on the surface of our understanding of ourselves?

Johnston argues that when the awareness of self and its singular needs is surrendered, then flashes our insight into the "Coincidence of Opposites." Perhaps then it becomes possible that the *all* becomes part of the self and the self becomes (precisely by not worrying about the external self) part of the *all* in which all persons are united and then one feels at home.

In the first "night of the senses," as William Johnston explains how he understands the sense of the personal unconscious,[3] he elaborates that it is through an emptying of personal fears and anxieties that each person moves toward a healing of self and paradoxically becomes more "individuated" and more able to pray. It would then be the normal hoped for pattern that the "second night," which we can come to know of the senses, is the still wider

need to assist in the purification of the "collective unconscious of
the world"—all the sins we face as persons who are linked together, manifested in all the dark actions of murder, greed and
selfishness constantly happening throughout the entire world. I
think if this is so it helps us to understand the process which allows us to pray and the deepening process which is radiated by
Merton's life and writings, seeking the true self which remains
united at its core with the Creator.

Many of the other essays which make up the section of this
book focused upon prayer develop ideas which often have to do
with prayer's specificity and immediacy. Both Kathy Hoffman
and Cynthia Bourgeault demonstrate this. Bonnie Thurston's
examination of Merton's insights gives us a clear view of the mature Merton pondering this fact. The article by Keith Egan, somewhat critical of Merton's early reading of St. John of the Cross, is
valuable *both* as an academic evaluation and as an indicator of
where Merton's analytical ability rested during the earliest part of
his career when he wrote *The Ascent to Truth*. Indirectly, Egan also
shows why Merton was skeptical about undertaking more extended formal theological study. For him prayer became more a
matter of living in a focused manner yet always within the context of a world never abandoned. Thus, David Belcastro and Phillip
Thompson remind us of Merton's prayerful engagement with the
world.

III

The three interviews included in this volume also may assist us to
triangulate on the importance of Merton's insights into the nature
of living prayerfully. Both the interviews of Fr. Kilian McDonnell
and Fr. Ray Pedrizetti provide first-hand insights about Merton,
yet, perhaps more importantly, they are valuable as evidence of
the importance of focused dedication to the kind of vowed religious life which Merton chose. Clearly, fidelity over an extended
period brings proof of the mystery of our longing for God. In my
own case as I have learned more about the mystery of Christian
belief, this also has proven to be true.

In addition to the group of articles about prayer included here,
we have two additional studies which demonstrate how the "mystic" side of Merton remained clearly related to the "prophetic" side
of Merton as critic and poet. The article by Gosia Poks makes it
clear that prayer cannot be withdrawal. The study by Professor

Davis about *Cables to the Ace* amplifies this point by demonstrating how playfulness can bring insights lost in a culture of formulas and actions.

Teilhard de Chardin, Merton, Karl Rahner, Hans Urs von Balthasaar, Hans Küng are, to my mind, most likely, the most significant Catholic theologians who lived the prophetic responsibility of a twentieth-century vision as projected prayerfully for our present century. They each did this because in separate instances— for Teilhard, pondering "future of man"; for Merton, seeking the "new man"; for Rahner, celebrating the importance of mysticism; for Balthasaar, constructing a theology of aesthetics; and, for Küng, finally, the absolute necessity of ecumenism—these five men all witness to the presence of God in our (sometimes unlikely) midst. We find God in all kinds of ways, yet clearly Merton and each of these other famous theologians would insist the discipline of prayer comes first.

Two recent publications, both tracing their origins straight back to Thomas Merton, can serve to establish a broader stage upon which we can observe some of the other players who engage in the examination of "theo-dramas" which also are reflected in this gathering of scholarly articles. No doubt prayer was always at the heart of Merton's life, but it was never just for himself. Six recently published study booklets or pamphlets, four of which I have seen, published as "Bridges to Contemplative Living with Thomas Merton"[4] by Jonathan Montaldo and Robert G. Toth, along with Augustine Roberts's revised edition of *Centered on Christ*: *A Guide to Monastic Profession*, demonstrate the significance of Merton's prophetic stance and his encouragement in the life of prayer for all persons who live in our contemporary culture. These two works, designed for two totally different audiences, are therefore excellent reminders of the continuing importance of Merton's thought for all serious Christians.

The pamphlets which Jonathan Montaldo and Robert Toth have jointly produced for use by discussion groups to develop "Contemplative Living" are a clear indication of the continuing wide appeal of Merton's thought for "ordinary" people. Clearly Merton has such continuing influence. (I must confess I did recently hear at a parish discussion, in Atlanta, that a Director of Religious Education was using *two* sessions per meeting to speed up the appreciation of the contemplative process!) Above all, through these study guides, we are reminded to find ways to make contemplative spaces, and to, thereby, feel at home.

The new edition of Augustine Roberts's *Centered on Christ*,[5] which began as a book based on Merton's own notes for novices, is now completely revised. This honed text is now used by many Cistercian Houses as a basic work which assists in monastic formation. Roberts's reworked and expanded text reflects Merton's careful thinking about preparation of novices as well as the test of time within this Benedictine-Cistercian framework of community. Because it is a revision of decades of continuing work by Roberts, it proves Merton's own systematic thinking remains of value.

In *Pax Intrantibus*,[6] a recent book of poetic meditations, which ruminate about Merton's quest as monk-poet, Fredrick Smock signals his readers about the enigmatic mystery of silence and humankind's often booming sound. Our being at home is disturbed in all kinds of ways. Smock writes about the mysteries of making poems amidst the impermanence of all that we love and see and breathe. What Merton does in his poems is a celebration often close to prayer. Merton's poetic temperament nurtured his talent which allowed him to enter into moments of intuitive seeing—whether this was to reflect some tiny thread of nature—which suggests wholeness and our desire for coming home, or the drifting of whole civilizations as they clash, dissolving still other cultures. Only in the now of focused poetry or prayer, Smock intimates, are we able to begin to find God.

This collection of essays and reviews includes several contributions which have a rather special meaning to me as editor which many readers most likely would not be able to notice the same way. Several of the writers are more than just scholars or authorities. Many of these contributors are scholars and authorities yet also they are true companion seekers. For example, Emile Farge has become a friend during the past several years. As a former priest he radiates a love of the Church. Emile's presence as a participant in the local Merton Reading Group for these years has been a gift. Bonnie Thurston's contribution reflects a different kind of growing relationship. She now lives quietly by herself, yet reaches out in many, including poetic, ways.

Among the reviewers here several have special relationships. The production manager, Glenn Crider, provides a review-essay of Br. (Ernest) Daniel Carrere's book, *Creating a Human World: A New Psychological and Religious Anthropology in Dialogue with Freud,*

Heidegger, and Kierkegaard. Brother Daniel himself, whom I first met in 1982, graciously edited the transcript of Merton included here. Glenn began his association with *The Merton Annual* in 2000 and his now seven years of Merton study has ranged from technical work to helping plan conferences; then editing, interviewing and more. I am pleased that he has been a steadfast presence, and especially as volumes 17 through 20 have been prepared.

Catherine Crosby's review-essay also deserves some brief comment. She and I were classmates (2004-2006) in the Spiritual Direction Program of Spring Hill College and her essay grew from what could have been just an objective review. Other reviews here have been written by persons, such as Martha Gross, now who have also become colleagues in the area of Spiritual Direction here in Atlanta.

In so many quiet and often indirect ways Merton has served as a catalyst in many of the developing relationships to which I allude. I am, of course, grateful for all the contributors who have made this book possible. Indeed, in closing, I must say this of all the contributors for the last twenty years.

Notes

1. Wendell Berry, *The Art of the Commonplace: The Agrarian Essays of Wendell Berry,* in "The Body and the Earth," ed. Norman Wirzba (Washington D.C.: Counterpoint, 2002), p. 120.

2. Thomas Merton, *Turning Toward the World: The Pivotal Years,* ed. Victor A. Kramer (San Francisco: HarperCollins, 1996), p. 74.

3. William Johnston, *Mystical Journey: An Autobiography* (Maryknoll: Orbis, 2006) p. 142 and pp. 157-58.

4. Jonathan Montaldo and Robert G. Toth, *Bridges to Contemplative Living* [4 pamphlets], Vol. One, *Entering the School of Your Experience;* Two, *Becoming Who You Already Are;* Three, *Living Your Deepest Desires;* Four, *Discovering the Hidden Ground of Love* (Notre Dame: Ave Maria Press, 2006). ISBN-10: 1-59471-089-9, (Vols. 1-4), $5.95, 63 pp. [Projected in this series: Vol. Five, *Traveling Your Road to Joy;* Six, *Writing Yourself into the Book of Life;* Seven, *Adjusting Your Life's Vision;* Eight, *Seeing that Paradise Begins Now.*]

5. Augustine Roberts, *Centered on Christ: A Guide to Monastic Profession* (Kalamazoo: Cistercian Publications, 2005), pp. 323 with Index. ISBN-10: 087907-074-9. $16.29 (paperback).

6. Frederick Smock, *Pax Intrantibus: A Meditation on the Poetry of Thomas Merton* (Frankfurt: KY, Broadstone, 2007), pp. 91.

Authentic Identity is Prayerful Existence:

A Short Commentary

by *Glenn Crider*

This tape, carefully transcribed and edited by Brother Daniel Carrere, O.C.S.O., was recorded by Thomas Merton during the last years of his life while he was living as a hermit. In its simplicity it does many valuable things. Above all, Merton reminds his listener that prayer cannot be a project which we undertake. Prayer is, in fact, always initiated by the mystery of God's presence. Prayer is a call just as any vocation is a call. Such a call is not initiated by us as individuals. Rather, it is something an individual hears and to which that person responds. Merton reminds us that no baby is ever aware of its nature and therefore no newborn consciously seeks to act as a baby should act. The child simply *is*—and in being so, the actions of the child are not different than our own entering into all life and prayer. Merton's analogy is to breathing. We do not consciously seek to breathe. We just do this natural action. So, he insists, should our prayer-life be—something which comes as a most natural part of our life. There are things which can be done to inspire the conditions of breathing and there are different kinds of moments when our breathing is different; yet Merton implies the best we can do is to realize there is no one single formula for prayer. Circumstances allow each person to pray in different ways—sometimes liturgically, sometimes in awe and silence. "Successful" prayer is not something to be evaluated.

Prayer and Identity[1]

by *Thomas Merton*
(Transcript of a taped conference)

A few things on the life of prayer ... Do we know why we want to live lives of prayer? Are we praying in such a way that our prayer is simply for "something else"? It's all very well to pray for intentions, and to pray for the world, and to pray for health and all

16

those things; still, a life of prayer tends to be an end in itself. It is right for prayer to be an end in itself insofar as it is entirely centered on God, who is our end, if we can still use those terms—I suppose people still believe that God is our end, in the sense of the goal toward which we orient all our lives, or should orient all our lives.

As religious we still think of our religious life as a life given to God, consecrated to God, oriented to God; and it is in prayer that we are most dedicated, consecrated, and oriented to God. In prayer everything in us is, so to speak, centered on God. It is in prayer that we are most ourselves, that we are most what we want to be, what we hope to be, what we are called to be. But this can easily become very confused, especially if we have some sort of implicit, confused ideas about what our prayer is all about, or what God is all about, and what kind of a thing the religious life is all about. When we are mixed up on these points everything tends to get mixed-up, and prayer can become a very mixed up and frustrating thing when it should be quite simple.

Basically, prayer should be as simple as breathing, as simple as living, but when we make a great issue out of prayer it tends to become confusing; it tends to get distorted. It becomes a cause, the great "cause of prayer," and then it becomes opposed to something else which is not prayer. You get into this break: prayer is something sacred and other things are secular, and you have to keep them apart—and that's a confusion.

As breathing is neither sacred nor secular—you just breathe—so prayer too should be neither sacred nor secular. I don't regard prayer as a specifically sacred activity. It's *life*; it is our life; it comes from the very ground of our life. I think it becomes a sacred activity when it gets to be quite public and formal and so forth, but we should not divide prayer against the rest of our life, and we should not make prayer a cause for which we are willing to fight and have crusades, so to speak. The danger is that our religious life, our prayer, our apostolate—things like that—become causes which we make to serve ourselves. We use them, perhaps, out of a spirit of self-glorification.

Anyway, let's start with the basic proposition that we belong to God, and we want to belong to God, and we want to affirm our belonging to God. We want to live in a consciousness that we belong to him. The great thing in our life is this awareness of our identity as children of God: he is our Father and we live in this constant relationship with him, with him from whom we come, to whom we return, to whom we belong. We belong to him most completely in prayer, and prayer should be the activity, therefore, in which we are most ourselves.

Right away we see that when prayer is not what it should be it becomes the activity when we're most *not* ourselves, when we're *least* ourselves. If we're not praying as we should, we are most artificial in prayer, and we feel that when we are praying we are phony in a certain sense; we're pretending. Of course, this is something we should at times feel because as soon as prayer becomes too much of a project, we do tend to pretend. Rather than praying, we pretend that we're praying. We discover some kind of a role, some part to play; we find some particular kind of prayer that we think we ought to furnish to God and we put ourselves in that role and try to act the part of somebody praying in that particular way. Well, then it's artificial, and one of the great curses of the life of prayer is that when it becomes a role (one learns how to play the part of a religious praying—I am so-and-so and I am praying—or worse still, the role of having a certain degree of prayer, which is all nonsense, and I put myself in that role and I play that) it gets to be very artificial.

This brings up the question of the understanding of ourselves, which is a big question today. Rightly or wrongly, whether we like it or not, we tend to be constantly questioning our understanding of ourselves and who we are, our vocation and whether we should stay or leave, whether we should consider ourselves this way or that way, whether we should look at ourselves from this or that point of view. We have a great variety of choices of identity offered to us today, and we tend to waver around which one are we going to be. We've got all these roles and we don't know which one we're supposed to be in. Well, if you don't know what role you're supposed to be in, you're having a hard time.

It isn't a question of a role; it's a question of a vocation. A vocation is not a role; it's not a part we play. It is a response to a personal call. God speaks and we answer. He doesn't give us a role; the function of being a child of God is not a part that we play; it's not a role. When a baby is born he doesn't start playing the role of baby. He doesn't know he's got a role to play—he hasn't.

This is a big problem. We are obsessed with this idea of understanding ourselves, and it's unavoidable that we are so, but we get that mixed up with prayer. We start trying to understand ourselves in prayer. Prayer becomes a time devoted to self-understanding, evaluation of ourselves; how are we doing? Well, that's what it should not be. It gets to be that to some extent, but we have to try to avoid this because it's wasteful, frustrating, and it's not what we want to do; it's not what prayer's for.

On the contrary, prayer should help us abandon ourselves, to be *not* occupied with ourselves, and to attain to a kind of wholeness, a kind of all-round acceptance, which I would say is a very important fruit of prayer—an all-round acceptance: acceptance of ourselves, acceptance of the world as it is, acceptance of our religious life as it is, not as it *may* some day be or we hope it will be (we have to accept it as it is if we are going to make it what it is going to be); and we really have to accept other people. Prayer is the great way of getting ourselves opened up to this attitude of acceptance and availability and not lamenting our lot so much— just being in it, being with it, being all there, and being ourselves. At the same time, we do have to recognize the fallenness and ambiguity of our state, the fallenness and ambiguity of our love.

The natural material of our prayer is our love, our capacity to love, our human heart. It's most important that our human heart as a whole should function in prayer. In some of the ancient monastic traditions the first thing about prayer is the ability to find one's heart, to seek and find one's own heart, one's true voice to speak to God with and to listen to God with, a true *center*—and not to be ambiguous about this. The fallen state that we are in is that we're ambiguous about our own heart.

To be in a fallen state is to be in a state where one's heart is double, self-contradictory. Even though we're baptized, and even though we are nourished with the bread of life, we maintain this state of ambiguity in spite of ourselves, at least psychologically. We can't get out of it altogether; we have to be saints before we are through with that, and even the saints aren't through with it. We also have to accept this fallenness and ambiguity of our love and of our hearts.

We come to prayer with ambiguous hearts, and we have in ourselves the same doubts as other people to some extent. We are not safely walled off from the world in a little religious universe where everything is secure. Our faith is not secure in the modern world, not that the modern world attacks our faith but that we are simply modern people and therefore ambiguous, and therefore, we tend to doubt. We don't have the simple, direct faith that people of another, less complicated, age were able to have, and we don't have to have that simple, direct faith. We are bound to have a certain element of doubt in our lives because we are ambiguous people, and it is simplicity to recognize this and not to pretend that we are totally out of it. Of course some are more simple and less complicated than others. You don't have a duty to be ambiguous. I'm not saying that your whole life has to become that of playing the role of an ambiguous, doubting person; but with the sincerity that we have in our own hearts, we must respond to God in prayer.

It is God who calls us to prayer. So prayer, first of all, is a response to a call from God, a personal call from God, and I think we should look at it that way even though we don't feel like praying. Let's admit that very often we don't feel like praying and that there are a lot of other things we'd rather do than pray.

God calls us to prayer, and he calls us to the particular kind of prayer that he wants of us. Some he calls to say the psalms; others he calls to a kind of loving attention to him; others he calls to biblical meditation on his word, deepening one's understanding of his word, one's identification with his love and loving will in his word. To learn how to pray is to learn how to respond to God's personal call to us to prayer, and of course the great place for learning this is in the public prayer of the Church, in the liturgy, and in the Bible.

Prayer is an inner awakening, the awakening of an inner self that God intends us to be and to have. It's an awakening of a God-intended self. Guardini has some good things on this in his book on Pascal.[2]

He talks about yielding to the call of God to prayer and the change that happens when one yields to this call and one answers God's call to come to prayer, which is a personal call that we have to listen for. Perhaps the beginning of all prayer (you aren't hit by a thunderbolt and immediately start praying) should be a certain amount of listening and praying that we may hear. When we begin the public prayer of the Church we say, "Lord, open Thou my lips"; well, let's perhaps think of our own meditative prayers as, "Lord, open my ears; open the ears of my heart so that I may hear you calling me to pray"—but the mere fact that I begin to pray is a call to prayer.

Guardini says that if the heart yields to the call, then something happens to it: for the first time appears the genuine center.

The *genuine* center, the counterpart of the divine center that is call-ing, for the first time awakens—the genuine God-intended self, the real self. So what we are aiming for in prayer—right now I'm talking especially of meditative prayer—is this awakening of a genuine center, an authentic personal center that is the counter-part to the divine center that is calling. They are both within us, and yet we don't find them by introspection. Introspection is usu-ally not helpful for prayer.

In this opening up and acceptance of God's call in our genuine center, our depth, Guardini says, the mystery of that absolute ini-tiative by which God reveals himself gives light, touches the bot-tom of the heart so effectively that it unbinds itself, opens, and recovers sight and freedom. So, a further development in our life of prayer is this interior opening up, this unbinding of the inner self at the touch of God, to recover sight and above all to recover freedom.

The *great* thing that we are all seeking today, especially in the Church, is this freedom of the sons of God, and there is no free-dom of the sons of God without prayer. So when this unbinding of the inner self takes place and we are, so to speak, liberated— liberated for what?—liberated to go to God, liberated to have free access to God and free speech with God (*parrhesia*, confident free speech), to have access to God and speak to him face to face in the dark (so to speak), to speak to him as sons to a father with all confidence and without any fear. Without *any* fear, except of course that reverential fear that gives us a deep *respect* for God as infinite, incomprehensible Presence—and yet without fear.

God wishes us to speak to him without fear, even though we are sinners, with perfect loving confidence as his children. This is what he asks us to come to prayer for: that we may walk right up to him without fear and say, "You are my father; I love you," and whatever else we believe that he wishes us to say. It isn't just that he dictates to us things to say; what we say to him comes from our own heart. We can invent new things to say to him, if there are things to say, and we can say nothing; we can just listen. There are many things we can do in the creative and inventive situation that is our mutual understanding with God in prayer. He wishes to establish us in a relationship of mutual understanding, realizing that he understands us and we understand him. He understands us to some extent in a way that we can understand: we know that he has a father's understanding of us and we know what that is.

It's not purely a mysterious, totally incomprehensible dark night of the soul thing, except sometime it is.

All these things we can confidently keep in mind as realities of the world of prayer.

This opening to God is an opening also to everything else. The Presence of God, which is so mysterious and so real and so intimate, does not exclude anything else; it doesn't block out other things necessarily, although sometimes it seems to. It also opens us to embrace the whole of life, the whole of the world. It opens us to everyone and to everything, and we embrace everyone and everything in God.

Of course here we come to the problem of the new consciousness of modern man, which is such a great problem because it is our problem to a great extent.[3] We all have this problem of modern man for whom, as they say, God is dead. Of course that can mean all kinds of things. It may mean just that modern man is unable to conceive God in any way and remains inarticulate before him. [Then there is] the so-called self-withholding of God that somebody has spoken of: that modern man is inevitably in a position where God withholds himself from modern man. But is this true? This is no dogma of faith; this is no axiom. We know that God does not withhold himself; but people who are too influenced by what other people are saying are soon going to be running around saying God is simply inaccessible to any of us: what's the use of trying to pray, what's the use of anything like this; we must find God in some totally different way—because he withholds himself we have no access to him, and so forth. This is not true; it just simply is not true, and we as Christians realize that even though we may at times have moments of great dryness and desolation and so forth and so forth, it doesn't mean a thing. God does not withhold himself from his children. We have received his Spirit; we live in Christ. Does God withhold himself? He gives us the Body and Blood of his Son. What do you mean, withholds himself? We don't need feelings of consolation to realize that God gives himself.

To confuse God's giving of himself with feelings of consolation, that's—well, it's an old-time mistake; we know that's delusive. But we have to realize that God is an infinitely higher reality than we are, and when a higher reality meets a lower one, Guardini says, this occurs in such a way that the higher reality appears questionable from the point of view of the lower reality, so we instinctively doubt God. It's understood that we *are* creatures of doubt, but doubt and faith in a certain way can coexist in the same person—not real theological doubt but *questioning*, self-questioning above all. We must not confuse our self-questioning with our questioning of God, our self-doubt with our doubt of God. We come to God in prayer with a great deal of doubt of ourselves, a great deal of doubt of our own authenticity, and we should because we're not totally authentic, but that should not become also a doubt of God.

Nevertheless, when we do come face to face with him we find that he is questionable from our point of view, until faith breaks through and, by his gift, that question is resolved: not by our figuring, not by our reasoning, not by our reading, and not by somebody else telling us, but simply by God resolving the difficulty.

On the other hand, if one consistently holds to a lower reality against a higher, one may develop a state of radical bad faith in which, constantly being suspicious of the higher reality, constantly questioning it and constantly rejecting it and pushing it away, there is formed a bad conscience. The doubt is suppressed and you get a doubt in another form now, the doubt that after all it may be something totally beyond us that is there and is speaking to us, and so forth, and we refuse to hear. This produces a state of resentment and a kind of inner bitterness and bad faith that we try to overcome with a sort of false liberty and resentment.

Sometimes this happens to a modern person, a person dominated by the way other people think, and by the way society thinks, and by the general agnosticism of the world in which we live, which is a normal thing today. You just can't avoid it; it's there. Dominated too much by this, we can't allow ourselves to really let go and believe, and yet we know somehow in us, in the depths of our being, something is calling us to believe; yet we can't do it. And so we hold back and then we're guilty about it and we accuse ourselves and then perhaps we are guilty and perhaps we don't believe.

The great thing is to get away from this preoccupation with ourselves, examining ourselves, examining our prayer, examining our good faith and our bad faith and our faith, and whether we believe and whether we don't believe, and whether God loves us and whether he doesn't love us—and all that stuff—and simply abandon our preoccupation with ourselves and let go, because

"He that would save his life must lose it, and he that would lose his life for my sake will save it,"[4] and that is the important thing.

Notes

1. Transcribed and edited by Ernest Daniel Carrere, O.C.S.O. The original and longer taped conference, generically titled "On Prayer" (no date), is available at the Thomas Merton Center of Bellarmine University in Louisville, Kentucky. The tape was prepared by Merton for cloistered nuns in Louisville.

2. Romano Guardini, *Pascal for Our Time*, trans. Brian Thompson (New York: Herder and Herder), 1966.

3. See Thomas Merton, *Faith and Violence* (Notre Dame, IN: University of Notre Dame Press, 1968), part four.

4. Mt 16:25; Lk 9:24

"Simply Go In And Pray!": St. Benedict's Oratory In RB 52

Terrence G. Kardong

Introduction

When a Benedictine monk is asked to contribute an essay about prayer for a gathering in *The Merton Annual*, it is only natural for him to turn to the *Rule of St. Benedict (RB)*. This sixth-century document is not only one of the most precious sources for all of Christianity; it is also a primary inspiration for all the Benedictine and Cistercian monks and nuns in the world today. We may not live according to the letter of the Rule, for that is not possible in the modern world, but we do consider it our basic optic for living a Christian life in this day and age.

Since the Benedictine Rule is written to guide the spiritual life of its adherents, it is reasonable to look to it for instruction on private prayer. When we do that, we find many chapters devoted to the Divine Office (RB 8-18), but very few given over to discussion of private prayer. RB 19 and 20 have some intriguing comments on the meaning of prayer, but they are very laconic and essentially devoted to public prayer. There is another little chapter, however, that is sometimes overlooked as a source of insight into Benedict's views on private prayer. It is RB 52, his chapter on the prayer-room, which we will quote in full here.

RB 52: On the Oratory of the Monastery

1. The oratory should be in fact what it is called, and nothing else should be done or stored there. 2. When the Work of God is finished, they should all leave in deepest silence and show reverence for God. 3. Thus will the brother who may wish to pray by himself not be hindered by the thoughtlessness of another. 4. But if someone perhaps wishes to pray privately at some other time, let him simply go in and pray, not in a loud voice but with tears and full attention of heart. 5. Therefore, whoever is not busy with this kind of work is not permitted to

25

remain after the Work of God in the oratory, as the place is
called. For the prayer of another should not be disturbed.[1]

St. Benedict normally does not talk about rooms. Of course, he
mentions several special rooms in his monastery such as the refectory, kitchen and dormitory, but he does not elaborate on the shape
or décor or equipment of those rooms. This is not surprising, since
a monastic *regula* is not an architecture treatise, but a blueprint for
living a monastic life. There is one chapter, however, that is ex-
pressly devoted to a given room, namely, RB 52 entitled "The Oratory of the Monastery."[2] Still, we will see that Benedict is not interested in the oratory as such, nor the things in it, but rather in
what is done there.[3]

In the first verse of the chapter, he insists that the oratory be
used for what its name suggests, nothing more. Although he does
not explicitly say so, the word "oratory" contains the Latin verb
orare, which means to pray. Even though everyday English no
longer uses this word, but rather synonyms like chapel, church
and sanctuary, in the time of Benedict *oratorium* meant a private or
public chapel.[4] At any rate, Benedict lays strong emphasis on the
"truth-principle," namely, that the thing actually be what it is called.
Apparently he is fond of this formulation, for he also uses it in
connection with the abbot.[5] He goes on to say that "nothing else is
to be done or stored there."

This remark that the oratory is for nothing else than prayer
can be taken as a sort of aphorism pointing to St. Benedict's conviction that prayer is of the greatest importance. Perhaps that is
something of a cliché coming from a monk, but monks are like
other people in this: they sometimes get distracted from the central purpose of their lives. Clearly, the focus of a monk's life is on
the spiritual, that is, God, so it is not unusual to find Benedict insisting on the centrality of prayer. In RB 43.3, we read: "Nothing
is to be put ahead of the Work of God." That injunction refers to
the public prayer of the community. Here in RB 52, the overriding
importance of private, personal prayer comes to the fore.

Actually, Benedict's programmatic statement about the name
and function of the oratory is not original. Rather, it is found in
one of his favorite sources, namely, the *Rule of Augustine*:

The place of prayer should not be used for any purpose other
than that for which it is intended and from which it takes its
name. Thus, if someone wants to pray there even outside the

appointed hours, in his own free time, he should be able to do so without being hindered by others who have no business being there.[6]

As we will see, this whole chapter of Benedict is heavily reminiscent of earlier patristic and monastic documents.[7] Although this might seem to us to lessen its value, that was not the opinion of ancient writers. They liked to lace their most careful formulations with references to well-known and prestigious documents.

Benedict's argument that nothing except prayer is to be done in the oratory shows that this activity of prayer must be very important for him. Benedict's monastery was probably quite poor,[8] and it certainly did not have a lot of space. No doubt other rooms had to double up in their functions, but not this one. Nothing was to be done in the oratory but prayer. In fact, this is typical of societies where religion is very important. They do not want "all-purpose" chapels; they want sanctuaries devoted exclusively to the things of God. Aquinata Böckmann, in her commentary on RB 52, remarks that even among the Base Communities of Brazil, which are composed of the poorest peasants, there is an insistence that there be a special place for prayer.[9] For people with barely a roof over their heads, this is an extraordinary expression of faith. "Nothing else is to be done or stored there!"

To return to the meaning of *oratorium*, it does not refer exclusively to private prayer. Even though RB 52 will address itself primarily to personal, individual prayer, in his second and third verses Benedict notes that monks who are exiting the oratory after the performance of the Divine Office are not to make so much noise as to disturb those who might wish to remain there to pray (RB 52.2-3). Here we can see at a glance that the room was used for both kinds of prayer, but the transition from one kind of prayer to the other could be problematic.

Some Relevant Aspects of Ancient Monastic Life

In order to explain this little chapter better, it will be helpful to provide some background on certain aspects of life among the early monks. To begin, Benedict's prohibition against work in the chapel may leave us wondering what he might mean. Modern people do not normally mix work and worship. But among the earliest cenobitic monks, it was quite common to engage in simple handwork such as rope-plaiting while praying the public Office. And so we read the following passage in the Egyptian *Rule of St. Pachomius*, the earliest of all the Christian monastic Rules (c. 340-60):

> 4. And when he begins to walk into the *synaxis* room (oratory), going to his place of sitting and standing, he should not tread upon the rushes which have been dipped in water in preparation for the plaiting of ropes, lest even a small loss should come to the monastery through someone's negligence.
>
> 5. But at night when the signal is given you shall not stand at the fire usually lighted to warm bodies and drive off the cold, nor shall you sit idle in the *synaxis*, but with quick hand you shall prepare ropes for the warps of mats, although exception is made for the infirmity of the body to which leave must be given for rest.[10]

Without going into too much detail, apparently it was the official practice for the Pachomian monks to plait and weave during the Office. Indeed, materials were set out to supply them for precisely this activity. Even though Pachomius has acquired an unearned reputation for being overly concerned for work and efficiency in his monastery, it is clear that this arrangement was not meant to boost monastic productivity. Rather, the purpose was to help keep the monks awake during the early morning liturgy. The reason why this was necessary might be seen in the fact that the earliest Office was largely performed by single chanters and readers with the rest of the congregation listening and occasionally responding with refrain antiphons.[11]

But not all of the early cenobitic legislators agreed with the practice of doing handwork during the psalmody. In the passage we quoted above, Augustine of Hippo, writing sixty years after Pachomius but a hundred years before Benedict, categorically precludes work in church. It could be that Augustine's Office gave the whole choir more to do and say, and therefore was less soporific. Or he simply may have not shared the peasant mentality of Pachomius that mixed plaiting and praying. At any rate, Benedict, although his monastery was more rural than Augustine's, chose to follow the African doctor and not the Egyptian pioneer in this matter.[12]

Another cultural factor that needs to be taken into account to fully understand RB 52 was the proclivity of ancient people to "think out loud." In contrast to our society, where it is seen as a mark of low education to read out loud, ancient people regularly

did so. That is why St. Benedict must warn his monks not to disturb others with their <u>private</u> reading during siesta period (RB
48.5). In his autobiographical *Confessions*, St. Augustine recalls that
he once saw St. Ambrose of Milan reading silently to himself. It
was the end of a long day, and the Bishop was too tired to do
anything else![13]

Apparently the old monks tended to treat prayer in the same
way. Like many people to this day in Asia and Africa, they saw
nothing unusual with praying aloud in the presence of other
people. Visitors to shrines in that part of the world speak of the
deafening atmosphere as pilgrims all pray aloud, but not together,
in the holy places. But not all the ancient monastic Rules agree
with this. The Rule of the Master, which is the principal source of
the Rule of Benedict,[14] will have none of this. When the monks
finish the public Office, the Master wants them to cease vocaliz-
ing:

Chapter 68. Immediately Upon Leaving the Oratory They Must Keep Complete. Silence.

1. As soon as the brothers leave the oratory they are to keep
silence 2. and not even repeat psalms as they come out 3. lest
what was said inside at the right time with reverence be sung
over and over outside at the wrong time with disrespect. 4.
Therefore let them keep quiet as soon as they leave the oratory, 5. because the time for the psalms is over with and that of
silence has begun, 6. as Scripture says: "A time for everything."[15]

It is clear that Benedict is influenced by this chapter of RM, as he is
by many other passages of that strange Rule, but even a cursory
glance at RM 68 shows that the Master's concern is quite restricted.
For his part, Benedict uses the problem of the transition from public to private prayer as an occasion to create a much richer, if equally
brief, chapter on private prayer.

In studying Benedict's insistence that the oratory be kept as
silent as possible for personal prayer, we should also note that it
was virtually the only place where the monk could be guaranteed
such an atmosphere. Unlike most modern monasteries, Benedict's
foundation provided no private rooms for the monks. His chapter on the common dormitory (RB 22) shows very clearly that this
was the case, but again there was no unanimity among the early

cenobites on this matter: Pachomius provided semi-private rooms for his monks, and some of the other monastic legislators at the time of Benedict did so as well.[16] Although he does not provide private rooms, Benedict seems to realize that the monks do need a very quiet place to pray. Hence his strong emphasis on silence in the chapel.[17]

A final background item that could stand some examination concerns the horarium. When St. Benedict sets out his rather detailed daily time-table for the community in RB 48, he seems to allow little or no free time. And yet here in RB 52, he urges the individual who wishes to pray to simply go into the oratory and do so. We might suspect that Benedict's daily schedule was not as air-tight as it looks on paper. It is hard to believe that people would agree to have every minute of the day programmed for them. But beyond that, the time set aside for *lectio divina* was certainly available for private prayer. According to RB 48, about three hours a day were devoted to the Bible and collateral reading, which was expected to kindle devotion and prayer.[18] Probably the ancient monks had plenty of time to visit the oratory for private meditation and prayer.

Of course, there are days when monks do not have a lot of discretionary time for personal prayer, but a permanently overloaded schedule is the bane of monasticism. Throughout Benedictine history, the correct balance of work and leisure for prayer and *lectio* has been a problem. The great difficulty is to find work that will sustain material life, but also allow sufficient time for contemplation. In our own time, when technology has not produced more leisure time as predicted but much less, monks often find themselves caught up in a rat-race of overwork. Sometimes it must be accepted that only a simpler, poorer life-style will allow more time for prayer and reading.

Sensitivity to the Needs of Others

One of the main themes of RB 52 is the importance of being aware of the needs of others, and accommodating them as much as possible. On the surface, it might seem that this is an elementary principle and not one that needs much elaboration. There is again the simple logic of the matter: the oratory is for prayer, therefore those who wish to pray there should not be disturbed. We have seen above that people in some cultures seem to feel less need for quiet during prayer, but St. Benedict is not one of those. He demands on behalf of his monks that they be afforded as much consideration as possible when they engage in the essential and difficult task of prayer.

Apparently Benedict feels quite strongly about this, since he uses some pungent language. For example, he labels the behavior of those who make noise in the oratory as *improbitas*. Now this is a word with a wide range of meaning, and it is not so easy to choose exactly the right translation for it. On one end of the scale, the word sometimes flatly refers to evil. It is hard to imagine someone deliberately and maliciously setting out to distract others at prayer, although the Devil might do so. But the rendition of "thoughtlessness," which I myself settled on in 1996, does not quite seem to do the job either.[19] It could be that someone is in the oratory for entirely the wrong reasons, as was indicated by St. Augustine in the passage of his Rule that we quoted earlier.[20] Still, who is to say that someone else does not belong in chapel? Nonetheless, an individual will find inconsiderate behavior intensely irritating at times and judge it quite harshly (*improbitas*).

Another linguistic clue to Benedict's views on mutual concern can be seen in the term *reverentia*. When he says that the monks exiting the oratory after Office should do so with reverence, he may be making a somewhat loaded comment. Our quote of the *Rule of the Master* showed that author using *reverentia* to refer to singing the psalms out loud at the right time, namely during the Divine Office. To sing them outside was for him a sign of "disrespect" (*extollantia*). Benedict may be playing on this usage, but he has modified it to his own purposes. For him it refers to a silent exit out of consideration for the recollection of those who have remained behind to pray.[21] Although Benedict normally uses the word *reverentia* to mean a respectful stance toward God, especially in the Liturgy (e.g. RB 9.7; 11.3; 20.1), here it seems he wants to inculcate a reverential attitude toward one's fellow monks.

Benedict, however, makes sure to address both sides of the question, for he warns the one who goes into the oratory for the right reasons not to become a nuisance himself. How can this happen? By "praying with a loud voice" (*clamosa voce*), in other words the very thing that one objects to in others! In deeply personal matters such as private prayer, it is not only possible, but all too easy, to lose a sense of proportion. Probably because I am very easily distracted, I may find the behavior of others off-putting. But it must be remembered that I too may be an impediment to others.[22] And the only way to make sure that this does not happen is to remain constantly aware of the needs of others around me. If it bothers people for me to click my rosary beads, then I don't do it—even if I think they would be better off if they too prayed the rosary!

Private Prayer

Finally we come to a couple of expressions that could be seen as the very heart of this chapter. After warning the monk not to pray with a loud voice, Benedict suggests that he pray with "tears and full attention of heart" (*lacrimis et intentione cordis*). Indeed, it could be said that in these two phrases, Benedict sums up his whole theology of prayer.[23] There is a parallel expression in RB 20.3: "We should also realize that it is not in much talking that we shall be heard, but in purity of heart and tearful compunction." We will see that those phrases are virtually synonymous with tears and full attention of heart.

Why does Benedict suggest that we should pray "with tears"? He cannot mean that we should give ourselves over to sobbing, for that would contradict what he has to say about silence in the rest of the chapter. Since this is at least the third time tears are mentioned as a desirable accompaniment of prayer (see also RB 20.3 and 49.4), we can say for sure that Benedict thought highly of them. Because it is rather unusual in our culture for people to weep during prayer, this point needs some attention.[24] For one thing, the ancients considered tears to be a precious gift of God granted to the religious seeker. One of the reports on the Egyptian Desert Fathers describes an ascetic whose chest was furrowed with tears shed in continuous weeping.

Since tears were seen as a grace of God, they could not be produced by sheer will-power. Nor were they restricted to highly emotional or susceptible personalities. Actually, tears were associated with many different aspects of the spiritual life. In his magnificent treatise on prayer, Cassian lists no less than four kinds of spiritual tears: 1) Sorrow for my sins; 2) Desire for eternal glory; 3) Fear of hell; 4) Sorrow for the sins of others.[25] To judge from this list, the ancient concept of tears covers a far wider gamut of experiences and emotions than our narrow notion of sorrow. Indeed, A. De Vogüé claims that the ancient idea of *penthos* really covers the whole range of spirituality.[26] Yet it is still probably true

that the primary meaning of tears in every age is compunction of heart for sins, as is evident in RB 20.3.

What are we to make of the expression "full attention of the heart"? First, we should note that the exact Latin expression is *intentio cordis*. Granted that "attention" and "intention" are close in meaning, they are not exactly the same. And since we have only these extremely spare expressions of Benedict as windows into his views on prayer, we have to peer through them very carefully. How rich this particular expression really is can be seen from the fact that Michael Casey has written a whole article, and a very good one, on it.[27]

Casey points out that the "heart" meant something rather different for the old Romans than it does for us. We think of it as the seat of emotion, but for them it was the center of decision and will. Consequently, it would be closer to our notion of "mind" than "heart." As for *intentio*, it has to do with focus, with aiming the mind at some object. When Benedict speaks of prayer characterized by *intentio cordis*, he means that the mind is focused on God alone. In other words, he demands full attention on our part. Anyone who has pursued a serious life of prayer knows that this is easier said than done, for distraction is an on-going problem. But we can also say that the person who sincerely <u>desires</u> to stay focused on God <u>is</u> by that very fact essentially focused on God. A parallel concept is found in RB 19.7, where Benedict insists that our minds be "in harmony with our voices" in the vocal prayer of the Divine Office.[28]

The main thrust of RB 19.7 is to accentuate the need for interior attention in addition to the external activity of the Divine Office. The importance of interiorization is probably the main overall theme of the voluminous spiritual writing of John Cassian, so it is no surprise that *intentio cordis* is one of his favorite expressions. Thus we find the term in no less than seven places in Cassian.[29] The use of this term by Benedict at this strategic juncture seems to bind his spirituality tightly to that of Cassian. Nevertheless, it is possible to overdo the idea of interiority. At least we can say that vocalized prayer is by no means inferior to the silent or wordless kind. Many people find that prayer-mantras, silent or spoken, help them precisely to stay focused on what they are doing, and thereby focused on God.

Before we conclude our exegetical remarks, we should note one more statement by Benedict in his final verse: "Therefore, whoever is not busy with this kind of work is not permitted to remain in the oratory, as the place is called." The reference to "this kind of work" seems to merit some comment. Since it refers to silent prayer, as mentioned in the previous two verses, we might be surprised. Has not Benedict made it quite clear that he does not want people doing "work" in the chapel? And is he not also contrasting personal prayer with public prayer, which is called "the work of God"?   Why, then, does he use this kind of language?[30]

Could it not be that he wants to show clearly that prayer, in whatever form it takes, is indeed hard work? This is a point of some confusion for many people, so it is worth sorting out. It certainly does not mean that just any kind of work, if done properly, is a form of prayer. That may be the case, but it is not the point here. Benedict urges the monk to put aside his work and devote himself exclusively to prayer at some times during the day. But that does not mean that prayer is easy. In fact, at times it is the hardest thing that a person can do. Therefore, we don't find Benedict saying "If you feel like it, be sure to drop in to the chapel now and then for prayer." He probably would rather say, "Even if you do not feel like it, be sure . . . ."

Conclusion

At the end of this survey of Benedict's brief chapter, we may feel somewhat unsatisfied. After all, we have had to glean insight into a very big subject from a very few words. And we have tried to derive some ideas on prayer from a little chapter that is not a formal treatise on the subject but rather a modest comment on the monastic chapel. Still, it could be that these terse remarks of Benedict shed light on this subject in a way that is not common in more formal treatments. Therefore, even in just a few well-chosen words, Benedict is able to convey quite clearly his great concern for the prayer-life of his monks. Absolutely nothing should be done in the monastery to impede this central activity of the monk. For if we cannot pray in the monastery, where can we do so?

Notes

1. My translation in *Benedict's Rule: A Translation and Commentary* (Collegeville, MN: Liturgical, 1996).

2. *De Oratorio Monasterii.* The titles in the Rule of St. Benedict appear to be original.

3. Actually, Benedict does mention several items that are found in the oratory in other places in his Rule: relics and altar (RB 58.19-20); benches and lectern (RB 9.5).

4. A. Blaise, *Dictionnaire Latin-Français des Auteurs Chrétiens* (Turnhout, Belgium: Brepols, 1954) s.v., gives the following references: Aug. *Ep.* 211.7; 221.11; Eugipp. *Vit.*, p. 56.3; Cassian, *Inst.* 3.7 tit.; Gelas. *Ep.* 14.25, p. 375; Vict.-Ton. *Chron.* P. 199.36; RB 38; 52. In RB 38.2-4, Benedict has the blessing of the kitchen-workers in the *oratorium*.

5. The reasoning in RB 2 is far less straightforward, however, than that in RB 52. In RB 2, the abbot is to imitate the leadership of Christ because he is called by Christ's name, that is, *abba* = father. But of course, Christ himself called his Heavenly Father *abba*. For a clear and comprehensive survey of the patristic theme of the Fatherhood of Christ, see C. Peifer, *RB 1980* (Collegeville, MN: Liturgical, 1981), pp. 356-363.

6. Augustine, *Praeceptum* (Rule for Male Religious) 2.2. The translation is by T. van Bavel in *The Rule of Augustine: with Introduction and Commentary* (Kalamazoo, MI: Cistercian, 1996), p. 13. The reference is found in M. Puzicha, *Kommentar zur Benediktusregel* (St. Ottilien, Germany: EOS 2002), p. 438.

7. What is more, the material on the abbot's name is copied directly from the *Rule of the Master* (RM 2).

8. We only have hints about the economic condition of Benedict's community: The monks are to bring in the harvest themselves if they are too poor to hire laborers (RB 48.7). They are not to grumble if local circumstances make it impossible to obtain wine for meals (RB 40.8). It is hard to see what, besides poverty, would make it impossible to obtain wine in Italy! On the other hand, the monks' clothing was not the poorest, for when it became worn, they were to give it to the poor (RB 55.9).

9. See "On the Oratory of the Monastery," *The American Benedictine Review* 49:1 [March, 1998], pp. 71-2.   She derives this information from her experience in Brazil and from Marcelo de Barros Souza, *Na Estrada do Evangelho, Uma Leitura communitarian e latino-americana de Regra de Sao Bento* (Petropolis, Brazil 1993), p. 111.

10. Found in *Praecepta* 4-5, translated by A. Veilleux in *Pachomian Koinonia* 2 (Kalamazoo, MI: Cistercian, 1981), pp. 145-46.

11. For an account of the primitive Office, see my remarks in *Benedict's Rule* (note 1), pp. 210-11.

12. Apparently the controversy was not over by the time of Benedict, for Caesarius of Arles, legislating for a convent of nuns he founded in the early sixth century (same time as Benedict) seems to be of two minds on this matter. In *Reg. Virg.* 10 he prohibits handwork in church, but RV 15 he recommends it—precisely to keep people awake. It might be noted that the monks of South Gaul were notorious for their long Offices. The

best modern study of Caesarius' monastic writings is found in Sources Chrétiennes 345 and 398, by A. De Vogüé and J. Courreau (Paris: Cerf, 1988-94). An English translation of the *Rule for Nuns* was done by M.C. McCarthy (Washington D.C.: Catholic U, 1960).

13. *Confessions* VI.3, 3.

14. For a succinct explanation of this controversial relationship, see *RB 1980*, pp. 71-72.

15. Translation of L. Eberle in *The Rule of the Master* (Kalamazoo, MI: Cistercian, 1977), p. 233.

16. Ferrandus, *Vit. Fulgentii* 43 and Aurelian, *Reg. Mon.*, 8; 33, favor private rooms for the monks, but Caesarius, *Reg. Mon.* 3 and *Reg. Virg.* 49, forbids them. The reasons that Caesarius gives for ruling out private cells refer to avarice and secularism. For a complete survey of the question of monastic cells, see De Vogüé, "Comme les moines dormiront: commentaire d'un chapitre de la Règle de Saint Benoît," *Studia Monastica* 7 (1965) 25-62. Although he recognizes the dangers of private rooms, Vogüé is vehemently in favor of them precisely because they provide an ideal place for contemplation.

17. Someone reading RB 6 on Silence might get the impression that all areas of Benedict's monastery were perfectly quiet, but that does not seem to have been the case. If it were, then why does he need to stress quiet and restrained speech in steps 9-11 of the Ladder of Humility (RB 7.56-61)? And why does he suggest that during Lent the monks avoid idle talk and needless jesting (RB 49.7)? See my further reflections in *Benedict's Rule* (note 1), pp. 126-29.

18. The classic formulation of this matter was made by Guigo (II) the Carthusian (died c. 1188), who delineated four steps in the process: reading, meditation, prayer and contemplation. See his *Ladder of Monks*, trans. E. Colledge and J. Walsh (London and Oxford, 1978).

19. *Benedict's Rule* (note 1) p. 415. The translator in *RB 1980* also wrestled over this one, as is evident in his note on p. 177, where he comes down on "insensitivity."

20. See note 6 above.

21. Böckmann (note 6) 73, notes that many of the old commentators mistakenly thought that *reverentia* in this passage meant a bow toward the altar. See Hildemar, *Expositio Regulae* ed. R. Mittermüller, (Regensburg: Pustet, 1880), p. 499.

22. *Impedimentum* is the exact word Benedict uses in this chapter; indeed, uses twice (RB 52.3 and 5). The etymology of this word refers to a stumbling block that one falls over. To become a stumbling block for other people who are trying to pray is not something anyone would want to have on his conscience.

23. Böckmann (note 6), p. 82.

24. But the phenomenon is not entirely unknown. In his book entitled *The Father and the Son* (New York: HarperCollins, 1999) Matt Murray describes the conversion experience of his father (James Murray) as characterized by copious weeping, not only during private prayer, but also at Mass. What strikes the reader is that James Murray is not at all a highly emotional man, but rather sober and even rationistic.

25. Conference 9.29, cited by M. Puzicha (note 5).

26. This is discussed in his one-volume spiritual commentary on RB entitled *The Rule of St. Benedict* (Kalamazoo, MI: Cistercian 1983; French original, 1977), p. 255. For a complete treatment of this topic, see I. Hausherr, *Penthos* (English translation: Kalamazoo, MI: Cistercian, 1982).

27. "Intentio Cordis: RB 52.4," in *Regulae Benedicti Studia* 6/7 (1981), pp. 103-120.

28. This connection is emphasized by A. Quartiroli in her study of RB 52 in *La Regola di San Benedetto* (Abbey of Praglia, Italy, 2002). She says "It is a call for sincerity and interiority of relations in prayer."

29. Conf. 1.7; 4.4; 9.6,7,12; 10.8; 23.11. See the concordance by M. Petschenig in his edition of Cassian in CSEL 13 and 17.

30. He calls prayer *simile opus,* "this kind of work." *RB 1980* avoids this literal translation, preferring "pray in this manner" but that ignores the word *opus.* I am pretty sure Benedict intends at least a gentle pun in this case.

Praying The Psalms:
A Layperson's Path to Contemplation

Kathy Hoffman

During the decades that preceded the reforms of the Second Vatican Council, scripture held a secondary role in the liturgy and life of the Roman Catholic Church. For the Catholic faithful, the sacrament of the Eucharist was the focus of the Mass, and prayer often centered on the rosary and other sacramentals. It seems unlikely that there would have been a significant audience for books devoted to the use of scripture in private prayer in the 1950s, yet Thomas Merton was responsible for two separate and successful efforts involving the use of the psalms in prayer and contemplation.

The material in *Bread in the Wilderness* was first published in 1950 as a series of articles in *Orate Fratres*.[1] Offered as a book in 1953, it was followed closely by *Praying the Psalms* in 1956. This article explores these literary efforts in relation to the following points: 1) as related to the background of the times and the framework of Merton's monastic experience and his vocation as writer and poet; 2) as a practical aid for personal piety and for meeting the challenges to prayer faced by Catholic laity in world of the twentieth-century; 3) as revelations about the nature of contemplation; 4) as aspects of thought that establish Merton's importance among the theologians of the twentieth century; 5) as keen insights into the psalms' value in prayer, which continue to be explored and developed by contemporary spiritual teachers and poets.

The Psalms: Merton's Background Music

By 1953, Thomas Merton had led a cloistered, monastic life for almost a dozen years, and he had been a best-selling author longer than he had been a priest. Merton's first breviary was purchased in 1940, as a response to his rejection by the Franciscans. Saying the Office became the icon representing his dream of entering the religious life, and praying the psalms kept alive his resolve to "live in the world as if I were a monk."[2] Real life in the monastery presented unexpected challenges, however. Passionate in the search for solitude and contemplation, Merton wrestled with a need for silence and detachment that often seemed incompatible with his literary career. However, by the 1950s, Merton had also clearly come to understand that his vocation as a Cistercian monk included a call to share the fruits of his experience of God with the world. He had already published *What is Contemplation?* in 1948 and *Seeds of Contemplation* in 1949.

Merton sometimes noted that Cistercian community life, with its emphasis on communal liturgy, work and study, could be an obstacle to true solitude and contemplation. At the same time, monastic prayer, centered on the chanting of the Divine Office, immersed Merton in the psalms. In 1947, Merton's journal shows evidence that saturation in psalmody had a profound effect on his thinking and writing. Verses from psalms spontaneously punctuate journal entries from this period, often as Merton struggled to maintain his focus on God in the midst of the distractions of the community and various writing projects.[3] In the entry of September 25, 1947, Merton expresses the pure joy he experienced in "saying the psalter all alone and looking at the hills in the cool morning shadows behind the Church." He voices the conviction that the psalms, said "wisely" and in solitude, will "stay with you all day afterwards." In the next line of this entry, solitude and the beauty of nature carry Merton away in a flood of psalm-prayer that culminates in a cry of desire and frustration: "My heart burns in my side when I write about contemplation … and I want to cast fire on the earth."[4] Already in April 1948, Merton had completed writing a pamphlet on contemplation which had met with criticism by his Cistercian censor for "the assertion that mystical contemplation was for everybody and was an integral part in Christian perfection." Even though the censor disagreed with the principle, Merton was allowed the freedom to express his conviction that contemplation was a fundamental and universal element of the Christian call to holiness.[5]

George Woodcock characterizes Merton's lyrical works of this period as "poetry of the choir" because the poet's monastic experience of the psalms is so clearly reflected. Woodcock observes that Merton's early poetry is more "ornate" than his later compositions (aptly named "poetry of the desert").[6] The poetry of the choir dominates Merton's work in the 1940s and many of these works reflect the structure, repetition, imagery, tone, and themes of the psalms.[7] Woodcock notes an "ecstatic expansiveness of the

Psalms that mainly rules the poems of the choir,"[8] which is evident in Merton's song of praise entitled "The Communion" (published in *Thirty Poems*, 1944):

> O sweet escape! O smiling flight!
> O what bright secret breaks our jails of flesh?
> For we are fled, among the shining vineyards,
> And ride in praises in the hills of wheat,
> To find our hero, in His tents of light!
> O sweet escape! O smiling flight![9]

The repetition of the first line of this opening stanza continues throughout the poem, which builds to a crescendo of praise for Jesus' transforming power.

"A Whitsun Canticle" (*A Man in the Divided Sea*, 1946) is Woodcock's choice as Merton's poem that most clearly illustrates the influence of psalmody. "It is a poem of laudation in which the poet calls upon man and nature to praise God…. One is immediately impressed by the sustained tone of joy, breathless, beyond breath, that provides the dominant feeling to the poem. It is a song of praise…. But in more than spirit is the Canticle in the true psalmodic tradition; the imagery, the diction, the prosody being there also."[10] Woodcock speculates that these early poems of the choir were the songs of Merton's personal rebirth into contemplative life,[11] and it seems as if the psalms acted as midwives in his birthing process. In "A Psalm" (*The Tears of the Blind Lions*, 1949), we glimpse the interplay of psalmody and contemplation in Merton's experience:

> When psalms surprise me with their music
> And antiphons turn to rum
> The Spirit sings: the bottom drops out of my soul
>
> And from the center of my cellar, Love, louder than
>   thunder
> Opens a heaven of naked air.
>
> New eyes awaken.
> I send Love's name into the world with wings
> And songs grow up around me like a jungle.
> Choirs of all creatures sing the tunes
> Your Spirit played in Eden.[12]

Walter Brueggemann has observed that the "movement of our life, if we are attentive, is a cycle of *orientation, disorientation*, and *reorientation*," and the psalms reflect this rhythm.[13] All growth necessarily involves a relinquishing of former, comfortable ways of life (*orientation*)—a process of *disorientation* that is painful, but essential. Eventually, a new way of living and being emerges (*reorientation*).[14] As Merton journeyed toward spiritual maturity, his poetry changed stylistically in ways that parallel Brueggemann's pattern, while also reflecting the inner silence of Merton's contemplative life.[15] His journals show a similar progression away from the breathless excitement of the early years to the constant struggle to find the balance between the active life and solitude, between sound and silence:

> I am more and more persuaded that our way of trying to be contemplatives by our individualism is utterly ruinous. But also, at the same time, what passes for community life and spirit can be just as ruinous…. What a disaster to build the contemplative life on the negation of communication. That is what, in fact, our silence often is – because we are obscuring it without really wanting it (yet needing it nonetheless) and without understanding what it is all about. That is why there is so much noise in a Trappist monastery….all this protests that we hate silence with all our power because, with our wrong motives for seeking it, it is ruining our lives. Yet the fact remains that silence is our life – but a *silence which is communication and better communication than words!* If only someone could tell us how to find it. The worse pity of all is that we think we know. What we have found is our own noise. No, that is not true. The Paradox is that in spite of all, we have found God and that is probably the trouble. Such a discovery is altogether too much and we beat a hasty retreat into any kind of protection.[16]

Merton's sometimes confusion and frustration are cries of disorientation. During this period of transition, it is not surprising that few poems from the 1950s display the elaborate qualities of the poetry of the choir;[17] however, echoes of biblical psalms remain. "Whether There is Enjoyment in Bitterness" (*The Strange Islands*, 1957) serves as a psalm of personal lament,[18] reflecting Merton's inner turmoil:

This afternoon, let me
Be a sad person. Am I not
Permitted (like other men)
To be sick of myself?

Am I not allowed to be hollow,
Or fall in the hole
Or break my bones (within me)
In the trap set by my own
Lie to myself? O my friend,
I too must sin and sin.

I too must hurt other people and
(Since I am no exception)
I must be hated by them.

Do not forbid me, therefore,
To taste the same bitter poison,
And drink the gall that love
(Love most of all) so easily becomes.

Do not forbid me (once again) to be
Angry, bitter, disillusioned,
Wishing I could die.

While life and death
Are killing one another in my flesh,
Leave me in peace. I can enjoy,
Even as other men, this agony.

Only (whoever you may be)
Pray for my soul. Speak my name
To Him, for in my bitterness
I hardly speak to Him: and He
While He is busy killing me
Refuses to listen.

Merton's words of self-pity evoke images of Psalm 38, "My wounds grow foul and fester because of my foolishness; I am utterly bowed down and prostrate; all day long I go around mourning."[19]   Both laments end with a faint ray of optimism that God's silence will eventually give way to mercy and help, displaying the classic pattern of movement from despair toward hope which is characteristic of the psalms.

The study portion of Merton's days at Gethsemani involved extensive reading of diverse works from a wide array of authors, ranging from his theological contemporaries to the Fathers of the Church. During this period, Merton's attention was drawn to the work of Jean Daniélou, a Jesuit priest and professor at the *Institut Catholique* in Paris, who was part of the "New Theology" movement centered in France. Daniélou's patristic scholarship and his ideas about liturgy and biblical exegesis had a strong influence upon Merton's understanding of the psalms. Significantly, Merton dedicated *Bread in the Wilderness* to Daniélou, and in a relationship maintained through correspondence, Daniélou remained a trusted friend and mentor until Merton's death in 1968. Merton's effort to share the riches of the psalms with a popular audience also mirrors Daniélou's desire to inspire the laity of the church toward a renewal of faith that would make Catholicism relevant in a rapidly changing world.[20]

Merton's Writings about the Psalms' Value in Prayer

Bread in the Wilderness was characterized by its author as "not a systematic treatise, but only a collection of personal notes on the Psalter . . . . One supposes that they might appeal above all to monks. But in this mysterious age, there is no telling whom the book may reach."[21] In fact, this general sense of almost confusion about the nature of the reader permeates the entire text. The prologue attempts to bridge the gap between monastic experience and that of the lay Catholic with a tone that is conversational and informative. However, the title of the first chapter reveals that Merton's primary focus remains a religious audience: *"The Problem: Contemplation in the Liturgy."*

Immediately, Merton discourses on monastic life, the search for God, and the wisdom found in the Church Fathers. Abstract concepts of "acquired contemplation" and "infused contemplation" are used without benefit of explanation, and countless references are made to reciting or chanting the Divine Office. A layperson of the period would have found little in common with Merton's experience of prayer. Themes of symbolism, typology, sacrament and liturgy all evidence strong influence by Daniélou and the "New Theology" of that period. The overall structure of the book and much of its content indicate a scholarly intent that would have been beyond the scope of the ordinary layperson's understanding of scripture and liturgy in this era.

Bread in the Wilderness hints at Merton's "separatist" mentality during this period. Lawrence Cunningham has noted that "his writings well into the 1950s are full of his disgust with contemporary secular culture."[22] Merton's initial entrance into the monastic community at Gethsemani was motivated by his desire to escape society's myriad evils. Yet even within the refuge of the monastery, dissatisfaction ultimately emerged. Merton's yearning for absolute dedication to God fueled a stubborn resistance to the Cistercian Rule's requisite limited contact with other monks. It is not surprising, therefore, to find that Merton's characterization of the world can seem to be very black and white: "Christ's Cross has become the key to a history whose purpose is to separate the City of God from the city of this world, which has Babylon for its symbolic name."[23] With Merton's focus on the institutional Church, liturgical prayer, and monastic life, the psalms become songs of the "City of God." Considering his own struggle to find peace in the context of his own monastic society, it is hardly surprising that Merton offers little practical help for the layperson struggling to survive in the world of "Babylon."

However, within this rather lofty view of Church, Merton occasionally establishes striking points of connection for the ordinary Christian. In one of his frequent warnings regarding a psychological approach to contemplation and the psalms, Merton emphasizes the importance for *all* the faithful to grasp the truth of the presence of Christ:

> The spiritual understanding of the Psalter will therefore not introduce us to some esoteric technique of prayer, nor will it tempt us to induce within our minds some peculiar psychological state. It will, above all, tell us not merely what we ought to be but the unbelievable thing that we already *are*. It will tell us over and over again that we are Christ in this world, and that He lives in us.[24]

Underneath the general piety and apparent focus on monastic life, Merton clearly senses that every human is on the same journey, which is a microcosm of the journey of the Church. That is why his two books on the psalms remain important today. There are many moments when he captures the essence of the connection between the Church and the singular soul finding his way in the world quite beautifully:

> Just as the whole people of God is still crossing the desert to the Promised Land, still passing through the Jordan, still building Jerusalem and raising God's temple on Sion, so each individual soul must normally know something of the same journey, the same hunger and thirst, the same battles and prayers, light and darkness, the same sacrifices and the same struggle to build Jerusalem within itself.[25]

Robert Waldron has observed that "every page of *Bread in the Wilderness* gives us a glimpse of Merton the poet," who has a keen appreciation for the lyric power, mystery and sacredness of the psalms. As "poems that spring from the depths of the soul where true religious experience abides," [26] the psalms mirror Merton's own poetic attempts to convey his experience of God. For all who embark on the soul-journey to unity with the cross of Christ, the psalms provide spiritual nourishment. As members of the Mystical Body of Christ, laypersons join those in religious life in singing these "songs of this City of God" and "become more fully incorporated into the mystery of God's action in human history."[27]

In addressing problems that are more widespread within human experience (such as distractions to prayer, unfamiliar language within the scriptures, and a universal aversion to suffering and pain) Merton successfully connects with his wider audience. He advises his readers to unite their personal struggles to those of the psalmist, offering the words of the sacred songs as their own prayer, rooted in personal, real-life experience. In this way, Merton establishes a common ground with the average Catholic layperson.

In 1956, Merton published an abbreviated treatment of the same topic for Liturgical Press' "Popular Liturgical Library" series. His *Praying the Psalms* is a thirty-eight page pamphlet, broken into seven untitled reflections on the value of the psalms in personal prayer. Merton's tone is much more conversational than in the earlier book, and the audience and intent are established in a question posed in the opening paragraph: "Why ... should the Christian layman turn to the Psalms and make use of them in his own prayer to God?"[28]

Praying the Psalms takes a basic look at the role of the psalms in the prayer of the Church and it also emphasizes their predominant theme of praise. Only a small section is devoted to the value of praise for contemplation. Significantly, Merton suggests the psalms are an untapped resource for family prayer, and he encourages Catholic parents (particularly fathers) to gain sufficient knowledge to discern the appropriateness of particular psalms to meet their family's specific daily needs.

By 1956, Merton seemed to have arrived at a new and clearer appreciation for the laity's ability to connect with the psalms. In *Bread in the Wilderness*, Merton struggled to imagine a laity capable of understanding the mystery and power of the psalms. Three years later in *Praying the Psalms*, Merton indicated that the layperson might actually have an *advantage* over those in religious life in appreciating the psalms.

Merton asserts that clerics, who often approach the psalms as an obligation or intellectual exercise, may be at a serious disadvantage in entering into them in any deeper way. Conversely, Merton imagines that any serious Christian can encounter God and connect with the psalmist's experience by developing a habit of reciting and meditating on a single psalm each day:

> The problem is therefore not to learn from the Psalms a totally new experience, but rather to recognize, in the Psalms, our own experience lived out and perfected, orientated to God and made fruitful, by the action of loving faith. Ultimately we do this by uniting our joys with the joys of Christ in the Psalms, our sorrows with the sorrows of Christ, and thus allowing ourselves to be carried to heaven on the tide of His victory.[29]

Merton devotes the last two sections of his essay, more than half its content, to identifying recurring themes within the psalms and providing excerpts to illustrate. Passages of scripture make up fifty percent of this portion of the text (a clear indication that the intended audience may lack proficiency in biblical study).

Merton also establishes recurring themes that are universal to the human condition: the delight and peace of following God's will; the struggle to surrender to God; suffering and trials; social and personal sin; and Messianic and eschatological visions of hope and deliverance. Throughout, he illustrates how one can appropriate the words of the given psalms as personal prayers for peace, strength, surrender, and healing, according to one's immediate need.

Aside from the previously mentioned reference to the world as "Babylon," *Bread in the Wilderness* makes no attempt to address the challenges faced by a layperson in living a contemplative life in secular society. No attempt was made to offer practical insights into how to incorporate the psalms into non-religious life. Nevertheless, while Merton's view of the world is sometimes bleak, hope is eternally present in Christ:

> It is not necessary for us to scale heaven to bring down Christ to us by some mysterious technique of contemplation. The Liturgy does not have to bring Christ from heaven. It is the manifestation of His presence and His power on earth. . . . It tells us that His Kingdom has already come. . . . It is established in full power in the midst of a godless humanity. Heaven is within us and all around us, even though we seem to be living in hell.[30]

Praying the Psalms is much more cognizant of the culture surrounding the reader, and the particular difficulties posed by mid-twentieth century society. With the media explosion that accompanied advances in television and radio, Merton questions whether advertising has irrevocably altered the meaning of praise and foreshadows some of his later work as a critic of culture. Judging most praise to be "cheap," "overdone" and "empty," he wonders if any superlatives remain to characterize the holiness of the Lord. The inability to break through this barrier presents a serious obstacle to experiencing the glory of God.

Merton views modern consumer-oriented society as a serious detriment to prayer:

> So we go to Him to ask help and to get out of being
> punished, and to mumble that we need a better job,
> more money, more of the things that are praised by the
> advertisements. And we wonder why our prayer is so
> often dead . . . But we do not really think we need
> God. Least of all do we think we need to praise
> Him.[31]

In Merton's view, the psalms contain a power to revive that spirit of praise in the human heart. By uniting one's daily struggles and joys with those of the psalmist, one can therefore once again recognize that not only is God *needed*, but that He is *everything*.

Since *Bread in the Wilderness* was apparently directed toward those in religious life, it discusses contemplation in much greater depth than *Praying the Psalms*. The prologue proposes a renewed appreciation for the mystical power of scripture (similar to the teaching of Vatican II in the next decade): "The reality which nourishes us in the Psalms is the same reality which nourishes us in the Eucharist, though in a far different form. In either case, we are fed by the Word of God."[32]

After a lengthy treatment of the multiple senses of scripture and the distinction between typology and allegory, Merton makes an important connection between the words of scripture and one's personal experience of God:

> The spiritual understanding of Scripture leads to a mystical awareness of the Spirit of God Himself living and working in our own souls, carrying out, by His mysterious power, in our own lives, the same salvific actions which we can see prefigured and then realized in the Old and New Testaments.[33]

Since the psalms are the words of God written by men under the inspiration of the Holy Spirit, Merton asserts, in reciting the psalms, one speaks the very words of God. Merton regards this truth as fundamental to the psalms' value for contemplation.

> The peculiar mystical impact with which certain verses of Psalms suddenly produce this silent depth-charge in the heart of the contemplative is only to be accounted for by the fact that we, in the Spirit, recognize the Spirit singing in ourselves.[34]

What is important is that Religious and laity alike can appreciate this excellent image of the mystery of contemplative prayer. Authentic contemplative experience widens one's consciousness of God and leads to greater love for others. In Merton's view, the value of one's contemplation can be measured in terms of growth of charity:

> Our growth in Christ is measured not only by intensity of love but also by the deepening of our vision, for we begin to see Christ now not only in our own deep souls, not only in the Psalms, not only in the Mass, but everywhere, shining to the Father in the features of men's faces. The more we are united to Him in love the more we are united in love to one another, because there is only one charity embracing both God and our brother.[35]

Here, also, we see evidence of Merton's personal growth as a monk and his developing thinking about relationships beyond the monastery. As he deepened his understanding of contemplation, he identified more strongly with Christ's presence in other people and moved away from the notion of the world as an evil to be avoided.

As noted, within the context of *Praying the Psalms*, Merton devoted less attention to discussing contemplative prayer. This word appears only three times in thirty-eight pages. In fact, Merton seems consciously to avoid terminology that might seem intimidating to a layperson:

> Let us prescind entirely from the whole question of mystical contemplation. Can we live the Psalms in this particular way without any special gift of God? Can we come to appreciate and "experience" the inner meaning of the Psalms without departing from the ordinary ways of prayer? Certainly we can. All that we need is the ability to understand the meaning of the Psalms, their literal meaning as poems, and to "echo" or answer their meaning in our own experience. Religious experience is born of loving faith. [36]

Praying the Psalms makes no attempt to instruct the reader about contemplation in the same manner evidenced in *Bread in the Wilderness*; however, the core of Merton's message is similar. Any deep experience of prayer (contemplation) involves an attitude of praise, a loving faith, and Christ's mystical presence in both the human heart and the words of scripture.

Both discourses on prayer carry a strong message about approaching the psalms with a focus on achieving a psychological or spiritual "experience." *Praying the Psalms* speaks directly to selfish intents. "If we seek only to 'get something out of them' we will perhaps get less than we expect, and generous efforts may be frustrated because they are turned in the wrong direction: toward ourselves rather than toward God."[37]

Bread in the Wilderness addresses its warning even more directly to seeking mystical contemplative experience: "It is useless ... to seek some secret esoteric 'method' of reciting the Psalter in order to 'get contemplation.' If we chant the psalms with faith, God will manifest Himself to us; and that is contemplation."[38] In both treatments, Merton insists that God's revelation is manifested to hearts that are centered only on God; it is a gift that may only be received, never taken.

The absence of published work devoted to the psalms during the last fifteen years of Merton's life might lead one to question whether his opinion of their value changed. As Merton's focus turned toward the outside world and its problems in the 1960s, his journals reflect less of the angst of his own interior journey than was more evident during his early years as a monk. With the granting of his request for more time of solitude (and, we assume, a corresponding decrease in choir participation), specific references to the psalms become infrequent. However, glimpses of the dialogue between the psalms and Merton's soul are still quite evident. In an entry from January 9, 1962, Merton shares a powerful moment of connection: "Deeply moved by this psalm in particular, in the night office. As if I have never seen it before (Ps. 55). Sometimes you get the impression a psalm is being given to you brand new, to be your own, by God."[39] Later in 1962 he returns to this same Psalm.

In July, 1965, as Merton joyfully anticipated full-time life in his hermitage, he regarded the Psalter an important point of connection between his own solitary life and the experience of the Desert Fathers: "In the evening began a perpetual Psalter.... Need for the continuity the Psalter offers – continuity with my own past and with the past of eremitism.... It is a deep communion with the Lord and His saints..."[40] Woodcock observes that Merton had a deep appreciation for the customs of the Desert Fathers in the formation of the monastic traditions of Christianity,[41] and it seems that his personal experience as a hermit drew him more deeply into the use of the psalms for prayer and meditation.

Eighteen months later, the silence of the hermitage had not eliminated Merton's interior struggles, but lessons from the psalms continue to emerge within Merton's journal:

> But one thing I know: as long as I am in the hermitage I can live according to my conscience, not anyone else's! I am not pure either, but at least I can struggle honestly with my ordinary dishonesty and not inflict my problems on other people. I know at least this solitude and this responsibility and this privileged silence. And the need to pray. Words of my Latin psalms have been driving themselves home to me lately... [42]

This passage concludes with five separate references to verses from the psalms related to the certainty of God's protection and the assurance of victory. Clearly this means Merton was, in a sense, living the Psalms.

Meanwhile, images of the psalms disappeared from much of the poetry in the 1960s. With the publication of *Original Child Bomb* in 1962, Merton's style of verse shifted dramatically from his previous work. With an increase in solitude and a profound concern about the perils of the nuclear age, "Merton himself had taken up poetic residence very near 'the moonlit cemeteries of surrealism,'"[43] says Woodcock. One could, however, argue that there are echoes of psalms in poetry as late as *Cables to the Ace*.

Contemporary Interest in Psalm Prayer

Merton's insights into the laity's interest in contemplative prayer, and particularly into the universal appeal of the psalms as an aid to contemplation, is supported by contemporary writings from a variety of sources. Cynthia Bourgeault, whose work in the field of contemplative prayer is well-known, observes that "contemplative prayer, once regarded as the pinnacle of monastic attainment, is now practiced daily by tens of thousands of Christians worldwide through simplified methods such as Centering Prayer and Christian Meditation."[44] She also characterizes the psalms as "some of the most ancient holy ground in our common Judeo-Christian heritage."[45] Brueggemann observes that "the Psalms are very much like our lives, which are seasons of scattering and gathering."[46] He regards the longevity of the psalms' use in liturgy as confirmation of their importance: "The community has found these words and modes of speech faithful, adequate, and satisfying because the original articulations of prayer have – in our judgement, in our faith, and in our experience – gotten it right."[47] Kathleen Norris agrees that "the psalms are holy in part because they are so well-used," and recognizes in them a "holistic" quality that insists that "the mundane and the holy are inextricably linked."[48] In reflecting the basic movements of human existence, the psalms offer a mirror for recognizing one's personal experience as part of the shared experience of God's people. Bourgeault observes that "the personal nature of the psalms is always in a creative tension with the collective…in a mysterious and dynamic way, the psalms still carry the heart and soul of the ongoing human adventure with God."[49] Praying with the psalms offers a unique opportunity to

reflect one's individual experience "back into community and tradition."[50]

While recognizing the value of the psalms for personal prayer,
Bourgeault also admits, "while the Divine Office may be the cen-
terpiece of the monastic program of spiritual transformation, it
continues to be a hard sell among contemporary lay
contemplatives."[51] It is important to remember that the Liturgy of
the Hours is designed to be a communal prayer, and the absence
of community can make praying the Office an arduous challenge.[52]
Followed systematically, the Office leads one through the entire
collection of one hundred fifty psalms in the course of just one or
two weeks. Norris suggests that this process is "disconcerting for
contemporary people...raised in a culture that idolizes individual
experience, they find it difficult to recite a lament when they're in
a good mood, or to sing a hymn of praise when they're in pain."[53]
However, the Divine Office provides a structure that is needed for
personal prayer. Arthur Boers claims that "the Office helps us
pray when prayer is hard," particularly during the discouragement of spiritual dryness.[54] Without structure and direction from
the wisdom of Christian tradition, he observes that modern Christians can find that they are isolated and disconnected from the
community of faith. A subjective and emotional focus in prayer
ultimately can result in a sense of being "increasingly disconnected
from God."[55]

Contemporary Christian debate continues regarding the usefulness of particular psalms which Brueggemann characterizes as
"the psalms of negativity" — complaints addressed to God that
demand vengeance upon Israel's enemies.[56] Norris reports recent
changes in some Benedictine communities of women, which have
led to the omission of some parts of the harsh, cursing psalms from
their public liturgy.[57] It is no surprise, then, that these psalms are
typically avoided in mainstream Christian worship. Such psalms
present a particular problem for many who resolve to use the
psalms as a meaningful part of their personal prayer. Norris characterizes this perspective as she asks, "How in the world can we
read, let alone pray, these angry and often violent poems from an
ancient warrior culture? At a glance they seem overwhelmingly
patriarchal, ill-tempered, moralistic, vengeful, and often seem to
reflect precisely what is wrong with our world."[58] Similar im-
pressions have surely led many readers to Nan Merrill's less shocking and more peaceful translation entitled *Psalms for Praying: An*

Invitation to Wholeness.   Originally released in September, 1997, Merrill's poetic rendering of the psalms has enjoyed considerable success and is currently offered in a newly revised tenth-anniversary edition.   While Merrill's beautifully tranquil images are attractive and soothing, her translations of these difficult psalms bear no resemblance to their biblical origins.   The striking contrast is evident in a comparative reading of Psalm 137:

By the rivers of Babylon—
   there we sat down and there we
      wept when we remembered Zion.
 On the willows there
   we hung up our harps.
 For there our captors
   asked us for songs,
 And our tormentors asked for mirth,
   saying,
 "Sing us one of the songs of Zion!"
                 (Ps. 137:1-3)
	Plunge into the Ocean of Love,
	   where heart meets Heart,
	 Where sorrows are comforted and
	   wounds are mended.
	 There, melodies of sadness min-
	   gle with dolphin songs of joy;
	 Past fears dissolve in deep
	   harmonic tones,
	   the future—pure mystery.
	 For eternal moments lived in
	   total surrender
	   glide smoothly over troubled
	      waters.

Merrill eliminates all references to the historical setting of the text and erases the bitterness of the psalmist's tone. The closing verses of this psalm, which present what may be the most disturbing and violent images in the entire Bible, are sanitized beyond recognition:

Remember, O LORD, against the
      Edomites
   the day of Jerusalem's fall,
 How they said, "Tear it down!
      Tear it down!"
   down to its foundations!"
 O daughter Babylon, you
   devastator!
 Happy shall they be who pay
   you back
   what you have done to us!
 Happy shall they be who take
   your little ones
   and dash them against the rock!
                 (Ps. 137:7-9)
	Hide not from Love, O friends,
	   sink not into the sea of despair,
	   the mire of hatred.
	 Awaken, O my heart, that I drown
	   not in fear!
	 Too long have I sailed where'ere
	   the winds have blown!
	   Drop anchor!
	 O, Heart of all hearts, set a
	   clear course,
	   that I might follow!
	 Guide me to the Promised Shore! [59]

Such attempts to reinterpret the psalms, rendering them less repugnant to modern sensibilities and more conducive to cultivating inner peace, are well intentioned; however, the result sometimes is verse that hardly seems to qualify as a "translation." (It should be noted that Merrill is careful to preface her work with the disclaimer that her verse is "in no way meant to replace the well-loved, still meaningful, and historically important Psalms of the Hebrew Scripture."[60]) While Merrill's volume is beautifully crafted poetic prayer, which in many instances is faithful to the original text, her treatment of the most disturbing psalms seems to support Brueggemann's assessment that modern Christian piety has become "romantic and unreal in its positiveness...seeking to go from strength to strength, from victory to victory. But such a way not only ignores the Psalms; it is a lie in terms of our experience... the honest recognition that there is an untamed darkness in our life that must be embraced – all of that is fundamental to the gift of new life." Observing that our society prefers to live in denial and avoidance, which results in a collective numbness, he claims that the recovery and use of these psalms could serve as a valuable reality check for our culture. He suggests that the spiritual crisis that resulted for many in the wake of the tragedies of September 11, 2001 illustrate "how urgent the descent into disorientation is for the practice of faith."[61]

Norris and Bourgeault are in agreement with Brueggemann that these psalms merit closer consideration because they hold an important key to an authentic prayer life. Norris asserts that the darker psalms force us to face the realities of the human psyche: "The psalms reveal our most difficult conflicts, and our deep desire, in Jungian terms, to run from the shadow. In them, the shadow speaks to us directly, in words that are painful to hear... They ask us to be honest about ourselves and admit that we, too, harbor the capacity for vengeance."[62] Bourgeault affirms the benefit that arises when these psalms take up residence in our consciousness and

> begin to create a safe spiritual container for recognizing and processing those dark shadows within ourselves, those places we'd prefer not to think about. There are times in the spiritual journey when anger is a very real part of our life, just as jealousy, abandonment, helplessness, rage and terror are. All of these emotions are in us, and they're all in the psalms.[63]

By acknowledging and validating the reality of these emotions, and connecting us to three millennia of shared human experience, these psalms remind us that others have walked through these same dark passages. Bourgeault believes engagement with these psalms offers an opportunity to acknowledge fully the emotions without "getting stuck in them." In a very real sense, praying these psalms can "serve as a kind of confessional, allowing us to place our shadow side on the altar of prayer and find our release there." She concludes that "contemporary revisionist criticism that finds fault with the violence of the imagery is misplaced in contemplative psalmody. The psalms are psychological tools. They describe the interior warfare, the desolation, the shadow and its transfiguration."[64]

Norris concurs that engaging the psalms in prayer offers the opportunity for transformation. Praying through destructive feelings like vengeance opens the possibility of diffusing these deadly forces, and (much to our surprise!) finding in them occasions for praise. The discomfort of encountering the psalms is in this tension between pain and praise.

> They don't allow us to deny either the depth of our pain or the possibility of its transformation into praise, [demanding] that we recognize that praise does not spring from a delusion that things are better than they are, but rather from the human capacity for joy. Only when we see this can we understand that both lamentation and exultation can be forms of praise... The psalms are evidence that praise need not be a fruit of optimism.[65]

Brueggemann agrees that a faith which attempts to bring even the most painful experiences to speech and use those experiences as a basis for conversation with God is a *"transformed* faith," which demonstrates a recognition of God's presence in even the darkest moments of human existence. However, he insists that the transformative power of the psalms extends beyond the personal to the communal dimension of spirituality, resulting in a deeper concern for social justice. Conventional, privatistic spirituality often fails to appreciate the issue of theodicy which is inherent in the prayers of ancient Israel. For Israel, *"communion with God* cannot be celebrated without attention to *the nature of the community,* both among human persons and with God." Unless the spirituality we find in the psalms causes us to confront questions of God's justice, we have missed a vital aspect of psalmic faith. "The Psalms crave for and mediate communion with God, but Israel insists that communion must be honest, open to criticism, and capable of transformation." Authentic Christian spirituality founded on the psalms must involve a "vigorous, candid and daring" dialogue with God about the state of our world and our own call to the pursuit of justice.[66]

While Thomas Merton's context for psalmody was rooted in the monastic choir, until recently little attention has been given to the relationship between the vocalization of the psalms and the contemplative experience. Since references to musical instruments and possible melodies are present in the titles to many psalms, it is curious that so little attention has been paid to music's contribution to the psalms' power to mediate an experience of God. Earlier references in Merton's journals clearly demonstrate that he had committed certain verses of the psalms to memory. An interesting question arises when one considers what effect the chanting of the verses may have had on Merton's ability to retrieve the words. Was it the words themselves, or the words in combination with the melody, which caused the psalms to sink into Merton's soul? The fact that words become more memorable when set to music is fact that few people would question. Whether attending a concert or listening to the radio in the privacy of their own cars, music-lovers can be found singing along with the words of their favorite tunes. By overlooking the musical accompaniment that has long been a part of the Christian tradition of psalmody, modern efforts to pray the psalms may be lacking a vital component of contemplation.

In recent years, modern culture has expressed an interest in several offerings of the psalms set to music. The CD *"Chant,"* a rendition of the Latin psalter produced by the monks of Santo Domingo de Silos in Spain, was a very popular success that renewed interest in Gregorian chant. The Taizé community in France, which welcomes between 2,500 and 6,000 pilgrims each week of the summer season, has also developed a following for their music. Taizé presents prayer that is beautiful in its simplicity, usually in the form of mantra-like chants formed by the blending of short texts from the psalms with a repetitive melody. Brother Jean-Marie of the Taizé community says their efforts are aimed at helping people discover that "there's something natural in prayer, something a little bit like breathing, like eating... We all need to find some way that God becomes—and faith becomes—a natural element of life." He observes that musicality adds to the experience of prayer: "There's a fullness to sung prayer, an element of wholeness."[67]

In *Chanting the Psalms*, Bourgeault characterizes the psalms as "soul music" and insists that "there's a hidden wisdom in psalmody that makes sense of the practice itself and pulls a lot of the other elements in the Christian contemplative path together." She acknowledges the challenges of learning to chant the psalms but insists that "there is a mysterious vital current that flows between the psalms and Christian inner awakening, each pole revivifying and intensifying the other" which makes the effort worthwhile.[68]   Certainly, contemporary interest in the psalms as a medium for prayer and contemplation is quite likely to continue.

Merton's Vision

Bread in the Wilderness and *Praying the Psalms* offer interesting insights into Merton's growth as a monk, a writer and a contemplative and in his desires to communicate about the psalms for laypersons. His reader catches brief glimpses of Merton's personal struggle to find solitude, even within the lifestyle of a monastic community. Longing to escape the world to rest in God alone, Merton was paradoxically drawn to share his journey with this same world through his writing.

Moving away from the scholarly, religious treatment of the psalms found in *Bread in the Wilderness,* a distinctly new approach was adopted in *Praying the Psalms,* as Merton's attention turned to the laity. As his own contemplation deepened with each passing year, so did his skill and his desire for bringing others to a more profound experience of God.

Neither *Bread in the Wilderness* or *Praying the Psalms* is considered among Merton's finest work, but re-examined in the context of the decade in which they were written, they establish Merton among the theologians of the twentieth century whose vision helped form the reforms of the Second Vatican Council. His concern for "active participation in the Liturgy"[69] is echoed in Vatican II's *The Constitution on the Sacred Liturgy* (14).

Merton's sense of scripture as the Word of God, equal to and inseparable from the reality of Christ in the Eucharist parallels the

Council's emphasis on the liturgy's "one table of the Word of God and the Body of Christ."[70] Through his effort to inspire Catholics toward a deeper experience of prayer, Merton advanced the same hope for the laity's power to transform the world that the Council expressed in the *Dogmatic Constitution on the Church* (31-38). The Church would not officially encourage the laity to personal study of the word of God until November, 1964,[71] but already a full decade beforehand, Thomas Merton was advocating daily meditation on scripture and especially the psalms as every Christian's most effective path to knowing and loving God.

As the Holy Spirit moved within the Church in preparation for Vatican II, Thomas Merton joined with leading theologians of the time to imagine a new vision of the Church which would address the issues faced by mankind in the twentieth century. In a rapidly changing world where silence and solitude were in short supply, Merton believed that both the laity and religious within the Church could experience God as he had: through contemplation and the words of sacred scripture. More than fifty years later, as distractions and noise remain an enduring plague for residents of the twenty-first century, the need to find meaningful expression and context for experiences of joy, fear, anger and pain is perhaps stronger than ever. While many well-meaning contemporary authors continue to follow in Merton's footsteps in offering advice to the masses on techniques of prayer (and even updated translations of the Hebrew psalms), many of these attempts to satisfy our spiritual hungers prove insufficient. As a new generation is discovering, and as Merton argued, the psalms provide authentic nourishment and offer a timeless pathway to prayer and contemplation.

Notes

1. Now entitled *Worship*.

2. Thomas Merton, *The Seven Storey Mountain* (New York: Harcourt, Brace, 1948) p. 300.

3. Thomas Merton, *Entering the Silence*, ed. Jonathon Montaldo (San Francisco: HarperCollins, 1996). See entries for 1947: May 4, 14, 29, June 24, July 6, August 20, Sept. 14, 24 (71, 73, 79, 87, 89, 102, 112, 122).

4. Merton, *Entering the Silence*, p. 122.

5. Merton, *Entering the Silence*, pp. 196-198.

6. George Woodcock, *Thomas Merton, Monk and Poet* (New York: Farrar, Straus & Giroux, 1978), p. 51.

7. Woodcock, *Thomas Merton*, pp. 55-58.

8. Woodcock, *Thomas Merton*, p. 61.

9. Thomas Merton, *The Collected Poems of Thomas Merton* (New York: New Directions, 1977), p. 40.

10. Woodcock, *Thomas Merton*, pp. 56-57.

11. Woodcock, *Thomas Merton*, p. 53.

12. Merton,*Collected Poems*, p. 220.

13. Walter Brueggemann, *The Psalms and the Life of Faith*, ed. Patrick D. Miller (Minneapolis: Fortress, 1995), p. 24.

14. Brueggemann, *The Psalms and the Life of Faith*, p. 31.

15. See Woodcock, *Thomas Merton*, p. 58.

16. Thomas Merton, *A Search for Solitude*, ed. Lawrence Cunningham (San Francisco: HarperCollins, 1996), p. 71.

17. Woodcock, *Thomas Merton*, p. 56.

18. Merton, *Collected Poems*, pp. 231-32. Brueggemann classifies psalms of disorientation into two general categories: communal and personal laments. See *The Message of the Psalms* (Minneapolis: Augsburg, 1984), pp. 51-77.

19. Psalm 38:5-6. All quotations are from *The New Oxford Annotated Bible*, New Revised Standard Version, 1994.

20. For further reading, see Jean Daniélou, *The Bible and the Liturgy* (Notre Dame, IN: University of Notre Dame Press, 1956) and *From Shadows to Reality: Studies in the Biblical Typology of the Fathers*, trans. Wulstan Hibberd (Westminster, MD: Newman Press, 1960).

21. Thomas Merton, *Bread in the Wilderness* (New York: New Directions, 1953), p. 4.

22. Lawrence S. Cunningham, *Thomas Merton and the Monastic Vision* (Grand Rapids, MI: Eerdmans, 1999), p. 26.

23. Merton, *Bread in the Wilderness*, p. 43.

24. Merton, *Bread in the Wilderness*, p. 38.

25. Merton, *Bread in the Wilderness*, pp. 89-90.

26. Robert Waldron, *Poetry as Prayer: Thomas Merton* (Boston: Pauline Books, 2000), p. 47.

27. Merton, *Bread in the Wilderness*, pp. 43-44.

28. Thomas Merton, *Praying the Psalms* (Collegeville, MN: Liturgical Press, 1956), p. 3.

29. Merton, *Praying the* Psalms, pp. 16-17.

30. Merton, *Bread in the Wilderness*, p. 136.

31. Merton, *Praying the Psalms*, p. 6.

32. Merton, *Bread in the Wilderness*, pp. 3-4.

33. Merton, *Bread in the Wilderness*, p. 37.

34. Merton, *Bread in the Wilderness*, p. 75.

35. Merton, *Bread in the Wilderness*, p. 92.
36. Merton, *Praying the Psalms*, p. 16.
37. Merton, *Praying the Psalms*, p. 31.
38. Merton, *Bread in the Wilderness*, p. 15.
39. Thomas Merton, *Turning Toward the World*, ed. Victor A. Kramer (San Francisco: HarperCollins, 1996), p. 193.
40. Thomas Merton, *Dancing in the Water of Life*, ed. Robert E. Daggy, (San Francisco: HarperCollins, 1997), p. 273.
41. Woodcock, *Thomas Merton*, p. 78.
42. Thomas Merton, *Learning to Love*, ed. Christine M. Bochen (San Francisco: HarperCollins, 1997), p. 170.
43. Woodcock, *Thomas Merton*, p. 56.
44. Cynthia Bourgeault, *Chanting the Psalms* (Boston: New Seeds, 2006), p. ix.
45. Bourgeault, *Chanting the Psalms*, p. 9.
46. Brueggeman, *Psalms and Life*, p. 31.
47. Brueggeman, *Psalms and Life*, p. 33.
48. Kathleen Norris, *Cloister Walk* (New York: Riverhead, 1996), p. 93.
49. Bourgeault, *Chanting the* Psalms, p. 16.
50. Norris, *Cloister Walk*, p. 100.
51. Bourgeault, *Chanting the Psalms*, p. 3.
52. Arthur P. Boers, "Learning the Ancient Rhythms of Prayer," *Christianity Today* 45 (2001): p. 42.
53. Norris, *Chanting the Psalms*, p. 101.
54. Boers, "Learning the Ancient Rhythms of Prayer," p. 41.
55. Boers, "Learning the Ancient Rhythms of Prayer," p. 40.
56. Brueggemann, *Spirituality of the Psalms* (Minneapolis: Fortress: 2002), p. xii.
57. Norris, *Cloister Walk*, p. 97.
58. Norris, *Cloister Walk*, p. 93.
59. Nan C. Merrill, *Psalms for Praying* (New York: Continuum, 2007), p. 275.
60. Merrill, *Psalms for Praying*, p. x.
61. Brueggemann, *Spirituality* xii, xv, 13.
62. Norris, *Cloister Walk*, p. 97, p. 104.
63. Bourgeault *Chanting the Psalms*, p. 41, p.43.
64. Bourgeault *Chanting the Psalms*, p. 44, p. 47.
65. Norris, *Cloister Walk*, p. 94, p. 96, p. 104.
66. Brueggemann, *Spirituality* 27, 59-74.
67. Brother Jean-Marie, "Prayer at Taizé: Singing and Silence," *Christian Century* 118 (2001), pp. 16-17.

68. Bourgeault, *Chanting the Psalms*, p. 6, p. 49.

69. Merton, *Bread in the Wilderness*, p. 42.

70. Austin Flannery, ed., *Vatican Council II, Dogmatic Constitution on Divine Revelation* (Northport NY: Costello, 1998), p. 21.

71. Flannery, *Dogmatic Constitution on the Church*, p. 37.

Thomas Merton's Approach to St. John of the Cross

Keith J. Egan

Julian [of Norwich] is without doubt one of the most wonderful of all Christian voices. She gets greater and greater in my eyes as I grow older, and whereas in the old days I used to be crazy about St. John of the Cross, I would not exchange him now for Julian if you gave me the world and the Indies and all the Spanish mystics rolled up in one bundle.

Thomas Merton made the above comment in a 1962 letter to Sister Madeleva Wolff, CSC, president of Saint Mary's College, Notre Dame, Indiana. Madeleva had chided Merton for omitting Julian of Norwich and other fourteenth-century English mystics from his notes "An Introduction to Christian Mysticism."[1] As is well known, Merton often expressed his enthusiasms extravagantly, some of which extravagances need to be taken with the proverbial grain of salt. Although Julian of Norwich would eventually capture his fancy, Merton turned early in his spiritual journey to John of the Cross. As Michael Mott wrote: "No writer and no religious authority meant more to Merton in the 1940s than St John of the Cross...."[2] In 1939, searching "to become a saint," Merton turned in earnest to John of the Cross:

So at great cost I bought the first volume of the Works of St. John of the Cross and sat in the room on Perry Street and turned over the first pages, underlining places here and there with a pencil. But it turned out that it would take more than that to make me a saint: because these words I underlined, although they amazed and dazzled me with their import, were all too simple for me to understand. They were too naked, too stripped of all duplicity and compromise for my complexity, perverted by many appetites. However, I am glad that I was at least able to recognize them, obscurely, as worthy of the greatest respect.[3]

Despite the above somewhat invidious comparison with Julian of Norwich, Thomas Merton's early attraction to the Spanish poet and mystic lasted throughout his lifetime.[4] In *Contemplative Prayer*, published posthumously in 1969, which Douglas Steere called Merton's "last testament," John of the Cross remains a significant voice and resource.[5] My essay in no way pretends to be a full-scale study of the influence of John of the Cross on Thomas Merton. That task would require a much longer inquiry than is possible for this brief undertaking. Rather I shall confine myself to a consideration of Merton's approach to John of the Cross in his two *ex professo* studies of the Carmelite poet and mystic: *The Ascent to Truth* and the essay "Light in Darkness: The Ascetic Doctrine of St. John of the Cross."

Thomas Merton was an important, perhaps the most important, North American voice in the revival of Christian spirituality that began in the mid-twentieth century and which continues to this day. David Tracy is convinced that Merton was "...one of the most influential proponents of the spiritual life in the twentieth century."[6] His early and on-going intense interest in John of the Cross, saint and doctor of the Church, was an important element in the renewed interest in the Spanish mystic that took place in the decades following Merton's death in 1968. Without Thomas Merton the retrieval of interest in mysticism and in a mystic's mystic like John of the Cross would certainly have been a quite different story. Merton's attraction to contemplation and mysticism inevitably led for many to the "turn" to the classics of Christian mysticism. Merton who devoured the classics of Christian mysticism became a prophetic voice that was heard by many and that sent these searchers to explore the spiritual riches of Christian classics from the gospels to Merton's own texts, some of which are already numbered among the classics.

The Ascent to Truth

Any inquiry into Thomas Merton's relationship with John of the Cross must take into account the Cistercian's book, *The Ascent to Truth*, published in September 1951, only three years after the appearance of *The Seven Storey Mountain*, two years after the publication of *Seeds of Contemplation*, eleven years before the opening of the Second Vatican Council. Merton dedicated his *Ascent to Truth* to Our Lady of Mount Carmel, and he said that this book was "...chiefly concerned with the doctrine of the Carmelite theolo-

gian, Saint John of the Cross."[7] Obviously the *Ascent* in the title of
the book was inspired by John of the Cross' *The Ascent of Mount
Carmel* which is the most cited of John's works in Merton's *Ascent
to Truth*; in fact, in some ways, Merton found it difficult to get beyond John's *Ascent*.

In 1964 Merton referred to *The Ascent to Truth* as "my wordiest
and in some ways emptiest book. ... it is a book about which I
have doubts. I think the material in it may be fairly good, but it is
not my kind of book, and in writing it, I was not fully myself."[8]
With *The Ascent to Truth*, Merton had attempted a book of theological justification, clearly not his métier. In 1967 the monk author evaluated his *Ascent* as "less good" among the books he had
published up till that date; indeed, Merton was a demanding critic
of his own writing. He awarded none of his books his highest rat-
ing of "best."[9]   In the preface to the 1958 French edition of *The
Ascent to Truth*, which Merton considered the definitive version of
this work, he wrote: "This book was written seven years ago. If I
were to attack the same subject at the present day (and I very probably would not), I might approach it very differently."[10] The manuscript of this book had several trial titles. On February 9, 1949,
Merton referred to it as *The Cloud and The Fire*,[11] while in 1951 within
less than a month he called the manuscript by two different names:
Fire Cloud and Darkness, then *The Ascent to Light*. He mentioned
these last two titles to Sister Thérèse Lentfoehr, SDS, on February
10, and March 1, 1951. On the former date he wrote to Sister
Thérèse, about what he called "at least the first draft," and added
that "it was your St. John of the Cross relic that did the trick! The
book is practically all about his doctrine. ... but only on the lower
reaches of Mount Carmel."[12] Sister Thérèse, who died in 1981,
shared with the writer of this essay that Merton regularly sent her
a relic or some manuscript and the like for what he mistakenly
thought was her birthday, July 16th, the feast of Our Lady of Mount
Carmel. His friend, Sister Thérèse, did nothing to set Merton
straight on the correct date of her birthday, which was July 18th.

At Gethsemani, in preparation for the priesthood Merton received a narrowly neo-scholastic theological education which was
at the time deemed adequate for those who would be monastic
priests; in fact, Lawrence Cunningham contends that these studies were "terribly unsatisfactory."[13] This neo-scholastic theology
inherited a sharp division between what were called ascetical and
mystical theology, two differing courses that the curriculum in

seminaries could not easily fit in their schedules. Catholic theological training at the time paid too little attention to scripture and to the writings of the Fathers of the Church as well as to the spiritual classics. By 1957 Merton acknowledged that these deficiencies had an effect upon his *The Ascent to Truth*, and he added that "scholasticism...is not the true intellectual climate for a monk."[14] Merton later laid out his vision for the formation and theological training of monks in an essay entitled "The Need for a New Education," in which he called for a sapiential theology for monks that would be broad and open. Merton understood from his own less than satisfactory theological training that there was a need for well-formed monks who could understand their monastic existence and the world beyond the monastery theologically.[15]

Goal of the Spiritual Life: Ascetical or Mystical?

A key to understanding Merton's approach to John of the Cross was this division into ascetical and mystical theology, a division that if applied too rigidly has unfortunate results. Bernard McGinn has shown that the texts of Giovanni Battista Scaramelli, S.J., 1687-1752, "were probably the most influential proponents in designating 'asceticism' and 'mysticism,' or ascetical and mystical theology." This terminology was in vogue at the time Merton composed *The Ascent to Truth*, and it certainly influenced his reading of the writings of John of the Cross. A book used in monastic formation and in seminaries when Merton was preparing for religious life and the priesthood was the ubiquitous manual of Adolphe Tanquerey entitled *The Spiritual Life: A Treatise on Ascetical and Mystical Theology*,[16] a study with which Merton was certainly acquainted. An anti-mystical era lasted in the Western Christian Church from the late seventeenth century until the middle of the twentieth century. The presumption of that era was that Christians were to be satisfied with an ascetical life since the contemplative or mystical life was usually beyond their reach, reserved for a few enclosed nuns. Within this milieu Merton became an interpreter of the teachings of John of the Cross. Eventually his interests in contemplation and mysticism would undo such a restrictive attitude, if not in his study of John, at least in his broader spiritual outlook.

John of the Cross never used the Spanish word *el ascetismo*, nor does this word appear in a Spanish dictionary that was published in 1611, a dictionary closest to the time of John of the Cross.[17]

The Ascent to Truth's citation from *Dark Night* 1.6.2 of undue physical mortification as nothing more than the "penance of beasts," is in the Spanish "la penitencia de bestias" To indicate what he meant by asceticism John of the Cross used words that in English translation appear as detachment, self-denial, mortification, annihilation, and purification. Moreover, John also used symbolic language to illustrate that one needs to be free of disordered attachments so that God may fill the empty space with God's love, expressions like emptiness, darkness, nakedness and poverty of spirit.

Thomas Merton, like most new students of John of the Cross, began by reading John's *The Ascent of Mount Carmel*. Among John's commentaries the *Ascent* appears first in collections of his writings. However, it is better to begin to read John of the Cross in a different order. Of John's four commentaries, *Ascent, Dark Night, The Spiritual Canticle* and *The Living Flame of Love*, the *Ascent* is the least well-crafted. John had not yet found his rhythm in this earliest of his commentaries. Moreover, in the *Ascent* John was dealing with one of the most difficult phases in the contemplative journey, where one must struggle to become free of what blocks one from being fully open to God's love. There is something in us humans that resists genuine spiritual freedom. John described this phase of the spiritual life in *The Ascent of Mount Carmel* as the time of the active nights of the sense and spirit. These active nights comprise what Merton and his time would refer to as the ascetical life. One needs to keep in mind that Merton belonged to the "Trappist" Order which, when he entered, put great stress on the penitential or ascetical character of the spiritual life. That had been so since the time of Armand de Rancé, who died in 1700, and the Trappists at that time gave much less attention to mystical prayer. Merton's gift to the Cistercian Order was to remind it of its contemplative heritage that had thrived so fully in the twelfth century when the Cistercian spirit was shaped by the likes of Bernard of Clairvaux and William of St. Thierry.

How much richer would Merton's understanding of John of the Cross have been if he had first found his way to the Spanish mystic by way of John's poetry, letters, and *Sayings of Light and Love*, then worked his way back to the *Ascent*, but only after first having studied John's *Living Flame of Love*, *The Spiritual Canticle* and *The Dark Night*? Read in this sequence one comes to *Ascent of Mount Carmel* knowing why the ascetical purification/liberation of the *Ascent* is crucial to anyone who seeks to be transformed in

God through love. That transformation is what the contemplative life is all about for John of the Cross. To limit one's vision to the ascetical life is to deny that one was created for the love that God pours into the liberated heart.[18]

For John of the Cross, the journey of *The Ascent of Mount Carmel* is but a prelude to the love that blooms in a heart that God has freed. Genuine freedom comes not through one's own efforts— the active nights. For John of the Cross, liberation from disordered attachments comes fully and finally through the purifying contemplative dark nights—the passive nights—that follow on what is described in *The Ascent of Mount Carmel*. Thomas Merton, though he knew better, seemed stuck in the active nights of the *Ascent* at least in his writing. However, as we have seen, Merton began his study of John with the first volume of the mystic's writings where he found the *Ascent* waiting for his own avid exploration.

John of the Cross: Thomist?

A serious detriment to an understanding of the doctrine of John of the Cross in *The Ascent to Truth* is Merton's presumption that John of the Cross was a thoroughgoing Thomist: "Here as everywhere Saint John of the Cross is a true Thomist."[19] In his *Ascent* Merton consistently argues that John's teaching was a doctrine that focused on reason and intellect. Steven Payne, OCD, who has studied this matter carefully, has this to say:

> ... even those familiar with scholasticism have often erred by assuming too readily that John was fundamentally a Thomist. More recent studies have shown that John disagreed with Aquinas on a number of substantive issues. And although his basic intellectual framework was undeniably scholastic, John was an original thinker who was not afraid to modify received views in order to deal with the spiritual life more clearly and accurately.[20]

In his claim that John was thoroughly a Thomist, Merton was following an opinion common at the time, and one that has prevailed among some until now.[21] In this regard Merton was especially influenced by Jacques Maritain's thomistic reading of John of the Cross.[22] My estimate is that John of the Cross was labeled as a Thomist because a Dominican like Reginald Garrigou-LaGrange (1877-1964), had linked "...the mystical wisdom of St. John of the Cross to the speculative wisdom of St. Thomas."[23] Jacques Maritain was influenced by Garrigou-Lagrange in his interpretation of John of the Cross. True, John of the Cross followed Thomas Aquinas in some ways, e.g., in his cognitional theory, but John is not a thorough-going Thomist by any means.

Basically John of the Cross is in the Augustinian tradition and a Platonist. One example of John's Augustinian affiliation is his use of the three faculties of the soul, intellect, will and memory rather than the thomist rendition of intellect and will as the soul's spiritual faculties. There is much else besides in John that identifies him with the platonic spiritual tradition of the middle ages, not the least of which was John's thorough adoption of the imagery and theology of the Song of Songs and the quite platonic *nachleben* or afterlife of The Song. John of the Cross, therefore, owed much to the Platonism, some would say the Neo-Platonism, of the Song of Songs tradition that began with Origen's middle Platonism. Teresa of Avila and John of the Cross introduced the Song of Songs tradition to Carmelite Spirituality and their example has had a lasting impact on Christian spirituality since then. To make John of the Cross a thoroughgoing Thomist puts his teaching in a context not faithful to his vision of the contemplative life. John was much more at home in the Platonic tradition.[24]

Thomas Merton characterized *The Ascent to Truth* as "...chiefly concerned with the doctrine of the Carmelite theologian, Saint John of the Cross."[25] The fact is John of the Cross was not a professional theologian. The Carmelite friar studied arts and philosophy for three years at the University of Salamanca and theology for only one year. John of the Cross' principal ministry was spiritual guidance, not theology. Whatever theological commentary appears in John's commentaries, and there is quite a bit especially in *The Ascent of Mount Carmel*, it was meant solely to ground his spiritual guidance. His writings, all of them, constitute a treasury of spiritual guidance, not theological commentary. John of the Cross dedicated *The Spiritual Canticle* to his dear friend Ana de Jesús, then prioress at Granada. In his prologue to this commentary he said to Mother Ana:

> ...although some scholastic theology is used here in reference to the soul's interior converse with God, it will not prove vain to speak in such a manner to the pure of spirit. Even though Your Reverence lacks training in scholastic theology, through which the divine truths are understood, you are not wanting

in mystical theology, which is known through love and by which these truths are not only known but at the same time enjoyed.[26]

Merton eventually became aware that his *Ascent* made too little use of scripture and the Fathers in his interpretation of John of the Cross. Had he done otherwise, he would have noticed that John regularly illustrated his teaching with a spiritual interpretation of texts: e. g, citing Job 7:2-4, John says that Job is speaking spiritually.[27] In speaking of prophecies about Christ, John wrote: "These prophecies about Christ should have been understood in their spiritual sense, in which they were most true."[28] John knew the literal sense of scripture but was much more interested in the spiritual or accommodated sense of scripture: "Guiding themselves, then, by the literal sense it was impossible for them to avoid deception."[29] John's studies at the University of Salamanca occurred during lively debates between traditionalists and those like Luis de León and Gaspar de Grajal who advocated the literal sense of scripture and the use of the vernacular.[30] John of the Cross followed professors like these in his use of the vernacular but not in a reliance on the literal sense of scripture.[31] John in one place even speaks of the baseness of the letter.[32] Elsewhere I have described John as having a biblical imagination,[33] an imagination shaped by his immersion in the bible.[34] Had Thomas Merton had a better and more extensive training in scripture, he would surely have appreciated the biblical grounding of the teachings of Saint John of the Cross and the necessity to attend to the way John's use of scripture affected the meaning of his spiritual doctrine.

A Tale of Two Poets

It is more than a little surprising that Thomas Merton the poet did not make more of the poetry of John of the Cross in *The Ascent to Truth*. Even when Merton quotes a stanza of the world-acclaimed "Spiritual Canticle,"[35] his emphasis is on the poem's commentary not on the poem as a poem.[36] What I think is at stake here, and elsewhere in Merton, was the prevailing chasm in Christianity between nature and grace. This separation of nature and grace left Merton unaware that one can theologize from poetry as well as from prose. An example of this wariness can be seen in the essay that Merton wrote for *Commonweal* on "Poetry and Contemplation" in 1947.[37] This essay shows Merton, like the Christian culture of this time, without an appreciation for the inner connection between the gift of poetry and the gift of grace, between poetry and prayer, between nature and grace and even the connection of nature and grace with glory. Merton did come in time to see that the sharp divisions between nature and grace carry a heavy price if one wants to lead a more integrated spiritual life. I think a more integrated view of nature and grace is evident in Merton's *Asian Journal*.[38] What a different book *The Ascent to Truth* would have been had Thomas Merton been able to tap into John of Cross' primary experience as imagined in his poetry. John wrote in his prologue to *The Spiritual Canticle* that the poem on which he was commenting was "...composed with a certain burning love of God"; that his poem contained "...expressions of love arising from mystical understanding...," and "...were composed in a love flowing from abundant mystical understanding."[39] It is regrettable that Thomas Merton did not feel free to use the poetry of John of the Cross as a *locus theologicus*, a place from which to explore and to express the compelling beauty of God. John's poems gave Merton every opportunity to find joy in the beauty of John's poetry and in the beauty of God.

> Let us rejoice, Beloved,
> And let us got forth to behold ourselves in your beauty
> To the mountain and to the hill,
> To where the pure water flows,
> And further, deep into the thicket.[40]

John of the Cross Apophatic?

It has been common, almost universal, to classify John of the Cross as an apophatic mystic. In *The Ascent to Truth*[41] Merton joined the chorus and referred to John of the Cross' theology as apophatic. A more nuanced way of understanding mysticism as apophatic or kataphatic was still a long way off in Merton's day. Yet, earlier in *The Ascent to Truth*[42] the Trappist author saw that "some of the greatest mystics—Ruysbroeck, Saint Teresa of Ávila, and Saint John of the Cross himself—describe both aspects of contemplation, 'light' and 'darkness.'" Merton, I think, had an inkling that it was too simplistic to designate any true mystic as simply apophatic or only kataphatic. What we now know is that the difference between the two designations is one of emphasis more than one of absolute division. The apophatic and the kataphatic are the other side of each other. An apophatic experience, in fact, depends on there being kataphatic experience.[43] Authors, however, have consistently labeled John of the Cross as apophatic without noting how much of John's poetry and other writings are filled with light and graphic imagery, especially imagery from the Song of Songs. Perhaps the ascetical character of John of the Cross' *The Ascent of Mount Carmel* and the darkness associated with John's *Dark Night* have been emphasized over the light, life and love for which the dark nights exist.[44] One should also keep in mind such characterizations of the Holy Spirit as the Living Flame of Love.[45] Indeed, John of the Cross clearly knows that experience of God is an experience of unknowing, an experience of mystery; yet, that profound mystery can be manifested in symbols of life, light and love.

Light in Darkness

In less than a decade after the publication of *The Ascent to Truth* Thomas Merton published a collection of essays entitled *Disputed Questions*.[46] This latter book, which Merton dedicated to Boris Pasternak, continues Merton's interest in the Carmelite tradition to which he devotes two of the studies in this book, including "Light in Darkness; The Ascetic Doctrine of St. John of the Cross."[47] Though the book's essays seem loosely connected, the author claimed that "...one theme, one question above all, which runs through the whole book...: [is] the relation of the *person* to the *social organization*.... [or] ...solitude vs. community."[48] That statement is important for the study of the Carmelite tradition; in fact, I contend that the basic motif of Carmelite spirituality is the creative tension between solitude and community.[49] This theme, which was so important in Merton's personal struggle over the relationship of eremitic life to cenobitic monasticism, may account in part for Merton's fascination with the Carmelite tradition.

In this essay "Light in Darkness: The Ascetic Doctrine of St. John of the Cross," Merton may have been responding indirectly to his own critique of *The Ascent to Truth*. As a matter of fact, Merton's essay "Light in Darkness" is a short, inadequate response to what Merton saw as the perception of John's harshness or, as Merton says, an asceticism that could be perceived as "...mechanical, cold, soulless and inhuman: a kind of mathematical exclusion of all spontaneity in favor of dreary and rigid self-punishment."[50] Merton, like John of the Cross, was an impatient writer with a yen to get on with what was next on his mind.

In this defense of John of the Cross Merton affirmed the biblical foundations of John's holiness and teachings. The Trappist monk was convinced that John's life and doctrine were derived from "...the New Testament, the Sermon on the Mount, the profound discourses in the Gospel of St. John, and particularly the mystery of the Passion and the Resurrection of the Son of God."[51] For Merton, John of the Cross' hard sayings were like the hard sayings in the Gospels. He argued that John's demands offered as an alternative to self-gratification "...love and the will of God." John, Merton explained, taught that one must prefer one to the other; one must make a choice.[52] Merton acknowledged that John of the Cross' asceticism "...may seem drastic, but it can lead one to the interior detachment and tranquility without which a fully contemplative life is impossible."[53] Merton was very much on target when he saw in John's asceticism a call to radical freedom, the freedom to love God and others as God intended creation and others to be loved. The Gethsemani monk wrote:

> If we read the saint carefully, and take care to weigh every word, we will see that he is preaching a doctrine of pure liberty which is the very heart of the New Testament. He wants us to be free. He wants to liberate us not only from the captivity of passion and egoism, but even from the more subtle tyranny of spiritual ambition, and preoccupation with methods of prayer and systems for making progress.[54]

I find that Merton's perception of John as advocating freedom fits exactly a careful reading of the Spanish Carmelite whose bottom line in the spiritual life is, I think, a call to freedom and love.

Merton in his "Light in Darkness" essay was still trying to apologize and explain what he saw as John of the Cross' asceticism; yet Merton felt the need to dispel John's reputation for severity. In this essay he shows a glimmer of going beyond the asceticism to John's mysticism. He cites John's *Living Flame of Love* where the soul walks "...in loving awareness of God...possessing this pure, simple and loving awareness, as one that opens his eyes with an awareness of love."[55] John of the Cross' contemplative goal is "loving attentiveness," *advertencia amorosa*, to the God of love.[56] The struggle for freedom in *The Ascent of Mount Carmel* is justified by the gift of loving attention to the God who is love.

At the conclusion of "Light in Darkness," Merton came close to, but still short of seeing the theological significance of John's poetry. He said that John's poems "...happily complete the aphorisms and cautions, and incite the reader to go on to the saint's great mystical treatises which are nothing but commentaries on his poems. The remarkable beauty of his poems shows that his asceticism, far from destroying his creative genius, had liberated and transformed it by dedicating it to God."[57] Nature and grace were still separated in Merton's mind. Would that the Trappist poet had been able to appreciate the primacy of John of the Cross' poetry and, in at least three of his poems, to see that these poems arose from John's mystical experience. Merton would then have been able to recommend to his readers the usefulness of John's poems as prayers in themselves and as a texts that can teach one how to pray. John of the Cross' poems are genuine resources for contemplative prayer; they open up the imagination to new horizons of belief in a merciful and loving God.

While "Light in Darkness" made some significant progress in his presentation of John of the Cross' teaching, Merton seems in the context of this essay to be eager to get on to other projects, which were many in 1960. I think the progress that Merton made in his understanding of John of the Cross there was the result of his position as master of scholastics at Gethsemani, 1951-1955 and his role as master of novices, 1955-1965. In these positions Merton was a guide to younger monks for whom he articulated what it meant to be a monk and, for him, especially what it meant to be a contemplative monk. Merton's interest in and admiration for John of the Cross helped him to guide young men into lives of contemplative prayer for which the Carmelite from Spain would have applauded the Trappist born in the Pyrennees.

An Afterword

I want to begin these concluding words with an act of contrition. I feel not a little uneasy critiquing somebody whose writings were, as far back as college days, and remain still, a powerful and abiding inspiration. Thomas Merton was, without a doubt, the architect of the North American retrieval of Christianity's spiritual heritage during the twentieth century. He brought the spiritual classics alive and shared his gift of a spiritual imagination that could see new possibilities for a joyful following of Jesus of Nazareth. I must count Thomas Merton as an important mentor in the spiritual life. So I am abashed at my impudence and seeming ingratitude in pointing out some shortcomings in his approach to Saint

John of the Cross. I take comfort in the realization that Thomas Merton had to be a man of his time and his culture, including the theological and monastic culture of his day that fostered much holiness, but like all cultures had its own drawbacks. I have pointed out some of these drawbacks that made it difficult for Merton to give a fuller picture of the spirituality of the Spanish mystic who so inspired the monk from Gethsemani. I do so with a sense of gratitude for his leading many of us to the writings of John of the Cross.

On the other hand, Thomas Merton was a prophetic and groundbreaking author who opened new vistas for God-seekers. What Thomas Merton did, besides much else, was to alert Christians to the significance of John of the Cross in an age that was beginning to show an interest in spirituality and contemplation. I believe that much of what Merton learned from John of the Cross was shared not only explicitly but implicitly in all of his writings. John of the Cross lies just below the surface of nearly all that Merton wrote. Merton democratized contemplation and made accessible what had seemed reserved to the few. The monk from Gethsemani who has been read by countless Christians would now want Christians to know that, as John of the Cross taught, the grace of contemplation is the very same grace that was poured into one's heart at baptism.[58] Merton also shared a vision of holiness that appreciates God's creatures everywhere, and a love of God and neighbor that cannot tolerate injustice. Merton's writings have and will continue to send his readers to Christian classics that reveal in new ways the wisdom of the gospels. Merton struggled with the demands that John of the Cross made in the quest for freedom and love. If one lets Merton lead one to the wisdom of John of the Cross, one will acquire a liberated heart that loves as God intended all of us to love. Thus did John of the Cross write:

> ...even though this happy night darkens the spirit, it does so only to impart light concerning all things; even though it humbles individuals and reveals their miseries, it does so only to exalt them; and even though it impoverishes and empties them of all possessions and natural affection, it does so only that they may reach out divinely to the enjoyment of all earth and heavenly things, with a general freedom of spirit in them all.[59]

There was no more ardent spiritual seeker in the twentieth century than Father Louis Thomas Merton who surely was deeply consoled at John of the Cross' conviction: "...if anyone is seeking God, the Beloved is seeking that person much more."[60]

Notes

1. Keith J. Egan, "Harvesting Seeds of Contemplation," *The Merton Annual* Vol. 16 (2003), pp. 53-54; this letter appears in Thomas Merton, *Seeds of Destruction* (New York: Farrar, Straus & Giroux, 1964), pp. 274-275; and in William Shannon, ed. *Witness to Freedom: The Letters of Thomas Merton in Times of* Crisis (New York: Farrar, Straus & Giroux, 1994), pp. 43-44. See Thomas Merton, *An Introduction to Christian Mysticism: Initiation into the Monastic Tradition*, ed. Patrick F. O'Connell (Kalamazoo, MI: Cistercian Publications, 2007).

2. Michael Mott, *The Seven Mountains of Thomas Merton* (Boston, MA: Houghton Mifflin, 1984), p. 78.

3. Thomas Merton, *The Seven Storey Mountain* (New York: Harcourt, Brace, 1948), pp. 238-39.

4. See references to John of the Cross in a book by Merton that consisted of "notes [that] add up to a personal version of the world in the 1960s." (p. 5): Thomas Merton, *Conjectures of a Guilty Bystander* (Garden City, NY: Image Books, 1968). References to John of the Cross: pp. 137, 271, 297, 320, 347.

5. Thomas Merton, *Contemplative Prayer* (New York: Herder and Herder, 1969); the Steere phrase is in the foreword, p. 14. This book was also published under the title *The Climate of Monastic Prayer* (Spencer, MA: Cistercian Publications, 1969).

6. David Tracy, "Recent Catholic Spirituality: Unity amid Diversity," Louis Dupré and Don Saliers, eds., *Christian Spirituality: Post-Reformation and Modern*, Vol. 18 of *World Spirituality* (New York: Crossroad, 1989), p. 160.

7. Thomas Merton, *The Ascent to Truth* (New York: Harcourt, Brace, 1951), p. ix.

8. Thomas Merton, *A Vow of Conversation: Journals 1964-1965*, ed. Naomi Burton Stone (New York: Farrar, Straus & Giroux, 1988), p. 56.

9. Thomas Merton, *Honorable Reader: Reflections on My Work*, ed. Robert Daggy (New York: Crossroad, 1989), Appendix 2. For comments on this graph see Lawrence Cunningham, *Thomas Merton and the Monastic Vision* (Grand Rapids, MI: Eerdmans, 1999), pp. 221-223.

10. Merton, *Honorable Reader*, p. 28.

11. Thomas Merton, *Entering the Silence: Becoming a Monk and Writer*, ed. Jonathan Montaldo, "The Journals of Thomas Merton, v. 2," (San Francisco: HarperSanFrancisco, 1995), p. 278.

12. Thomas Merton, *The Road to Joy: The Letters of Thomas Merton to New and Old Friends*, ed. Robert Daggy (New York: Farrar, Straus & Giroux, 1989), p. 206.

13. Cunningham, *Thomas Merton and the Monastic Vision*, p. 34.

14. Merton, *Honorable Reader*, p. 28.

15. Thomas Merton, "The Need for a New Education," *Contemplation in a World of Action* (Notre Dame, IN: University of Notre Dame Press, 1998, originally Doubleday, 1971), pp. 193-199.

16. Tournai: Desclée, 1930. See McGinn, "Asceticism and Mysticism in Late Antiquity and the Early Middle Ages," pp. 58-74 in Vincent Wimbush and Richard Valantasis, *Asceticism* (New York: Oxford University Press, 1995).

17. Sebastián de Covarrubias Horoxco, *Tesoro de la Lengua Castellana o Española* (Navarra: Vervuert, 2006; originally Madrid, 1611).

18. See *The Living Flame of Love* 1.1; 1.3; and *The Spiritual Canticle* B, 29.3 in *The Collected Works of Saint John of the Cross*, rev. ed., eds. Kieran Kavanaugh and Otilio Rodriquez (Washington, DC: Institute of Carmelite Studies, 1991).

19. Merton, *Ascent to Truth*, p 283; p. 132.

20. Steven Payne, *John of the Cross and the Cognitive Value of Mysticism: An Analysis of Sanjuanist Teaching and its Philosophical Implications for Contemporary Discussions of Mystical Experience* (Boston: Kluwer, 1990), p. 17.

21. David Perrin, "Asceticism: The Enigma of Corporal Joy in Paul Ricoeur and John of the Cross," *Pastoral Sciences* 16 (1997) pp. 153, note 83: "John's anthropology is essentially based on the writings of Thomas Aquinas (and therefore based on Aristotle....)"

22. Jacques Maritain, *Distinguish to Unite or The Degrees of Knowledge*, trans. from 4th French edition under supervision of Gerald Phelan (New York: Charles Scribner's Sons, 1959), chapters 8 and 9. The fourth French edition appeared in 1946.

23. See Gerald McCool, "Garrigou-Lagrange," *Biographical Dictionary of Christian Theologians*, eds. Patrick Carey and Joseph Lienhard (Westport, CT: Greenwood Press, 2000) p. 206.

24. Payne, *John of the Cross*, p. 17.

25. Merton, *The Ascent to Truth*, p. ix.

26. *The Spiritual Canticle* B, Prologue 3.

27. *Dark Night* 2.11.6, *hablando spiritualmente*.

28. *The Ascent of Mount Carmel*, 2.19.7.

29. *The Ascent of Mount Carmel* 2.19.7, *el sentido literal*, *Collected Works of Saint John of the Cross*, p. 216.

30. On scripture as formative of John's spirituality, see Iain Matthew, 'The Knowledge and Consciousness of Christ in the Light of the

Writings of St. John of the Cross," D. Phil. Thesis, Oxford University, 1991, pp. 81ff. On John and biblical studies at the University of Salamanca, see Melquiades Andrés Martím, "La teología en Salamanca durante los estudios de San Juan de la Cruz (1560-1570)," *Juan de la Cruz, Espíritu de Llama*, ed. Otger Steggink (Rome and Kampen: Institutum Carmelitanum, Kok Pharos, 1991) pp. 213-230.

31. John of the Cross' poetry and prose were in the vernacular; for his change from Latin quotations to vernacular quotations of the Bible, see *The Ascent of Mount Carmel* 2.27.6, n.2 and *The Spiritual Canticle, Prologue* 4, n. 2, in *Works of Saint John of the Cross*.

32. *Ascent of Mount Carmel* 2.19.8.

33. Keith J. Egan, "The Biblical Imagination of John of the Cross in *The Living Flame of Love*," *Juan de la Cruz, Espíritu*, pp. 507-521; see in the same collection John Welch, "The Imagination of St John of the Cross," pp. 847-862.

34. Jean Vilnet, *Bible et Mystique chez Saint Jean de la Croix*, "Études Carmélitaines," (Bruges: Desclée de Brouwer, 1949).

35. I cite John's poetry in quotation marks and his commentaries in italics.

36. Merton, *Ascent to Truth*, p. 313.

37. *Commonweal* 46 (July 4 1947), pp. 280-286.

38. See Thomas Merton, *The Asian Journal of Thomas Merton*, eds. Naomi Burton, Patrick Hart and James Laughlin (New York: New Directions, 1973).

39. Prologue, *The Spiritual Canticle*, 1-2.

40. *The Spiritual Canticle*, B, Stanza 36.

41. Merton, *Ascent to Truth*, p. 243.

42. Merton, *Ascent to Truth*, pp. 25-26.

43. For discussions of the apophatic and the kataphatic, see Oliver Davies and Denys Turner, *Silence and the Word: Negative Theology and Incarnation* (Cambridge: Cambridge University Press, 2002).

44. See *The Ascent of Mount Carmel*, Prologue 1.

45. *The Living Flame of Love*, 1, 1.

46. Thomas Merton, *Disputed Questions* (New York: Farrar, Straus and Cudahy, 1960).

47. This essay has appeared in editions of *Counsels of Light and Love*, 1960, 1978, 2007 and in *The Power and Meaning of Love*, 1976. The other Carmelite essay is entitled "The Primitive Carmelite Ideal," *Disputed Questions*, pp. 218-263.

48. Merton, *Disputed Questions*, p. viii.

49. Keith J. Egan, "The Solitude of Carmelite Prayer," *Carmelite Prayer: A Tradition for the 21st Century*, ed. Keith J. Egan (New York: Paulist Press, 2003), pp. 38-62.

50. "Light in Darkness," p. 209.
51. "Light in Darkness," p. 208.
52. "Light in Darkness," p. 209
53. "Light in Darkness," p. 211.
54. "Light in Darkness," p. 214.
55. "Light in Darkness," p. 215, quoting *The Living Flame of Love*, 3.32.
56. *Living Flame of Love*, 3. 65.
57. "Light in Darkness," pp. 216-217.
58. *The Spiritual Canticle* B, 23.6.
59. *The Dark Night*, 2.9.1.
60. *The Living Flame of Love*, 3.28.

Ignatian and Puritan Prayer: Surprising Similarities; A Comparison of Ignatius Loyola and Richard Baxter on Meditation

E. Glenn Hinson

I may have been rather brash thirty years ago, when I introduced *The Saints Everlasting Rest* as "Baxter's 'Spiritual Exercises'" and commented that it was "closely analogous in both origin and content" to Loyola's *Spiritual Exercises*.[1] I went on to point out that, although Baxter did not go through the same emotional struggle as the Spanish saint, he did "write 'out of the depths'" when stricken with what was expected to be a terminal illness when serving as a chaplain in Cromwell's army. In his *Autobiography* Baxter described the circumstances of its composition:

> Whilst I was in health I had not the least thought of writing books, or of serving God in any more public way than preaching. But when I was weakened with great bleeding, and left solitary in my chamber at Sir John Cook's in Derbyshire, without any acquaintance but my servant about me, and was sentenced to death by the physicians, I began to contemplate more seriously on the everlasting rest which I apprehended myself to be just on the borders of. And that my thoughts might not too much scatter in my meditation I began to write something on the subject, intending but the quantity of a sermon or two (which is the cause that the beginning is in brevity and style disproportionable to the rest); but being continued long in weakness, where I had no books nor no better employment, I followed it on till it was enlarged to the bulk in which it is published. The first three weeks I spent in it was at Mr. Nowel's house at Kirkby Mallory in Leicestershire; a quarter of a year more, at the seasons which so great weakness would allow, I bestowed on it at Sir Thomas Rous's house at Rous Lench in Worcestershire; and I finished it shortly after at Kidderminster. The first and last parts were first done, being all that I intended

for my own use; and the second and third parts came afterwards in besides my first intention.

This book it pleased God so far to bless to the profit of many that it encouraged me to be guilty of all those scripts which after followed. The marginal citations I put in after I came home to my books; but almost all the book itself was written when I had no book but a Bible and a Concordance. And I found that the transcript of the heart hath the greatest force on the hearts of others. For the good that I have heard that multitudes have received by that writing, and the benefit which I have received by their prayers, I humbly return my thanks to him that compelled me to write it.[2]

The Aim of "Spiritual Exercises"

You will recognize, I am sure, that Ignatius's *Spiritual Exercises* and Baxter's *Saints Everlasting Rest* have a very different look about them. On the surface the two may seem far apart because of the language and the handbook format of *The Spiritual Exercises*. Ignatius's language was much more steeped in tradition, Baxter's in the Bible. Ignatius was fashioning a handbook for spiritual formation, Baxter a long, long sermon or exhortation based on a biblical text. If interpreters of these documents are correct, however, Loyola and Baxter shared the principal goal of perfection in the love of God. Both would recognize that humans will not achieve such a goal in this life, but they may have a foretaste, as it were, and thus must concentrate their energies now on preparation. What *raison d'etre* have we in this life other than to glorify God and serve God forever?

Ignatius outlined a program for an intensive four-week retreat; Baxter framed a daily regimen he thought every devout believer should pursue. *The Spiritual Exercises* are concise and pointed; *The Saints Everlasting Rest* profuse and verbose (almost 800 pages long!). Catholics had not gotten caught up in the typographic revolution that exploded with the invention of moveable type in 1456 to the extent Protestants, especially Puritans, had.

As you might expect also, Loyola and Baxter expressed their goals in different ways even if they envisioned rather similar goals. Ignatius stated at the outset that the aim of his spiritual exercises was "to overcome oneself, and to order one's life, without reaching a decision through some disordered affection." "To overcome oneself" accentuated the negative purpose—to set aside sins or faults which get in the way of the main goal. Jesuit scholars, however, have debated what the central aim of ordering one's life means. One school, "electionists," contend that the object is to help a sincerely devout person make a wise choice of vocation in which to serve God. The other, "perfectionists," argue that the goal is intimate and complete union with God. Ignatius himself seems to have pursued both ends in his use of the text. With beginners he used it to achieve the first; with advanced the second.[3]

Baxter did not state his purpose so succinctly as Loyola did, but the major one appears many times throughout *The Saints Everlasting Rest*. He wanted readers not merely to read what he had written but to "set upon this work [of attaining the rest as set forth in Heb. 4:1], and [to] take God in Christ for thy only rest, and fix thy heart upon him above all." Loving God and delighting in God should be "the work of our lives."[4] What is the saints' rest? It is "the most happy state of a Christian; or it is, the perfect endless enjoyment of God by the perfected saints, according to the measure of their capacity, to which their souls arrive at death, and both soul and body most fully after the resurrection and final judgment."[5] Baxter, however, would have agreed enthusiastically with Ignatius's assertion that "Human beings are created to praise, reverence, and serve God our Lord, and by means of this to save their souls."[6]

Ignatian and Puritan Examen

Format aside, similarities of the whole process of formation are more striking, beginning with self-examination. Although Baxter did not expound on a method so rigorous as Ignatius's examination of conscience three times a day during the first week of a Lenten retreat, like most Puritans he placed much emphasis on self-scrutiny as a part of daily meditation. His brief examples show that he kept his own behavior under careful watch and was keenly conscious of failure to live up to what the "saints' rest" would demand. His expectations would come close to those set forth in Francis de Sales' adaptation of *The Spiritual Exercises* in his *Introduction to the Devout Life*. Those wishing to live a devout and holy life must first forsake sin, purge themselves of a bad conscience, and free themselves from earthly attachments.[7] Baxter devoted one whole chapter to self-examination as the means of determining whether one would be worthy of the saints' rest. He gave directions for this which might have earned the approval of Ignatius himself:

> Empty thy mind of all other cares and thoughts, that they may not distract or divide thy mind. This work will be enough at once, without joining others with it.—Then fall down before God in hearty prayer, desiring the assistance of his Spirit, to discover to thee the plain truth of thy condition, and to enlighten thee in the whole progress of this work.—Make choice of the most convenient time and place. Let the place be most private; and the time, when you have nothing to interrupt you; and if possible let it be the present time. Have in readiness, either in memory or writing, some scriptures containing the descriptions of the saints and the gospel terms of salvation; and convince thyself thoroughly of their infallible truth. Proceed then to put the question to thyself. Let it not be whether there be any good in thee at all? Nor whether thou hast such or such a degree and measure of grace? But whether such or such a saving grace be in thee in sincerity or not. . . . If after all thy pains thou art not resolved, then seek out for help. Go to one that is godly, experienced, able, and faithful, and tell him thy case, and desire his best advice. . . . But don't make it a pretence to put off thy own self-examination.[8]

That scheme is not far from Loyola's five-step procedure: (1) Give thanks to God for benefits; (2) Ask for grace to know sins and rid oneself of them; (3) Ask an account of the soul from arising to the present; (4) Ask pardon of God for faults; (5) Resolve, with God's grace, to amend them and close with the Our Father.[9] It is worthy of note that both Baxter and Ignatius ascribed the success of the self-examination to grace or the Holy Spirit. Ignatius *required* a spiritual director, Baxter *encouraged* seeking one.

One Ignatian exercise which one will not find matched in *The Saints Everlasting Rest*, but which Baxter would have approved, is meditation on Hell. Ignatius underscored vivid imagination entailing all five senses. In imagination the retreatant should *see* the huge fires and souls within the bodies full of fire; *hear* the wailing, shrieking, cries, and blasphemies of the damned; *smell* the smoke, the sulfur, the filth, and the rotting things; *taste* the bitter flavors of hell—tears, sadness, and the worm of conscience; and *touch* how the flames burn souls. Like Loyola, Baxter did make much use of antithesis, but he relied much more on contrasting life on earth here and now—its painfulness, sinfulness, uncertainties, gloominess, terrors—with the saints' rest. Nothing on earth can match the joys and glories of heaven.

Making Imagination Work for You

What stands out most vividly in these two classics is their consensus regarding the whole process of effecting obedience to God. Ultimately it is our will which determines how we behave. Although we depend on God's grace to see that we will the Good, what God wills, we know that human emotions or affections influence the will either for good or for bad. If we are to "work together with God" to do what is right, therefore, we must influence our emotions through the proper use of imagination. Because imagination can impact emotions both negatively and positively, however, we must rely on our rational faculties, "consideration," to direct imagination, and the safest place to turn our imaginations would be toward the scriptures, for Ignatius especially the Gospels, in which we may discover "the mind of Christ," for Baxter the texts on the "saints' rest" in which we can see our goal.

"Consideration": Directing Imagination[10]

Both Ignatius and Baxter seem to have had a strong awareness of the erratic nature of emotion and sought to safeguard against it through "consideration." Ignatius does not explain in detail, as Baxter does, how consideration would work, but the exercises themselves make clear that the whole process originates in and proceeds from the rational faculty. Baxter, however, perhaps because Calvinist theology would have less confidence in human reason, elaborated at some length on how consideration would keep the whole process on the right track toward obeying God.

"Consideration is the great instrument by which this heavenly work is carried out," he said. "This must be voluntary and not forced. . . . Great is the power which consideration hath for moving the affections and impressing things on the heart, . . ."[11] In typically Puritan fashion he proceeded to expound the step-by-step process: (1) Consideration "opens the door between the head and the heart" by taking received truths and laying them on the memory and thence conveying them to the affections; (2) It "presents to the affections those things which are most important"; (3) "in the most affecting way": here Baxter throws in an added note that consideration is not simply *human* reason at work—rather, by virtue of the tie with scriptures, it "is but the reading over and repeating God's reasons to our heart"; (4) It "exalts reason to its just authority" and "helps to deliver it from its captivity to the senses and sets it again on the throne of the soul"; (5) Consideration "makes reason strong and active"; (6) It "can continue and persevere in this rational employment. Meditation holds reason and faith to their work and blows the fire till it thoroughly burns."[12]

In Baxter's elaboration of the way consideration influences reason one can see the Calvinist caution. Consideration is not the same faculty as reason; it is more the God-guided mind. "When reason is silent, it is usually subject; for when it is asleep, the senses domineer. But consideration awakens our reason . . . . Spiritual reason excited by meditation, and not fancy or fleshly sense, must judge of heavenly joys."[13]

A Chain of Command

Both Ignatius and Baxter envisioned a sort of chain of command in the process of achieving the object of meditation. Consideration would arouse Memory; Memory would lead to Meditation; Meditation would arouse the Affections. By itself, consideration alone will not affect the heart, Baxter concluded. It requires the arguing of a case with oneself (soliloquy) and prayer.

Imagination the Key Tool

The use of imagination as the key tool in meditation on scriptures is not surprising in the Catholic tradition that is rich in art—mosaics, paintings, stained glass windows, statuary, *et al*. It comes as something of a shock to find the imagination holding a central place in the writing of "Mr. Puritan," Richard Baxter. Part of the "purification" which the Puritans intended was to remove all images from their worship. Cromwell's "round heads" could scarcely pass a church during the English Civil War (1642-1646) without trying to bust out windows or remove statues and effigies. True, Baxter did insert a warning about the use of images drawn from the physical senses. We should keep images in the mind and not put them on canvas or in statues. "Don't, like the papists, draw them in pictures," he directed.[14] Despite this caution, however,

Baxter restricted imagination based on scriptures only in insisting on directing it by consideration.

The *Spiritual Exercises* obviously sought to get the exercitants to recognize their human failings and need of God's help to change, then to enter into the Jesus story in imagination and let it do a job on them, and finally to experience the transforming love of God manifest in the Cross and in the Resurrection. The effectiveness of the exercises lay both in their schematic nature and in Loyola's insistence on vividness of imagination in going through the Jesus story. Each contemplation required preparatory prayer; preludes imagining history and place and asking for what you desire; reflection on several questions; and then a colloquy in which you make a case for yourself. Vividness depended on the use of all five senses. "If you are imagining a scene where there are animals," Ignatius insisted, "smell the manure."

Once again, you will find surprising congruity between the Ignatian and the Baxterian approaches. Both were firmly convinced that meditation holds great value for the spiritual life. "Say not," Baxter said, "how can mortals ascend to heaven! Faith hath wings, and meditation is its chariot."[15] He touted it as "that duty by which all other duties are improved and by which the soul digesteth truths for its nourishment and comfort."[16] It does for the soul what digestion does for the body, "turns the truths received and remembered into warm affection, firm resolution, and holy conversation."[17] Meditation is not just a work of understanding and memory.

The Process

Like most spiritual guides, Baxter attended to details that would make this exercise effective. It should occur at stated times, frequently, and on special occasions. The fittest place would be "some private retirement."[18] Preparation for meditation is all important. We can see in Baxter's counsels concerning "Preparations of Your Heart" how closely his aims coincided with Ignatius's. He demanded two preparations: (1) "Get thy heart as clear from the world as thou canst."[19] The reason for that is that the enjoyment of God in contemplation "depends on the capacity and disposition of thy heart" and thus you must seek God "with all thy soul."[20] (2) "Be sure to set upon this work with the greatest solemnity of heart and mind."[21] To do this, you must strive "to have the deep-

est apprehension of the presence of God and [God's] incomprehensible greatness" and to realize the importance of contemplation. Thus, you must consider "with what a spirit thou shouldst
meet the Lord and with what seriousness and awe thou shouldst
daily converse with him."[22]

Given Puritan fear of violating the second commandment, it
may come as a surprise to hear that Baxter devoted one lengthy
chapter to how heavenly contemplation may be "assisted by sen-
sible objects" and "guarded against a treacherous heart." Sound-
ing very Ignatian, he directed: "For helping of thy affections in
heavenly contemplation, draw as strong suppositions as possible
from thy senses."[23] By no means should meditators actually draw
pictures. They should instead "get the liveliest picture of them in
the mind that thou possibly canst by contemplating the scripture
account of them till thou canst say, 'Methinks I see a glimpse of
glory!'"[24] In addition, they could compare "the objects of sense
with the objects of faith." Comparing and contrasting things of
earth and things of heaven, based on scriptures, of course, would
be the key. Focus on scriptures related to the saints' eternal rest
rather than the life of Jesus would give a different cast to Baxter's
meditation, but the style of argumentation is remarkably similar
to Ignatius's "points." In both cases, the aim is to direct one's
mind toward higher, that is, godly, things.

Baxter gave an extended list of comparisons or contrasts: "the
corrupt delights of sensual men to the joys above"; "the delights
above, with those we find in natural knowledge"; "the delights
above with the delights of morality and of the natural affections";
"the excellencies of heaven with those glorious works of creation
which our eyes now behold"; "the enjoyments above with the
wonders of Providence in the church and world"; "the joys above
with the comforts thou hast here received in ordinances"; "the joy
thou shalt have in heaven with what the saints have found in the
way to it and in the foretastes of it"; "the glory of the heavenly
kingdom with the glory of the church on earth and Christ in his
state of humiliation"; "the glorious change thou shalt have at last
with the gracious change which the spirit hath here wrought on
thy heart"; and "the joys which thou shalt have above with those
foretastes of it which the Spirit hath given thee here."[25]

For a meditation scheduled for the first day of the second week
of retreat on the Incarnation Ignatius included three points, all
comparing and contrasting earth and heaven.

The First Point. I will see the various persons, some here, some there.

First, those on the face of the earth, so diverse in dress and behavior: some white and others black, some in peace and others at war, some weeping and others laughing, some healthy and others sick, some being born and others dying, and so forth.

Second, I will see and consider the Three Divine Persons, seated, so to speak, on the royal throne of their Divine Majesty. They are gazing on the whole face and circuit of the earth; and they see all the peoples in such great blindness, and how they are dying and going down to hell.

Third, I will see Our Lady and the angel greeting her. Then I will reflect on this to draw some profit from what I see.

The Second Point. Here I will listen to what the persons on the face of the earth are saying; that is, how they speak with one another, swear and blaspheme, and so on. Likewise, I will hear what the Divine Persons are saying, that is, "Let us work the redemption of the human race," and so forth. Then I will listen to what the angel and Our Lady are saying. Afterward I will reflect on this, to draw profit from their words.

The Third Point. Here I will consider what the people on the face of the earth are doing: How they wound, kill, go to hell, and so on. Similarly, what the Divine Persons are doing, that is bringing about the most holy Incarnation, and other such activities. Likewise, what the angel and Our Lady are doing, with the angel carrying out his office of ambassador and Our Lady humbling herself and giving thanks to the Divine Majesty. Then I will reflect on these matters, to draw some profit from them.[26]

Similarities in the process do not stop here. Ignatius proposed ending each meditation with a *colloquy*. He explained that it "is made, properly speaking, in the way one friend speaks to another, or a servant to one in authority—now begging a favor, now accusing oneself of some misdeed, now telling one's concerns and asking counsel about them."[27] For the meditation just cited, he explained: "I will think over what I ought to say to the Three Divine Persons, or to the eternal Word made flesh, or to our Mother and Lady. I will beg favors according to what I feel in my heart, that I may better follow and imitate Our Lord, who in this way has recently become a human being."[28] Baxter recommended a *soliloquy* "or a pleading the case with thyself" in order to "quicken they own heart." "Enter into serious debate with it," he insisted.[29] Soliloquy is "preaching to oneself."[30] In practice, I suspect that soliloquy and colloquy would differ little from one another.

Finally, both proposed ending the meditation with prayer, Ignatius the "Our Father," Baxter a more spontaneous prayer. Persons acquainted with *The Spiritual Exercises* will know that Ignatius appended three methods of prayer: (1) on the ten commandments, seven mortal sins, three powers of the soul, and five senses of the body; (2) contemplation of each word of a prayer; and (3) rhythmical recitation of a prayer. These provided a flexibility for the assistance of persons not well equipped to do the full *Exercises*. He undoubtedly expected spiritual directors to guide retreatants with reference to prayer. Baxter thought that ejaculatory prayers "may very properly be intermixed with meditation as a part of the duty." He explained why:

> As God is the highest object of our thoughts, so our viewing of [God], speaking to [God], more elevates the soul and excites the affections than any other part of meditation. . . . Thus in our meditations to intermix soliloquy and prayer; sometimes speaking to our own hearts and sometimes to God is, I apprehend, the highest step we can advance to in this heavenly work. Nor should we imagine it will be as well to take up with prayer alone and lay aside meditation. For they are distinct duties and must both of them be performed.[31]

How to Explain Such Surprising Similarities

It is quite surprising, shocking even, to find such similarities of concepts and practices of prayer in these antagonists and adversaries of the sixteenth and seventeenth centuries. When Richard Baxter penned *The Saints Everlasting Rest* in 1646 during a protracted illness, no group could have gotten a chillier reception and put themselves at greater risk by coming to England than the Jesuits. Edmund Campion (1540-1581), a convert to the Roman Catholic Church in 1571 who entered the Society of Jesus in 1573 and joined Robert Parsons (1546-1610) in the first Jesuit mission to England in 1580, was put on the rack and martyred at Tyburn on December 1, 1581. Parsons escaped by fleeing to the continent. One could hardly find a period subsequently when anti-Catholic sentiment reached a higher peak than the English Civil War (1642-

1646) during which Baxter wrote, and none surely would have spoken more harshly of "popish religion" than Puritans. In trying to account for correspondences between Jesuit and Puritan meditation, therefore, I doubt whether anyone could establish that Baxter self-consciously sought to learn from the great Spanish spiritual master. The Puritans deliberately went back to medieval sources to find help in effecting the "further reformation" they sought in England, but they would have had a different view of Jesuit writings and activities. Not even Baxter, a scholarly pastor, would have sought out and adopted the views and customs of so inveterate an enemy.

Since it is highly unlikely that Baxter would have consulted Loyola's *Spiritual Exercises* directly, we need to look in another direction to explain correspondences. A more fertile field in which to search would seem to be the vast contemplative tradition that nurtured *both* Jesuits and Puritans. Innovation would have been the last idea to have forced its way into the mind of Ignatius in a day when the Spanish inquisition loomed threateningly over every new movement that stirred. By spending a year at a Dominican convent at Manresa Ignatius surely would not have intended to diverge far from that great tradition.

What Ignatius did was to feed the vast corpus of contemplative thought and practice through his own mind and heart in a different context and to integrate it into a spirituality that would guide the Catholic faithful through the traumatic years of the Reformation and beyond.[32] Similarly, the Puritans arrested the wild scuttling of ancient practice in which the early Protestant reformers engaged and started rooting around in early Christian and medieval closets to find methods of prayer which could effect the "further reformation" they so earnestly yearned to bring about in England.[33] Similar exigent circumstances a century apart turned out to be the mother of invention.

Notes

1. E. Glenn Hinson, "Editor's Introduction to *The Saints Everlasting Rest*," in *Doubleday Devotional Classics*, ed., E. Glenn Hinson (Garden City, NY: Doubleday, 1978), p. 3.

2. Richard Baxter, *Autobiography*, Ch IX; Everyman's Library, pp. 94-95.

3. George E. Ganss, SJ, *Ignatius of Loyola: Spiritual Exercises and Selected Works*, *Classics of Western Spirituality* (New York, Mahwah: Paulist Press, 1991), pp. 390-91, n. 10.

4. Richard Baxter, *The Saints Everlasting Rest*, Ch 1, Sect 1.

5. Baxter, *Saints Everlasting Rest*, Ch 1, Sect 2.

6. Loyola, *Spiritual Exercises* 23; in *Classics of Western Spirituality*, p. 130.

7. Francis de Sales, *Introduction to the Devout Life*, trans. Michael Day (London: J.M. Dent & Sons Ltd; New York: E.P. Dutton & Co Inc, 1961), pp. 17-23.

8. Baxter, *Saints Everlasting Rest*, VIII.12; *Doubleday Devotional Classics*, I. pp. 86, 87.

9. Loyola, *Spiritual Exercises* 32-44; *Classics of Western Spirituality*, pp. 132-5.

10. For an excellent introduction to the Ignatian perspective see Robert W. Gleason, SJ, "Introduction to the Spiritual Exercises," in *The Spiritual Exercises of St. Ignatius*, trans. by Anthony Mottola (Garden City, NY: Doubleday Image Books, 1964), pp. 11-31.

11. Baxter, *Saints Everlasting Rest*, XIV.2; *Doubleday Devotional Classics*, p.142.

12. Baxter, *Saints Everlasting Rest*, XIV.3-8; *Doubleday Devotional Classics*, pp. 142- 4.

13. Baxter, *Saints Everlasting Rest*, XIV.6; *Doubleday Devotional Classics*, p. 144.

14. Baxter, *Saints Everlasting Rest*, XV.3; *Doubleday Devotional Classics*, p. 159.

15. Baxter, *Saints Everlasting Rest*, XI.10; *Doubleday Devotional Classics*, p. 102.

16. Baxter, *Saints Everlasting Rest*, XIII.3; *Doubleday Devotional Classics*, pp. 130-131.

17. Baxter, *Saints Everlasting Rest*, XIII.3; *Doubleday Devotional Classics*, pp. 130-131.

18. Baxter, *Saints Everlasting Rest*, XIII. *Doubleday Devotional Classics*, p. 18.

19. Baxter, *Saints Everlasting Rest*, XIII. *Doubleday Devotional Classics*, p. 140.

20. Baxter, *Saints Everlasting Rest*, XIII. *Doubleday Devotional Classics*, p. 20.

21. Baxter, *Saints Everlasting Rest*, XIII. p. 21; *Doubleday Devotional Classics*, p. 141.

22. Baxter, *Saints Everlasting Rest*, XIII. p. 21; *Doubleday Devotional Classics*, p. 141.

23. Baxter, *Saints Everlasting Rest*, XV.3; *Doubleday Devotional Classics*, p. 158.

24. Baxter, *Saints Everlasting Rest*, XV.3; *Doubleday Devotional Classics*, p. 159.

25. Baxter, *Saints Everlasting Rest*, XV.3; *Doubleday Devotional Classics*, pp. 159-168.

26. Loyola, *Spiritual Exercises*, pp. 106-8; *Classics of Western Spirituality*, pp. 148-49.

27. Loyola, *Spiritual Exercises*, p. 55; *Classics of Western Spirituality*, p. 138.

28. Loyola, *Spiritual Exercises*, p. 109; *Classics of Western Spirituality*, p. 149.

29. Baxter, *Saints Everlasting Rest* XIV.21; *Doubleday Devotional Classics*, p. 155.

30. Baxter, *Saints Everlasting Rest*, XIV.21; *Doubleday Devotional Classics*, p. 156.

31. Baxter, *Saints Everlasting Rest*, XIV.22; *Doubleday Devotional Classics*, pp. 156-57.

32. Alexandre Brou, SJ, *Ignatian Methods of Prayer*, translated by William J. Young, SJ (Milwaukee: Bruce, 1949), p. 2, remarks that, although earlier teachers of prayer didn't use the word method, "the author of the *Exercises* was not without forerunners." Methodical prayer began with contemplatives of the twelfth century and got away from generalities in the thirteenth. Bonaventure, for instance, taught a method not far removed from Loyola's "three powers of the soul." By the time Ignatius came along methodical prayer was well developed. What he did, Brou concluded, is to popularize it by simplifying and reducing it to essentials. He placed such exercises within the reach of all. Others, such as Francis de Sales, carried the popularization further. "And the work of St. Ignatius which was the end of a movement that had its beginning in the heart of the Middle Ages is also the beginning of the movement that has lasted down to our own day" (Ibid. p. 11).

33. A number of studies have pointed to this, but, with apologies, I cite my article on "Puritan Spirituality" in *Protestant Spiritual Traditions*, edited by Frank C. Senn (New York and Mahwah: Paulist Press, 1986), pp. 165-182. My conclusion on this issue is: "Puritans were to Protestantism what contemplatives and ascetics were to the medieval church. They parted company with their medieval forbears chiefly in the locus of their efforts. Where monks sought sainthood in monasteries, Puritans sought it everywhere—in homes, schools, town halls, shops as well as churches. Sometimes knowingly, at other times unknowingly, they employed virtually the same methods monks used to obtain the same goal—'the saints' rest,' heaven, or 'full and glorious enjoyment of God.' Like the monks, they were zealous of heart religion manifested in trans-

formation of life and manners. Impatient with halfway commitments, they kindled fires for unreserved, enthusiastic embracing of the covenant. Everything they did, they did with solemnity and determination" (Ibid. p. 165).

From Thomas Merton's "Contemplation" to Ignatius of Loyola's "Contemplation to Obtain Love": A Personal Prayer Journey

Richard J. Hauser

Foreword

Frequently I give workshops on aspects of spirituality. In a recent workshop entitled "Deepening Personal Prayer" I heard myself telling the participants that I came to an understanding of Ignatian prayer, particularly his Contemplation to Obtain Love,[1] through an understanding of Thomas Merton's understanding of contemplation. A workshop participant suggested I might write my reflections.[2] Hence these reflections are autobiographical. I am reflecting on my own prayer journey; I cannot presume to speak for anyone else. Perhaps I am writing my "confessions."

Autobiographical Background

As a Jesuit priest and a university professor I teach, write and lecture on Christian spirituality. My primary mentor for personal prayer has been Thomas Merton. For some this may seem scandalous. Ought not a Jesuit's primary prayer mentor be Ignatius Loyola and the prayer methods enshrined in his *Spiritual Exercises*? Yet I must acknowledge that Merton has been the dominant influence in my approach to personal prayer. More accurately it was Merton's approach to contemplation that ultimately gave me my entrée to Ignatius' Contemplation to Obtain Love.

From 1969 to 1972 I did graduate studies in theology which concluded with a dissertation involving Thomas Merton and Abraham Maslow. Writing the dissertation gave me the opportunity to grasp intellectually Merton's approach to spirituality, especially contemplation; I knew little about him before. But it is also important to note that during my graduate studies I simultaneously became interested in Abraham Maslow's self-actualization psychology, especially in his approach to religious experiences which he calls "peak experiences." My dissertation compared

Merton and Maslow in their approaches to religious experience (see note 18).

Having concluded my degree I began university teaching. I discovered that many aspects of Merton's thought made sense in conjunction with my personal experience so I gradually began appropriating his spiritual synthesis and using his language to name my own experiences. Indeed Merton became my primary guide as I began teaching university spirituality courses.

Why did I use Merton and not Ignatius as my primary spiritual guide? I entered the Society of Jesus in 1955. During the nineteen-fifties and sixties we Jesuits were indoctrinated into a Jesuit spirituality characteristic of the pre-Vatican II period. The indoctrination focused on guidelines for daily living and guidelines for personal prayer. The guidelines for daily living centered on obedience to the external laws and rules of the Society of Jesus. Since these laws and rules were the will of God the ideal goal of spirituality presented to us was perfect conformity with them: "You keep the rules and the rules will keep you." Additionally, since the will of the superior was also the will of God the indoctrination focused on perfect conformity to his will also. I can even remember applying the obedience principle to the type of haircut we received. It is not an exaggeration to say that my formation introduced me to a law-centered spirituality. Even now I can recall experiencing anxiety which was often accompanied by migraine headaches because of my inability to observe these guidelines fully.

The guidelines for daily prayer focused on the Ignatian methods of meditation and contemplation found in the *Spiritual Exercises*. We were given Jesuit-authored meditation books that presented scriptural passages for each day of the year; we were instructed to focus on the texts using memory, imagination, understanding and will in order to extract insights. We prayed for fifty minutes each morning beginning at 5:30. I found these early morning periods very difficult and did not look forward to them. They seemed totally irrelevant to my life; I regularly experienced distraction, boredom and sleep.

Please note that these approaches are no longer dominant in Jesuit formation. Vatican II invited religious orders to renew their spirituality according to the original charism of their founders. We Jesuits have responded fully and have rediscovered the authentic Ignatian spirituality. The theme of my reflections centers on how my Merton orientation led me, eventually, to an authentic understanding of Ignatian spirituality, especially Ignatian prayer.

The Holy Spirit and Merton

Before personally appropriating Merton's spirituality, however, and subsequently Ignatius', I was given a great grace: the realization of the centrality of the Holy Spirit in all Christian spirituality. That realization occurred through the study of the documents of Vatican II. Without these insights I doubt I could have internalized either Merton or Ignatius. The passages such as the following from the "Constitution on the Church" began to revolutionize my understanding of spirituality:

> When the work which the Father had given the Son to do on earth (cf. Jn. 17:4) was accomplished, the Holy Spirit was sent on the day of Pentecost in order that He might forever sanctify the Church and thus all believers would have access to the Father through Christ in the one Spirit (cf. Eph. 2:18). . . .The Spirit dwells in the Church and in the hearts of the faithful as in a temple (cf. 1 Cor. 3:16; 619). In them he prays and bears witness to the fact that they are adopted sons (cf. Gal.4:6; Rom. 8:15-16 and 26). The Spirit guides the Church into the fullness of truth (cf. Jn. 16:13) and gives her a unity of fellowship and service.... He furnished and directs her with various gifts, both hierarchical and charismatic, and adorns her with the fruits of His grace (cf. Eph. 4:11-12; 1 Cor. 12:4; Gal. 5:22). [3]

Intellectually, I had always understood that the Holy Spirit is our sanctifier: the Father creates, the Son redeems, the Holy Spirit sanctifies. However, I had never grasped that the indwelling of the Spirit had actual concrete effects in daily life and daily prayer. Now Vatican II was teaching that the Spirit dwells in the Church and that we are the Church; therefore the Spirit dwells in us and not only in the hierarchy! Now I began asking about the concrete effects of this indwelling. Very soon I made the link between the Holy Spirit and daily living and daily prayer.

Merton provided the occasion for my recognizing for the first time the role of the Spirit in daily prayer. In 1975 I published an article entitled "Personal Prayer: Contemporary Themes."[4] The themes pulled together my insights on praying and attempted to articulate this renewed understanding using Merton's language.

The article was a significant milestone on my own prayer journey. It was Merton who gave me the words to enshrine my experience. And I do think I was faithful to Merton. The five themes treat were: Prayer as Letting the Spirit Speak, as an Expression of the Whole Self, as an Experience of the Whole Self, as the Discovery of God in the Depths of the Self, and as Resting in the Lord.

The first theme, Prayer as Letting the Spirit Speak, is the most significant. The subsequent themes are simply elaborations. The theme reflects on Paul's famous passage in *Romans*:

> The Spirit too helps us in our weakness for we do not know how to pray as we ought; but the Spirit himself makes intercession for us with groanings that cannot be expressed in speech. He who searches hearts knows what the Spirit means, for the Spirit intercedes for the saints as God himself wills (Rom. 8:26-27).[5]

Since Merton died in 1968, most of his writing pre-dated Vatican Council II's reappropriation of the role of the Holy Spirit in Christian life. Yet all Merton's writing assumes this presence of the Holy Spirit, and frequently Merton does incorporate Holy Spirit language. Let the following Merton quote stands for all his passages that explicitly cite the role of the Holy Spirit in personal prayer.

> It can therefore be said that the aim of mental prayer is to awaken the Holy Spirit within us, and to bring our hearts into harmony with His voice, so that we allow the Holy Spirit to speak and pray within us, and lend Him our voice and our affections that we may became, as far as possible, conscious of His prayer in our hearts.[6]

Why was my article enshrining Merton's insights revolutionary for me? Very simply, I had a Pelagian understanding of prayer. All my life I had assumed that praying well was a result of my hard work. In prayer, I made efforts to avoid distractions and focus on the scriptural texts and to use my memory, understanding, will and imagination to produce suitable thoughts, insights, images and affections about the Lord. When I did pray well—experience suitable insights and affections—I attributed it to the conscientious use of my faculties. I have to confess that the understanding of Ignatian prayer I had developed during my years of formation as a Jesuit seemed to reinforce this approach. In any case, I didn't begin intellectually questioning seriously this theology until my study of Merton.

Now Merton—and Saint Paul and Vatican Council II—are saying that prayer is the work of the Spirit!

I should note in passing that Merton also provided my first insights into the role of the Holy Spirit in daily life. The transformation of our hearts by the Holy Spirit in contemplation flowed out into our daily life, transforming our actions. I recall being struck by Merton's image of the spring and the stream.

> Action and contemplation now grow together into one life and one unity. They become two aspects of the same thing. Action is charity looking outward to other men, and contemplation is charity drawn inward to its own divine source. Action is the stream, and contemplation is the spring. The spring remains more important than the stream, for the only thing that really matters is for love to spring up inexhaustibly from the infinite abyss of Christ and of God.[7]

I began to realize that the "spring" for all goodness is the Holy Spirit. Actions are holy to the degree they are transformed by the Holy Spirit. Merton's reflections on the "true self" versus the "false self" were central. I realized that true understanding of the self acknowledges the role of the Holy Spirit; any false understanding does not.

> Every one of us is shadowed by an illusory person: a false self. This is the man that I want myself to be but who cannot exist, because God does not know anything about him. And to be unknown of God is altogether too much privacy. My false and private self is the one who wants to exist outside the reach of God's will and God's love—outside of reality and outside of life. And such a self cannot help but be an illusion.[8]

These insights of Thomas Merton about the role of the Holy Spirit in prayer and in daily life led to a profound reconsideration of my attitude to spirituality. I began to realize that my entire understanding of spirituality flowed from erroneous cultural assumptions of the relationship between myself and God. I, erroneously, saw myself as initiating all good actions in order to please God and so be rewarded by God for my fidelity. Merton helped me realize that, in reality, God through the Holy Spirit initiates all good within us and we in turn respond to the Spirit, not only in personal prayer but also in daily life: "I am the vine; you are the branches; without me you can do nothing."

These insights led me to articulate two models of the self which I dubbed the "Western Model" and the "Scriptural Model." The Western Model accepted my erroneous cultural assumptions and ignored the role of the Holy Spirit; the Scriptural Model challenged these cultural assumptions and acknowledged the centrality of the Holy Spirit.

The year 1975 was a watershed in my personal appropriation of Christian spirituality. Merton's approach, reinforced by Vatican Council II's theology of the Holy Spirit, had revolutionized my understanding of spirituality. I could hardly believe what I was discovering on the role of the Holy Spirit. Yet it was clearly the teaching of the New Testament echoed throughout history by the formal teaching of the Church, and most recently by Vatican Council II, especially in its Dogmatic Constitution on the Church. My excitement spilled over into dozens of articles and eventually into three books.[9]

Merton and Contemplation

Though I resonate with Merton's entire spiritual synthesis, one of its most attractive aspects is his approach to contemplation. I have to confess that though I had an intellectual grasp of the concept of contemplation while writing my dissertation it was not until I began university teaching in 1972 that I began to recognize contemplation in my own experience, and consequently was able to help others identify it in theirs. His approach was entirely new for me. It became key in providing the link to Ignatius' "Contemplation for Obtaining Love."

When I began university teaching I was assigned to teach a course on mysticism in the graduate theology program, since I had done a dissertation on Merton. Naturally enough contemplation emerged as a central concept and I used Merton as my guide. The opening chapters of *New Seeds of Contemplation* provide Merton's best descriptions of contemplation. His reflections transformed my understanding.

I learned that contemplation is the human being fully functioning. It is not limited to special types of people, such as cloistered monks and nuns.

Contemplation is the highest expression of man's intellectual and spiritual life. It is that life itself, fully awake, fully active, fully aware that it is alive. It is spiritual wonder. It is spontaneous awe at the sacredness of life, of being. It is gratitude for life, for awareness and for being.[10]

I learned that contemplation can happen anywhere and anytime and need not be restricted to formal prayer periods and to specifically religious topics. Indeed I noted that most of Merton's own experiences seemed to happen through creation and daily events.

Hence contemplation is a sudden gift of awareness, an awakening to the Real within all that is real. A vivid awareness of infinite Being at the roots of our own limited being. An awareness of our contingent reality as received, as a present from God, as a free gift of love. This is the existential contact of which we speak when we use the metaphor of being "touched by God."[11]

I learned that contemplation is really not the result of strenuous human effort to pray well using memory, understanding, will and imagination but, rather, comes most unexpectedly as a gift when we are relaxed and centered in God's presence.

It is awakening, enlightenment and the amazing intuitive grasp by which love gains certitude of God's creative and dynamic intervention in our daily life. Hence contemplation does not simply "find" a clear idea of God and confine Him within the limits of that idea, and hold Him there as a prisoner to Whom it can always return. On the contrary, contemplation is carried away by Him into His own realm, His own mystery and His own freedom.[12]

I learned that contemplation is an experience that can never adequately be put into words. Merton couldn't be clearer: contemplation is not thinking. It is not a function of the self that thinks rationally and logically. Merton illustrates his insight by contrasting contemplation with the *cogito ergo sum* ("I think therefore I am") of Descartes.

For the contemplative there is no *cogito* ("I think") and no *ergo* ("therefore") but only SUM, I AM. Not in the sense of a futile assertion of our individuality as ultimately real, but in the humble realization of our mysterious being as persons in whom God dwells, with infinite sweetness and inalienable power.[13]

I learned that contemplation is a knowing of God that occurs through an intuition into reality that happens when the circumstances are conducive and God gives the gift. Merton notes that the more objectively and scientifically we try to analyze contemplation the more we empty it of its real content, for the experience of contemplation is beyond verbalization and rationalization.

> The "I" that works in the world, thinks about itself, observes its own reactions and talks about itself is not the true "I" that has been united to God in Christ. It is at best the vesture, the mask, the disguise of that mysterious and unknown "self" whom most of us never discover until we are dead.[14]

He concludes that "The only way to get rid of misconceptions about contemplation is to experience it."[15]

So even while writing my dissertation I began asking myself whether I had ever had this amazing intuitive awareness of God's presence in my life. I concluded that I had not. I assumed these experiences were present only in people like Merton who were called to live cloistered contemplative lives in monasteries. I assumed they were not present in the lives of active Christians living in the world like myself.

However, during my graduate studies I took courses in the psychology of Abraham Maslow. I was interested especially in his theory on religious experiences which he calls "peak experiences."[16] Maslow describes the characteristics of peak experiences in an appendix entitled "Religious Aspects of Peak Experiences":

> -it is quite characteristic in peak experiences that the whole universe is perceived as integrated and unified whole; to have a clear perception that the universe is all of a piece and that one has his place in it can be so profound and shaking an experience that it can change the person's character.
>
>   -there is a tremendous concentration of a kind that does not normally occur.
>   -it can be relatively ego-transcending, self-forgetful, egoless, unselfish.
>   -there is a very characteristic disorientation in time and space, or even the lack of consciousness of time and space.

-the world is seen only as beautiful, good, desirable, worthwhile and is never experienced as evil or undesirable.

-emotions as wonder, awe, reverence, humility, surrender, and even worship before the greatness of the experience are often reported.[17]

I was fascinated by Maslow's descriptions of peak experiences and his observations that healthy persons normally do experience them. So I began asking myself even while writing my dissertation whether I had these experiences. I concluded that I did. I noted four circumstances occasioning my peak experiences: 1) solitude in natural beauty, especially by oceans or mountains; 2) encounters with close friends; 3) satisfaction during or after effective spirituality presentations; 4) realization of God's love during morning prayer.

This was the first time in my life that I distinguished my ordinary daily experiences from my peak experiences. In retrospect, naming these peak experiences and distinguishing them from my ordinary daily thinking was an important first step toward recognizing contemplation in my life. However at no time did I interpret these experiences as religious, except for the ones occurring during formal prayer, nor did I identify them with Merton's understanding of contemplation.

However, when I began reflecting on my experiences while teaching university courses on mysticism my interpretation of these experiences changed. I began acknowledging similarities between Maslow's peak experiences and Merton's contemplation—always, of course, understanding that the experiences were gifts of the Holy Spirit. I soon concluded I was being "touched by God" in a way not only fulfilling Maslow's criteria for peak experiences but also Merton's criteria for contemplation.

Ignatius of Loyola and the Contemplation to Obtain Love

When the time came to choose a dissertation topic I was drawn toward reflecting on religious experience using Maslow's peak experiences. The chair of my department suggested I compare Maslow with a Christian approach. Since I was a Jesuit, he suggested I use Ignatius of Loyola. I discarded this suggestion immediately because of my negative attitude toward Ignatian prayer. Even though I had been living the Jesuit vocation for almost twenty years before writing my dissertation, I had never been attracted to any of the Ignatian methods of prayer. In 1970 dissertations on Merton were in vogue so I chose to use Merton instead. My dissertation compared Maslow and Merton in their approaches to religious experience.[18]

Why did I summarily reject Ignatius' approach? I was still carrying very negative attitudes toward Ignatian prayer developed in my Jesuit formation. The methods presented were all thinking-centered. I found these methods tedious. Most did not connect to my life and so did not engage me. But I did remain conscientious in using these approaches for the first nine years of my Jesuit life—I knew no other method to fill up the time allotted for daily meditation. I should note that I was familiar with Ignatius' Contemplation to Obtain Divine Love but I saw it then as simply an elaboration of the same Ignatian methods that had not been working for me.

Fortunately my understanding and practice of personal prayer and contemplation changed; this was radically affected by two breakthroughs. The first breakthough occurred long before I was ever familiar with Merton's approach to contemplation; the second after I arrived at the university and I had begun teaching courses in mysticism.

The first breakthrough occurred nine years after I entered the Jesuits. I was assigned to teach at a mission for Native Americans the Jesuits ran in South Dakota. Life there was very difficult. Each day we young non-ordained Jesuit teachers arose at 5:00 A.M. and spent an hour in personal prayer in the community chapel, with the mission superior kneeling behind us. I conscientiously attempted to use the Ignatian methods of prayer I had been taught. The time was usually uneventful for me, due to tiredness, cold, and lack of interest in the topics I was praying over using the meditation books.

Life at the mission was also very difficult and often very frustrating. Never in my life had I experienced so many personal challenges both in my Jesuit community life and in my ministry. The students showed little interest in the religion courses I was teaching, not to mention the daily mass program and other activities I ran. I was very discouraged and even began wondering whether I had chosen the right vocation for my life.

However, very soon after I arrived at the mission I began taking walks alone at night down the remote country road late to pour out my discouragement to the Lord. I had never felt so lonely, so frustrated, so unappreciated—and I let the Lord know. All alone under a star-lit sky in the middle of nowhere I unloaded my frustrations to the Lord, often crying out loud.

These walks stabilized me; I looked forward to them and would not miss them if at all possible. Frequently after having poured out my troubles, I experienced a profound stillness and peace in the pitch darkness under the starry skies. Indeed, looking back now I can recognize that I was being "touched by the Lord" in a way fulfilling Merton's description of contemplation. I regularly left the walks energized, determined to continue to serve the Lord, even in that difficult situation. My encounters with the Lord made it all worthwhile.

Initially, however, I did not consider these walks personal prayer—they were surely not the Ignatian prayer I was supposed to be doing.

Then the superior left for a month and no one monitored the 5:30 A.M. meditation hour. I needed sleep so badly that I decided to stay in bed, skip meditation, and get up in time for 6:30 mass. But soon my conscience began to bother me. I had been told that daily meditation was the most important part of our day, and I was skipping it. But one day during this period I had the realization that I was not skipping daily prayer; I was doing it at night walking down the road!

From that moment on my attitude toward personal prayer changed. Prayer did not have to be a tedious reflection from a meditation book on some aspect of scripture using memory, understand, will and imagination. Simply being with the Lord and allowing Him to touch me wherever I was in my life was prayer. I wasn't sure whether theologians would agree with me—and this wasn't the "Ignatian prayer" I was taught—so I kept my ideas to myself. But it was working for me so I continued it. My first breakthrough taught me that my daily life was the best starting point for my daily prayer.

My second breakthrough occurred several years after I began teaching university courses on mysticism—I was, of course, familiar with Merton's approach to contemplation. I learned that the daily prayer I had been accustomed to doing since my time at the mission was not only genuine prayer but indeed genuine Ignatian prayer. My previous understanding of Ignatian prayer confining it to the use of memory, understanding, imagination and will flowing from reflection on scripture passages was too limited. Though these methods were indeed appropriate for retreatants making the thirty-day Spiritual Exercises, they were not as appropriate for regular daily prayer. I was relieved to discover that Ignatian prayer ought not be identified solely with them.

It happened this way. Sometime in the late nineteen-seventies—I do not remember the exact year—I was ending my annual eight-day retreat using the prescribed Contemplation to Obtain Divine Love. Ignatius presents this Contemplation as a concluding prayer experience of his thirty-day Spiritual Exercises; it is frequently used also for eight-day retreats. His two preliminary observations are important: first, love is manifested more by deeds than by words, and, second, the lover shares with the beloved all that he or she has. We are instructed to stand before the Lord and ask for interior knowledge of how much God the Lover has shared with us the beloved. First Ignatius asks us just to recall all gifts received through creation, redemption and even individual personal gifts. Then Ignatius directs us to reflect on how God dwells in these gifts and sustains them in existence, giving life to plants, sensation to animals, intelligence to humans—and "making me his temple, since I am created as a likeness and image of the Divine Majesty."[19] Further, Ignatius suggests we reflect on how God not only creates and sustains these gifts but actually labors and works for us through them and even manifests Infinite power and beauty in some way through each created gift. The purpose of these reflections: to be stirred to a profound gratitude that we may better love and serve the Lord.

I had always understood that this prayer should focus on the high points of my relationship with Jesus and stir me to be grateful for blessings, such as faith, redemption, vocation, daily graces to be faithful to my calling for yet another year. But then I found myself being moved in a different direction. I began asking what was the greatest blessing of the past year for which I was grateful. The answer surprised me. It was a specific and moving relationship with a sophomore student.

The student had lost his father in high school but never permitted himself to grieve because as the oldest boy he wanted to be strong for his mother, sisters and younger brothers. One day after class he followed me to my office, eyes red, but said nothing was wrong. Next class he also followed me to my office, eyes red, and finally broke down and told me about his father's death, acknowledging for the first time to another person his great loss. I remained his confidant throughout the year as he continued to share his personal and family concerns; we grew close. But the next year another tragedy struck the family: in a freak accident, his sister died. At his suggestion his mother asked me to do the funeral. This nineteen year old was now attempting to cope with two great losses. The coping involved alcohol. So not long after his sister's funeral he was arrested for driving while intoxicated, his second driving-under-the-influence arrest. At his court hearing a compassionate judge, a graduate from our law school, asked if he knew any Jesuits on campus that might serve as his probation officer. So he came by my office to ask if I would be his probation officer—and his father!

What was the greatest gift God had given me this year? A young student. All the blessings of creation and redemption and my vocation came together for me as I reflected upon our relationship the past two years. Effortlessly I recognized God's gift to me in this student. Effortlessly I was grateful for God's creating, sustaining and laboring through each of us – laboring especially through the power of the Holy Spirit within us to draw us together in love. It was all here: the blessings of creation and redemption and my vocation.

I realized that my experiences of being "touched by God" through this student throughout these two years frequently fulfilled not only Maslow's criteria for peak experiences but also Merton's criteria for contemplation.

And I realized that this was also genuine Ignatian prayer, indeed, an excellent example of Ignatius' Contemplation to Obtain Love! I began realizing that the prayer rhythm I discovered at the mission was not only genuine prayer but was even Ignatian prayer because it flowed from daily life. I had too narrowly identified Ignatian prayer with the formal meditation and contemplation methods presented in the texts of the *Spiritual Exercises*. Indeed, Ignatius presents, even in the *Spiritual Exercises*, a much more comprehensive approach to prayer, one that arises naturally from ordinary daily life—the Contemplation for Obtaining Love.

My Debt to Merton

As I conclude my "confessions," I realize that I am indebted to Thomas Merton in two inestimable ways. First, I am indebted to Merton for giving me a theological foundation for revitalizing my

understanding and practice of personal prayer and contemplation.

What did I learn from Merton?

I learned that daily prayer is not primarily a religious obligation superimposed on our nature but rather a natural spontaneous expression of our truest self. Until Merton, I viewed formal
prayer most often as a religious duty, a duty to which I was committed but did not relish.

I learned that normally prayer is easy, requiring being before
the Lord honestly and allowing the Holy Spirit to bring us into
communion—not unlike being with a friend. Prayer does not have
to be a strenuous attempt to concentrate on scripture using memory,
understanding, will and imagination.

I learned that the beauty of creation and the ordinary events of
daily life are the best starting points for daily prayer, rather than
scriptural texts unrelated to daily life. Merton's prayers as recorded
in his journals are usually occasioned by just such experiences of
creation or the human situation.

I learned that normally the best way to pray is to reduce personal efforts of thinking, willing and imagining and to allow ourselves to be present to the Holy Spirit, listening to this voice rising
up within us. This voice often leads to communion with Jesus:
"My sheep hear my voice."

I learned that prayer is enjoyable because communion with
God often flows over to deep peace and well-being. And I learned—
to my great surprise—that this communion sometimes becomes
contemplation. And I learned that these contemplative moments
happen outside of my formal prayer time as well as during it. I
discovered that my richest human experiences were also religious
experiences—no separation between the sacred and the secular.

Second, I am indebted to Merton for bringing me "home" to
Ignatius. I realize that my off-hand remark about Merton's approach to contemplation leading me to Ignatius' "Contemplation
to Obtain Love" was accurate. Primarily through Merton's reflections on contemplation I have "come home" to Ignatian prayer
and contemplation. I should note that by the mid nineteen-eight-
ies I was squarely in the Ignatian camp, owning my own Ignatian
spirituality and communicating it to others.

Observations of Ignatius at prayer, like the following recollection from one of Ignatius' first companions, assure me I'm on the
right track.

At night he would go up on the roof of the house, with the sky there up above him. He would sit there quietly, absolutely quietly. He would take his hat off and look up for a long time at the sky. The he would fall on his knees, bowing profoundly to God. Then he would sit on a little bench because the weakness of his body did not allow him to take any other position. He would stay there bareheaded and without moving. And the tears would begin to flow down his cheeks like a stream, but so quietly and so gently that you heard not a sob nor a sigh nor the least possible movement of this body.[20]

I ask myself why this journey took so long. I've always known intellectually that "finding God in all things" and being "contemplatives in action" were hallmarks of Ignatian spirituality and prayer. I recognize now that I was blocked from grasping this dimension of Ignatius by invalid assumptions flowing both from my pre-Vatican II orientation and from my early Jesuit formation. I needed someone to address these assumptions directly. In God's Providence Thomas Merton was that person.

And I realize now that Merton, Ignatius and I are brothers in prayer and contemplation, seeking God in daily lives and in creation—in all things!

Notes

1. Ignatius presents the "Contemplation to Obtain Love" as the concluding spiritual exercise of his thirty-day retreat. See George E. Ganss, *The Spiritual Exercises of Saint Ignatius: A Translation and Commentary* (St. Louis: Institute of Jesuit Sources, 1992), pp. 94-95.

2. The participant was Victor A. Kramer, ed.: *The Merton Annual: Studies in Culture, Spirituality and Social Concerns* (Louisville: Fons Vitae).

3. Walter M. Abbott, Editor, *The Documents of Vatican II* (New York: Guild Press, 1966), "Dogmatic Constitution on the Church," para. 4, p. 17.

4. "Personal Prayer: Contemporary Themes," *Review for Religious* (March 1975), pp. 256-265.

5. *The New American Bible* (New York: Thomas Nelson, 1970).

6. Thomas Merton, *Spiritual Direction and Meditation* (Collegeville: Liturgical Press, 1960), p. 79.

7. Thomas Merton, *No Man Is an Island* (New York: Harcourt, Brace, 1955), p. 70.

8. Thomas Merton, *New Seeds of Contemplation* (New York: New Directions, 1961), p. 34.

9. Richard J. Hauser, *In His Spirit: A Guide to Today's Spirituality* (New York: Paulist Press, 1982); *Moving in the Spirit: Becoming a Contemplative in Action* (New York: Paulist Press, 1986); *Finding God in Troubled Times* (Chicago: Loyola Press, 2002).

10. *New Seeds of Contemplation*, p. 1.

11. *New Seeds of Contemplation*, p. 3.

12. *New Seeds of Contemplation*, p. 5.

13. *New Seeds of Contemplation*, p. 9.

14. *New Seeds of Contemplation*, p.7.

15. *New Seeds of Contemplation*, p. 6.

16. Abraham H. Maslow, *Religions, Values and Peak-Experiences* (New York: Viking Press, 1970). This book contains Maslow's theory on the relationship between peak experiences and religious experiences.

17. *Religions, Values and Peak Experiences*, Appendix A, pp. 59-68. Appendix contains twenty-five characteristics of peak experience. I have paraphrased six.

18. Richard J. Hauser, S.J., *The Value of Abraham H. Maslow's Personality Theory for Understanding the Approach to Christian Prayer in Selected Writings of Thomas Merton* (Ann Arbor, MI: University Microfilms, 1973).

19. *Spiritual Exercises*, p. 95. I have paraphrased Ganss' translation.

20. W. W. Meissner, S.J., *Ignatius of Loyola: The Psychology of a Saint* (New Haven: Yale University Press, 1992), p. 280.

"Rising Up Out of the Center":
Thomas Merton on Prayer

Bonnie Thurston

In a way, everything Thomas Merton wrote, said, and did was "about prayer," because, as I hope to demonstrate, he made no fundamental distinction between "life" and "prayer." As he remarked toward the end of his life, "you pray with your whole life."[1] That being the case, it is curious that there is so little secondary literature on Merton and prayer. Studies abound on Merton and monasticism, mysticism, contemplation, solitude and silence, but the most important secondary sources on prayer *per se*, of which I am aware, consist of the articles in *The Merton Encyclopedia*, John Higgins' 1973 book *Thomas Merton on Prayer*[2] and a series of essays by John Teahan.[3] Because there is so much primary Merton material on prayer, I have limited this essay fundamentally, though not exclusively, to things Merton wrote in the 1960s and particularly to his correspondence with Abdul Aziz and with Etta Gullick, a record by Br. David Steindl-Rast, O.S.B., of Merton's conversation with a group gathered in California on the eve of his Asian journey, and the talks he gave in Alaska in September and October, 1968. These last have been much underused by Merton scholars and are a rich source for his mature thought on prayer. One in particular, "Prayer and Conscience," is an extremely good summary of Merton's practical teaching on prayer.[4]

Br. David Steindl-Rast begins his essay "Man of Prayer" in the 1974 volume *Thomas Merton, Monk* by explaining that a small group of people had gathered in California to meet with Merton before he left for Asia. The plan was to discuss renewal in religious life, and the group had asked Merton to speak on prayer. Br. David records that Merton insisted "nothing that anyone says will be that important. The great thing is prayer. Prayer itself. If you want a life of prayer, the way to get to it is by praying."[5] That last sentence summarizes the general concerns of the present essay.

By the word "prayer" I do not think Merton meant "saying prayers." For him prayer was the disposition of the whole person

God-ward. That is, prayer is an attitude or a mode of being as much as it is a specific activity.[6] As Merton noted in another conference given late in his life at the Monastery of the Precious Blood in Alaska, "Prayer is not really just a way of addressing God out there somewhere. Prayer is opening up ... deepest conscience and consciousness...."[7] This echoes what he had written years earlier in *Thoughts in Solitude*: "Prayer is ... not just a formula of words ... it is the orientation of our whole body, mind and spirit to God in silence, attention, and adoration."[8] And this attitude is consistent with what he writes much later in *Contemplative Prayer*: "By 'prayer of the heart' we seek God himself present in the depths of our being and meet him there...."[9] Contemplation, he notes, "is essentially a listening in silence, an expectancy."[10]

Merton's writings do not evince any particular interest in prayer as the word is commonly used, that is, in petitionary prayer, coarsely understood as "asking God for things." As John Teahan notes in his article "Meditation and Prayer in Merton's Spirituality," "Merton gave little attention to the prayer of petition." "... he preferred silent prayer to vocal prayer."[11] I suggest one reason for this is Merton's awareness that we can hide behind words. As he put it in *Thoughts in Solitude*, "We put words between ourselves and things. Even God has become another conceptual unreality in a no-man's land of language that no longer serves as a means of communion with reality."[12]

What Merton does say about prayer of intercession is very beautiful and helpful. "We are not rainmakers, but Christians. In our dealings with God he is free and so are we. It's simply a need for me to express my love by praying for my friends; it's like embracing them. If you love another person, it's God's love being realized. One and the same love is reaching your friend through you, and you through your friend."[13] This echoes a remark in *Thoughts in Solitude:* "Prayer uses words to reverence beings in God."[14]

Merton's basic understanding is that our intercessory prayer for our friends is the way we love them. But more than this, it is the way God's love is brought to bear on human situations; "it's God's love being realized," as he says. Such a view undercuts any dualistic understanding of prayer, any sense of me / other / God, because self and other are both understood to be "in God" since "one and the same love is reaching your friend through you, and you through your friend."[15] There is no other love than God's, because there is nothing else but God.[16] In the talk entitled "Prayer and Conscience," which was given in Alaska, Merton put this point as follows:

> If I am going to pray validly and deeply, it will be with a consciousness of myself as being more than just myself when I pray. ... I am not just an individual when I pray .... When I pray I am, in a certain sense, everybody . .... because this deep consciousness when I pray is a place of encounter between myself and God and between the common love of everybody.[17]

Another reason Merton may have been less interested in vocal prayer than in wordless prayer was his own struggles with the liturgy and the offices in Cistercian life which for him seemingly tended toward dualism. Writing on Holy Thursday, April 3, 1947, Merton reflected, "As soon as I get to choir I am overwhelmed by distractions. No sense of the presence of God. No sense of anything except difficulty and struggle and pain. Objectively speaking I suppose it is more perfect to thank God through the liturgy. The choral office should be the best way of continuing one's Communion. For me it is the worst."[18] The operative words here are "should be." Merton felt he *ought* to be able to pray deeply in choir. But in fact, he could not always do so. Multiple entries in his journals in 1947, 1948 and 1949 bear this out. As Merton matured in monastic life and as a Christian, he realized that the life of prayer cannot be forced. For each of us, it is what it is. Allowing for that variousness and individuation is crucial to the success of real, deep and profound prayer.

About ten years later (ca. 1957) Merton wrote, "There has never been any question, in Christian tradition, of the fact that the most propitious atmosphere for real contemplation is the solitude of a hermit's cell. Corporate and liturgical prayer are indeed important in the life of the Church and of the monk but they do not of themselves satisfy the deep need for intimate contact with God in solitary prayer...."[19] From our vantage point, knowing as we do that Merton was moving toward life as a hermit, the passage has an authentic, autobiographical ring. He had heard the call of the hermitage early in his monastic life.

Having noted his difficulty with the choir offices, it is still true that the Psalms were at the heart of Merton's prayer during the whole of his monastic life. As Erlinda Paguio notes in her important article "Thomas Merton and the Psalms," "in the monastic life the prayer of the community is made up above all of psalms."[20] In the 1950s Merton wrote two works on the Psalms, *Bread in the Wilderness* (1953), reflections on the Psalter intended primarily for monastics whose life is built around chanting them, and *Praying the Psalms* (1956), a pamphlet for laypersons. The Psalms, Merton reflected, "bring our hearts and minds into the presence of the living God" Who "will give Himself to us through the Psalter if we give ourselves to Him without reserve, in our recitation of the Psalms."[21] In the Psalms, Merton suggests, we recognize "our own experience lived out and perfected, orientated to God and made fruitful."[22] "There is no aspect of the interior life, no kind of religious experience, no spiritual need ... that is not depicted and lived out in the Psalms."[23]

Perhaps for this reason, even though he had difficulty chanting the Psalms in choir with the community, the Psalter itself was crucial to Merton's life of prayer for the whole of his life. On July 5, 1965 he spoke of the "greatest 'comfort' ... in the Psalms which face death as it is, under the eye of God, and teach us how we may face it—and bring us at the same time into contact, rather communion, with all those who have so seen death and accepted it. Most of all the Lord Himself who prayed from Psalm 21 on the Cross."[24] On July 19, 1965 Merton notes in his journal that he began a perpetual Psalter, "a necessity ... to keep the Psalter going from now on until I die (or can no longer do it). Need for the continuity the Psalter offers—continuity with my own past and with the past of eremitism."[25] Merton notes he will pray the Latin Psalter, and this is born out by a journal entry of December 15, 1966 that says "Words of my Latin psalms have been driving themselves home to me lately."[26]

I have suggested that for Merton prayer is turning of the whole person toward God, the opening of the heart to God: "...you cannot pray with your mind," he said, "You pray with your heart or with the depths of your being."[27] Clearly, as he understood and prayed it, the Psalter allowed him to turn and open to God "with the depths" and in communion with the whole Church. But Merton's own prayer life was also individuated, and so we turn now to the one account we have in which Merton describes his own prayer practice to see what can be learned from it about Merton's thinking on prayer. This will be an exercise in "theology gleaned from experience," although at one remove in that the experience is Merton's; the analysis is my own.

In November, 1960, upon the advice of the great Islamic scholar, Louis Massignon, a Pakistani Sufi, called Abdul Aziz, wrote to Merton. The resulting long correspondence was a very important one as it was Aziz who encouraged Merton's study of Sufism and subsequently his lectures on that subject to the monks at Gethsemani. The Merton-Aziz letters are one of the most complete records of a genuine Islamic-Christian dialogue on the personal level that the twentieth century offers. And it was to his friend, Abdul Aziz, the Pakistani Muslim, that Merton most fully revealed his own life of prayer. On January 2, 1966, in response to a question from Aziz about his own prayer practice, Merton wrote:

> ...you ask about my method of meditation. Strictly speaking I have a very simple way of prayer. It is centered entirely on attention to the presence of God and to His will and His love. ...it is centered on *faith* by which alone we can know the presence of God. One might say this gives my meditation the character described by the Prophet as "being before God as if you saw Him." Yet it does not mean imagining anything or conceiving a precise image of God, for to my mind this would be a kind of idolatry. ...it is a matter of adoring Him as invisible and infinitely beyond our comprehension, and realizing Him as all. My prayer tends very much toward what you call *fana.* There is in my heart this great thirst to recognize totally the nothingness of all that is not God. My prayer is then a kind of praise rising up out of the center of Nothing and Silence. If I am still present "myself" this I recognize as an obstacle about which I can do nothing unless He Himself removes the obstacle. If He wills He can make the Nothingness into a total clarity. If He does not will, then the Nothingness seems to itself to be an object and remains an obstacle. Such is my ordinary way of prayer, or meditation. It is not "thinking about" anything, but a direct seeking of the Face of the Invisible, which cannot be found unless we become lost in Him who is Invisible. I do not ordinarily write about such things and I ask you therefore to be discreet about it.[28]

This is a most remarkable passage in its personal intimacy, in what it reveals about Merton's assumptions about the practice of prayer and in its depth of understanding of Islamic spirituality. It is extraordinarily sensitive to Islam, its radical monotheism and abhorrence of *shirk* (idolatry, the cardinal sin in Islam). It uses the language of Sufism (for example, *fana* which means "annihilation" or nullification of ego-consciousness) to express a very Christian concept, that of *kenosis*, the self-emptying of Jesus which, in Philippians 2:6-11, St. Paul holds up as the model for all Christians. The excerpt from Merton's letter suggests that in prayer the great Christian, Thomas Merton, emptied himself of all that was not God in order to be present to God Who is ALL.

Of the many things this passage reveals, I have isolated and will discuss the following five principles of prayer which are inherent in Merton's practice as he describes it to Aziz:

1. God is with us.
2. Prayer is a gift and as such cannot really be taught.
3. In prayer it is absolutely crucial to be present. We start where we are.
4. Two fundamental and relatively common difficulties in prayer are distractions and self-consciousness.
5. Intentionally and potentially, all of life is prayer.

God is with us.

The idea that God is with us is a fundamental assertion of Christianity. Indeed, we call our Lord "Emmanuel," meaning "God with us" (Matthew 1:23). Merton's description of his prayer suggests it was primarily a matter of "attention to the presence of God."[29] St. Teresa of Avila is reputed to have said that all difficulties in prayer begin with the assumption that God is somewhere else. Merton made no such assumption; for him there was no *Deus absconditus*, no absent God. God is present to those who pray in three senses. First, God is present in an adjectival, geographic sense: here, at hand, "among us" to use St. Luke's happy turn of phrase. Second, God is present in an adverbial, temporal sense: now, existing at this moment. Third, God is present in a nominal sense: as gift, voluntarily given. This is why Merton stresses "*faith* by which alone we can know the presence of God."[30] God is present, here and now, *as* a present, a gift to the one who prays. God's presence in prayer is entirely gratuitous, given, not earned or forced or manipulated. As the Latin adage has it, *vocatus atque non vocatus, Deus aderit* which, loosely translated, means "whether we like it or not, God is with us."

Prayer is a gift and as such cannot really be taught.

Merton's prayer is centered on attention to the presence of God known by faith. Thus, like faith, prayer is a gift. In *Contemplative Prayer* Merton notes that true prayer "is not a psychological trick but a theological grace. It can come to us *only* as a gift, and not as a result of our own clever use of spiritual techniques."[31] The logical implication of this fact is that prayer cannot really be "taught." One might be able to help another to be disposed toward receiving the gift of prayer, but one cannot teach another person how to pray. And this is both because prayer is not a "technique" to be learned and perfected and because authentic prayer is as individualized as a fingerprint. Each of us must find our own way to pray. Indeed, the task of religious maturity is to find one's own language of prayer.

This simply highlights a point that Merton made several times in his writings. In the preface to *Spiritual Direction and Meditation* (1959) Merton begins, "You cannot learn meditation from a book. You just have to *meditate*." He speaks of the informality of the hints he will provide and of his "aversion to conventional and rigid systems." He is not, he says, opposed to discipline, but "it should be *one's own* discipline, not a routine mechanically imposed from the outside."[32] "Meditation is really very simple and there is not much need of elaborate techniques to teach us how to go about it."[33]

Similarly, writing to Etta Gullick (an Oxford-educated English woman with whom Merton corresponded extensively) on June 15, 1964 Merton says, "I do not think contemplation can be taught, but certainly an aptitude for it can be awakened." "... it is a question of showing ... in a mysterious way by example how to proceed. Not by the example of doing, but the example of being, and by one's attitude toward life and things."[34] Writing to Gullick on September 12, 1964 about contemplative prayer in the novitiate, Merton stated, "I don't use special methods. I try to make them [the novices] love the freedom and peace of being with God alone in faith and simplicity...."[35] This sounds remarkably like his own prayer as described to Abdul Aziz, and it continues to reflect Merton's reaction against overly rigid systems of prayer that do not take account of individual differences.

In prayer is it absolutely crucial
to be present. We start where we are.

If, as Merton has said, prayer is attention to the presence of God, then being present is crucial to prayer, *is* in some sense prayer. Merton writes to Abdul Aziz that he places himself "before God as if [he] saw Him."[36] Put slightly differently, Merton makes himself present to the present God. Indeed, this is what he also said in the 1959 book on meditation: "In order to meditate, I have to withdraw my mind from all that prevents me from attending to God present in my heart."[37] Br. David Steindl-Rast remarked that "to *start where you are* and to become aware of the connections ... was Thomas Merton's approach to prayer"(emphasis mine).[38] Brother David reports that Merton also said, "In prayer we discover what we already have. You start where you are and you deepen what you already have, and you realize that you are already there. We already have everything, but we don't know it and we don't experience it. Everything has been given to us in Christ. All we need is to experience what we already possess."[39]

The implication is that one must be present where she is, must give both time and the fullness of one's self to prayer. "If we really want prayer," Merton said, "we'll have to give it time. We must slow down to a human tempo." "...We live in the fullness of time. Every moment is God's own good time, his *kairos*. The whole thing boils down to giving ourselves in prayer a chance to realize that we have what we seek. We don't have to rush after it. It is there all the time, and if we give it time it will make itself known to us."[40]

This is exactly the advice he had given to Sr. Thérèse Lentfoehr when he wrote to her about prayer on August 29, 1949:

> ...have you a garden or somewhere that you can walk in, by yourself? Take half an hour, or fifteen minutes a day and just walk up and down among the flower beds .... Do not try to think about anything in particular and when thoughts about work, etc. come to you, do not try to push them out by main force, but see if you can't drop them just by relaxing your mind. Do this because you "are praying" and because our Lord is with you. But if thoughts about work will not go away, accept them idly and without too much eagerness with intention of letting our Lord reveal His will to you through these thoughts....[41]

Merton articulated the same point more generally in 1958 in *Thoughts in Solitude*: "If we want to be spiritual ... let us first of all live our lives. Let us not fear the responsibilities and the inevitable distractions of the work appointed for us by the will of God. Let us embrace reality and thus find ourselves immersed in the life-giving will and wisdom of God which surrounds us everywhere."[42]

Two fundamental and relatively common difficulties in prayer are distractions and self-consciousness.

For Merton prayer is basically attentiveness to the presence of God which is a gift given in the present moment. One hears in this understanding the influence of his studies of Buddhism, and particularly of Zen, which stresses "being present where we are." To be fully present is not as easy as it may sound. Most of us are not where we are. We are "somewhere else," for example, dwelling in regret about the past or anxiety about the future. Such attitudes are real hindrances to prayer, hindrances which are traditionally termed "distractions" and "self-consciousness."

The matter of distractions in prayer has been alluded to in the letter to Sr. Thérèse Lentfoehr already quoted. Very simply, distractions are the thoughts that fill our heads when we attempt to pray, when we attempt to become fully present in the moment and open to God. In the life of prayer such distractions are inevitable. The important thing is not to give them energy by "fighting" them. That would be like trying to put out a fire by pouring gasoline on it. Merton's advice that distractions should be accepted "idly and without too much eagerness"[43] is extremely practical. He said nearly the same thing in an Alaskan conference: "What do you do with distractions? You either simply let them pass by and ignore them, or you let them pass by and be perfectly content to have them. If you don't pay attention to them, the distractions don't remain."[44] That is, one recognizes the thought or feeling that is a distraction, but doesn't think or feel it; one simply lets it "pass through." Merton continues, "If you don't wrestle with distractions wildly and just let them go by for a while, they get less and less, and after a while there is nothing much left."[45]

One reason people have so much trouble with distractions in prayer involves self-consciousness. Merton alluded to it in his letter to Abdul Aziz when he spoke of *fana* (annihilation of ego, becoming lost in God). The obstacle is being present to myself. Specifically, it is the problem of "watching ourselves" as we pray, and the more general problem of being self- absorbed in our own spiritual quest and with our own spirituality. In the sort of prayer of which Merton writes to Aziz, "self" recedes, as Merton noted: "If I am still present 'myself' this I recognize as an obstacle...."[46] Writing to Etta Gullick on October 29, 1962, Merton noted, "There is too much conscious 'spiritual life' floating around us, and we are too aware that we are supposed to get somewhere. Well, where? If you reflect, the answer turns out to be a word that is never very close to any kind of manageable reality. If that is the case, perhaps we are already in that where."[47] In short, self-consciously worrying about making progress in prayer (as if one were learning to bowl or play tennis!), first, makes one self-conscious and, second, deflects one from the truth of the Presence in the present into which one simply "relaxes" or even "melts."[48]

On August 1, 1966 Merton returned to this same idea in his correspondence with Mrs. Gullick. Obviously once again (at her prompting?) addressing "progress in prayer" he says, "the chief obstacle to progress is too much self-awareness and to talk about 'how to make progress' is a good way to make people too aware of themselves. In the long run I think progress in prayer comes from the Cross and humiliation and whatever makes us really experience our total poverty and nothingness, and also gets our mind off ourselves."[49] (Those who worry about Merton's orthodoxy might note the profoundly Christian groundedness of this formulation.) In his letter to Abdul Aziz Merton had said of his own prayer, "If I am still present 'myself' this I recognize as an obstacle," but this obstacle is one about which he can do nothing himself. He must wait for God to remove the obstacle, not struggle with it or against himself. In short, prayer is modeled by the *kenosis* (self-emptying) of Jesus and is received as a grace God gives.

In *Thoughts in Solitude* Merton wrote, "A man knows when he has found his vocation when he stops thinking about how to live and begins to live."[50] For our purposes a paraphrase might read, "A person knows she has 'learned' to pray when she stops thinking about prayer and worrying about herself and her 'progress' and prays." And that leads to Merton's understanding that, ultimately, all of life is prayer.

Intentionally and potentially, all of life is prayer.

As Merton describes it to Abdul Aziz, prayer is as much a state of being (being present) as it is a particular, differentiated activity.

This is because, as Merton already noted in *Thoughts in Solitude*, "As soon as a man is fully disposed to be alone with God, he is alone with God no matter where he may be...."[51] If, as Christians assert, God is Emmanuel, with us, and if, as Merton asserts, prayer is being disposed toward God in the present, then it is actually possible, as St. Paul commanded the Thessalonians, to "pray ceaselessly" (1 Thessalonians 5:17) by maintaining the prayer disposition or attentiveness constantly.

One can be constantly turned toward and open to God. Indeed, for Merton this is the whole object of the spiritual life. "What I object to about 'the Spiritual Life,'" he wrote to Etta Gullick, "is the fact that it is a part, a section, set off as if it were a whole. It is an aberration to set off our 'prayer' etc. from the rest of our existence, as if we were sometimes spiritual, sometimes not." "...Our 'life in the Spirit' is all-embracing, or should be."[52] Therefore, as he noted in *Contemplative Prayer*, "A false supernaturalism which imagines that 'the supernatural' is a kind of Platonic realm of abstract essences totally apart from and opposed to the concrete world of nature, offers no real support to a genuine life of meditation and prayer. Meditation has no point and no reality unless it is firmly rooted in *life*."[53]

One of the great, frequently commented upon and written about themes in Merton's writing is that of identity. Many people have been greatly helped by Merton's articulation of the false and true self, "little-s" self and "big-S" self, so clearly presented, for example, in chapters 4-7 of *New Seeds of Contemplation*.[54] The connection to our discussion is that Merton points in the direction of understanding prayer as one's authentic, Christian identity: we are our prayer. In prayer, "we seek first of all the deepest ground of our identity in God."[55] Thus, as he taught in Alaska, we pray with our entire life ("...you pray with your whole life."[56]). As Brother David Steindl-Rast remarked, "Finding your true self and living a life of prayer were not two things for Thomas Merton, but one."[57] Chapter 12 of *Thoughts in Solitude* opens with this very important observation: "If you want to have a spiritual life you must unify your life. A life is either all spiritual or not spiritual at all. No man can serve two masters. Your life is shaped by the end you live for. You are made in the image of what you desire."[58]

The need to overcome dualisms like self/other or self/God or life/prayer is one of Thomas Merton's most profound insights. His mature teaching on prayer strikes at the heart of all dualism because he teaches that being present *is* prayer. As he said in *Contemplation in a World of Action*, "The real purpose of prayer ... is the deepening of personal realization in love, the awareness of God."[59] Merton thinks that we are already *in* a state of prayer, *in* God. We must "wake up to it" so to speak. In centering "entirely on attention to the presence of God and to His will and His love," directly "seeking the Face of the Invisible,"[60] we can, indeed, be "made [or I would say "re-made"] in the image of what [we] desire."[61] The process of being re-formed in God's image by prayer is what Orthodoxy calls "deification in Christ." In my view, it is this to which Merton's most mature teaching on prayer calls us. "What you have to do," Merton says, "is have this deeper consciousness of here I am and here is God and here are all these things which all belong to God. He and I and they are all involved in one love and everything manifests His goodness. Everything that I experience really reaches Him in some way or other. Nothing is an obstacle. He is in everything."[62]

As he was leaving for Asia, as he embarked on his final journey, speaking to that small group of men and women seeking renewal in religious life, Merton asked rhetorically, "What do we want, if not to pray? O.K., now, pray."[63] And then he asked the more profound question, and the one that haunts me: "What is keeping us back from living lives of prayer? Perhaps we don't really want to pray. This is the thing we have to face."[64]

Notes

1. Robert E. Daggy, ed., *Thomas Merton in Alaska* (New York: New Directions, 1989) p. 129.

2. John J. Higgins, S.J., *Thomas Merton on Prayer* (Garden City, NY: Doubleday, 1973). The work was first published by Cistercian Publications in 1971 under the title *Merton's Theology of Prayer*.

3. These include "A Dark and Empty Way: Thomas Merton and the Apophatic Tradition," *Journal of Religion* 58 (1978), pp. 263-287; "Meditation and Prayer in Merton's Spirituality," *American Benedictine Review* 30 (1979), pp. 107-133; "Solitude: A Central Motif in Thomas Merton's Life and Writings," *Journal of the American Academy of Religion* 50 (1982), pp. 521-538.

4. The essay appears in *Thomas Merton in Alaska* and was also published in *Sisters Today* 41 (1971).

5. Br. David Steindl-Rast, O.S.B., "Man of Prayer," in *Thomas Merton, Monk,* Br. Patrick Hart, O.C.S.O., ed., (New York: Sheed and Ward, 1974), p. 79.

6. For an exposition of this idea see my article "Prayer: A Mode of Being" published serially in *Spirituality* 10/52 (2004) and 10/53 (2004).

7. Daggy, *Thomas Merton in Alaska,* pp. 130-131.

8. Thomas Merton, *Thoughts in Solitude* (New York: Farrar, Straus & Cudahy, 1956), p. 48.

9. Thomas Merton, *Contemplative Prayer* (New York: Doubleday/ Image, 1969/71), pp. 30-31. The masculine references are Merton's. In the interest of accuracy, if not of inclusivity, I maintain Merton's exact usage throughout this essay.

10. Merton, *Contemplative Prayer,* p. 90.

11. Teahan, "Meditation and Prayer in Merton's Spirituality," p. 114.

12. Merton, *Thoughts in Solitude,* p. 85.

13. Hart, *Thomas Merton, Monk,* p. 88.

14. Merton, *Thoughts in Solitude,* p. 69.

15. Hart, *Thomas Merton, Monk,* p. 88.

16. This, of course, is the logical conclusion of radical monotheism of the sort that Merton encountered in Sufi literature, especially in the writing of Al Hallaj.

17. Daggy, *Thomas Merton in Alaska,* pp. 134-135.

18. Thomas Merton, *The Sign of Jonas* (New York: Harcourt, Brace, 1953), p. 37.

19. Thomas Merton, *The Silent Life* (New York: Farrar, Straus & Cudahy, 1957), p. 149.

20. Erlinda Paguio, "Thomas Merton and the Psalms," *The Merton Seasonal* 22/4 (1997), p. 12.

21. Thomas Merton, *Bread in the Wilderness* (New York: New Directions, 1953), pp. 13 and 47.

22. Thomas Merton, *Praying the Psalms* (Collegeville, MN: Liturgical Press, 1956), p. 16.

23. Merton, *Praying the Psalms,* p. 31.

24. Robert E. Daggy, ed., *Dancing in the Water of Life: The Journals of Thomas Merton 1963-1965* (San Francisco: Harper San Francisco, 1995), p. 264.

25. Daggy, ed., *Dancing in the Water of Life,* p. 273.

26. Christine M. Bochen, ed., *Learning to Love: The Journals of Thomas Merton 1966-1967* (San Francisco: Harper San Francisco, 1997), p. 170.

27. Daggy, *Thomas Merton in Alaska,* p. 81.

28. William H. Shannon, ed., *Thomas Merton, The Hidden Ground of Love, Letters* (New York: Farrar, Straus and Giroux, 1985), pp. 63-64.

29. Shannon, *Hidden Ground of Love*, p. 63.
30. Shannon, *Hidden Ground of Love*, p. 63.
31. Merton, *Contemplative Prayer*, p. 92.
32. Thomas Merton, *Spiritual Direction and Meditation* (Collegeville: Liturgical Press, 1959). No pagination in the Preface
33. Merton, *Spiritual Direction and Meditation*, p. 68.
34. Shannon, *Hidden Ground of Love*, p. 367.
35. Shannon, *Hidden Ground of Love*, p. 368.
36. Shannon, *Hidden Ground of Love*, p. 63.
37. Merton, *Spiritual Direction and Meditation*, pp. 68-69.
38. Hart, *Thomas Merton, Monk*, p. 80.
39. Hart, *Thomas Merton, Monk*, p. 80.
40. Hart, *Thomas Merton, Monk*, p. 81.
41. Quoted in Christine M. Bochen, ed., *Thomas Merton: Essential Writings* (Maryknoll: Orbis Books, 2000), p. 83.
42. Merton, *Thoughts in Solitude*, pp. 46-47.
43. Bochen, *Thomas Merton: Essential Writings*, p. 83.
44. Daggy, *Thomas Merton in Alaska*, p. 138.
45. Daggy, *Thomas Merton in Alaska*, p. 139.
46. Shannon, *Hidden Ground of Love*, p. 64.
47. Shannon, *Hidden Ground of Love*, p. 355.
48. The terms "relaxes" and "melts" are mine, not Merton's, but I think they accurately describe what he is suggesting.
49. Shannon, *Hidden Ground of Love*, p. 376.
50. Merton, *Thoughts in Solitude*, p. 87.
51. Merton, *Thoughts in Solitude*, p. 96.
52. Shannon, *Hidden Ground of Love*, p. 357.
53. Merton, *Contemplative Prayer*, p. 39.
54. Thomas Merton, *New Seeds of Contemplation* (New York: New Directions, 1961).
55. Merton, *Contemplative Prayer*, p. 67.
56. Daggy, *Thomas Merton in Alaska*, p. 129.
57. Hart, *Thomas Merton, Monk*, p. 85.
58. Merton, *Thoughts in Solitude*, p. 56.
59. Quoted in *Thomas Merton: Essential Writings*, p. 86.
60. Shannon, *Hidden Ground of Love*, pp. 63-64.
61. Merton, *Thoughts in Solitude*, p. 56.
62. Daggy, *Thomas Merton in Alaska*, p. 140.
63. Hart, *Thomas Merton, Monk*, p. 84.
64. Hart, *Thomas Merton, Monk*, p. 85.

PRAYING THE QUESTIONS
Merton of Times Square,
Last of the Urban Hermits

David Joseph Belcastro

If there is one ambition we should allow ourselves, and one form of strength, it is perhaps this kind of wholehearted irony, to *be* a complete piece of systematic irony in the middle of the totalitarian lie—or the capitalist one. And even the official religious one.

Letter from Thomas Merton to Czeslaw Milosz[1]

Introduction

As a consequence, perhaps, of an extended crisis about stability, Thomas Merton was granted permission to meet with Dr. Gregory Zilboorg at St. John's University during July of 1956 at a conference on monasticism and psychology. While Merton never mentions the second session with the psychoanalyst in his journals, Dom James Fox, who was present at this meeting, did, and apparently on more than one occasion, thus influencing ecclesiastical opinions of Merton for years to come. While previous conversations between the two men had not gone particularly well, the second encounter greatly disturbed Merton. Pressing his opinion that Merton's desire to be a hermit was almost pathological, Zilboorg declared, "You want a hermitage in Times Square with a large sign over it saying 'HERMIT.'"[2] *

---

* Editor's note: An overarching problem with the Merton / Zilboorg meeting arguably makes it an unreliable topic for discussion: the arrangement and public knowledge of this meeting reveals a compromise of integrity between those involved. Regardless of how or why Merton's meeting with Zilboorg was disclosed to the public, the point is that its very disclosure shows that either Merton or Zilboorg (probably both) did not respect or understand the nature and purpose of their meeting. If one interprets this deficit psychoanalytically, one sees that both Merton and Zilboorg idealized and therefore distorted one another's identity.

Zilboorg was, at least in part, correct. Certainly, he was correct to observe a fundamental contradiction in Merton's monastic life. Zilboorg, however, failed to understand how the opposite poles of this contradiction, urban and hermit, might authentically converge in the person of Thomas Merton. Zilboorg's preconceptions about Merton and monasticism prevented him from understanding the man sitting before him.[3]   His judgement, consequently, was wide of the mark. There was a contradiction in the urban Merton, yet the contradiction was anything but pathological.[4]   As we shall see, it was Cardinal Larraona's light-hearted dismissal of Zilboorg's diagnosis with a Spanish proverb that most likely moves us in the right direction and closer to the truth with regard to Merton as an urban hermit: *De poeta y de loco tenemos todos un poco* (We all have a bit of poetry and a bit of madness in us).[5]

This article suggests that the idea of Merton as someone like a hermit in Times Square may be correct, not, however, as descriptive of a troubled personality but rather as indicative of an essential aspect of this particular monastic vocation. In order to make a case for this opinion, several intersecting lines of inquiry into Merton's life will be explored: 1) a question he lived; 2) a contradiction he embodied; 3) and a hidden wholeness he offered the world in his silent prayer and protest against the crimes and injustices of political tyranny.

It needs to be noted as well that Merton's meeting with Zilboorg was *not* a psychoanalytic session, and no diagnosis occurred. Had they begun an actual analytic relationship, the general public would never have known it. Excluding specific homicidal disclosure, psychoanalysts and their analysands are ethically bound to hold their relationship in confidence. Also, non-psychoanalytic sources (including Merton) addressing Zilboorg's alleged diagnosis of Merton show basic misunderstandings about narcissism and psychoanalytic pathology. The Merton / Zilboorg relationship lacked what is required to take seriously the nature and process of a therapeutic relationship. Their meeting likely amounts to little more than a clash between two high-profile figures who were unwilling or unable to dialogue about their vastly different worldviews. Consequently, there is a serious question to be raised regarding the legitimacy of using the Zilboorg / Merton meeting as a basis of any discussion other than to say that their meeting shows itself as fallacious. [GC]

A Lived Question

Dom André Louf is known for saying that a monk is a person who begins every day by asking, "What is a monk?" Dom Benedetto Calati restates the question with a sharper focus. After reviewing Merton's publications, he asked an appropriate question, "If a monk, what kind of a monk is he?"[6] Merton was a monk who lived this very question and struggled with the questions raised and the answers offered by others regarding his life and work. His writings provide ample evidence of an unfailing desire to find an answer. He eventually discovered, however, that the question he lived was the answer he sought. "Untitled Poem" expresses the importance of this question, informing as it does the obscure theology of God's presence at work throughout his life.

> All theology is a kind of birthday
> Each one who is born
> Comes into the world as a question
> For which old answers
> Are not sufficient.
>
> Birth is question and revelation.
> The ground of birth is paradise
> Yet we are born a thousand miles
> Away from our home.
> Paradise weeps in us
> And we wander further away.
> This is the theology
> Of our birthdays.
>
> Obscure theology
> On the steps of Cincinnati Station:
> I am questioned by the cold December
> Of 1941. One small snowflake
> Melts on my eyelid like a guess
> And is forgotten.
> (Across the river my meaning has taken flesh
> Is warm, cries for care
> Across the river
> Heaven is weeping.)

> Heaven weeps without cause
> Forever if I do not find
> The question that seeks me . . .[7]

Beginning with the remembrance of his stopover at Cincinnati Station during the train ride from St. Bonaventure to the Abbey of Gethsemani, the poem weaves together recollections that inevitably return to this fundamental question that sought Merton. Even though this speaker sets out to construct a "theology of will" that would allow him to be "a man without doubts," Wisdom makes of his theology "a broken neck of questions." Wisdom is described as a fire smouldering, a flower growing, a bird flying in the center of his monastery, here named "Fort Thomas Kentucky" where "all the gates are shut" and "everything … is certain." It is Wisdom that undoes such a "stone wall Eden" and awakens the speaker to love and the way of not knowing. "Untitled Poem" reveals the movement of Merton from a theology of answers to a theology of questions; a theology that he believed would lead to a "way home to where we are / Epiphany and Eden."

Merton had come to learn that previous answers to the question, as well as those formulated by others like Zilboorg, were and would continue to be insufficient. He had come to realize that if he were to ever discover the nature and meaning of his life as a monk, he must live the questions that surfaced in his life, obscure and contradictory as they might at first appear. By the mid 1960's, this had become apparent to him. A journal entry from the January 31, 1964 reads:

> The new *Monastic Studies* is out, only one copy in the house, in the Chapter Room. A long review takes in that Italian collection of monastic conferences in which Dom [Benedetto] Calati discusses me as precisely what? As utterly out of his world. And of course, he is right. I do not belong to his monastic world at all, am no part of it—the world where the status quo is just all right. On the other hand I do not rebel against it either, I am just not concerned with it. And thus from many points of view I am "not a monk." In general that is all right with me, since I need only to be concerned with loyalty to my own graces and my own task in life, not with being recognized by "them" in "their" categories.[8]

And, nearly a year later, on December 9, 1964, he writes in his journal about an unexpected discovery with regard to his vocation:

> Last night after a prayer vigil in the novitiate chapel (didn't do a good job—was somewhat disorganized and distracted), went to bed late at the hermitage. All quiet. No lights at Boone's or Newton's. Cold. Lay in bed realizing that what I was, was *happy*. Said the strange word "happiness" and realized that it was there, not as an "it" or object. It simply was. And I was that. And this morning, coming down, seeing the multitude of stars above the bare branches of the wood, I was suddenly hit, as it were, with the whole package of meaning of everything: that the immense mercy of God was upon me, that the Lord in infinite kindness had looked down on me and given me this vocation out of love, and that he had always intended this, and how foolish and trivial had been all my fears and twistings and desperation. And no matter what anyone else might do or say about it, however they might judge or evaluate it, all is irrelevant in the reality of my vocation to solitude, even though I am not a typical hermit. Quite the contrary perhaps. It does not matter how I may or may not be classified. In the light of this simple fact of God's love and the form it has taken, in the mystery of my life, classifications are ludicrous, and I have no further need to occupy my mind with them (if I ever did)—at least in this connection.[9]

With these journal entries in mind, it becomes apparent that Merton's defense of Boris Pasternak is as appropriate for himself as it was for the Russian writer:

> But the important thing to realize is that here, as with all deeply spiritual thinkers, to concentrate on a strict analysis of concepts and formulas is to lose contact with the man's basic intuitions. The great error, the error into which the Communists themselves plunge headlong at the first opportunity, is to try to peg genius down and make it fit into some ready-made classification. Pasternak is not a man for whom there is a plain and definite category. And we must not try to tag him with easy names . . .[10]

Abandoning easily prescribed definitions of what a monk is, Merton takes a different path; one less certain but more promising, one guided not by an established theology of answers but by one led by Wisdom into deeper and more complicated questions. There is a line in *Opening the Bible* where Merton says that religious thought does not move from question to answer but rather from question to question, with each new question opening a larger field of vision for understanding oneself in relation to God and the world.[11]

This particular strain of religious thought is further clarified by recalling what Rilke says in a letter to a young poet, a letter most certainly familiar to Merton, that one must live the question and, if one lives long enough, one may live into an answer.[12] In other words, a person's life becomes the answer to the question as the question shapes the person who lives it. And so it was with Merton who lived the question of his vocation and the paradoxes unique to it. By living this question, a question for which there was no definitive answer but only more questions, the mystery of Merton's vocation would unfold, obscurely but nonetheless authentically. Perhaps this is what he had in mind while writing "Learning to Live." While he is never able to say exactly who he is or what kind of monk or hermit he might be, he was none-the-less aware of how living the question moved him in the direction of becoming more authentically human, free and alive in relation to and for the sake of the world in which he lived. Recalling his early formation at Columbia, he writes:

Life consists of learning to live on one's own, spontaneous, freewheeling: to do this one must recognize what is one's own—be familiar and at home with oneself. This means basically learning who one is, and learning what one has to offer to the contemporary world, and then learning how to make that offering valid. The purpose of education is to show a person how to define himself authentically and spontaneously in relation to his world—not to impose a prefabricated definition of the individual himself, still less an arbitrary definition of the world. The world is made up of the people who are fully alive in it: that is, of the people who can be themselves in it and can enter into a living and fruitful relationship with each other in it. The world is, therefore, more real in proportion as the people in it are able to be more fully and more humanly alive: that is to say, better able to make a lucid and conscious use of their freedom. Basically, this freedom must consist first

of all in the capacity to choose their own lives, to find themselves on the deepest possible level.[13]

Merton finally had discovered that his vocation could only be
understood by discerning the dark path of questions along which
he journeyed; questions that obscurely revealed the grace of God
at work within his life. Following the trajectory of questions emerging from a person's life is a far cry from Zilboorg's approach, an
approach not unlike those who tried, according to Merton, to categorize Pasternak. Zilboorg failed to see the relevance of the questions emerging from Merton's struggle to be a monk according to
his own graces and tasks. His preoccupation with institutional
definitions and psychological categories prevented him from hearing, and assisting Merton in hearing, how Merton was answering
the question, "If a monk, what kind of a monk?" Zilboorg would
have better served Merton had he focused their attention on the
questions that were emerging from this one question that was central to Merton's life by simply saying, "Ah, I see you as a hermit in
Times Square. What an odd image, Merton. What are you to make
of it?"

An Embodied Contradiction

Had Zilboorg raised such a question, Merton may have recognized
the contradiction that was inherent in his vocation. And, if Matthew Kelty had been there, he would have confirmed their observation by saying, as he would later say, "While many have tried to
categorize Merton, he cannot be placed in one category of monk
or another because he was a contradiction, a man who lived at the
center of the cross."[14] This being the case, if a category is to be
offered, it must be one for which contradictions are an essential
aspect. Before turning to such a category, the two parts of the
contradiction presented by Zilboorg's image of Merton as a hermit in Times Square need to be addressed.

Contradictions result from establishing boundaries that define
human experience by way of opposites. Once established, boundaries determine inclusion and exclusion. So it is with urban and
hermit. What urban includes, hermit excludes and vice versa.
Urban includes society, public discourse, and commerce. Hermit
includes solitude, silence, and self-sufficiency. Consequently, according to this way of thinking, a predominantly Western and
modern way of thinking, hermits do not live in Times Square or

any other public place. Merton was aware of this. In *The Silent Life*, he writes:

> Let us face the fact that the monastic vocation tends to present itself to the modern world as a problem and as a scandal. In a basically religious culture, like that of India, or of Japan, the monk is more or less taken for granted. When all society is oriented beyond the mere transient quest of business and pleasure, no one is surprised that men should devote their lives to an invisible God. In a materialistic culture which is fundamentally irreligious the monk is incomprehensible because he "produces nothing." His life appears to be completely useless.[15]

Merton, of course, had problems with this way of seeing things. The boundary that separated the two worlds disturbed him. This was not a consequence of being maladjusted but something deeper and of greater significance. It had to do with a valid objection to the way in which the Western world had been defined into opposites of sacred and profane, religious and secular, and so forth. Such a way of defining the world was contrary to what he was discovering in his life at Gethsemani and, in particular, his experience at Fourth and Walnut:

> In Louisville, at the corner of Fourth and Walnut, in the center of the shopping district, I was suddenly overwhelmed with the realization that I loved all those people, that they were mine and I theirs, that we could not be alien to one another even though we were total strangers. It was like waking from a dream of separateness, of spurious self-isolation in a special world, the world of renunciation and supposed holiness. The whole illusion of a separate holy existence is a dream. Not that I question the reality of my vocation, or of my monastic life: but the conception of "separation from the world" that we have in the monastery too easily presents itself as a complete illusion: the illusion that by making vows we become a different species of being, pseudo-angels, "spiritual men," men of interior life, what have you.[16]

It is commonly understood that the intersection of Fourth and Walnut in Louisville marks the place where Merton's understanding himself and his relation to the world radically changed. While some distance from Times Square, on that day, he was clearly an urban hermit who was able to see with the eyes of a contemplative the world in which he lived and of which he was a part. His account of the experience continues:

> Then it was as if I suddenly saw the secret beauty of their hearts, the depths of their hearts where neither sin nor desire nor self-knowledge can reach, the core of their reality, the person that each one is in God's eyes. If only they could all see themselves as they really *are*. If only we could see each other that way all the time. There would be no more war, no more hatred, no more cruelty, no more greed . . . . I suppose the big problem would be that we would fall down and worship each other. But this cannot be *seen*, only believed and "understood" by a peculiar gift.[17]

It was also at this intersection that one might say Merton runs into Czeslaw Milosz and Albert Camus. Of course this did not actually occur. What did happen, however, was no less significant. Two years following the experience at Fourth and Walnut, Merton initiated correspondence with Milosz and, by Milosz's encouragement, began reading Camus. I emphasize these relationships because of the role they play in the further formation of Merton as an urban hermit, which might—going one step further—be called an urbane hermit. At the heart of both "conversations" was a search for a position in the world that was true to the deepest dimension of the Fourth and Walnut experience, i.e *le point vierge*, "the gate of heaven" that "is everywhere."[18] While a contemplative's vision, it also becomes for Merton the ontological grounding of his engagement with that world. In a letter to Milosz dated December 6, 1958, Merton writes:

> It seems to me that, as you point out, and as other writers like yourself say or imply (Koestler, Camus etc.) there *has to be* a third position, a position of integrity, which refuses subjection to the pressures of the two massive groups ranged against each other in the world. It is quite simply obvious that the future, in plain dialectical terms, rests with those of us who risk our heads and our necks and everything in the difficult, fantastic job of finding out the new position, the ever changing and moving "line" that is no line at all because it cannot be traced out by political dogmatists.[19]

The search for *le point vierge* and the third position became primary concerns for Merton as evidenced by his correspondence with Milosz and his essays on Camus. This third position is the intersection of opposites that opposes the illusion of separateness manifested by a world artificially defined and compartmentalized. It is this search that makes Merton an urban hermit. Unable to accept the division between religious life and political action, he holds the two together. Note, for example, how his photographing of Kanchenjunga and pilgrimage to Polonnaruwa eventually lead to the city of Bangkok where he addresses himself to:

> . . . the monk who is potentially open to contact with the intellectual, the university student, the university professor, the people who are thinking along lines that are going to change both Western and Eastern society and create the world of the future, in which inevitably we are going to have to make our adaptation.[20]

The awareness of the other side of the mountain that cannot be reduced to a postcard and the dharmakaya exploding from the stone Buddhas, brought Merton to an urban setting in which he offered, once again, a contemplative's vision of the world; a vision that was full of promise, new life, and, as Merton stated in "Untitled Poem" "a way home to where we are / Epiphany and Eden."

If Merton were placed within the Alexandrian tradition, the odd image of urban hermit would not appear so strange. It clearly has historical precedence in the West. Philo Judaeus, a contemporary of Jesus and Paul, was as at home with the Therapeutae, contemplative community, as he was in the streets of Alexandria. He could be found in the synagogue reading the Torah, as well as in the library reading Plato; and reading *Timaeus* and Genesis in light of one another. A highly imaginative biblical scholar who created commentaries for Jews living in a Hellenistic culture, he was equally skilled at writing political tracts and leading embassies to see Gaius in Rome. At the heart of Philo's life and work was an effort to integrate a contemplative vision of the world with social and political action. In a sense this is what Merton did best.

While Merton only makes passing reference to Philo, he devoted considerably more attention to another figure from that ancient city. While desiring to live as a hermit, Merton appears in many ways far more like Clement of Alexandria than Anthony of the Desert. Confessing his love for and affinity with Clement,

Merton's admiration is more than apparent from the numerous references to this Alexandrian as "a great mind and a great Christian, noble and broad and belonging to antiquity, yet new."[21] He draws Jean Leclercq's attention to Clement as a source for renewal of monastic spirituality in the twentieth century.[22]

His essay on Clement's *The Protreptikos* reveals what he found of great value in this early Christian theologian.

> The voice of Clement is the voice of one who fully penetrates the mystery of the *pascha Christi*, the Christian exodus from this world in and with the Risen Christ. He has the full triumphant sense of victory which is authentically and perfectly Christian: a victory over death, over sin, over the confusion and dissensions of this world, with its raging cruelty and its futile concerns. A victory which leads not to contempt of man and of the world, but on the contrary to a true, pure, serene love, filled with compassion, able to discover and to "save" for Christ all that is good and noble in man, in society, in philosophy and in humanistic culture. This is the greatness and genius of Clement, who was no Desert Father. He lived in the midst of Alexandria, moved amid its crowds, knew its intellectual elite, and loved them all in Christ.[23]

Clement was able to live within the city, presenting the Christian faith in terms comprehensible to the world in which he lived because, as Merton explains, he was:

> . . . a man of unlimited comprehension and compassion who did not fear to seek elements of truth wherever they could be found. For truth, he said, is one. And consequently its partial and incomplete expression is already something of the great unity we all desire. The full expression is found most perfectly in the Divine Logos, the Incarnate Word, Jesus Christ.[24]

In order to illustrate this, Merton points to how Clement would have worked with Plato.

> Gnosis is . . . the full experience of Christ revealed and living in His Church. But this full experience could not be attained without a thorough preparation, both cultural and spiritual. Here is Clement's special contribution: he felt that Greek philosophy could and did assist this preparation. But Christian gnosis was far beyond Plato, and to enter into the Divine light

one had to leave Plato's cave. Nevertheless, Plato himself had not failed to realize the existence of the cave, or the fact that he realities "seen" there were only shadows cast by a light from elsewhere.[25]

Within these paragraphs, we find the theology and pedagogy that formed the foundation for the contradiction of Merton's vocation as a hermit in Times Square. Truth is one. While fully revealed in Christ, it is nonetheless present everywhere. Recognizing the truth presented by persons from other traditions and representing alternative perspectives, prepares the way for the Gospel. Consequently, it is necessary for those who bear the responsibility of sharing the Gospel to be in the midst of the city fully engaged in the conversations of the day. It is somewhat amusing to note that Merton laments that there have not been more Clements in the history of the Church; amusing because it is not at all difficult to see him as a Clement engaging the world in dialogue and thereby awakening within the hearts and minds of his contemporaries the hidden Logos.[26] Merton's seven essays in response to the literary work of Albert Camus provide an excellent example of this.[27] Recognizing a certain affinity with Camus, Merton referred to him as the "Algerian Cenobite."[28] Believing that Camus was a prophetic voice that the Church needed to heed, Merton sought to clarify Camus' message. In these essays we observe a pattern that is remarkably similar to what we find in Clement's response to the intellectuals of his day. First, there is an expression of respect for Camus as a person and writer. Second, there is acceptance and approval of Camus' ideas. This acceptance, however, is seldom without reservation. Consequently, there is a third part to the pattern where Merton indicates that Camus is fine as far as he goes but Camus needs to go further. Like Plato, he must move beyond the shadows to the light of the Gospel.

While Zilboorg was correct to identify two dimensions of Merton's vocation, urban and hermit, he was unable to see how they paradoxically might be true for Merton. Unaware of the Alexandrian tradition, he failed to grasp the significance of his image of a hermit in Times Square. Had he said, "Ah, I see you as a hermit in Times Square. What an odd image, Merton. What do you make of it?", Merton might very well have responded, "Clement of Alexandria."

A Hidden Wholeness

There is more, however, to Merton than a twentieth-century reincarnation of an ancient Alexandrian. While looking at Clement
may have shed some light on the image of an urban hermit, it is
not sufficient for fully grasping the significance of this image for
Merton. I noted earlier Matthew Kelty's opinion that Merton could
not be categorized. I also indicated that I would nonetheless suggest a category but one that by its very nature embodies contradictions.

Before turning to that category, a brief mention of Nicholas of
Cusa's notion of coincidence of opposites will suggest that it is
not unreasonable to believe that contradictions such as urban and
hermit might converge into an authentic whole. Simply stated,
the coincidence of opposites is a state in which opposites no longer
oppose each other but converge into a harmonious union. While
perceived as a coincidence, the unity, not the distinction, is the
deeper reality that we, for a brief and passing moment, are able to
glimpse. With this in mind, it becomes possible to consider ways
in which urban and hermit might converge to reveal a hidden
wholeness in Merton's life. One such way is suggested by Lewis
Hyde in his book entitled *Trickster Makes This World; Mischief, Myth,
and Art*.[29] Hyde points out that the trickster is an embodiment of
contradictions who provides an invaluable service to society by
opening the deeper dimension of life that has become closed off
by formidable boundaries constructed by custom and practice. As
we shall see, it is not at all difficult to understand how urban and
hermit converge in Merton to reveal his essential and hidden
wholeness as a trickster.

The trickster embodies the playful and disruptive side of the
human mind; the wild and creative imagination that breaks up
static ways of thinking and with them rigid institutions and traditions that no longer allow for the dynamic processes of authentic
life, freedom, and joy. The old myths tell us that dying cultures
are transformed by the subversive innovation of tricksters. In these
stories, the trickster is always up against those who are intent on
building a more perfect and ideal world; one without the natural
complexities, ambiguities, and paradoxes of life. The trickster is
an anti-idealist. He is in and for the world of imperfections. He
speaks and acts out about those things that a society has deemed
unfit, that is, do not fit together according to the prevailing ways

of seeing the world. Consequently, the trickster and the establishment are locked in an endless cycle of constructing and
deconstructing worlds. On the one hand, officials plan, build, and
manage business-as-usual. On the other hand, the lone trickster
emerges from "nowhere" to ensure the continuation of life in its
full mystery by disarranging everything. Needless to say, for most,
tricksters are bothersome [as Merton was to Zilboorg]. Few understand them, many dislike them, but paradoxically history tells
us that they are indispensable cultural heroes whose stories have
been told from antiquity: Hermes in Greece, Loki in Scandinavia,
Eshu in Africa, the Monkey King in China, and Coyote in North
America, to name just a few. And, now with Hyde's book, the life
and work of still more recent tricksters are recalled: Pablo Picasso,
John Cage, Allen Ginsberg, and Frederick Douglass. All these characters, fictional and real, are described by Hyde as follows:

> . . . trickster is a boundary-crosser. Every group has its edge,
> its sense of in and out, and trickster is always there, at the gates
> of the city and the gates of life, making sure there is commerce.
> He also attends the internal boundaries by which groups ar-
> ticulate their social life. We constantly distinguish - right and
> wrong, sacred and profane, clean and dirty, male and female,
> young and old, living and dead - and in every case trickster
> will cross the line and confuse the distinction. Trickster is the
> creative idiot, therefore, the wise fool, the gray-haired baby,
> the cross-dresser, the speaker of sacred profanities. Where
> someone's sense of honorable behavior has left him unable to
> act, trickster will appear to suggest an amoral action, some-
> thing right/wrong that will get life going again. Trickster is
> the mythic embodiment of ambiguity and ambivalence,
> doubleness and duplicity, contradiction and paradox.[30]

Hyde identifies here four characteristics of the trickster. The trickster is a boundary-crosser, a confuser-of-distinctions, a cross-
dresser, and an embodiment-of-ambiguity. These characteristics
are true for Merton and can be seen as the characteristics of someone who longed to be a hermit, but also as someone whose attraction to the urban and urbane remained basic. The designation of
boundary-crosser can be misleading. It may suggest that the trickster simply crosses boundaries. He does more than this. He works
his way in-between established boundaries. That is to say, his work
is done not on one side or the other but in the middle. Perhaps, it

would be better to describe him as a playful criss-crosser who moves back and forth, weaving connections where there had not only previously been none but where such connections were more than likely prohibited. Crisscrossing boundaries like a thief in the night, the trickster employs any crafty measure available to create something new and totally unexpected. While many will see his play as whimsical, disoriented, foolish, and even immoral, he is playing true to a deeper sense of order, harmony, and beauty; playing true to his own intuitions and graces. His tricks are for the sole purpose of making new and odd connections and thereby opening up the deeper dimensions of life that had become closed off by the rigid structures of a society. Merton was a boundary-crosser who worked his way in-between established traditions and institutions which had been closed to one another for ages. This is so apparent from his writings, there is no need to list them all. It was so characteristic of his life and work that it is difficult, if not impossible, to think of Merton without conjuring up an image of a man-between-something-or-another. Locating himself in-between mutually exclusive worlds, he went about opening dialogue, imaginations, and ways of thinking to the vast array of possibilities for an authentic human community grounded by grace in a freedom offered by life unbounded.

As a boundary-crosser, the trickster is also a confuser-of-distinctions. He erases those carefully drawn lines that have been used to distinguish persons, things, and activities from one another. His favorite area of play is the intersection of human and divine. When the relation between humanity and the gods becomes too distant and, consequently, meaningless, the trickster is there to renew the presence of the divine in the daily activities of human life on earth. In order to do this, the trickster must erase the line that has been drawn between the sacred and the profane, the eternal and the temporal, heaven and earth. Merton was a confuser-of-distinctions. That is to say, he took great pleasure in turning things upside down and around to see what new forms could be created. For example, in his poem entitled "Five Virgins," he intentionally confuses the distinctions that we make between the sacred and the profane, piety and play, vigilant virgins and good looking women who know how to dance. Merton knew the dangers of a religious life whereby the joy of heaven could be lost by over-emphasis on being responsible, prepared, and ever-vigilant virgins. While there is nothing wrong with these virtues

in and of themselves, if practiced to the exclusion of human foolishness in all its rich earthiness, they can become the death of the
Spirit that is intended to create life, freedom, joy within us and
our communities. Consequently, we see in this poem a confusing
of distinctions between wise and foolish virgins so that the reader
may discover *holy folly*.[31]

> There were five howling virgins
> Who came
> To the Wedding of the Lamb
> With their disabled motorcycles
> And their oil tanks
> Empty
>
> But since they knew how
> To dance,
> A person says to them
> To stay anyhow.
>
> And there you have it:
> There were five noisy virgins
> Without gas
> But looking good
> In the traffic of the dance.
>
> Consequently
> There were ten virgins
> At the Wedding of the Lamb.

In order to crisscross boundaries and reconnect heaven and earth,
the trickster must be a cross-dresser; that is to say, a master of disguises. His life is marked by happenstance. He must be able to
take advantage of the unexpected coincidence. Consequently, one
moment he appears this way and the next another. To an onlooker,
the trickster will appear a shifty character, aimless and without
purpose. In reality, the trickster is simply playing the moment for
all it is worth by adapting to the situation. Nonetheless, he keeps
his wits about him and his eye on the primary objective of opening the place up. Merton was a cross-dresser, a master of disguises.
Perhaps this is best seen in his correspondence. Facing all four
corners of the globe, he wrote letters to Latin American poets in
the South, Buddhist monks in the East, Beat writers in the West,
and Russian dissidents in the North. In these letters we observe

with what great ease he became all things to all people. A casual reading of the letters reveals Merton's vast array of voices and disguises. After a while, you cannot help but ask, "Which was the true Merton?" If we understand him as a trickster, we have to say Merton was honestly "playing" whatever he was at that moment, sincerely and authentically engaging his world in conversation. He was able to move between communities, make connections and open possibilities for dialogue.

There is one more characteristic that must be considered. A trick or two, now and then, does not make someone a trickster. The trickster must embody the ambiguities of his age. The trickster has internalized the contradictions of his world. He is acting them out. He is trying to make a place for himself in the world that has no place for him. As one might imagine, his acting out of these internal conflicts inevitably disturbs the peace and quiet of the community or communities through which he is passing. Even though the trickster's behavior is deeply rooted within himself and has much to do with his own unresolved issues, his acting out always has social consequences. As he struggles to make a place in the world for himself, he opens the doors for others. In this struggle, he becomes his own place within the world, his own geography, his own pattern of life; his own and yet oddly enough not his own for he has become the embodiment of life with all of its questions, ambiguities, and paradoxes. And, so in his struggle, he gains for his contemporaries a new-found freedom for discovering life at its deepest level and experiencing for themselves the fullness of life in all of its complexities. Merton was an embodiment of the ambiguities of his age. The opening lines of *The Seven Storey Mountain* articulate this most clearly: "Free by nature, in the image of God, I was nevertheless the prisoner of my own violence and my own selfishness, in the image of the world into which I was born."[32] These few words describe the birth of a trickster in our world who would eventually combust with the contradictions of our age. Reflecting back on his autobiography, Merton writes:

> . . . the monastery is not an "escape" from the world. On the contrary, by being in the monastery I take my true part in all the struggles and sufferings of the world. To adopt a life that is essentially non-assertive, non-violent, a life of humility and peace is in itself a statement of one's position. But each one in such a life can, by the personal modality of his decision, give his whole life a special orientation. It is my intention to make

my entire life a rejection of, a protest against the crimes and injustices of war and political tyranny which threaten to destroy the whole race of man and the world with him. By my monastic life and vows I am saying NO to all the concentration camps, the aerial bombardments, the staged political trials, the judicial murders, the racial injustices, the economic tyrannies, and the whole socio-economic apparatus which seems geared for nothing but global destruction in spite of all its fair words in favor of peace. I make monastic silence a protest against the lies of politicians, propagandists and agitators, and when I speak it is to deny that my faith and my Church can ever seriously be aligned with these forces of injustice and destruction.[33]

In the World

Merton could not understand monasticism as simply a retreat from the world. On the contrary, for Merton, to be a monk meant also to be in the world and, for him, this meant to be in the world in a way unique to the monastic vocation. He understood the monk as "essentially someone who takes up a critical attitude toward the world and its structures," believing "that the claims of the world are fraudulent."[34] This did not mean for Merton a rejection of the world. For Merton, it meant taking up a middle position, the third position, a position in-between worlds.

> I think we should say that there has to be a dialectic between world refusal and world acceptance. The world refusal of the monk is something that also looks toward an acceptance of a world that is open to change. In other words, the world refusal of the monk is in view of his desire for change.[35]

All this underscores the opinion that Merton was a trickster-monk set loose in the world; a hermit talking about silence and solitude in Times Square. It is perhaps this lived contradiction that caused a restless search that eventually led to Albert Camus in whom he found a mentor and model of silence as a language of resistance and a source for social change.

> With all my silence I shall protest to the very end. There is no reason to say, "It had to be." It is my revolt which is right, and it must follow this joy which is like a pilgrim on earth, follow it step by step.[36]

While we might be inclined to identify this quote with Merton, it was actually written by Albert Camus. A notebook entry dated the September 9, 1937, it represents a youthful Camus' early reflections on a position that he would later develop in several collections of essays entitled *The Myth of Sisyphus*, *The Rebel*, and *Resistance, Rebellion and Death*, as well as, in plays, short stories, and novels. It is, however, quoted by Merton in "Terror and the Absurd: Violence and Nonviolence in Albert Camus"; the third essay in a series of seven essays by Merton on Camus. Merton was looking seriously at Camus' position of revolt as valid for himself as a monk living in the twentieth century. Referring to this notebook entry, Merton indicates that he had found in Camus the pure rebel who refuses to accept with passive and unreasoning resignation a falsification of authentic life; who protests the destruction or mutilation of life in the name of something else, whether it be patriotism, the economy, or religion; and who resists the numerous forces of alienation that separate humans from one another and from life itself.[37] It is interesting to observe, however, that Merton appears to have overlooked the opening words of the notebook entry. Even though Merton belonged to an order that valued silence, he took no notice of Camus' words, "With all my silence I shall protest to the very end." This, as is obvious from the context, is *not* the despairing silence of resignation but the affirming silence of protest on behalf of life. Camus' rebel is grounded in this silence, speaks out of this silence, and embodies this silence. While Merton does not make anything of this in "Terror and the Absurd: Violence and Nonviolence in Albert Camus," it is clearly articulated in his "Message to Poets." In this address, Merton calls upon a new generation of Latin American writers to be rooted in "fidelity to *life* rather than to artificial systems."[38] He points out that they are a generation who are "not in tutelage to established political systems or cultural structures" and, as a consequence, may "dare to hope in their own vision of reality and of the future."[39] Because they remain outside all socially constructed categories, outside where life unfolds in "all its unpredictability and all its freedom,"[40] he declares that they, like himself, are "monks," "ministers of silence," and "children of the Unknown"[41] whose words "point beyond all objects into the silence where nothing can be said."[42] It is out of this silence, Merton tells them, that they will be able to resist with innocence, love, and solidarity the alienation, violence, and deceptions that are inherent in the social structures of their day.

Whether it was the notebook entry or something else, it is clear from "Message to Poets" that Merton and Camus were on the same page with regard to silence as the language of resistance.

In order to gain a clearer understanding of what this might possibly mean, we could look at Merton's "Rain and the Rhinoceros" and Camus' "The Growing Stone." Both works explore in similar ways silence as the language of resistance. Nature is presented as a witness that invokes an awareness of the ineffable that extends beyond all social constructs. This awareness silences all declarations of what is and what ought to be. In Camus' story, the murmuring of a river running through the jungles of Brazil silences social customs and ecclesiastical traditions that had long alienated the indigenous peoples. In Merton's essay, the strange rhythms of rain baptizing his hermitage in the hills of Kentucky silences technological enterprises that make for progress and war. Both narratives awaken within the reader an awareness of an interior silence that echoes the silence of the universe. The awareness of this interior silence to which nature and these two works of literary art witness, long forgotten in the West, was understood by Camus and Merton as the essential protest necessary for the protection of life in the postmodern world.

While silence as resistance is explored in these two works, neither Camus or Merton present systematic studies but simply express, as stated by Merton, intuitions which cannot be easily defined because they are "obscure and ironic."[43] Consequently, "The Growing Stone" and "Rain and the Rhinoceros" leave the reader with difficult questions to consider. These questions, however, if pursued, offer an opportunity to discover new horizons for humanity as it approaches the end of the modern era. How does the silent gesture of a French engineer carrying a stone overcome alienation and create community with the poor and oppressed? Why should we consider the silent presence of a hermit in the woods a valid and effective protest against alienation? Of what do a river in Brazil and rain in Kentucky speak? Who are we who are silenced by a simple gesture, a hermit in the woods, a murmuring river, or the rhythms of falling rain?

Luce Irigaray, a French feminist philosopher, provides a perspective from which we can consider "The Growing Stone" and "Rain and the Rhinoceros," the questions these works raise, and silence as the language of resistance. In her book, *Between East and West: From Singularity to Community*, Irigaray presents a theory on gender as a paradigm for an appreciation of diversity, a respect for differences, and a commitment to solidarity.[44] She understands human identities to be grounded in the fecundity of nature and therefore irreducible to stereotypes, class distinctions, and social customs. The witness of nature appears and reappears everywhere in the random murmurings of running streams, unrecognizable rhythms of falling rains, and sundry other ways. Nature, according to Irigaray, challenges us to welcome the diversity it represents and, to do so, in the spirit of democracy.[45] Consequently, nature silences all forms of authoritarianism and totalitarianism that have dominated human life in modern times. Nature witnesses to the possibility of a community woven from the differences of age, gender, and race, as well as, the diverse religious symbols that vary from one culture to another.[46] For this to happen, she suggests an "education of the body"[47] by which learning comes through the sensual experiences of the whole person immersed in nature. Here, she believes, is the possible refoundation of the human community "at the level of the least constructed, at the most intimate level of being human itself and of its living relations with the pregiven world that surrounds it: nature, other living beings."[48] While sharing much in common with Merton and Camus on nature, silence, and resistance, Irigaray has moved beyond these two, presenting a more systematic study. Her perspective on silence and human relations can be summarized in three parts.

First, silence is always an essential aspect of the human experience. George Steiner in *Silence and Language: Essays on Language, Literature, and the Inhuman* has noted that language only deals meaningfully with a restricted segment of reality. The rest, and he presumes this to be the much larger part, is silence.[49] Irigaray situates this silence within human relations. She sees the recognition, establishment, and nurture of this silence as necessary for all authentic ways of relating. In "The Growing Stone," Camus essentially says the same thing. Here he describes a situation in which a traditional Christian ceremony processes unexpectedly outside the church and the town to a primitive hut by a river where an engineer from France and indigenous peoples simply sit together in silence. In "Rain and the Rhinoceros," Merton, while reflecting on the immediate experience of the rain falling in the woods around his hermitage, remembers Ionesco's play *Rhinoceros* seemingly to suggest that the silent presence of a hermit, impervious to the gigantic snorting sounds of progress, lives in fidelity to the rhythms of his own life.

The second aspect of Irigaray's perspective is an extension of the first and may be summarized: in silence the socially constructed one becomes two with each standing as unique and a mystery before the other. That is to say, for example, in silence, I cannot be reduced to you or you to me but each stands separate, a mystery to one another. The same is true for other human differences. Identity, at the deepest and truest level, according to Irigaray is always open rather than closed; open to seemingly endless possibilities. Human identity, like life itself, is undefinable and therefore free to be explored and discovered in new ways. So, in Camus' "Growing Stone," the native peoples are no longer seen as members of a European empire but are present as distinct and unique and, consequently, an unknown to be discovered rather than predefined. Likewise, Merton in "Rain and the Rhinoceros" makes a point of distinguishing himself from the culture that would try to define him and what he does, believing, as he says, to know what he was doing in the hermitage.

The third aspect of Irigaray's perspective is simply the reverse of the second: silence is where two resists one. Irigaray believes that from within silence emerges a natural resistance of the two to reduction to the socially constructed one. The resistence is essential for the unfolding of the uniqueness and mystery of the individual. This silence prevents a person or group of persons from defining others in ways that restrict, alienate, and oppress them, thereby preventing the human community from flourishing. All such social constructs become meaningless when dwarfed as they are by the expansive unknown reality of the ineffable to which silence witnesses. Furthermore, this aspect of silence becomes the ground for a solidarity of resistance but one that does not require uniformity but the openness of wonder, exploration, and acceptance. So, with Camus' "Growing Stone" we find in the closing scene that while the distinctive differences are more than apparent a community nonetheless is present. And, in Merton's "Rain and the Rhinoceros," Merton understands that while he is distinctively different, he is nonetheless inescapably a member of a larger community with the task of protesting.

Thoreau sat in *his* cabin and criticized the railways. I sit in mine and wonder about a world that has, well, progressed. I must read *Walden* again, and see if Thoreau already guessed that he was part of what he thought he could escape. But it is not a matter of "escaping." It is not even a matter of protesting very audibly . . . .[50]

Merton's recognition that neither he nor Thoreau can escape the social constructs of their times is important.

Merton understands the monk's vocation to be in but not of the world; a situating of oneself that is characteristic of the trickster figure who lives on the boundary between the socially constructed world and the vast unknown, and thereby becomes a portal between the two. It is in taking up this position that his very presence becomes a protest against the social constructs and a witness to life, to the virgin point that cannot be analyzed by social scientists but only discovered as the place where the dance of life happens.

Viewing Merton and Camus on silence as resistance through the lens provided by Irigaray, we see that both writers recognized the problem with social constructs and the need to awaken within the human experience an awareness of that which lies outside the boundaries of all constructs and, while beyond comprehension, nonetheless real, speaking as it does of our true identity as unknown, undefinable and unfolding in contrast to ideologies that define human identity as knowable and set. Nature, as represented by the stone and rain, witnesses to this dimension without boundaries, beyond analysis, before all constructs. An engineer's silent gesture and a hermit's silent presence draw our attention to this witness. Their silence speaks of the vast unknown, calling us to live within and out of this mystery that silences our illusions of grandeur, and calls us to live and speak out of it and its unpredictability and the freedom it offers. Here, as suggested by Irigaray, a new horizon for life is to be found. Here we discover the importance of silent gestures, a hermit's vocation, and the deepest dimension within ourselves that is awakened by murmuring rivers and the rhythms of falling rain to enter the dance of life.

While Merton acknowledged his agreement with Camus, he also recognized how they differed. While both may agree on silence as the language of resistance, Camus proceeds no further than the human heart and the happiness one must imagine Sisyphus knew as he resisted death and despair with each step up the hill. Merton, on the other hand, understands the human heart and its deepest joy and capacity to love in a world of sorrow and hate to be grounded in the hidden work of God in Christ. Even so, the distance between the two men may not be as great as it appears. Czeslaw Milosz in his obituary essay on Camus stated that all of Camus' work, not just his academic thesis on Augustine, might very well have been "marked by a suppressed theological bent."[51] This "bent" has been acknowledged by others who have found in Camus themes of grace and redemption, although without reference to the Christian God that Camus says he was unable to accept as long as their was one innocent child in this world suffering.

Whether the distance between these two men could ever have been bridged is the subject of another study. For this article, however, it should be noted, that Merton and Camus would have no difficulty sitting together with whatever disagreement may have existed. Each, I am sure, would have respected and valued the uniqueness of the other. Merton's essays on Camus testify to this and Camus' "The Unbeliever and Christians" does so as well. And, I have no doubt that there would have been an authentic solidarity between the two; a solidarity emerging not from conformity of thought but out of a deep intuition of the ineffable diversity they embodied together. Both understood, perhaps obscurely, this irony that Irigaray would later so clearly articulate in her writings.

Conclusion

The relation with Camus, as well as with Milosz and many others, places Merton in the Alexandrian, rather than the Desert, tradition. This makes him no less a contemplative, a monk, or even a hermit. His unique vocation embodied the contradictions of contemplation and action, monk and writer, longing to be hermit and connected to the urban.   Merton became a contemplative whose silence included, not excluded, conversation with the world in which he lived. The same could be said of his solitude. It was never an exclusive solitude but rather a solitude grounded in the solidarity of Christ with all humanity. The world was his hermitage. And, for a brief moment in history, he was the world's hermit.   In every relation and situation, varied as they might be, Merton witnessed to the ineffable presence of God in the world and the unbounded possibilities of life lived in the Spirit of that God. This witness, as we have seen, was not limited to essays on monastic life but extended into the public domain as a protest against humankind's propensity for violence, exploitation, and death.

Living these contradictions involved Merton in a lifetime of questioning and more searching for answers that could only be discovered in his prayerful lived experience. These contradictions, however, were not his alone but those of the world in which he lived and sought to serve. By living the contradictions of his age, he opened for his contemporaries a new way of being religious within the world; a way that extended far beyond the sectarian divisions of the past, the classifications of sacred and profane, and the limitations of modern thought.

Merton's struggle was not pathological as Zilboorg would have us to believe. While his observations were correct, his conclusion was wrong. When we compare Zilboorg's observations as recorded by Merton[52] with Hyde's description of a trickster, we discover that the collective wisdom of mythology provides a far more interesting perspective on Merton than that provided by psychoanalysis. When we consider the way in which Merton lived the question of his vocation and the contradictions that he embodied, we come to see that his "poetry and craziness" were expressions of a hidden wholeness; the hidden wholeness of a trickster who was both urban and hermit. Merton moved between the monastic world and modern life with the intention of opening the twentieth century to deeper dimensions of life that it had forgotten.

Postscript

After working his way in-between so many worlds, erasing the barriers which bound and separated humanity in the twentieth century, and thereby opening for us new ways of seeing life's possibilities when lived as grace and mystery, Thomas Merton, far from home, on December 10, 1968, after talking about monasticism and Marxism, had a coke and disappeared . . . which is the way of tricksters. Tricksters erase lines and, then, themselves. The trickster cannot stay around long. He is always outside, in-between, and on-the-road. Sooner or later, for his work to be completed, the trickster must disappear. This last act is essential. In the last act of the trickster's play, his audience is lured into the trap that will set them free. By his absence, the audience is left alone, puzzled and perplexed by the crazy antics of someone who has rearranged their world. Alone, the audience discovers something that could never have been found had the trickster remained. The audience becomes aware that they too may have wild and creative imaginations that can see beyond the confines of their old world.

Notes

1. *Striving Towards Being: The Letters of Thomas Merton and Czeslaw Milosz*, ed. Robert Faggen (New York: Farrar, Straus & Giroux, 1997), p. 56.

2. For an account of Merton's meetings with Zilboorg, see Michael Mott, *The Seven Mountains of Thomas Merton* (Boston: Houghton Mifflin Company, 1984), pp. 290-99, 339.

3. Regarding Zilboorg's lack of objectivity, see Mott, *The Seven Mountains*, pp. 291-93.

4. Mott does not agree with Zilboorg's diagnosis. See Mott, *The Seven Mountains*, p. 366. And, apparently, Fr. John Eudes Bamberger did not agree that Merton's desire for solitude was pathological. See Thomas Merton, *Witness to Freedom: Letters in Times of Crisis*, ed. William H. Shannon (New York: Farrar, Straus & Giroux, 1994), p. 212.

5. Thomas Merton, *The Hidden Ground of Love: The Letters of Thomas Merton on Religious Experience and Social Concerns*, ed. William H. Shannon (New York: Farrar, Straus & Giroux, 1985), p. 135.

6. Dom Benedetto Calati, *The Theory of Monasticism in the Literature of the Last Thirty Years* in *Problemi e orientamenti di spiritualita monastica, biblica e liturgica* (Rome: Edizioni Paoline, 1961), pp. 337-497.

7. Thomas Merton, *Eighteen Poems* (New York: New Directions, 1985).

8. Thomas Merton, *Dancing in the Water of Life*, ed. Robert Daggy (San Francisco: HarperSanFrancisco, 1997), p. 68.

9. Merton, *Dancing in the Water*, pp. 177-78.

10. Thomas Merton, *Disputed Questions* (New York: Farrar, Straus and Cudahy, Inc., 1960), p.23

11. Thomas Merton, *Opening the Bible* (Collegeville, MN: Liturgical Press, 1970), p. 19-20.

12. Rainer Maria Rilke, *Letters to a Young Poet*, trans. and ed. Stephen Mitchell (New York: Modern Library, 2001), p. 34.

13. Thomas Merton, *Love and Living*, ed. Naomi Burton Stone and Brother Patrick Hart (New York: Farrar, Straus & Giroux, 1979), p. 3.

14. *A Taste of Gethsemani: Trappist Monks Remember Merton* (Video of Panel Discussion at Bellarmine University in Louisville, Kentucky by The Thomas Merton Center Foundation: December, 1997).

15. Thomas Merton, *The Silent Life* (New York: Farrar, Straus and Cudahy, Inc., 1957), p. viii.

16. Thomas Merton, *Conjectures of a Guilty Bystander* (New York: Doubleday, 1966), pp. 140-141.

17. Merton, *Conjectures*, p. 142.

18. Merton, *Conjectures*, p. 142.

19. *Striving Towards Being*, p. 4.

20. Thomas Merton, *The Asian* Journal, ed. Naomi Burton, Patrick Hart & James Laughlin (New York: New Directions, 1973), p. 328.

21. Thomas Merton, *Clement of Alexandria; Selections from the Protreptikos* (New York: New Directions, 1962), p. 3.

22. *Survival or Prophecy? The Letters of Thomas Merton and Jean Leclercq*, ed. Brother Patrick Hart (New York: Farrar, Straus & Giroux, 2002), p. 76.

23. Thomas Merton, *Clement of Alexandria; Selections from the Protreptikos* (New York: New Directions, 1962), pp. 1-2.

24. Thomas Merton, *Clement of Alexandria*, p. 3.

25. Thomas Merton, *Clement of Alexandria*, p. 5.

26. Thomas Merton, *Clement of Alexandria*, p.10.

27. *The Literary Essays of Thomas Merton*, ed. Brother Patrick Hart (New York: New Directions, 1981), pp. 181-301.

28. *The Literary Essays*, p. xv.

29. Lewis Hyde, *Trickster Makes This World; Mischief, Myth, and Art* (New York: North Point Press, 1999).

30. Lewis Hyde, *Trickster Makes This World*, p. 7.

31. For Merton's understanding of *folly*, see Mott, *The Seven Mountains*, pp. 419f.

32. Thomas Merton, *The Seven Storey Mountain* (New York: Harcourt, Brace, 1948), p. 3.

33. Thomas Merton, *"Honorable Reader"; Reflections on My Work*, ed. Robert Daggy (New York: Crossroad, 1989), pp. 65-66.

34. Merton, *The Asian Journal*, p. 329.

35. Merton, *The Asian Journal*, pp. 329-30.

36. Albert Camus, *Notebooks 1935-1942* (New York: Alfred A. Knopf, 1963) p. 54.

37. Thomas Merton, "Terror and the Absurd: Violence and Nonviolence in Albert Camus" in *The Literary Essays*, p. 239.

38. Thomas Merton, "Message to Poets" in *The Literary* Essays, p. 372.

39. Merton, "Message to Poets," p. 371.

40. Merton, "Message to Poets," p. 373.

41. Merton, "Message to Poets," pp. 373-374.

42. Merton, "Message to Poets," p. 374.

43. Thomas Merton, *Raids on the Unspeakable* (New York: New Directions, 1966), p. 2.

44. Luce Irigaray, *Between East and West: From Singularity to Community* (New York: Columbia University Press, 2002), p. 137.

45. Irigaray, *Between East and West*, p. 140.

46. Irigaray, *Between East and West*, p. 140.

47. Irigaray, *Between East and West*, p. 70.

48. Irigaray, *Between East and West*, pp. 11; 55.

49. George Steiner, *Language and Silence* (New Haven: Yale University Press, 1998), p. vii.

50. Merton, *Raids on the Unspeakable* (New York: New Directions, 1964), pp. 12-13.

51. Tony Judt, *The Burden of Responsibility: Blum, Camus, Aron, and the French Twentieth Century* (Chicago: The University of Chicago Press, 1998), pp. 93-94.

52. Mott, *The Seven Mountains*, pp. 295-96.

Centering Prayer and Attention of the Heart

Cynthia Bourgeault

In the thirty years now since Centering Prayer first moved beyond the walls of St. Joseph's Abbey in Massachusetts and became a lay groundswell, it has certainly implanted itself deeply and (one hopes) permanently in the canon of Christian contemplative practice. Yet it still jostles somewhat uneasily against the walls of received tradition. I am not speaking here of fundamentalist-generated fear ("The devil will get you if you make your mind a blank"), but rather, of serious reservations on the part of some deeply formed in the Christian contemplative tradition that this prayer is somehow "breaking the rules." In its classic presentations, Christian prayer is "progressive"; it passes through stages. And the contemplative stage is traditionally regarded as the highest, or most subtle. In the concluding words of a recent, thoughtful article by a well-prepared commentator, "One does not take the kingdom by force."[1] Contemplation is approached by a gradual path leading from purgative to illuminative to unitive; from cataphatic to apophatic. The "ladder" of spiritual ascent is so deeply engrained on the Christian religious imagination that it seems virtually impossible to conceive of the journey in any other way. Contemplative prayer is "higher," and it is approached only gradually through a long journey of purification and inner preparation.

But is this in fact really so?

> "You have to experience duality for a long time until you see it's not there," said Thomas Merton at a conference given to the nuns of the Redwoods shortly before boarding the plane to Asia on the last leg of his human journey. "Don't consider dualistic prayer on a lower level. The lower is higher. There are no levels. At any moment you can break through to the underlying unity which is God's gift in Christ. In the end, Praise praises. Thanksgiving gives thanks. Jesus prays. Openness is all."[2]

Certainly these words of unitive, realized mastery make it clear that Merton "got there." But how? Was this breakthrough insight

151

the result of his long tread up the traditional ladder of ascent—in other words, is he "exhibit A" of the assertion that the classic monastic model works? Or is his unitive awakening something more akin to Dorothy in the final scene of *The Wizard of Oz*, when she realizes that all along the shoes that would carry her home have been right there on her feet?

This is, of course, an impossible question to answer, and I do not intend to do so directly; only to use it as a kind of leverage. In the words of the poet Philip Booth, "How you get there is where you arrive," and Merton's journey could only have been Merton's. And yet the door, once he found it, can only be seen as the timeless and universal gate. Like a few others before him and a few significant monastic others following in his wake (Thomas Keating most prominently), he simply, in my estimate, came upon that hidden back door or "wormhole" within the Christian path that transports one out of the "progressive " journey in linear time into the instantaneous, seamless fullness from which prayer is always emerging.

And he found it in the same way that all who find it do so: in the gathering awareness that the cave of the heart is entered not only or even primarily through purification and concentration, but through surrender and release. This is this hidden, backdoor path that I wish to explore in the following essay. My thesis is that there has always been an alternative within Christian spiritual practice to the "ladder of ascent": perhaps not as well known, but fully orthodox and in the end even more reliable, since it derives, ultimately, from the direct teaching and self-understanding of Jesus himself. It is from this alternative pathway that Centering Prayer derives its legitimacy and its powerful capacity to heal and unify.

Centering Prayer as self-emptying love

First, let me give a quick summary of Centering Prayer, for those unfamiliar with its somewhat unusual methodology. As a method of meditation situated within the Christian contemplative tradition, Centering Prayer is founded entirely on the gesture of surrender, or letting go. The theological basis for this prayer lies in the principle of *kenosis* (Philippians 2:6), Jesus's self-emptying love that forms the core of his own self-understanding and life practice. During the prayer time itself, surrender is practiced through the letting go of thoughts as they arise. Unlike other forms of meditation, neither a focused awareness nor a steady witnessing presence is required. There is no need to "follow" the thoughts as they arise; merely to promptly let them go as soon as one realizes he or she is engaged in thinking (a "Sacred Word" is typically used to facilitate this prompt release).

With committed practice, this well-rehearsed gesture of release is inwardly imprinted and begins to coalesce as a distinct "magnetic center" within a person; it can actually be experienced on a subtle physical level as a "drop and release" in the solar plexus region of the body and as a tug to center. Of its own accord it begins to hold a person at that place of deeper spiritual attentiveness during prayer time. Not long after this initial "tethering of the heart" has set in, most experienced practitioners begin to feel the tug even outside their times of prayer, in the midst of their daily rounds, reminding them of the deepening river of prayer that has begun to flow in them beneath the surface of their ordinary lives. The intent of Centering Prayer is not to "access" God through contemplative stillness or mystical experience, but to teach its practitioners how to align spontaneously with Jesus's own continuously creative and enfolding presence through emulating his kenotic practice in all life situations.

Thus the real measure of this prayer is not found during the prayer time itself; Centering Prayer neither seeks nor accepts[3] what is commonly known as "mystical experience." Instead, it is found in the gradual but steady capacity to conform a person to "the mind of Christ," and the life attitudes of compassion, generosity, and freedom that flow from this gesture.

"God should be with you like a toothache!" proclaimed the nineteenth-century mystic Theophan the Recluse.[4] And while most of us might have preferred a different metaphor, it does speak forcefully to the fact that our concept of God is *sensate*. Remembrance of God is not a mental concept; it exists deeply embodied as a vibration, a homing frequency to which we can become increasingly sensitively attuned.

This growing experiential awareness of magnetic center is very important, not only for one's spiritual development but because of the new light it sheds on the ancient and venerable *desideratum* of the Western spiritual path: the goal of "putting the mind in the heart." As I hope to show, it is against this backdrop that Centering Prayer's powerful and innovative contribution to the received wisdom of Western spirituality becomes fully visible. But let us return to Merton.

The Way of the Heart

It is by now established that during the final decade of his life
Merton was deeply drawn not only to Buddhism, but equally to
Sufism, that mystical arm of Islam in which so much of the original heart and flavor of Jesus's Near-Eastern kenotic spirituality
came to reside.[5] In particular, during those years he had come upon
Louis Massignon's commentary on a treatise on the heart by al-
Hallâj, a ninth century Sufi saint. Merton refers to this writing both
in his journals and throughout his *Conjectures of a Guilty Bystander*
(1966), and Massignon's vision of the "point vierge," that mysterious liminal ground equally shared between creator and created,
forms the basis for those stirring final paragraphs of "A Member
of the Human Race":

> Then it was as if I suddenly saw the secret beauty of their hearts,
> the depths of their hearts where neither sin nor desire nor self-
> knowledge can reach, the core of their reality…. Again that
> expression, *le point vierge*, (I cannot translate it) comes in here.
> At the center of our being is a point of nothingness which is
> untouched by sin and by illusion, a point of pure truth, a point
> or spark which belongs entirely to God, which is never at our
> disposal, from which God disposes of our lives, which is inac-
> cessible to the fantasies of our own mind or the brutalities of
> our own will. This little point of nothingness and of *absolute
> poverty* is the pure glory of God in us. It is so to speak His
> name written in us, as our poverty, as our indigence, as our
> dependence, as our sonship. It is like a pure diamond, blazing
> with the invisible light of heaven. It is in everybody, and if we
> could see it we would see these billions of points of light com-
> ing together in the face and blaze of a sun that would make all
> the darkness and cruelty of life vanish completely.[6]

Merton's intuitive mystical grasp of this teaching contexts it fault-
lessly, it seems, within the lineage of the Christian *via negativa*. But
so seamless and evocative is his transposition, that one may overlook the fact that the passage also has a context within its own
Islamic frame of reference. This "point of nothingness and of absolute poverty" within al-Hallâj's treatise is in fact the *sirr*, the final veil covering the heart.[7] What looks like a mystical metaphor
within Merton's prose-poetry actually belongs to a rigorous
anatomy of the heart as a spiritual instrument of perception—or,
as Massignon puts it, "the Quranic notion that the heart is the or-

gan prepared by God for contemplation."[8] And it is just here that the point becomes interesting. For as one conceives the heart, so one conceives the transformative journey.

With regard to this "Quaranic notion of the heart," perhaps the clearest elucidation comes from a modern Sufi master, Kabir Helminski. In his *Living Presence* Helminski writes:

> We have subtle subconscious faculties we are not using. Beyond the limited analytic intellect is a vast realm of mind that includes psychic and extrasensory abilities, intuition; wisdom; a sense of unity; aesthetic, qualitative, and symbolic capacities. Though these faculties are many, we give them a single name with some justification because they are operating best when they are in concert. They comprise a mind, moreover, in spontaneous connection with the cosmic mind. This total mind we call "heart."[9]

The heart's job is to look deeper than the surface of things, deeper than the jumbled, reactive landscape of our ordinary awareness, and to beam in on the deeper, ensheltering spiritual world in which our being is truly rooted (Jesus calls it "the Kingdom of Heaven"). As the heart becomes clearer and stronger, we are able to come into alignment with divine being and are able to live authentically the dance of divine self-disclosure which is our true self. Helminski goes on to explain:

> The heart is that antenna that receives the emanations of subtler levels of existence. The human heart has its proper field of functioning beyond the reactive, superficial ego-self. Awakening the heart, or the Spiritualized mind, is an unlimited process of making the mind more sensitive, focused, energized, subtle and refined, of joining it to its cosmic milieu, the infinity of love.[10]

It is clear that Merton absorbed this basic concept of the heart as an organ of spiritual perception—the whole "antenna" aspect—and was deeply impressed with it. In his marvelous lectures on Sufism to the novices of Gethsemani, he speaks over and over of that "little kernel of gold" (Massignon's *le point vierge*, al-Hallaj's *sirr*), which is not only our deepest reality, but also a kind of homing signal through which we can stay aligned with that reality. As he sees it,

The real freedom is to be able to come and go from that center, and to be able to do without anything that is not connected to that center. Because when you die, that is all that is left. When we die, everything is destroyed except this one thing, which is our reality that God preserves forever. He will not permit its final destruction.

And the thing is, that we know this. This is built into that particular little grain of gold, this spark of the soul, or whatever it is. It *knows* this. And the freedom that matters is the capacity to be in contact with that center. For it is from that center that everything else comes.[11]

But make no mistake: Merton is not embracing an Islamic anthropology; rather, in the mirror of Sufism he is able to recognize the heart he has already come to know intimately through his years of Christian contemplative practice. And in that same moment of recognition, he also understands intuitively that the way to remain in contact with "that little grain of gold, this spark of the soul" is simply to be able to let go of whatever it is that jams its signal.

Surmounting Love by Love

For most Western Christians, the heart would more readily be associated with the capacity to *feel*. Its genius is emotional empathy. Even that old pop psychology cliché, "being in the heart" versus "being in the head," rests on our staunch conviction that the heart mirrors the real person through its capacity to feel, to love, to empathize. If it has a capacity for spiritual perception, it is exercised through love. Hence the immortal instructions in the *Cloud of Unknowing*: "God may be reached and held fast by means of love, but by means of thought never."[12]

It is not surprising, then, that overwhelmingly in the Western tradition, the core methodology for "putting the mind in the heart" can be described as *the concentration of affectivity*. In both the Christian East and the Christian West, the basic strategy for spiritual transformation begins by engaging the heart's natural capacity to feel. Once the heart has been stirred by strong emotions, it is a surprisingly short step to concentrate and purify these emotions through spiritual practice and harness their vibrant energy for spiritual awakening.

You can see the strategy already at work in John Cassian in the fifth century, particularly in his Tenth Conference, where he urges the continuous use of the prayer sentence from Psalm 70, "O Lord, come to my assistance, Oh God make speed to save me." Cassian goes on to explain: "It is not without good reason that this verse has been chosen from the whole of Scripture as a device. It carries within it all the feelings of which human nature is capable."[13] By embracing the full intensity of these feelings, an ardor is generated that catapults the heart free and clear of its egocentric orbit and straight into the heart of God.

In fact, as Christian contemplative masters have consistently observed from the Desert times right down into our own, without that critical intensity of ardor, it is all but impossible to escape the centrifugal force of human egotism. It takes gold to make gold; a heart that burns, even with carnal love, can be directed toward contemplation of higher things, but a heart of stone travels nowhere. As St. John Climacus observed with keen insight:

> I have seen impure souls who threw themselves headlong into physical *eros* to a frenzied degree. It was their very experience of that *eros* that led them to interior conversion. They concentrated their *eros* on the Lord. Rising above fear, they tried to love God with insatiable desire. That is why when Christ spoke to the woman who had been a sinner he did not say that she had been afraid, but that she had loved much, and had easily been able to surmount love by love.[14]

This goal of "surmounting love by love," or in other words, uniting the devotional and perceptive aspects of the heart in a single mystical flame, reveals the secret of why Christianity has always embraced affectivity as the gateway to inner awakening. We see this same predilection at work in *lectio divina*, where the third stage, *oratio*, is intended to take the concentrated attention of a mind that has gathered itself through *meditatio* and fan it to a level of emotional intensity wherein the boundaries of egoic consciousness are essentially melted, at least for the duration of the prayer. We see it again in the Jesus Prayer, classically understood, which while superficially resembling a mantra, in fact gains its force through the concentration of affective love.

This is also the underlying reason, I believe, that Christian tradition has never taken easily to meditation, and has never rested entirely comfortably with a methodology that seems to go against the grain of one of its most basic presuppositions: that it is not possible to reach the apophatic without first going through the cataphatic—i.e., via the concentration of affectivity. Working with *eros* as its transformational quicksilver, the journey necessarily entails a long, tough slog through the gristmills of purification and inner preparation before the soul is ready to "bear the beams of love" (in the words of William Blake) in pure contemplation. By an overwhelming majority, the pedagogy of both the Christian West and the Christian East has favored this developmental trajectory.

Attention of the Heart

But majority is not the same thing as exclusive. While "concentration of affectivity" clearly dominates the field in Christian spirituality, there is also a different pathway to center, and one who was onto it was Simeon the New Theologian. His curiously little known essay, "Three Forms of Prayer and Attention," is one of the most important resources available for locating Centering Prayer within the wider tradition of Christian interior prayer and for validating its innovative yet entirely orthodox starting points.[15]

I have spoken of Simeon extensively in my book *Centering Prayer and Inner Awakening*, but let me briefly recap some of the essential points. Simeon was one of the most brilliant spiritual theologians of his day, or of any day. His lifespan (949-1022) places him almost exactly a thousand years ago, but the issues he was grappling with in the eleventh century are still cutting edge in our own times. Essentially, Simeon insisted on the dimension of *conscious presence* in our human relationship with the divine—or as he called it, "attention of the heart."

Developing this kind of attention is all-important, Simeon maintains, for otherwise, "It is impossible to have purity of heart; impossible to fulfill the Beatitudes."[16] Only when the mind is "in the heart," grounded and tethered in that deeper wellspring of spiritual awareness, is it possible to live the teachings of Jesus without hypocrisy or burnout. The gospel requires a radical openness and compassion that is beyond the capacity of the anxious, fear-ridden ego.

But how to swim down to these deeper waters? Simeon lays out three possibilities. The first is the classic path of "concentration of affectivity" as we have just described it:

> If a man stands at prayer and, raising his hands, his eyes, and his mind to heaven, keeps in mind Divine thoughts, imagines celestial blessings, hierarchies of angels and dwellings of the

saints, assembles briefly in his mind all he has learnt from the
Holy Spirit and ponders over all this while at prayer, gazing
up to heaven and thus inciting his soul to longing and love of
God, at times even shedding tears and weeping, this will be
the first method of prayer.[16]

The problem with this traditional method, Simeon asserts, is that
it relies on a high level of excitement of the external faculties, which
is ultimately self-delusional and can become addictive, leading
one to depend on lights, sweet scents, and "other like phenom-
ena" as evidence of the presence of God. "If then such a man give
himself up to silence," Simeon adds bluntly, "he can scarcely avoid
going out of his mind."[17]

The second method he explores is self-examination and the
collecting of thoughts "so that they cease to wander"—the classic
methodology of a practice based on awareness. This approach relies heavily on the practices of inner attention, self-remembering,
and the examination of consciousness. But the fatal flaw in this
methodology, Simeon observes, is that such a practitioner "remains
in the head, whereas evil thoughts are generated in the heart."[18]
In other words, the aspiring seeker is likely to be blindsided by
the strength of his unconscious impulses.

Simeon designates the third method as *attention of the heart* and
describes it as follows:

You should observe three things before all else: freedom from
all cares, not only cares about bad and vain but even about
good things...your conscience should be clear so that it denounces you in nothing, and you should have a complete absence of passionate attachment, so that your thought inclines
to nothing worldly.[19]

The importance of Simeon's observation here is extraordinary, for
he has essentially described the practice of kenotic surrender. That
greatest *desideratum* of the spiritual life, attention of the heart, is
achieved, he feels, not so much by concentration of affectivity as
by the simple release of all that one is clinging to, the good things
as well as the bad things. He proposes that we start with that bare
gesture of letting go. Attention of the heart can certainly be engaged through concentrated affectivity. But it can also, just as well,
be engaged through relinquishing the passions and relaxing the
will.

While Simeon is clearly describing an integrated practice combining both prayer and daily life, it is uncanny how closely his words dovetail with the basic methodology of Centering Prayer. As a person sits in Centering Prayer attempting to "resist no thought, retain no thought, react to no thought," (the instructional formula offered in all introductory training sessions), he or she is actually progressing in small but utterly real increments toward "freedom from all cares" and "the absence of passionate attachments." This is Simeon's "attention of the heart," which he states is inseparable from true prayer and true conversion. In fact, the case can be made that what Thomas Keating has really succeeded in doing is to give meditational form to Simeon's attention of the heart, thereby providing a powerful new access point to the traditional wisdom of the Christian inner path. His approach, like Simeon's, is innovative but entirely orthodox once you understand where he is coming from. The tie-in between Centering Prayer and Simeon's attention of the heart is simply another link in the chain situating Centering Prayer firmly within the lineage of Christian kenosis understood as spiritual path.

Finding the Way to the Heart

"Keep your mind there [in the heart]" remarks Simeon, "trying by every possible means to find the place where the heart is." In his *Lost Christianity*, Jacob Needleman immediately picks up on the irony of this: that as we begin, we do not know where the heart is. We must learn, through the process of repeated tuning in.[20]

My hunch is that this describes the actual journey of both Thomas Merton and Thomas Keating—and undoubtedly Simeon as well. During their respective monastic novitiates "the first method of attention and prayer" was what was available, and they each practiced it to its fullness. (And even in the early days of Centering Prayer teaching, the Sacred Word was initially described as a "love word": affectivity in capsule form, or in other words, an intense, concentrated version of "all those feelings known to man."[21]) It was ultimately through the experience of contemplation itself that these spiritual masters came to their realization that all along it has been the surrender carrying them home.

In his inimitable way, Merton puts words to the barebones truth of this timeless moment: the "aha" realization that solves Simeon's (and Needleman's) koan of "the Way to the Heart:"

> This act of total surrender is not simply a fantastic intellectual and mystical gamble; it is something much more serious: it is an act of love for this unseen Person Who, in the very gift of love by which we surrender ourselves to His reality, also makes Himself present to us.[22]

If what he glimpses in this remarkable insight is true, then the response to those overly concerned that Centering Prayer is violating the traditional pedagogy can only be a gentle "All shall be well, and all manner of things shall be well. " For ultimately, as this "unseen person" becomes present, the knee of the heart will instinctively bow— and the rest will somehow work itself out.

It is indeed true that ego-driven spiritual ambitiousness can wind up in very bad places. But it is important never to lose sight of the fact that *spiritual ambitiousness and attention of the heart are mutually exclusive categories.* The proud may fall, but it will not be through following the Way of the Heart, for the heart has its inbuilt safeguard: it perceives only in the modality of surrender (which means, literally, to "hand oneself over," to entrust oneself entirely). In other words, the heart can fulfill its function as organ of spiritual perception only to the degree that it is able to bring itself into moral alignment with "the infinity of love" (in Helminski's words); to the extent that it is willing and able to coincide with love, to become love itself. For love is the ultimate, and ultimately the *only,* purification. But this "Love which moves the sun and the stars" (as Dante calls it) is not a feeling, an *eros*-fixated-upon-God; it is rather the alchemical *agape* which comes into being when *eros* becomes whole in the act of giving itself away. Whenever and wherever along the pathway of prayer this great secret is learned, it instantaneously reorganizes the playing field.

Notes

1. Peter Feldmeier, "Centering Prayer and the Christian Contemplative Tradition," *Spiritual Life* (Winter 2003), p. 239.

2. David Steindl-Rast, "Man or Prayer," in Patrick Hart, ed., *Thomas Merton, Monk* (New York: Sheed & Ward, 1974), p.90.

3. For more on this point see my *Centering Prayer and Inner Awakening* (Cambridge, MA: Cowley Publications, 2004), Chapter 5: "Spiritual Non-Possessiveness."

4. Robin Amis, ed., *Theophan the Recluse: Writings on Prayer of the Heart* (Newburyport, MA: Praxis Press, 1992), p. xx.

5. The word Islam itself means "submission"—i.e., the complete kenosis of self-emptying before God. For a brilliant and comprehensive study of Merton's late-life immersion in Sufism, see Rob Baker and Gray Henry, eds., *Merton and Sufism: The Untold Story* (Louisville, KY: Fons Vitae, 1999).

6. Thomas Merton, "A Member of the Human Race," *Conjectures of a Guilty Bystander*, (New York: Doubleday, 1966, p. 158. Quoted from *A Thomas Merton Reader*, ed. Thomas P. McDonnell, rev. ed. (Garden City, NY: Image Books, 1974), pp. 346-47.

7. See Sidney H. Griffith, "Merton, Massignon, and the Challenge of Islam," in *Merton and Sufism*, pp. 64-65.

8. *Merton and Sufism*, p. 65.

9. Kabir Helmiski, *Living Presence: A Sufi Way to Mindfulness and the Essential Self* (New York: Tarcher/Putnam, 1992), p. 157.

10. *Living Presence*, pp. 157-58.

11. Thomas Merton, "True Freedom," transcribed by the author from the cassette series *Sufism: Longing for God* (Kansas City: Credence Cassettes, 1995).

12. *The Cloud of Unkowing*, ed. Ira Progoff (New York: Delta Books, 1957), p. 72.

13. John Cassian, *Conferences*, trans. Colm Luibheid (Mahwah, NJ: Paulist Press, 1985), p. 133. Cassian's full explanation is as follows: "It carries within it a cry to God in the face of every danger. It expresses the humility of a pious confession. It conveys the watchfulness born of unending worry and fear. It conveys sense of our frailty, the assurance of being heard, the confidence in help that is always and everywhere present."

14. Quoted from Joseph Chu Cong, OCSO, *The Contemplative Experience* (New York: Crossroad, 1999), p. XX. This goal, in fact, comprises the basic pedagogy of monastic love mysticism, which has flowed like a great underground river through the spirituality of the Christian West, reaching its culmination in the writings of St. Bernard of Clairvaux. Chu Cong's book is a profound yet accessible introduction to this great tradition.

15. This essay is found in E. Kadloubovsky and G. E. H. Palmer, eds., *Writings from the Philokalia on Prayer of the Heart* (London and Boston: Faber and Faber, 1951, 1992), pp. 152-61.

16. *Philokalia*, p. 153.

17. *Philokalia*, p. 153.

18. *Philokalia.*, p. 154. In this context the word "heart" obviously refers to what we would today call "the unconscious," a nuance unavailable to Simeon.

19. *Philokalia*, p. 158.

20. Jacob Needleman, *Lost Christianity* (New York: Doubleday, 1980), p. x. The quotation from Simeon is from the *Philokalia*, p. 158.

21. This aspect of the Sacred Word has been consistently emphasized in the teachings of Father Basil Pennington. For further comments, see my Preface to Thomas Keating and Basil Pennington, *Finding Grace at the Center* (Woodstock VT: Skylight Paths, 2007).

22. Thomas Merton, *The Inner Experience*, ed. William H. Shannon (San Francisco: HaperCollins, 2003), p. 44. The work was originally published as a series in several successive issues of *Cistercian Studies* in 1984 (vols. 18-19). My original introduction to this quotation was through a photocopy of one of these articles loaned to me by a monk of St. Benedict's Abbey, Snowmass, Colorado, in 1995; the quotation is found in the third article: 18: 3 (1983), p. 209.

Thomas Merton and Paramahansa Yogananda: Two Prayerful Mergings of Cult and Culture

Emile J. Farge

Readers of Thomas Merton have known that while being a faithful member of the Catholic Church he was certainly also catholic in the broader meaning. His final journey was like the cymbal crash at the end of symphony of many years of prayerful investigating of different religions and many schools of thought. During his last months he visited with Hindus, Buddhists and other groups in his Asian tour. Such encounters bore equal weight with his participation at the conference where he gave what was to be his last sharing of insights about monastic life. At what turned out to be Merton's last address, he pointed out that monasticism from the Christian or Eastern traditions were equally concerned with "...penetrat[ing] by detachment and purity of heart to the inner secret of the ground of ... ordinary experience, [and thus] attain to a liberty that nobody can touch, that nobody can affect, that no political change of circumstances can do anything to." [1]

The title of his talk on December 10, 1968 was "Marxism and Monastic Perspectives," and it suggested many direct parallels with Buddhist thought and prayer, and, importantly, concludes, "...I believe that by openness to Buddhism, to Hinduism, and to these great Asian traditions, we stand a wonderful chance of learning more about the potentiality of our own traditions." [2] In his journal Merton mentions that he discussed points in this planned talk with the *Dalai Lama*.

The tenet we investigate here is that there is a striking consonance of Merton's teaching with the Hindu person who is perhaps the most published in the US, and in perhaps the entire western hemisphere, Paramahansa Yogananda. The contention of this study is that there is a spiritual union of complementarily that, when explored, will prove helpful both to readers of Merton and to readers of Yogananda.

The question, of course, immediately presents itself: "Is this a forced fit?" A corollary might be "Where do they meet in any way that one can truthfully assert such spiritual unity?" Table 1 presents a biographical and personal comparison. They were born only twenty-two years apart, Merton having early education in Europe and in the US and Yogananda in India. Both, however, spent a goodly portion of their time in countries other than those of their birth (UK and US for Merton, US for Indian-born Yogananda).   The French-born Merton lived for fifty-four years and Yogananda for fifty-nine; both amassed many followers during their lives, and more followers than ever after their deaths. Both of these visionaries wrote books that are today being read more than ever, and are ever being translated into new languages. Yogananda has "centers" and "temples" and a non-denominational church dedicated to his teaching. There are academic centers, societies and "chapters" and "reading rooms and libraries" along with The International Thomas Merton Society to cherish, hold and propagate Merton's works.

Table 1

	Merton	Yogananda
Birth	Jan, 1915	Jan, 1893
Date bodily death	Dec. 8, 1968	Mar.7, 1952
Time "in body"	53.8 years	58.2 years
Life altering event	1938, age 23	1909, age 16
Autobiography published	1948	1946
Age @autobio. publication	33	53
Books written	45+	15+
Poems written	hundreds	hundreds
Artistic renderings	hundreds	unknown
Copies sold	tens of millions	tens of millions
Languages of autobiography	dozens	dozens
Occasion of bodily death	after speech, quickly	after speeck, quickly
Today's followers	worldwide	worldwide
Type of follower	monastics, but mostly lay persons	monastics, but mostly lay persons
Center of prayer life	liturgy, meditation	yoga, meditation
Taught system of meditation	no	yes
Lived under human guru	no	yes
Served as guru to followers	no	yes

Both of these spiritual masters had their autobiographies published in the nineteen-forties, post-WWII, and both books continue to sell and be translated widely sixty years later. At this writing Yogananda's *Autobiography of a Yogi*[3] *and* Merton's *The Seven Storey*

Mountain[4] both remain in print in many languages, and continue to be the prime sellers of the authors' many works. The influence of both is growing with no sign of waning. Each was highly evolved, and had a major event to trigger a deeper spiritual life: Merton's was his preparation for and receiving his Baptism[5] (age twenty-three) and Yogananda's his search for and finding his guru[6] (age seventeen).   Merton had lost his mother at age six and Yogananda at age eleven.

Merton's Baptismal preparation had such intensity as to include recitation of the Divine Office, meditation, and certain aspects in his daily routines which most may associate only with monastic life. He had made inquiries of various churches, including the Quakers, the Mormons, and the Church of England without any lasting interest. His reading of Étienne Gilson[7] had piqued his respect for the Catholic notion of God. Later, in 1951, he wrote to Gilson to thank him his influence.[8] His love for Blake's poetry had led him to Gerard Manley Hopkins. Upon reading Hopkins' letter to Cardinal Newman about becoming a Catholic Merton states "….something began to stir within me, something began to push me, to prompt me … like a voice. 'What are you waiting for?…Why don't you do it'?"[9] To quell the voice he smoked a cigarette (as was his wont) but the voice repeated "What are you waiting for?" His nine-block walk in the rain followed, leading to his visit with Father Ford at Corpus Christi Parish, the discussion, and departing the priest's house with three books and appointments for twice-a-week instructions.

During Merton's instruction period in 1938 he had frequent visits with Dan Walsh, the philosophy professor and friend, who introduced him also to St. Anselm, St. Bernard, St. Bonaventure, and Hugh and Richard of St. Victor as well as Duns Scotus. He was a recent graduate of literature at Columbia, and a graduate student in the same field. "I now began to burn with desire for Baptism, and to throw out hints and try to determine when I would be received into the Church." [10] On November 16, 1938, during the ceremony of Baptism, he recalled "…I had entered into the everlasting movement of that gravitation which is the very life and spirit of God: God's own gravitation towards the depths of His own infinite nature, His goodness without end."[11]

Yogananda (born Mukunda lal Ghosh) sought a pathway to channel his severe need for a life of prayer and meditation by spending time in an ashram recommended to him.   He followed the ashram's rules, meditated faithfully, but had no inward satisfaction from communication with the leader, swami Dayananda. One day in 1910, at age 17, he prayed "Merciful Mother of the universe, teach me thyself through vision, or through a guru sent by Thee." After some hours he reports "...suddenly I felt lifted as though bodily to a sphere unsubscribed: 'Thy Master cometh today.'"[12] At that moment one of the priests sent him and another postulant on an errand to the market. He continues "as Habu and I moved on, I turned my head (and) a Christ-like man in the ocher robes of a swami stood motionless at the end of the lane." Thinking he was mentally confused (for he had already a master at his ashram) he continued. "After ten minutes, I felt heavy numbness in my feet. As though turned to stone, they were unable to carry me farther, (and he said) the saint is magnetically drawing me to him." He returned and the swami was still there. Mukunda shouted "Gurudeva!" ("Beloved Guru"). The teacher responded, "O my own, you have come to me...How many years I have waited for you."[13] They both promised unconditional love, and Yogananda promised life-long obedience to his guru as the first words from his mouth.

After their different launchings into their respective states (baptized Catholic and Hindu disciple) both dedicated the major effort of their days and indeed their lives to prayer and to writing. Merton and Yogananda have both had many books written about their thought and their teachings. The influence of both is still growing at this writing several decades after their deaths. Regarding their public life, Yogananda was a public speaker whose lectures on yoga and self-realization filled large venues on three continents. Merton spoke quite selectively and nearly always to small groups, yet of course he is now recognized world-wide.

The Hindu man arrived in Boston in 1920 and continued his work until his death thirty-two years later in the United States. The European-born Merton came to live in New York in 1936 and continued his work for thirty-two years until his death. Both died after giving addresses on cross-cultural matters, addresses which they wanted to give for many years: Merton on "Marxism and Monastic Perspectives"[14] and Yogananda on "My India / My America."[15] Merton died in Bangkok, Yogananda, in Los Angeles. Consistent with the catholic character of both, the "Westerner" died in Asia; the "Asian" died in America.

This Author's Lens

It is difficult to describe the biases and assumptions of the comparison of these two remarkable men of God without some personal admission or confession. As a seminarian who went through the pre-Vatican II seminary curriculum for secular priests (1954 to 1961) leading to my ordination, I read *The Seven Storey Mountain*, *The Sign of Jonas*, (1953) and *No Man Is an Island*[16] (1955). During those years we had a daily twenty-minute morning meditation and twenty-minute afternoon quiet chapel visit, but were not taught that contemplation would be central to our life-style. As seminarians we were perhaps trained rather than educated in spiritual matters, and assumed that the "real meditative life" was for monastics.

As an "activist" priest for the next nine-plus years I knew of Merton's support for the reforms of the Vatican Council, his ecumenism and his backing of the peace movement,[17] but did not really "discover" him until some thirty years later as an ex-priest. Having just retired from work I became aware of a local ITMS chapter in Atlanta which met monthly to discuss Merton's books and ideas. Such a discovery meant that in addition to knowing Merton as a fine writer and critical observer of the social and ecclesial milieu, it began to become clear that this remarkable monk was preparing monastics as well as lay and ordained Christians— in fact, all humankind—toward the life of prayer and meditation as a desirable life-style for all God-seekers. He was quite more catholic than most in our church. His death in late 1968 freed him from the dilution by the Roman Curia of much of the Spirit-content of Vatican II. The still promising re-evangelizing of his beloved Catholic church voted by the Ecumenical Council was to be ignored in large measure for the next four decades.

I discovered Yogananda in 2000 (My wife had bought his *Autobiography of a Yogi* in 1980) when I found the book on my shelf shortly after beginning to attend the Merton discussion group. From that day until now it is a rare day that I don't read from both of these inspired teachers. Little by little I have perceived the Christ of the New Testament very clearly known, loved and explained equally well both by this Hindu man, and by this worldly convert. I became active in a meditation/study group at the Self-Realization Fellowship Center in Atlanta in 2002 and after a few years of study was initiated into Kriya Yoga.

A Common Sense of Urgency

For both Yogananda and Merton the interest in both Eastern and Western spirituality was laced with urgency. Yogananda's interest in the West is recounted several times in his *Autobiography*. After spending some time in the ashram of his guru, Swami Sri Yukteswar, the basic sameness of all true religions had become clear to him; that is, that there is a basic core of truth, wisdom and spiritual desire present in all God- seekers. In an unusual encounter with his paramguru (guru of his guru), some twenty years previously, Yukteswar quotes Mahavatar Babaji as saying "East and West must establish a golden middle path of activity and spirituality combined; you…have a part to play in the coming harmonious exchange between Orient and Occident. Some years hence I shall send you a disciple whom you can train for yoga dissemination in the West…I perceive potential saints in America and Europe, waiting to be awakened."[18]

While Merton did not have his interest in Eastern spirituality pre-announced by any guru, his vision was no less clear. In *Mystics and Zen Masters* he recalls: "A hundred years ago America began to discover the Orient and its philosophical tradition.... America did not have the patience to continue what was happily begun. The door that had opened for an instant, closed again for a century….[and now] seems to be opening again…. It is imperative for us to find out what is inside this fabulous edifice."[19] Later in the same essay ("Love and Tao") he concludes, "The horizons of the world are no longer confined to Europe and America. We have to gain new perspectives, and on this our spiritual and even our physical survival may depend."[20]   This can easily be seen today as a prescient statement given the large overlap in culture and economy of today's Europe and America in the West and China, and Japan in Asia.

Today some half-century after the death of these two remarkable men of God we who choose to study their works can begin to see how each contributed to the bridge between East and West which is becoming more and more needed to maintain the human understanding in our ever-shrinking world. Seeing through the outward differences to the core of unity among God-seekers is key to understanding our two monks. Merton might be described as joyously conflicted by knowing that his personal calling from God was to be a monk, but indeed one who eventually longed more for a hermitage than a monastery. He also knew that due to the unique role he played in the lives of faithful God-seeking persons his every word was likely to be published, which was joyous because he saw that his mission was to share the contemplative life with others. This led quite naturally to his lifelong need to understand the spiritual orientation of persons who were so obviously on a God-ward path ("by your fruits they will know you"), yet were not directly associated with Christianity.

As a Christian humanist Merton concluded that the spiritual teaching guiding non-Christian seekers must indeed be from the Holy Spirit. Thus Christian seekers must learn of and from them. As the airplane taking him on his 1968 journey eastward lifted off, he wrote in his journal that he was departing "...with Christian mantras and a great sense of destiny" and added "May I not come back without having settled the great affair." He continued "I am going home, to the home where I have never been in this body."[21]

It might be hyperbole to compare him to a mendicant with his begging bowl seeking the rice of their spiritual wisdom, but still he was going as a brother, a fellow contemplative, to learn and to share the ways in which other seekers find unity with God.

Yogananda reached his own catholicity by the route of his guru, Swami Sri Yukteswar. Born in 1893, he was seventeen when he met Yukteswar and asked to be his disciple upon their first meeting. After some years, Yogananda matriculated at the local university and obtained a degree.

After receiving his university degree (Calcutta University, 1915), Mukunda continued at the ashram but asked to be made a monk in order to remove the family pressures to enter into business and become a householder, which is the Indian position for those who marry and raise a family. Yukteswar happily agreed and at the ceremony of initiation said "Forsaking your family name of Mukunda lal Ghosh, henceforth you shall be called Yogananda of the Giri branch of the swami Order."[22] "Yogananda" means "bliss from yoga."

After some years of preparation and fund-raising, Yogananda founded the Ranchi School for Boys (for teaching skills in academics, living, and yoga) and was its headmaster for some three years. That was the time when Yukteswar was to give him his "commission" which was to consume the balance of his time on earth.

Yukteswar had received an invitation to represent Indian mysticism at an international congress of religious leaders in Boston in the fall of 1920. The group asked for Yukteswar to deliver a talk on "The Science of Religion" or to name a delegate in his stead. Sri Yukteswar had been expecting the day when he would fulfill the prescient word of Babaji given to him in the city of Allahabad on the occasion of the Kumbha Mela (the decennial, largest gathering of swamis, disciples, Hindu religious persons in the world) many years previously. So he commissioned Yogananda to represent him. Through a sizable gift from his father, Yogananda undertook the long boat journey to Boston, where his address was enthusiastically received. He remained in Boston some three years to learn American culture and ways. He was a learner and a teacher, and gained followers.

That same year he founded Self Realization Fellowship (SRF) "to disseminate among the nations knowledge of definite scientific techniques for attaining direct personal experience of God."[23] In 1924 he undertook a lecture tour of the country, going east to west and attracting much publicity and large crowds in many cities. Ending in California, he set up the international headquarters for SRF, where it remains today. Since that date several dozen temples and centers have been opened in over thirty countries, some four-hundred monastics serve the community of those practicing yoga and meditation techniques of self-realization as taught by Yogananda.

Shared Spiritual Themes

There are many common topics shared by Merton and Yogananda. Here follow some that have such commonalities as to make our basic tenet easily seen.

1. Centrality of Nicodemus' encounter and "new birth"

Although Jesus attracted the masses of humble Jews, he also drew the attention of some of the best known rulers and scholars, among them Nicodemus. Merton is perhaps at his most catholic and mystical center when he writes of the need for Rebirth, which he describes as the "answer [to] a deeper need in man: a need that cannot be satisfied merely by the ritual celebration of man's oneness with nature."[24]

Nicodemus came and expressed, "Rabbi, we know that you are a teacher who comes from God; for no one could perform the signs that you do unless God were with him."[25] Merton notes that

Christ brushes aside Nicodemus' compliment that he is a "true master," and that Jesus "… says there is something of much more crucial importance than being the disciple of a spiritual master…. A man must be born again, or in a better translation, 'born from above' (John 3:3)."[26] Merton underscores that Jesus makes very clear from the outset that the old (false) self must die to the new man. Nicodemus, the scholar, asks, "How can a grown man be born? Can he go back into his mother's womb…?"[27]

So eager was Jesus to have this fine, but obviously fearful, Jew understand that he went on to clarify that what is born of flesh is flesh, what is born of Spirit is Spirit. This mystery is a new kind of birth, and Merton, understanding the ardor of Christ to help Nicodemus grasp its importance, underscores Jesus' insistence for "a renewed transformation, a 'passover' in which man is progressively liberated from selfishness."[28] In fact being a Christian demands one "To become completely transparent and allow Love to shine by itself is the maturity of the 'New Man.'"[29]

Merton concludes his commentary on rebirth and the new man, insisting that the reborn Christian renounce his own will to dominate and let the Spirit act secretly in and through him. He then adds that "This aspect of Christianity will…be intelligible to those in an Asian culture…. For the religions of Asia also have long sought to …initiate [man] into the full and complete reality of an inner peace which is secret and beyond explanation."[30] Many readers of Merton will also recall the new birth in Christ as revealed in the meditations of his pivotal work by the same name of *The New Man* in 1961, and in his last unfinished work, *The Inner Experience*.[31]

Yogananda's stress on the "second birth of man – in Spirit" is no less clear or intense. In the posthumously published two volumes entitled *The Second Coming of Christ*,[32] there are seventy-five chapters (called discourses), and three are dedicated to the new birth as outlined in the visit of Nicodemus. Yogananda perceives Jesus' insistence on the second birth as "…the necessity of which Jesus speaks, [and which therefore] admits us to the land of intuitional perception." This is parallel with Merton's "renewed transformation" which Yogananda compares to the faith of "illumined Christian mystics – St. Thomas Aquinas, Bonaventure, Jan van Ruysbroeck, Meister Eckhart, Henry Suso, Johannes Tauler…"[33] All of these spiritual thinkers also found liberal citations in

Merton's own works, including *The Seven Storey Mountain*,[34] *The Inner Experience*,[35] *Conjectures of a Guilty Bystander*.[36]

Yogananda perceives Jesus' handling of Nicodemus' objection to "rebirth" in terms of "…removing the debris of karma [effects of one's past actions] from the individualized God-image of his soul."[37] Such is quite consistent with Yogananda's assumption of reincarnation. In other words Jesus was stressing that after "Man's soul becomes incarnate—born of water or protoplasm—he should transcend the moral impositions of the body by self-development. Through awakening the 'sixth sense' of intuition, and opening the spiritual eye, his illumined consciousness can enter into the kingdom of God."[38]

In his third chapter on the secret visit by Nicodemus, Yogananda concludes with a cogent explanation of Christ's words that "…as Moses lifted up the serpent in the wilderness, even so must the Son of man be lifted up; that whosoever believeth in him should not perish, but have eternal life"[39] with the awakening of the kundalini. To Yogananda, new birth in the Spirit happens when the kundalini (coiled-up serpentine) power of the lower chakras moves to the higher chakras of consciousness of the Son of Man. The self-awareness that Christ had of his union with the Father is the most desirable end-point which he modeled for us. Jesus was instructing Nicodemus that such a union is possible and indeed the necessary end-point for all to be "born again." This very overt yogic / Hindu reference is an obvious difference from Merton's explanation of the Christ-Nicodemus encounter, yet it is nonetheless clear that each one of these monk-mystics perceived the Jesus-Nicodemus encounter as epitomizing the struggle of humankind to return to God, its Source.

At this point the basic difference in approach to spiritual matters between the two might be underscored. This author is unaware of explicit mentioning of man's cerebro-spinal energy centers in Merton's writings. These energy centers (chakras) are central to many practices of Eastern traditional medicine (e.g., acupuncture and acupressure are fully dependent on this cerebro-spinal grid), yoga practices and systems of meditation and contemplation. Merton readers recall the Dalai Lama's questioning of Merton about posture of meditation, since the straight spine in meditation is the fundament of all oriental methods of centering prayer.[40]

Yogananda, however, expounds on the chakras in myriad places in his writings. He even considers that the mention in St. John's "Book of Revelation" of the "seven seals, seven stars, seven churches with their seven angels and seven golden candlesticks"[41] are all very direct references to the chakras, or energy grid in every human.

In *The Bhagavad Gita* Yogananda explains that the "spiritual spine" (Sanskrit "sushumna") "…extends from the coccygeal center (muladhara chakra) to the brain. This spiritual or astral spine controls the sympathetic nervous system of the gross physical body."[42] The five spinal chakras are described as "wheels" and are located at the coccygeal, the sacral, lumbar, dorsal, cervical areas of the spine. The two cerebral chakras are located at the medulla oblongata, and between the eyes, called "spiritual eye" or the "Christ consciousness center." Yogananda uses this latter term literally thousands of times in his writings. God's grace energizes and magnetizes the sushumna in order to facilitate the meditation process to assist the meditator to ascend more and more from the basic human functions to the direct knowledge of God. Here follows the yogic premises of such development.

Table 2: The Chakras and their Functions

Cerebro-spinal #	Chakras	Positive Powers	Relate to physical cosmos parts:	Negative Powers
7	1000 Petalled Lotus	Christ consciousness	Astral/Causal Cosmos	False ego, greed
	House of Lords			
6	Medulla	Thinking	Super ether	Evil thoughts
5	Cervix	Vocalizing	Ether	Cruel, dishonest speech
4	Dorsal	Peaceful Sensation	Air	Sensuous Touch
	House of Commons			
3	Lumbar	Tactile sense	Fire	Material attachments
2	Sacrum	Reproduction	Water	Indescriminate sex
1	Coccyx	Elimination	Earth	Retains poison

The "climbing" up the ladder of chakras is the spiritual journey of everyman. Previous to entering the God-ward path the life force is most identified with chakra 1, in which energy flows outward, focusing on safety and survival issues. The five senses occupy the large part of one's attention. Reason enters more directly in the second chakra, freeing attention to be aware of wellness, quality of life and need for ethical behavior. After success in habitually avoiding evil and seeking good, the third chakra energies move toward the interior freedom of seeking personal honor, self-esteem and sensitivity.

As the thinking person perfects these basic life skills, he is prepared to move from the "House of Commons to the House of Lords, the fourth to sixth chakras."[43] By meditation the devotee starts on the spiritual path of re-uniting with God as his Source. The fourth chakra (dorsal area, corresponding to the heart-center or thymus gland area) is the beginning of experiencing the soul's realizing that it is associated with the bliss which is God. "I am he" is an ancient chant known to yogic meditators.[44] More devotion and deeper meditation will free the devotee from bodily matters into the blissful world of limitless bliss (samadi) and indeed to union with Christ in this life. Here one is living from and seeing with the spiritual eye,[45] so often referenced by Yogananda as the Christ-centered spiritual eye invisibly present between the eyebrows.

While the Merton reader has no overt citations of such concepts, he receives some strong ideas of the East-West possible union from the inclusion in his *Asian Journal* of Appendix IV, "Monastic Experience and East-West Dialogue."[46] The notes for a paper to have been delivered in Calcutta sum up Merton's thoughts on the rapprochement between monastics of both traditions, written previous to his last departure from home and prior to those inchoate ideas gleaned from the journey itself. He remarks that there exists a real possibility for exchange of a transformation of religious consciousness of both groups. Merton immediately adds that at our current state of "religious maturity" one can indeed remain perfectly faithful to a Christian monastic life and yet learn in depth from, say, a Buddhist or Hindu discipline and experience, and finishes the discussion by saying, "…I believe that some of us need to do this in order to improve the quality of our own…life and even help in the task of…renewal."[47]

2. Gandhi's spiritual mission to the modern world

Gandhi's profound influence on both Merton and Yogananda is evident not only in that each stresses the same central ideas of ahimsa (non-violence) and satyagraha (holding on to truth), but that both see him as the very embodiment of Christian and human virtues as preached and lived by Jesus himself.

Born on October 2, 1869 in Porbandar, province of Kathiawad, at a time when India was owned and operated by Britain, Mohandas Gandhi was a loyal subject of the crown. He attended Indian schools, and subsequently studied law in England. His work in South Africa led him to see the extraordinary evil involved in discrimination based not on capability but on race, class, caste or religion. His many experiences in S. Africa, along with his discovery of the *Bhagavad Gita*[48] in the English translation of Sir Edwin Arnold, led him to his lifelong, historic battle for peace. His weapons were prayer and fasting.

Merton's *Gandhi on Non-Violence*[49] consists of a twenty page essay followed by selections from Gandhi's *Non-Violence in Peace and War*,[50] with commentary. Merton briefly notes that his early life had prepared Gandhi more for activity than contemplation. His fully unexpected encounter with racism in South Africa while traveling on a totally different legal matter politicized the young London-educated lawyer. This led to his helping to liberate parts of Africa from such obvious abuse, and to the turning, or more properly returning to his Indian/Hindu roots.

In section one of his essay, Merton demonstrates in detail that Gandhi's *ahimsa* (loosely translated as "non-violence" or peace in all circumstances) is not a means to an end (freedom and independence for India), but rather is the result of his *satyagraha*, a term coined by Gandhi meaning "holding on to truth," and entailing resistance by non-violent means.[51] Satyagraha was the very core of Gandhi's life, which resisted by non-approval and civil disobedience to unjust laws, yet always performed in the spirit of love for oppressor and oppressed. Violence in action and even in thought had no place in satyagraha.

Even though Gandhi concentrated on equality and freedom for the lowest of all classes, the Harijan (untouchables), Merton observes that *"the people of India were awakening in him.... It was not 'Indian thought' or 'Indian spirituality' that was stirring in him, but India herself. It was the spiritual consciousness of a people that awakened in the spirit of one person."*[52] Merton therefore sees Gandhi as the ultimate renunciant dressed in homespun even though "...surrounded not only by respect but by worship." [53]

In the Mahatma ("great soul"), Merton sees Christianity and Hinduism as melded, along with activity and contemplation. With some comparison to Christ as well as to Aquinas and to Erasmus, Merton sums up Gandhi's lesson and legacy to the world: "The evils we suffer cannot be eliminated by a violent attack in which one sector of humanity flies at another in destructive fury. Our evils are common and the solution of them can only be common."[54] And then he sees this Hindu as so close to the heart of Christ, stating that Gandhi taught us that "To forgive others and to forget their offense is to enter with them into the healing mystery of death and resurrection in Christ."[55]

Yogananda devoted a chapter of his *Autobiography of a Yogi* and a chapter in *The Divine Romance*[56] to his 1935 visit to Gandhi's ashram in Wardha.[57] He gives a detailed account of the eleven vows (the Satyagraha) observed in a spirit of humility by the disciples of Gandhi at the ashram as: truth, non-stealing, celibacy, non-possession, body labor, control of the palate, fearlessness, equal respect for all religions, use of home goods (made in India), freedom from unsociability.[58] Among the twenty-five disciples in the ashram were those of lowly castes as well as the high-born British woman Madelyn Slade, who spun cloth from cotton, served the poor and fit into the group with all naturalness.

Yogananda sees Gandhi as the father of a nation, who encapsulated all of the Hindu qualities of the vows above with a full and joyous spirit, having no self-seeking, and indeed distributing his goods to the poorest when he began his ashram in Wardha. Gandhi discussed the celibacy vow taken by himself and his wife after the birth of their fourth child, and how he saw the control of the palate as a necessary means to self-control.

In response to Yogananda's request to "...tell me your definition of ahimsa," Gandhi replied "the avoidance of harm to any living creature in thought or deed," further explaining that "I could not kill a cobra without violating two of my vows – fearlessness and non-killing. I cannot lower my standards to suit my circumstances."[59]

Gandhi asked and received Kriya yoga from Yogananda[60] and spent their day together talking of the ahimsa and the satyagraha, the very terms to be selected by Merton in 1964 for explaining the Mahatma's philosophy. Issued in 1946, the *Autobiography* added a page "in memoriam" in later editions, recalling Einstein's tribute to Gandhi, stating that the "generations to come may scarce believe that such a one as this ever in flesh and blood walked upon the earth."

In the same section Yogananda also quotes the Vatican dispatch that "...the assassination caused great sorrow [to the Church];

Gandhi is mourned as an apostle of Christian virtues."[61] Yogananda had himself spoken of the mahatma during his lifetime in Christian terms, stating that he "...is reestablishing the Christian doctrine. All men—white, brown, yellow and black—are descendants of Adam and Eve, our common grandparents, and as such have one blood flowing in their veins."[62]

3. Ecstatic Moments

Merton and Yogananda both undoubtedly had occasions when the sense of time and place evaporated into the Christ-conscious state. The unity of mankind can be called the most telling characteristic of such an event. Here perhaps are the two best known examples. Many Merton students recall his journal when he wrote:

> In Louisville, at the corner of Fourth and Walnut, in the center of the shopping district, I was suddenly overwhelmed with the realization that I loved all those people, that they were mine and I theirs, that we could not be alien to one another even though we were total strangers. It was like waking from a dream of separateness, of spurious self-isolation in a special world, the world of renunciation and supposed holiness. The whole illusion of a separate holy existence is a dream....The conception of separation from the world [is] a complete illusion ... [I]t cannot be explained. There is no way of telling people that they are all walking around shining like the sun.[63]

Yogananda, some months after joining his guru's ashram, recounts the following:

> One morning at Sri Yukteswar's hermitage, I experienced a divine state in which I was in tune with everything. I could not distinguish between my brother and anyone else. Later, when I went to Master, he said, 'your training is finished. You feel the same love for all.' Master knew my thoughts and feelings. My guru was not interested in what people were saying, but in what they were thinking. He was always conscious of everything that was going on, always calm he had expanded his consciousness into Christ Consciousness.[64]

By this Paramahansa means that just as with Christ, others can expand consciousness to a point beyond everyday experience.

Both stressed that having visionary experiences of cosmic consciousness, while possible for all God-seekers, was not an outcome to be sought. More central to the seeker is the peace and the constant striving to do God's work, while being detached from any consolation or outcome of the work.

4. False self and attachment vs. true self and detachment

These two masters spent a large part of their effort in teaching and encouraging their readers to develop their most authentic self, and showing that this can be possible only by a highly evolved sense of detachment. For Merton to build and live by the "true self" one must replace the "false self" that is part of the human illusion of separateness from God and from each other.

Merton contends: "The secret of interior peace is detachment," and that even if one desires the interior life, constant recollection and prayer, "…You will never be able to have perfect interior peace and recollection unless you are detached even from the desire of peace and recollection. You will never be able to pray perfectly until you are detached from the pleasures of prayer."[65]

He urges that we take this hard lesson from those who have continued to seek God first and always, saying that even the mystic "…lives in emptiness, in freedom, as if he had no longer a limited and exclusive 'self' that distinguished him from God and other men." Thus detachment is a function not of the sweetness and peace that sometimes accompany our prayer, but of the "… resoluteness, the determination to renounce all things for the love of God, without which….we remain aghast at our own weakness, our own poverty, our evasions…."[66]

By continuing in one's resolve, Merton contends that "…the false, exterior self is caught in all its naked nothingness and immediately dispelled as an illusion."[67] And then "If we enter into ourselves, find our true self, and then pass 'beyond' the inner 'I,' we sail forth into the immense darkness in which we confront the 'I AM' of the Almighty…. For us, there is an infinite metaphysical gulf between the being of God and the being of the soul, between the 'I' of the Almighty and our own inner 'I.' Yet paradoxically our inmost 'I' exists in God and God dwells in it."[68] Such is the consolation he gives to the struggling prayerful seeker.

The utter centrality of detachment to enabling the God-seeker to experience deep prayer and self-realization was also a constant part of Yogananda's instructions to his monks and followers. "Scripture" to Yogananda consisted in three sacred canons of writings: the Yoga *Sutras* of Patanjali, the *Bhagavad Gita* from the times of the Ancient Vedas and Hindu rishis, and the Old and New Testament of the Judeo-Christian Bible.

In his commentary on the *Bhagavad Gita*, he cites Lord Krishna's admonition to his disciple: "…renunciation, O mighty Arjuna, is difficult to achieve without God-uniting actions [yoga]. By the practice of yoga, the muni ["he whose mind is absorbed in God"] quickly attains the infinite. "No Taint [karmic involvement] touches the man of action who …has conquered ego consciousness, who is victorious over his senses, and who feels his self as the Self existing in all beings."[69]   He teaches that "attachment is the offspring of desire," and only "desire-less action" in which one follows God's will without any personal attachment to the outcome of his prayer or of his activity, is bound for God. He will perceive his self as the Self existing in all things. Over and over he perceives desire as leading to "anger and lust"[70] whereas performing right action without regard to the outcome leads to the soul-perfection, which transforms the little self (ego) into the divine self (soul), and only thus does the God-seeker perceive his unity with God, perceiving "the self as the Self."

Continuing in Volume Two of the same work on the *Bhagavad Gita* he minces no words, stating "Good actions…that are performed with any motive in the conscious or subconscious minds other than the desire to please God are …done with longing for their fruit. No matter how noble the activity, if it diverts one from the Supreme Goal by its consequent karmic bondage it does not belong to the category of the highest dutiful actions."[71]   A priest serving in India applied this very notion from the *Gita* text of detachment to Thomas Merton, calling his work and spirit of personal detachment that of "a modern Arjuna."[72]

As stated above, Yogananda named his non-denominational church "Self-Realization Fellowship," and all centers, temples and other entities bear that same title today. In his commentary on the original sin of Adam and its consequences for all humans, Merton used that term thus: "Contemplation is the highest and most paradoxical form of self-realization, attained by apparent self-annihilation."[73] His usage in this one instance describes quite precisely the return to man before his separation from God, which is the goal of Yogananda's self-realization movement.

Conclusion

Many more likenesses appear in the writings of these men of God, but the above will serve to show the basic tenet we are investigating, that there is much consonance and harmony between these two spiritual masters. By implication one can also infer that same harmony in true religions and among spirit-filled persons, rather than seeing sectarian biases which have often been recognized in the past.

We have attempted to show the sameness of many central spiritual themes of these two strangers and their perceptions of: Christ's message to Nicodemus, Gandhi as a modern Christ in Hindu clothing, the vast overlap of East and West in so many ways (perhaps a subtle updating of R. Kipling!), as well as the deep similarities in their concepts of detachment and the need to develop and realize the true Self. We have also noted (*supra*, p.173) that we find no mention of the cerebro-spinal plexes with its *seven* energy centers, so central to Yogananda, in Merton's writings. Still one who knows the multi-layered mind of Merton will smile when thinking about the title he gave to his autobiography, *The Seven Storey Mountain*.

Notes

1. Thomas Merton, *The Asian Journal of Thomas Merton*, eds., Naomi Burton Stone, Br. Patrick Hart & James Laughlin (New York: New Directions), pp. 342.

2. Merton, *The Asian Journal of Thomas* Merton, p. 343.

3. Paramahansa Yogananda, *Autobiography of a Yogi* (Los Angeles: Self-Realization Press, 1946).

4. Thomas Merton, *The Seven Storey Mountain* (New York: Harcourt, Brace, 1948).

5. Merton, *Seven Storey Mountain*, pp. 222-23.

6. Yogananda, *Autobiography of a Yogi*, pp. 106-107.

7. Merton, *Seven Storey Mountain*, p. 171.

8. Merton's gratitude to Gilson is perhaps better expressed in a private correspondence of Nov. 12, 1951. Merton says in part "...I want to do what I should have done long ago—write you a line to assure your of my recognition of a spiritual debt to you which I too sketchily indicated in the pages of *The Seven Storey Mountain*—...To you...I owe the Catholic faith. That is to say I owe you my life. This is no small debt" (Thomas Merton, *The School of Charity*, ed., Br. Patrick Hart [New York: Farrar, Straus & Giroux, 1990], pp. 30-31).

9. Merton, *Seven Storey Mountain*, p. 215.

10. Merton, *Seven Storey Mountain,* p. 217.

11. Merton, *Seven Storey* Mountain, p. 225.

12. Yogananda, *Autobiography of a Yogi,* p. 105.

13. Yogananda, *Autobiography of a Yogi,* pp. 106-107.

14. Merton, *The Asian Journal of Thomas Merton,* pp. 326-43.

15. Merton, *Seven Storey Mountain;* Thomas Merton, *Sign of Jonas* (New York: Harcourt, Brace, 1953); Thomas Merton, *No Man Is an Island* (New York: Harcourt, Brace, 1955).

16. International Publications Council of Self-Realization Fellowship, *Personal Accounts of Master's Last Days* (Los Angeles: Self-Realization Press, 1958), p. 67-69.

17. Many references, such as Thomas Merton, *The Nonviolent Alternative* (New York: Farrar, Straus & Giroux, 1980), pp. 67, et seq.

18. Yogananda, *Autobiography of a Yogi,* pp. 389-91.

19. Thomas Merton, *Mystics and Zen Masters* (New York: Farrar, Straus & Giroux, 1967), p. 69.

20. Merton, *Mystics and Zen Masters,* p.80.

21. Merton, *The Asian Journal of Thomas Merton,* pp. 4-5.

22. Yogananda, *Autobiography of a Yogi,* p. 258.

23. See "Aims and Ideals of Self-Realization fellowship," in Yogananda, *Autobiography of a Yogi,* p. 573.

24. Merton, *Love and Living,* eds., Naomi Burton Stone & Br. Patrick Hart (New York: Farrar, Straus & Giroux, 1979), p. 194.

25. John 3:14-15.

26. Merton, *Love and Living,* p. 197.

27. Merton, *Love and Living,* p. 197.

28. Merton, *Love and Living,* p. 199.

29. Merton, *Love and Living,* p. 199.

30. Merton, *Love and Living,* p. 202.

31. Thomas Merton, *The Inner Experience,* ed., William H. Shannon (San Francisco: HarperCollins, 2003), p. 62.

32. Paramahansa Yogananda, *The Second Coming of Christ* (Los Angeles: Self-Realization Fellowship Press, 2004).

33. Yogananda, *The Second Coming of Christ,* p. 241.

34. Merton, *Seven Storey Mountain,* pp. 30, 173, 175, 186, 200, 218ff., 230, 238, 242, 261, 267, 288, 290, 303ff., 327, 333, 337ff., 352ff., 418, 428ff.

35. Merton, *The Inner Experience,* pp. 13-14, 75, 82, 84, 86, 157, 162.

36. Thomas Merton, *Conjectures of a Guilty Bystander* (Garden City, NY: Doubleday, 1966), pp. 42-43, 115, 121, 168-70, 182, 184-90, 200, 241, 267, 290, 293.

37. Yogananda, *The Second Coming of Christ,* P. 244.

38. Yogananda, *The Second Coming of Christ,* P. 245.

39. John 3:14-15.

40. Merton, *The Asian Journal of Thomas Merton*, pp. 112-13.

41. Yogananda, *The Second Coming of Christ*, p. 109.

42. Yogananda, *The Bagavad Gita: Royal Science of God-Realization*, pp. 60-62.

43. Yogananda, *The Bagavad Gita: Royal Science of God-Realization*, pp. 16-21.

44. Yogananda, *The Bagavad Gita: Royal Science of God*-Realization, pp. 985-87.

45. Yogananda, *Autobiography of a Yogi*, pp. 243, 316, 319, *et alibi*.

46. Merton, *The Asian Journal of Thomas Merton*, pp. 309-317.

47. Merton, *The Asian Journal of Thomas Merton*, p. 313.

48. Sir Edwin Arnold, *The Bhagavad Gita* (New York: Truslove, Hanson & Comba, 1900.)

49. Thomas Merton, *Gandhi on Non-Violence* (New York: New Directions, 1965).

50. M.K. Gandhi, *Non-Violence in Peace and War* (New York: Associated Advertisers and Printers, 1942).

51. Gandhi, *on Non-Violence*, p. 4.

52. Gandhi, *on Non-Violence*, p. 5.

53. Gandhi, *on Non-Violence*, p. 7.

54. Gandhi, *on Non-Violence*, p. 16

55. Gandhi, *on Non-Violence*, p. 18.

56. Paramahansa Yogananda, *The Divine Romance* (San Rafael: Self-Realization Press, 1986) pp. 117-29.

57. Yogananda, *Autobiography of a Yogi*, pp. 497-513.

58. Yogananda, *Autobiography of a Yogi*, p. 498.

59. Yogananda, *Autobiography of a Yogi*, p. 507.

60. Yogananda, *Autobiography of a Yogi*, p. 508. Kriya yoga is an ancient system of yoga revived by Lahiri Mahasaya in 1861 and was brought to widespread public awareness through Yogananda's *Autobiography of a Yogi*. The system consists of a number of yogic techniques that are believed to hasten the practitioner's spiritual development and to help to bring about a deeper state of communion with God.

61. Yogananda, *Autobiography of a Yogi*, p. 517.

62. Yogananda, *The Divine Romance*, pp. 117-29.

63. Merton, *Conjectures of a Guilty Bystander*, pp. 140-41.

64. Yogananda, *Autobiography of a Yogi*, p. 166.

65. Thomas Merton, *New Seeds of Contemplation* (New York: New Directions, 1961), pp. 207-208.

66. Merton, *New Seeds of Contemplation*, pp. 210, 212.

67. Merton, *The Inner Experience*, p. 10.

68. Merton, *The Inner Experience*, pp. 11-12.

69. Yogananda, *The Bagavad Gita: Royal Science of God-Realization*, p. 537.

70. Yogananda, *The Bagavad Gita: Royal Science of God-Realization*, pp. 542-43.

71. Yogananda, *The Bagavad Gita: Royal Science of God-Realization*, p. 587.

72. Veliyathil, Paul, "East-West Dialogue: Thomas Merton, a Modern Arjuna," *Spirituality Today*, Vol. 39, (1987), pp. 293-304.

73. Thomas Merton, *The New Man* (New York: Farrar, Straus & Cudahy, 1961), p. 19.

Prayer in a High Tech World

Phillip Thompson

> Just in terms of time resources, religion is
> not very efficient. There's a lot more I could
> be doing on a Sunday morning.[1]
> Bill Gates

> He who is controlled by objects
> Loses possession of his inner self.[2]
> Chuang Tzu

What is the Problem?

Many cultural influences currently challenge our spiritual lives. This article will focus on one of these influences, the recent flood of new communication technologies, and their impact on one aspect of the religious life, prayer. I am well aware of the complexity of this problem as a Catholic intellectual employed at a public, engineering university.[3]

Thomas Merton's writings on the intersection of faith and technology provide important insights for this exploration. Let us begin with the primary goal of a Christian life as defined by Merton. Laboring under the "truth and the judgments of God," Christians seek "the manifestation of God's transcendent and secret holiness." The "truth and the judgments of God" also apply to our temporal actions. Hence, Christians have a prophetic role in assuming a "critical attitude toward the world and its structures" because, Merton argues, many of the claims of the world are fraudulent. One source of falsity is a technological mentality that can become an autonomous imperative without any grounding in ultimate reality. In exposing and confronting this technological mentality, there are serious traps and dangers in discerning and expressing the "truth and judgments of God." For example, the truth of God may more often than not reflect the prejudices of the interpreter. Such caveats provide valuable warnings, but they are not a call to inaction. Unless we select the "Amish option" of attempted seclu-

185

sion, we can not isolate ourselves from engaging the world; the world will come in anyway.[4]

Although prophetic at times, Merton's style is not that of the ancient Hebrew prophets. His slashing criticisms of technology are often mixed with humorous observations.[5] Technology can be a source of wry amusement, because its promoters are unaware of its limitations and ironies. Merton was asked by two teenage girls if he could write a prayer to a computer. His bemused response was:

> Write a prayer to a computer? But first of all you have to find out how It thinks. *Does It dig prayer?* More important still, does It dig me, and father, mother, etc., etc.? How does one begin: "O Thou great unalarmed and humorless electric sense..."? Start out wrong and you give instant offense. You may find yourself shipped off to the camps in a freight car. Prayer is a virtue. But don't begin with the wrong number.[6]

The stance of prophet and amused observer was balanced by an admission, particularly in his later years, that technology was an inevitable aspect of our world. He once observed in a lecture as novice master that

> the first thing that we have to make quite clear: there is absolutely no point whatever in monks or anybody else standing back and saying we are not going to have any technology... There's no way around it. We are living in a technological world."[7]

Technologies and their applications allow for mixed possibilities, dependent on the wisdom or folly of our choices in development and application.

> Technology could indeed make a much better world for millions of human beings. It not only can do this, but it must do it. We have an absolute obligation to use the means at our disposal to keep people from living in utter misery and dying like flies.... What I am "against" then is a complacent and naive progressivism which pays no attention to anything but the fact that wonderful things can be and are done with machinery and with electronics.[8]

In his personal life, the judgment on a technology was determined by its compatibility with the monastic vocation. Merton initially detested the camera as a tool of prying visitors to the Abbey of Gethsemani who wanted a picture of the famous monk of *The Seven Storey Mountain*. Yet, he eventually discovered that the camera could become a vehicle for art, for capturing moments of divine creativity present in our daily lives. On his many walks, he photographed whatever came across his path, particularly the random object, as its Creator had left it. The "Zen camera" then became a "catalyst for contemplation." It could create a "heightened awareness very similar to meditative prayer." [9]

Merton's stance, that I would term prophetic ambivalence, remains a thoughtful approach for assessing technologies with all of their profound dangers and constructive possibilities. Employing this paradigm, I will delineate some observations about prayer in a high-tech world. If I am successful, there may be some insights for a broad range of persons struggling to nourish their spiritual lives within our current cultural context.

The Communications Tsunami

Before considering Merton's approach on the issue of prayer, I will briefly outline our current predicament. The first point is perhaps an obvious one. We have experienced an accelerating explosion of communication technologies since the passing of Thomas Merton in 1968. Consider the following list:

The Media Explosion-Communication Devices

1968	2007		
Telephone	Telephone-cellphone	Laptop Computers	Palm Pilot
Telegraph	Internet/email	Power point	Fax
Television	Television-cable/ satellite	I-Pod	Cassette player
Radio	Radio	CD	Blackberry
Record player	Personal computer	MP3 player	

There are not only more devices, but each new technology reaches a majority of the population much faster. It took sixty-seven years for the telephone to reach 75% of the American population. In contrast, the VCR reached 75% of the American population in twelve years. Internet usage went from 15% in 1994 to 73% by 2006. [10]

These rapidly spreading devices are used by millions of people in the United States who receive massive amounts of largely unfiltered data in every conceivable form in their i-pods, the internet,

etc. What is the cognitive impact of these devices and their messages? Some experts believed that computers would ride to the
rescue of education, but like earlier proposed technological "cures"
such as film and television, they do not seem to be producing more
intelligent or better-informed students. Vast amounts of data can
now be accessed by students, but there is little filtering of the form
or content. Blogs are used as equivalent citation sources with peer
reviewed journals or texts. Partly for these reasons, some school
districts are dropping their laptop programs.[11] Outside of the classroom, the communications flood is also expanding. Consider these
statistics:

- College students spend 11 hours per day engaged with media;
- College students spend 3.5 hrs per day emailing,
  instant messaging and web surfing;
- 34% of college students reported spending at
  least 10 hrs a week on-line.[12]

By way of contrast, the average child in the United States spends
only forty-five minutes per day reading. Less than 6% of adult
Americans read more than one book a year and 60% of adult Americans do not read a book of any kind during a year. Daily newspaper readership in the United States has declined from 67% in 1965
to 31% by 2000. The loss of serious reading to the new technologies has assisted the decline in basic levels of common knowledge.
Less than half of Americans know that the earth revolves around
the sun in a year. Such intellectual decay is matched by declining
levels of critical thinking or imagination. The positive impact on
such skills from examining serious works of literature, philosophy, etc. is often replaced in the best-case scenario with challenging movies and at worst with computer games, Utube, and South
Park.[13] The sociologist, Todd Gitlin, in his book, *Media Unlimited:
How the Torrent of Images and Sounds Overwhelms Our World*, describes the impact of this constant massaging of our collective psy-
ches.

> The most important thing about the communications we live
> among is not that they deceive (which they do); or that they
> broadcast a limited ideology (which they do); or emphasize
> sex and violence (which they do); or convey diminished im-
> ages of the good, the true, and the normal (which they do); or
> corrode the quality of art (which they also do); or reduce lan-

guage (which they surely do)—but with all their lies, skews, and shallow pleasures they saturate our way of life…streaming out of screens large and small, or bubbling in the background of life, but always coursing onwards. To an unprecedented degree, the torrent of images, songs, and stories has become our familiar world.[14]

This immersion in battering waves of questionable sights and sounds is quite common, but it is only fair to consider that such devices also provide manifold means to communicate worthwhile information and projects to other human beings and this impulse might provide a powerful counterweight to cultural diminishment. And to be fair, there are some wonderful instances of charity and human connection because of these technologies. Yet, the evidence of a significant negative impact remains troubling. Ironically, in an age of so many communication possibilities, there seems to be a greater isolation of individuals and unhealthy social development. Mental health problems among the communications generation continues to spiral upwards. In one of the wealthiest and most politically stable societies in the history of the world, the use of psychotropic drugs in the United States by children tripled in the 1990s. A rising tide of mental health problems, including suicides and violence, is hitting our college campuses.[15]

There are other less severe, but still worrisome problems. The communication age allows us to be more anonymous, selecting the images we wish to view and answering only those e-mails and text messages that we wish to answer. Teenagers can text message their feelings to one another without the same fear that arises from expressing themselves before an embodied reality that can not be immediately shut down or discarded. These contacts may produce less meaning, but they also require less emotional exposure.

This ability to shape our communications allows us to believe that we can organize our lives and create our identities in our own auto-culture. Even in his life, Merton observed this phenomenon, declaring that modern life nurtured the belief that every person can act like a "little autonomous god, seeing and judging everything in relation to [ourselves]". We seek to make our individual lives interesting and controlled as we abandon community bonds with their tiresome demands and requirements. As Robert Putnam explored in *Bowling Alone*, participation in the community and civic life of the United States has been in decline for several decades and the media torrent, albeit not the sole cause, has contributed to the precipitous decline of our common life.[16]

Why do we accept this atomization of our selves? The truth is that we have been impacted by a series of new communication processes dating back to the printing press. Isn't this current phase just one more turn of the inventive process? The exponential increase of the scale and speed of communication technologies, however, is unprecedented. We have reached the epoch of the nanosecond. "Speed is the form of ecstasy the technical revolution has bestowed on man" laments the Czech novelist Milan Kundera, who concludes that modern man is "caught in a fragment of time cut off from both the past and the present; he is wrenched from the continuity of time; he is outside of time…."[17]

The speed and pervasiveness of the media torrent has too often distended our sensibilities and alienated us from our fellow human beings, but it is seductive because we can now construct a virtual world of our own imagining, full of entertainment and sensation signifying virtually nothing. This communications environment is not particularly hospitable to ancient truths and religious practices. Indeed, the media offensive washes such positions in a cynical acid and refuses to allow special efficacy to anything except forms that can pierce the relentless background noise with new forms of stimulation. The trend in movies reflects this reality as they become louder, more vulgar, more violent, and more cynical each year. If you doubt this fact, then randomly select and watch five movies in the same genre that are at least forty years old. The difference is startling. A recent attempt of Christianity to compete with this nouveaux sensationalism, Mel Gibson's, *The Passion of the Christ*, seeks to beat the current trend at its own game by its graphic violence, its luxuriating in pain. Such efforts are at best a mixed blessing for the faithful. The Church will not win in any effort to produce more visual sensation than Hollywood and would no doubt become a sorcerer's apprentice in the attempt. God's kingdom, whatever it may be, is not likely to be revealed in such a sensationalistic movie.

Christianity and other religions must recognize that the media torrent appeals to an anthropology that reduces human beings to largely autonomous creatures that are self-centered and addicted to the constant massaging of our sensations and desires. The often feckless and infantilizing dimensions of these messages were revealed to Merton when he passed a television one day.

Once when I did happen to pass in front of a set I saw the commercial that was on: two little figures were dancing around worshipping a roll of toilet paper, chanting a hymn in its honor… We have simply lost the ability to see what is right in front of us: things like this need no comment.[18]

Seeds of Hope

Just as Merton depicted the errors of television, we must speak truth to inanity, superficiality, and idolatry in the current media revolution. Such messages poison our mental ecology in which we seek to pursue our faith, including our prayer life. To counter such trends in our culture, we must effectively present the case for thick forms of religious life that can sustain our faith such as art, literature, ritual, charity, contemplation, natural and spiritual cycles, sacraments, study, moral reflection, and of course prayer.

Let me begin with the prophetic task of critique. There are a number of possible paths. Humor, drama, critical thinking, and the development of community can help us to resist the worst aspects in the drift of contemporary culture. In the development of critical thinking, the Jesuit theologian, Bernard Lonergan, privileges the act of the intelligent agent who appropriates the cognitive path to understanding that sustains our resistance to a culture that presents "superficial minds with superficial positions" and can ignite "flights from understanding."[19]

Perhaps the religious artist also has a special duty to awaken us from the numbing influence of the surrounding white noise. The novelist, Walker Percy, advised that a Christian novelist has a unique role and approach in such a context. To pierce the simulacrum of false cultural idols, "he calls on every ounce of cunning craft and guile he can muster from the darker regions of his soul. The fictional use of violence, shock, comedy, insult, the bizarre are everyday tools of his trade. How could it be otherwise?" Percy noted that if such strategies awaken us to our plight then we have taken the first steps on the road to being a "sovereign wayfarer," of entering into the pilgrimage of the Christian in a disoriented post-modern age.[20]

Merton would certainly appreciate the paths of Lonergan and Percy. He did not exclude a path through study, reflection, or literature and indeed was a contributor to these approaches. They could oppose communication technologies like television that fostered "a descent to a sub-natural passivity" when the goal should be a "supremely active passivity in understanding and love." The desire to reject the numbing passivity of the media barrage present in Lonergan and Percy is thus keenly felt by Merton.

> Therefore, if a man is going to make authentic judgments and do some thinking for himself, he is going to have to renounce the passivity of a subject that merely sits and "takes in" what is told him, whether in class, or in front of the TV, or in the other mass media. This means serious and independent reading, and it also means articulate discussion.[21]

As Merton suggests, it is not enough merely to be cultural critics. Another part of the solution must be to develop alternatives, thick spiritual communities where the mental ecology will be more compatible with a contemplative life. We must redevelop our sense of community with neighbors, parishes, civic associations, clubs, and families. Instead of autonomy, solidarity should be our watchword. What would be the impact of giving preference to communal activity over the hours in front of the television and computer or on the cell phone? Merton provides other antidotes to this cultural affliction such as reviving the measured and creative craft traditions like those of the Shakers.[22] These actions could help to foster a true community and reawaken a sense of the transcendent in our midst.

The most powerful antidote, however, would be contemplation. It is in the moments of quiet reflection and prayer that the loud hum of the 24/7 media buzz invading our senses is silenced and the soul can seek comfort, rest, and connection to the divine. Merton has his doubts and is not certain that contemplation can "still find a place in the world of technology and conflict which is ours." Admittedly, the path will not be easy. We must place ourselves outside the convenient illusions and facile seductions of the media onslaught. Instead, we must struggle and make "one of the most terrible decisions possible to man: the decision to disagree completely with those who imagine that the call to diversion and self-deception is the voice of truth…." The call to superficial diversions, so prominent in our world, is problematic because they block our connection to our "inmost truth—the image of God in [our] own soul." The movement to a dedicated prayer life as part of this contemplative choice is thus a counter-cultural act that calls upon each of us as spiritual agents to seek a different path.[23]

The technological mentality of our age nurtures still another harmful dimension that blocks our contemplative path. While a consumer mentality may foster a "sub-natural" passivity in the recipients of the deluge of images, the production of all these images, sounds, etc. are also the consequence of a hyper-productive mentality of an age of global competitiveness. The creation of so many products including diverse communication forms is the result of technological innovations that are pushing forward at astonishing rates. The epigraph of Bill Gates for this essay reflects the impact of this restive desire for product development. Gates is frustrated that religion seems so inefficient, so unproductive. Who can blame him? Gates is used to results, concrete tangible results—new products, market share, profits. What does a religious service or prayer give you? Merton abhorred such a mentality of productivity that had at times even infected the monastery, with monks running out to their fields like a football team to maximize productivity. Likewise, he mocked the seriousness of efforts to sell monastic cheese. Behind these humorous observations, he detected troubling assumptions. The monks who worked with the machinery had a special difficulty adjusting to silence. With the advent of a technological mentality, "everything becomes centered on the most efficient use of machines and techniques of production, and the style of life, the culture, the tempo and manner of existence responds more and more to the needs of the technological process itself."[24]

Indeed, the spirit of productivity, formulas, and efficiency can enter into prayer life. This is true even of spiritual directors, whose calling is to assist the life of prayer. While they should be guides and sources of questions and insights, they have often assumed a technological mentality of expertise in their counseling.

> The "director" is thought to be one endowed with special, almost miraculous, authority and has the power to give the "right formula" when it is asked for. He is treated as a machine for producing answers that will work, that will clear up difficulties and make us perfect.... Such spiritual direction is mechanical, and it tends to frustrate the real purpose of genuine guidance. It tends to reinforce the mechanisms and routines with which the soul is destroying its own capacity for a spontaneous response to grace.[25]

Merton's warnings ring especially true for me because they remind me of a silent retreat that I took many years ago. During the retreat, I was committed to not speaking or watching television, but I wanted to schedule my spiritual life. I created a detailed list of structured activities for each day that included reading, prayer, religious services, walking, lectures, etc. I yearned for constant structure and activity, because I was pressing to be productive and ward off the silence. My objective was to get something more—grace perhaps—than others by maximizing my efforts, efficiently using my time. I would leverage my spiritual assets and obtain an optimal effect. And of course I did not.

A "sub-natural passivity" or a "Six Sigma" approach to the spiritual life are both problematic for nurturing a contemplative life. God will not provide streaming video of the divine nor are spiritual outcomes improved through the refinements of technique as though we are doing a systems analysis of a production line. Merton offers some guidance to mitigate and perhaps elude these contemporary traps. First, we must develop a sense of what is meant by prayer. Prayer is the "raising of heart and mind to God." By the act of prayer, we enter into a mystery. This process is difficult because we are comfortable with the glitzy, constantly mutating images of our daily bath of media. In contemplative prayer, there is a move away from images and sounds. Instead, we must focus our attention on the mystery which is the "presence of God and ... His will and His love." We will not be given exact images or sets of images which would be a form of idolatry. Indeed, God is "infinitely beyond our comprehension." It is only through a purgation of all objects such as images that we can recognize the divine in reality beyond our nothingness.[26]

In addition to praise, meditative prayer or a prayer of the heart is not a search for God, but "a way of resting in him whom we have found, who loves, who is near us, who comes to us to draw us to himself." This form of prayer requires the finding of a person's deepest center, an awakening of our deepest being in the presence of God. The climate for this type of prayer is one of "awareness and gratitude and a totally obedient love that seeks nothing but to love God." Solitude is critical so that there can be a void that can be then filled by God's presence. We must put aside the "emptiness and futility" of those forms of "distraction and useless communication" which do not contribute to a life of prayer.[27] So, the enervating flow of images and sounds of the media deluge is not a hospitable environment for such a prayer life. Moreover, our mental habits developed while absorbing these images and sounds may make our efforts at prayer much more difficult. For example, if praise is at the heart of prayer, the concept of praise may be troubling because of its cultural associations. The praise that is so imprinted in our minds is that of advertising. Praise becomes "cheap" when it is associated with the "official hollow enthusiasm" of an announcer for a variety of "gadgets which are supposed to make life more comfortable." Who can use this term when it is associated with the praise of trifles, useless objects?[28]

There are still other dimensions of prayer at odds with our cultural assumptions. A contemplative connection with the divine in prayer is a gift. We are afraid of this process because we can not control it or obtain it by technical means, nor can we remain numbly passive as we do with the torrent of media images. The contemplative process requires us to abandon the software of our current communication experiences and enter into a new form of experience. We must learn how to wait, watch, and listen attentively. Because of our life of streaming images and communications, the contemplative prayer life at first may seem boring, empty, and dry. The process may even seem pointless and unproductive for quite some time. Indeed, prayer life is not terribly productive in our current sense of the term.

> In technology you have this horizontal progress, where you must start at one point and move to another and then another. But that is not the way to build a life of prayer. In prayer we discover what we already have. You start where you are and you deepen what you already have, and you realize that you are already there. We already have everything, but we don't know it and we don't experience it. Everything has been given to us in Christ. All we need is to experience what we already possess.[29]

Thus, in our prayer life, we must be willing to let go of our false sense of control. In the end, progress in this endeavor is not within our command. This is also a foreign concept to an age in which we seek our own self-help answers at every turn. We are comfortable with our ability to know ourselves through our own actions. If we just get the right book, the right technique—all will be well. So, we may not be thrilled with Merton's suggestion that "progress in prayer comes from the Cross and humiliation and whatever makes us really experience our total poverty and nothingness, and also gets our mind off ourselves."[30]   The false self, the self of diversions and control that must be annulled in order to open us to being filled with a divine reality restrains us.

Merton's analysis of contemplation can be annealed by the cultural insights of Josef Pieper, an intellectual deeply admired by Merton in his lifetime. We know his esteem for the German theologian because Merton recommended his works as valuable to a fellow Novice Master and in a favorable book review in the journal, *Cistercian Studies*. Pieper proposes the ressourcement of an ancient ideal of leisure in order to heal the cultural milieu of the modern world. Josef Pieper reminds us that leisure is a foundation for a culture that can nourish the contemplative life. Modern culture has become obsessed with work as the central focus of our daily lives and discursive thought as the highest intellectual virtue. The contemporary culture of work and reason assumes an "outwardly directed, active power," a readiness to suffer pain, and "the adoption of a rationalized program of useful social organization." While not denying some merit to these activities, the modern world has lost the best part of life, that of the intellectus, the ability to simply look and be receptive to a more profound vision that encompasses temporal *and* spiritual realities. We can then acquire through our receptive attention in contemplation a very special gift. This divine gift is not a matter of our intellectual or physical labors; it is not the product of a special technique. The gift is an awareness of how God, operates or to use a word favored by Aquinas, "plays" throughout the world, a world of divine festivity. Because of this recognition, we can accept "a whole preserve of true, unconfined humanity: a space of freedom, of true learning, of attunement to the world-as-a- whole."[31]

Finding Space for the Contemplative Life

While Merton's approach and Pieper's insights may be correct about contemplation and the proper form of a culture, we confront the problem of following his path in a media age that is in some fundamental sense oppositional to such a quest. How do we get our minds out of the communication deluge and away from its mental habits such as a numbing passivity or a quest for productivity? The answer is not necessarily to abandon the technological age. Merton came to realize that technology is inevitable in some form and can often be desirable as long as we remember that, "Technology can elevate and improve man's life only [if] it remains subservient to his *real* interests; that it respects his true being; that it remembers that that the origin and goal of all being is in God."[32]

How do we achieve this subservience? Perhaps, it is prudent to seek intentionally to limit the footprint of technology in our lives and its impact on our cognitive habits and mental states. There must be room for silence, for the presence of the divine. Practically, what might this mean in our daily actions? Perhaps, we could limit or eliminate the use of the media technologies at certain times. How about no television, cell phone or computer use on Sundays? Or for an hour or two, each day? In its place, we could replace it with activities that better nurture contemplative moments such as:

- Spending time in nature or a garden.
- Recreation with friends and family.
- Listening to sacred or inspirational music.
- Reading poetry or a worthwhile book.
- Resting with no goal or objective.
- Waiting, watching and listening for the divine.
- Visiting those in need.
- Prayer.

Merton certainly saw the advantages of many of these kinds of activities as sources for renewal of the contemplative life and prayer, and not just on Sunday. For example, the realization of the divine is possible in our meditation on nature; it can be a form of meditative prayer.

> When your mind is silent, then the forest suddenly becomes magnificently real and blazes transparently with the Reality of God…. And we who are in God find ourselves united in Him with all that springs from Him. This is prayer, and this is glory![33]

So in order to develop a vibrant prayer life in a frenetic age of expanding forms of communication, we must slow our pace when and where we can. We must accept the value of our prayer life and give primacy to those moments. In our lives and in our institutions, we must promote the preconditions for contemplation. Of course, we must begin with ourselves. We can make new choices for our time. For example, Merton observed that "there is nothing to prevent a layman from taking just one Psalm a day, for instance in his night prayers, and reciting it thoughtfully, pausing to meditate on the lines which have the deepest meaning for him."[34]

In addition, it is possible to imagine that our institutions could be more compatible with such a life. In Montreal, there is a company, Cordon Bleu, owned by Robert Ouimet, who has installed meditation rooms in his plants where every person of faith is free to seek these contemplative moments in their own way in their breaks at work.[35] Perhaps such openness to spiritual possibilities can become more widespread. Robert Ouimet and Cordon Bleu are very small compared to Bill Gates and Microsoft, yet as is often noted in the Bible, size and apparent power are often illusions. Unusual things can grow from the seeds of spiritual possibility that are always, as Merton noted, with us.

In the end, we all stand before our walls of immanence built in part with the white noise of discordant sounds and transmuting images of our media culture. This wall is one that Merton would recognize, for he too lived in an age of "crisis" of "special searching and questioning." Such an age needs meditation and prayer, because only prayers of "humble supplication" can turn our despair into a "perfect hope." [36] So, we yearn to go beyond the walls and the abyss of sights and sounds they seem to encompass. This action is not a physical one, but a spiritual journey; it is not in the world, but in us. And so we pray. In the end, as Saint Augustine observed, we can feel the pull and respond in prayer because our hearts are restless until they rest in thee, oh my God.

*I would like to dedicate this paper to the deeply religious journeys of so many students at Georgia Tech. Here at the most technological and scientific of institutions, these young people are searching for a spiritual basis for their lives and in doing so remind their elders of the joy and merit of such a quest.

Notes

1. Walter Isaacson, "In Search of the Real Bill Gates" *Time Magazine* (January 13, 1997).

2. Thomas Merton, *The Way of Chuang Tzu* (New York: New Directions, 1965), p. 137.

3. Strictly speaking, Georgia Tech is an institute, not a university, but I thought this might confuse the reader. If in Atlanta, do not de-

scribe the Georgia Institute of Technology as a university to any student, faculty, or staff there. You may be summarily corrected.

4. Perhaps this humorous style is peculiar to American Catholic intellectuals. Merton once wrote that the Catholic novelist, Walker Percy, had a "merry kind of nausea." He told his novices that he would like to be known as the "Santa Claus of loneliness." Thomas Merton, "Letter to Walker Percy" (January, 1964), *The Courage for Truth*, Christine M. Bochen, ed. (New York: Farrar, Straus & Giroux, 1993), p. 282; Thomas Merton, "Poetry and Imagination" (#8 Credence Cassettes, 1994).

5. Thomas Merton, *The Asian Journal of Thomas Merton* (New York: New Directions, 1973), p. 329; Thomas Merton, *Disputed Questions* (New York: Farrar, Straus and Cudahy, 1960), p. 222.

6. Thomas Merton, *Cables to the Ace* (New York: New Directions, 1968), pp. 5,6. This piece was initially prepared in response to the request of high school student, Suzanne Butorovich from Campbell, California, for her "underground" newspaper, the *Clique Courier*. Thomas Merton, "Letter to Suzanne Butorovich" (July 18, 1967) in Thomas Merton, *The Road to Joy*, ed. Robert Daggy (New York: Farrar, Straus & Giroux, 1989), p. 310.

7. Thomas Merton, The Christian in a Technological World. (Electronic Paperback Series).

8. Thomas Merton, "Circular Letter, Lent 1967" in *The Road to Joy*, pp. 98-99.

9. Thomas Merton, (September 26, 1964) in Thomas Merton, *Dancing in the Water of Life*. vol. 5, Robert E. Daggy, ed. *The Journals of Thomas Merton* (San Francisco: HarperCollins, 1997), p. 149. The later interest stands in contrast to Merton's boredom with photography in 1939 when he visited a Museum of Modern Art exhibit of Charles Scheeler. The photographs were "so neat and so precise and so completely uninteresting." Thomas Merton, *Run to The Mountain*, Vol. 1. Patrick Hart, ed., *The Journals of Thomas Merton* (San Francisco: HarperCollins, 1995), p. 68; Patrick Hart, "Photography and Prayer in Thomas Merton," *The Merton Seasonal* 7.2 (Summer, 1982), pp. 2-5; John Howard Griffin, *A Hidden Wholeness: The Visual World of Thomas Merton* (Boston: Houghton-Mifflin, 1970), p. 49.

10. Robert Putnam, *Bowling Alone* (New York: Simon and Schuster, 2001), p. 217; Steve Metz, "Editor's Corner," *The Science Teacher* (October, 2006), p. 8.

11. Against the educational trend to viewing computers as the key to improving education and society, there stand a few dissenting voices. Clifford Stoll, *High Tech Heretic: Reflections of a Computer Contrarian* (Anchor Press, 2000); Todd Oppenheimer, *The Flickering Mind: Saving Edu-*

cation from the False Promise of Technology (New York: Random House, 2004); Larry Cuban, *Oversold and Underused: Computers in the Classroom* (Cambridge: Harvard University Press, 2003); Jessica E. Vascellaro, "Saying No to School Laptops" *Wall Street Journal* (August 31, 2006), p. D1; Winnie Hu, "Seeing No Progress, Some Schools Drop Laptops," *New York Times* (May 4, 2007), pp. A1,A23.

12. Survey by Burst Interactive Media www.burstmedia.com/about/news.

13. Morris Berman, *The Twilight of American Culture* (New York: W.W. Norton, 2000), p. 36; Todd Gitlin, *Media Unlimited: How the Torrent of Images and Sounds Overwhelms Our World* (New York: Henry Holt, 2002), p. 18. The impact of the changing forms of communication has been detailed in the last half century by a variety of prophetic voices. See Marshall McLuhan, *Understanding Media: The Extensions of Man* (New York, McGraw-Hill, 1964); Neil Postman, *Amusing Ourselves to Death* (New York: Penguin Books, 1986); Thomas De Zengotita, *Mediated: How the Media Shapes Your World and the Way You Live in It* (New York: Bloomsbury, 2005).

14. Gitlin, *Media Unlimited,* p. 6.

15. J. Zito, et. al., "Psychotropic Patterns for Youth: A Ten Year Perspective" (157) *Archives of Pediatric and Adolescent Medicine* (2003), pp. 17-25. In a national survey, of the American College Health Association, almost 10% of students had contemplated suicide. A Study at Kansas State University discovered that between 1988 and 2001 the number of students being treated for depression and suicide nearly doubled. Richard D. Kadison, "Mental Health Crisis: What Colleges Must Do" 51 *Chronicle of Higher Education* (December 10, 2004), p. B20.

16. Gitlin, *Media Unlimited,* pp.39-41; There are of course those who claim that there has been the creation of real communities online, but these communities seem very content-thin. Sensation and online visual quests provides a limited basis for human connection. Edward Castranova, *Synthetic Worlds: The Business and Culture of Online Games* (Chicago: University of Chicago Press, 2005); Merton, *Dancing in the Water of Life* (April 3, 1965), p. 224; Thomas Merton, *New Seeds of Contemplation* (New York: New Directions, 1962), pp. 14, 30; Thomas Merton, *Learning to Love.* Vol. 6, Christine M. Bochen, ed. *The Journals of Thomas Merton* (San Francisco: HarperCollins, 1997) (October 27, 1966), p. 151; Robert Putnam, *Bowling Alone.* (New York: Simon and Schuster, 2001), pp. 216-246.

17. James Glieck, *Speed* (New York: Little, Brown & Co., 1999), p. 6; For a fictional account of the media fog, see Don DeLillo, *White Noise* (New York: Penguin, 1986).

18. Thomas Merton, "Letter to Czelaw Milosz" (March 28, 1961) in Merton, *The Courage for Truth,* p. 72.

19. Bernard Lonergan, *Insight* (San Francisco: HarperCollins, 1957), pp. xii-xvi, 472-475; Bernard Lonergan, *Method in Theology* (Toronto: Toronto University Press, 1971), p. 317.

20. Walker Percy, *The Message in the Bottle* (New York: Farrar, Straus & Giroux, 1987), p. 118.

21. Thomas Merton, "Letter to Mr. L. Dickson" (September 12, 1965) in Thomas Merton, *Witness to Freedom*, ed. William H. Shannon (New York: Harcourt Brace & Co., 1994), p. 169.

22. Judith Flournoy, "Thomas Merton and the Shakers" *The Merton Seasonal* 22.1 (Spring, 1997), pp. 7-11.

23. Merton "Preface" to Japanese edition of *Seeds of Contemplation*" in Thomas Merton, *"Honorable Reader": Reflections on My Work*, ed. Robert F. Daggy (New York: Crossroad, 1989), p. 86; Merton, Thomas. "The Other Side of Despair," in Thomas Merton, *Mystics and Zen Masters* (New York: Farrar, Straus & Giroux, 1967), pp. 255-80; Merton, *Disputed Questions*, p. 183. For an incisive analysis of monastic prayer in Merton, see Anne Carr, *A Search for Wisdom and Spirit* (Notre Dame: University of Notre Dame Press, 1988), pp. 108-120; Merton, *New Seeds of Contemplation*, p. 86.

24. Thomas Merton, "Answers for Hernan Lavin Cerda" 2 *The Merton Annual* (1989), p. 6.

Thomas Merton, "CHEE$E" in *The Collected Poems of Thomas Merton* (New York: New Directions, 1977), pp. 799-800. Thomas Merton, "Letter to Dom Gregorio Lemercier"(October 23, 1953) in *The School of Charity*, ed. Patrick Hart, O.C.S.O. (New York: Farrar, Straus & Giroux, 1990), pp. 68,69; Thomas Merton, *Conjectures of a Guilty Bystander* (Garden City: NY, Doubleday, 1966), p. 16.

25. Thomas Merton, *Spiritual Direction and Meditation* (Collegeville, MN: Liturgical Press, 1960), pp. 10-11.

26. Thomas Merton, "Letter to Abdul Aziz" (January 2, 1966) *The Hidden Ground of Love*, William H. Shannon, ed. (New York: Farrar, Straus & Giroux, 1985), pp. 63-64.

27. Merton, *Contemplative Prayer* (New York: Herder and Herder, 1969), pp. 32-38.

28. Thomas Merton, *Praying the Psalms* (Collegeville, MN: Liturgical Press, 1956), p. 5.

29. David Steindl-Rast, "Man or Prayer," in Patrick Hart, ed. *Thomas Merton, Monk: A Monastic Tribute* (New York: Sheed & Ward, 1974), p. 80.

30. Merton, "Letter to Etta Gullick" (April 6, 1966) *The Hidden Ground of Love*, p. 376.

31. Thomas Merton, Letter to Father Mark Weidner (April 15, 1959) in *The School of Charity*, 119; Thomas Merton book review of Josef Pieper,

In Tune with the World in 1 *Cistercian Studies* (1966), 108-109; Josef Pieper, *Leisure: The Basis of Culture* (South Bend: St. Augustine's Press, 1998), 11-27,37.

32. Merton, *Conjectures of a Guilty Bystander*, p. 230.

33. Thomas Merton, *Entering the Silence.* Vol. 2. Jonathan Montaldo, ed. *The Journals of Thomas Merton* (San Francisco: HarperCollins, 1996), p. 471.

34. Merton, *Praying the Psalms*, p. 14.

35. This information is based on my visits with Robert Ouimet in Montreal. He holds an annual conference on spirituality and work and I have attended several of the conferences.

36. Merton, *Contemplative Prayer*, pp. 25, 28.

In Memoriam: "We are Life, Its Shining Gift"

ROGER JONATHAN CORLESS
(26 June 1938—12 January 2007)

Harry Wells

Roger Jonathan Corless died on January 12, 2007, in San Francisco, California from complications associated with cancer. Born in Merseyside, England in 1938, he began studying religion at the age of sixteen, understanding himself as being Buddhist, though attending Christian churches. He studied theology at King's College at the University of London, receiving a Bachelor of Divinity in 1961. In wrestling with the Hebrew and Greek texts of the Bible, and particularly in the sacrament of the Eucharist, Roger experienced God's presence. He was baptized into the Roman Catholic Church in 1964 after coming to the United States to pursue a Ph.D. in Buddhist Studies at the University of Wisconsin-Madison from which he received that degree in 1973. From there, he joined the Department of Religion at Duke University and remained there until his retirement in 2000.

In 1980, Roger took refuge as a Gelugpa Buddhist under Geshela Lhundup Sopa, having first obtained permission from his Catholic spiritual director and having explained to Geshela what he was doing. His refuge or dharma name was Lhundup Tashi, "spontaneous fortune" or "luck." Later, Roger also became a Benedictine oblate, taking Gregory as his Oblate name after Pope Gregory, whose instruction to Augustine of Canterbury was not to destroy the pagan temples, but to bring them into the church by trying to find what was good and preparatory to the Gospel. Roger understood himself as a dual practitioner, but did not seek to blend the two practices or traditions. Rather, he sought to be present to each in their own irreconcilable differences and deep riches.

Roger was always reflecting and writing on something, wanting to be open to the insights emerging from his studies and practices. His works are prolific. Over the past thirty years, he published three monographs (*The Art of Christian Alchemy: Transfigur-*

ing the Ordinary Through Holistic Meditation, Paulist Press, 1981; *I am Food: The Mass in Planetary Perspective*, Crossroad, 1981 and Wipf and Stock 2004; *The Vision of Buddhism: The Space Under the Tree*, Paragon House, 1989), one edited volume (with Paul Knitter, *Buddhist Emptiness and Christian Trinity: Essays and Explorations*, Paulist Press, 1990), essays in 31 books, 37 articles in 20 journals, articles in six encyclopedias, along with 27 papers. Before his death, he had also completed six additional essays, forthcoming in edited volumes, and a draft of another monograph, *Where Do We Go From Here?: The Many Religions and the Next Step*. Over the years, his works examined Buddhist teachings and practices, Christian teachings and practices, Buddhist-Christian dialogue, interreligious dialogue, and more recently his focus had turned to queer dharma topics and same-sex issues.

A memorial service, *We are Life, Its Shining Gift*, was held for Roger on March 10, 2007 in San Francisco. Friends and colleagues spoke of Roger's life and accomplishments and his impact on their lives. There was Buddhist chanting and Christian hymns, with the service opening and closing with two musical pieces selected by Roger for that purpose, "The Swan of Tuonela" by Jean Sibelius and "The Lark Ascending" by Sir Ralph Vaughn William.*

Remembering Roger Corless

Roger Corless, who was a bridge between East and West enjoyed telling a story which he cherished. It was based upon the words of his English mother, who commented to him once about his appearance at birth. I can almost visualize Roger again smiling with his eyes not quite in a happy squint. His mother had remarked, "Yes, you looked yellow." He loved telling that story which suggested reincarnation.

Roger had, in addition to a facility with a wide range of scholarly and religious interests, a cultivated sense of humor about life, and the way scholars' minds work. Of course, he also cultivated his own wry sense of his own complexity and enjoyed playing the role of mediator (between East and West).

We were fortunate to have Professor Corless make contributions to six volumes of *The Merton Annual*. These six contribu-

---

*Monetary memorial gifts are being received by the Society for Buddhist-Christian Studies to be used toward the 8th International Buddhist-Christian Dialogue to be held in 2009. Gifts should be sent to SBCS Corless Memorial Fund, CSSR Executive Office, Rice University MS 156, P. O. Box 1892, Houston, TX   77251-1892, or to donate by credit card, call 713-348-5721.

tions consistently raised healthy questions about the intersections of religious tradition, belief, and intellectual inquiry.

In honor of Roger J. Corless we are including a slightly abridged version of his "The Christian Explanation of non-Christian Religions: Merton's Example and Where it Might Lead." We do this because upon his death, Professor Corless, in the very spirit of the article included below, was preparing another article to be included for this volume about "Hinduism and Prayer." In place of that we are pleased to offer our readers this essay which is done so well in the best manner of Roger Corless and in the spirit of Merton.

(V.A.K.)

The Christian Exploration of Non-Christian Religions: Merton's Example and Where It Might Lead Us

Roger Corless

Merton was a bellwether for the Catholic Church. His thinking changed constantly throughout his life and with each change he was always slightly ahead of important movements in the reform of Catholic spirituality in the twentieth century. It was significant that he was only *slightly* ahead of his time. Had he been too far ahead of the church he might have been ignored or condemned, but somehow, he managed to be the first to express what was on the tips of the tongues of many Catholics. This, I believe, is the secret of his popularity, both during his life and now, so many years after his death.[1]

I have suggested that he went through a number of stages, trailing, like the Pied Piper, the church (even, *mirable dictu*, the Vatican itself) behind him, beginning, after his rejection of secularism, with what I have called Romantic Medievalism, marked by the publication of his best-selling *The Seven Storey Mountain* (New York: Harcourt, Brace & Co., 1948). His next stage was Romantic Orientalism in which he became enamored of a variety of East Asian religious traditions, notable Philosophical Taoism (Lao Tzu and Chuang Tzu) and Buddhism. At first, he learnt much of Buddhism from his contact with D.T. Suzuki, an important but, as we are beginning to see, ambiguous figure in the dissemination of the Buddha Dharma to the West.[2] Suzuki was regarded in the West as a Zen Master, and although he did not claim the title he did nothing to deny it. He was never authenticated as a Zen teacher, he may never have attained the *satori* (Zen awakening) to which his later writings allude, and in Japan he is known as an adherent of Shin, the form of Buddhism which advocates trust in and surrender to Amida Buddha over what it regards as the ineffectiveness of so-called 'miscellaneous practices' such as Zen sitting and *koan* practice.

Merton was able to recover from the unreliable information he received from D.T. Suzuki, which was not Buddhism as much as it was a triumphalist form of Sino-Japanese monism,[3] during his travels in Asia, where he met Theravadin and Tibetan monks, including HH Dalai Lama XIV.[4] His experience at Polonnaruwa, Sri Lanka, which we might call a 'buddhophany', rings true to the essential teaching of all Buddhist lineages on the lack of inherent existence, the fundamental openness, of reality-as-it-is (called Self-lessness [*anatta*] in Theravada and Emptiness [*shunyata*] in Mahayana).[5] However, he did not stay long with this insight. His speech in Bangkok, which in the event became his final testament, revealed his growing interest in Marxism, and may have presaged a move, cut short by his untimely death, towards Liberation Theology, which was beginning to gain popularity in South and Central America. Since his time, Liberation Theology has undergone many changes, partly in response to Vatican attacks. Had Merton lived, he might have participated in these changes (as Novice Master he taught Ernesto Cardenal and was much influenced by him) or he might have moved on to something quite different.

We are still trying to follow, and catch up with, Merton. This essay will attempt to build on Merton's suggestions, focusing on his interaction with Buddhism, the non-Christian religion which interested him the most.[6] I have already published my analysis of the strengths and weaknesses of Merton's interactions with Buddhism, in the two articles mentioned above, and I respectfully refer the reader to them for a more detailed introduction. Here, I will propose where his insights might lead us.

Exclusivism and Inclusivism

It is sometimes said that Christians have no business conversing with other religious traditions: Christianity is the truth from God, other religions are false or are the deceptions of the devil, and non-Christians are damned to hell. On the other hand, it is claimed that, since God is the God of all and wills the salvation of all, no-one is outside the love of God. These two views, of exclusivism and inclusivisn, are found in the Bible, and they have existed side by side throughout Christian history. In the early church, inclusivism was the more popular view—the Fathers generally maintained that God's salvific grace was brought to fulfillment in Jesus but that it had been at work before his appearance. The classic statement is that of Justin Martyr. Basing himself on Jn. 1.1-18, Justin said, 'And those who live according to Principle (Logos) are Christians, even though accounted atheist.'[7] During the Middle

Ages, inclusivism lost ground and the statement *extra ecclesiam nulla salus est* ('outside the church there is no salvation') based upon St. Augustine's theology of universal sin, became popular.[8] At the Reformation, this was picked up by John Calvin, who claimed that works done out of Christ are worthless, and it dominated Tridentine Catholic missiology. St. Francis Xavier, for example, lamented that there were so many heathens in India to be baptized (who would otherwise go to hell) that he did not have time to eat, sleep, or pray.[9]

Recently, the Catholic Church has revived the inclusivist position and given it official recognition, beginning with the Second Vatican Council which proclaimed that 'the Catholic Church rejects nothing of what is true and holy in these [non-Christian] religions' and that they 'often reflect a ray of that truth which enlightens all men.'[10] On the basis of this, Pope Paul VI set up the Secretariat for Non-Christian Religions in 1964. In 1989 it was reorganized, and given permanent status, as the Pontifical Council for Interreligious Dialogue (PCID). The PCID is now the principal actor in an ongoing commitment by the Vatican to dialogue, rather than confrontation, with those who do not explicitly own to faith in Christ. Stimulated by the PCID, Catholic monks and nuns have engaged in profound and fruitful exchanges with Buddhist monks and nuns under the auspices of the Monastic Interreligious Dialogue (MID) program.[11]

However, these recent developments at the official level have not resolved, but rather intensified, the theological tension between exclusivism and inclusivism. Raising dialogue to prominence by giving it a permanent Vatican office has put the exclusivists on the alert. Too much dialogue, they fear, dilutes the claim that Jesus (the personal, individual Jesus, not the universal Logos) is the one and only Savior. Several Vatican documents now propose some version of inclusivism (under the rubric of 'dialogue') and exclusivism (variously called 'mission,' 'proclamation' or 'announcement') simultaneously, insisting that they must be balanced, but not explaining how to effect this balance. For example, *Redemptoris Missio* (7 December 1990) baldly states 'salvation comes from Christ...dialogue does not dispense from evangelization,' leaving it up to us to decide what that means in practice.[12] Most recently, *Ecclesia in Asia* (6 November 1999), the papal response to the Synod for Asia held in April 1998, has deepened the mystery. Father Michael Amaldoss, SJ of Vidyajyoti College of Theology,

New Delhi, shrewdly notes that 'one can pick up encouraging quotes [from *Ecclesia in Asia*] to support any activity in which the church is engaged.'[13]

Merton, already in his day ahead of the church, was definitely on the side of universalism. His legacy is encapsulated in his remark that 'by openness to Buddhism…we stand a wonderful chance of learning more about the potentiality of our own traditions.'[14] We can now enter into his legacy and ask how we can move beyond it, considering how the church can be as open as possible to the fullness of Buddhism (dialogue) without compromising the fullness of the Christian message (proclamation).

Beyond Merton's Legacy

In the Christian exploration of Buddhism there are, as I see it, three levels in the movement from contact with to full dialogue between Buddhism and Christianity. At the most basic level, Christianity can learn from Buddhism, and Buddhism can in turn learn from Christianity; secondly, Christianity and Buddhism can renew themselves on the basis of their mutual education; and finally, Buddhism and Christianity, thus renewed, can participate in a global spiritual renewal.

The first level is open to all Christians who come into contact with Buddhism from an inclusivist perspective, and it happens more or less automatically. True dialogue differs from monologue in that both parties strive to listen to each other, to learn from each other, and to allow themselves to be challenged and changed. It is a mark of a living system that it changes, and it is a sign of maturity in a person, or system, that there is no fear of change in and of itself. From a theological perspective, the renewal of the church is a work of the Holy Spirit that it would be sinful to quash. In this essay I will restrict myself to suggesting some ways in which Christianity can learn from Buddhism and postpone to a later date suggestions on how Buddhism can learn from Christianity.

Having learnt from each other, and begun to change because of what they have learnt, Christianity and Buddhism can renew themselves to the point that they will cease to exist as we know them at present. This is not as radical as it might sound—it has already happened many times. It is a truism that even the most radically reformist Christians never imagine that they are literally, in every respect, down to the language and customs, restoring the church, or churches, as it was or they were in the days of St. Paul.

In a real sense, the church of the Apostles, the church of the Middle Ages, and so forth, have ceased to exist so that the church of today could come into being. We seem to be at another point in history where the church will undergo such a change that, were we able to see the future, we might say that the church had disappeared.

These two levels of dialogue are like the warm-up band that prepares the audience for the featured artists. Having gone through the mutual learning and renewal process, the transformed traditions will be able to assist, provoke, and participate in, the spiritual renewal of the entire planet.

In what follows I will expand and build upon some of my earlier suggestions about renewal, to which I again respectfully refer the reader who is unfamiliar with my work.[15] I will arrange my suggestions broadly in accordance with the three ascending levels of dialogue, but since the levels are interdependent, and their categories somewhat porous, I will not rigidly tie any one suggestion to a particular level of dialogue. The reader should, however, notice a movement upwards (or inwards) towards an ever richer sense of communion between Christianity and Buddhism.

Anonymous Dualism

Officially, Christianity is not dualistic. Indeed, it stigmatizes dualists as Gnostics, Bogomils, Cathars, and so forth, and has in the past tried to exterminate them, proclaiming the incarnation of the God-Man as the definitive answer to such heresies. In practice, Christianity is often very dualistic, but it is not in the habit of admitting or even recognizing it. Paul Knitter has called this 'anonymous dualism' and has suggested that an examination of Merton's dialogue with Buddhism might help to cure the church of its unofficial schizophrenia.[16] I agree, but I enter a caveat.

Much of the dialogue (especially in Europe, as noted above) has been between Benedictines and Japanese Zen Buddhists. This seems to work well at first, since everyone gets along so famously. Benedictines, with their motto of *Pax*, do not with to offend, and the Zen Buddhists, being Japanese, are culturally conditioned to be courteous. But these social strengths are also theological weaknesses, since no one is ready for the cut-and-thrust of lively doctrinal debate. Worse still, Zen Buddhists have a tendency to deemphasize doctrine in favor of aestheticism, lapsing into a version of the uncritical Sino-Japanese monism which bedeviled the books of D.T. Suzuki. It is fairly soon obvious that this does not go anywhere.[17] The formalities of introduction completed, we need to bring on the theologians and dharmologians.[18] When Jesuits are true to their heritage (and a surprising number of them have fallen victim to Sino-Japanese esthetic monism) they like to debate, and they are good at it. Their worthy adversaries in debate are not the Zen Buddhists but the Tibetans, the T'ien-t'ai (Tendai) Buddhists of East Asia, and the Theravadin specialists in Abhidhamma.

The Tibetan Buddhists, especially those of the Gelugpa lineage (the lineage to which the Dalai Lama belongs) are trained in debate as an important part of their monastic formation. They are in principle opposed to the formless (imageless or aniconic) sitting practices of Zen, regarding them as dangerous temptations to grasp on to Emptiness as a concept or idea, thus becoming, as Nagarjuna said, incurable:

> Emptiness has been declared by the Conquerors
> (i.e., the Buddhas) as
> The purgative of all viewpoints; whoever regards Emptiness
> itself as a
> Viewpoint is declared incurable.[19]

In order to use Emptiness as a medicine the Gelugpas engage in spirited, noisy, but precisely regulated, debate. The aim is not to destroy the opponent but to sharpen the insight of both the protagonist and the antagonist. The goal is wisdom, the motivation is compassion—since, without wisdom, unskillful actions will continue to produce suffering. Buddhist-Christian debate could learn much from this approach. Upon the successful conclusion of such a debate there would be no aesthetically pleasing but intellectually mushy monism or unrecognized dualism, there would be greater insight. Particularly, the subtlety and strength of the positions on each side would be brought out. It would help to reassure both Buddhists and Christians that indifferentism is not the goal of dialogue, but rather mutual understanding. A major point of mutual understanding concerns the presence or absence of God in the two systems. There are Christians who assume that, whatever a Buddhist might say, there is a belief in God hidden somewhere in the Dharma. Most Buddhists are too polite to object that this view is quite erroneous, and it took a Gelugpa teacher to call it like it is.[20]

The Tien-t'ai Buddhists of China belong to a lineage which was formed to contain all the doctrines and practices of all the varieties of Buddhism known to the founder, Chih-i (531-597), and to balance study and meditation. Ch'an Buddhism is a fragment which broke out of the grand synthesis of T'ien-t'ai, and Zen, the Japanese derivative of Ch'an, developed into a lineage with a more or less exclusive concentration on one or two practices (*zazen* and *koan*), rendering it unsuitable for extended dialogue with more comprehensive traditions such as Catholic Christianity. It has to be realized that the Japanese Buddhist traditions, particularly as they regrouped during the Kamakura Shogunate (a grouping that largely survives to the present day), which have up to now dominated the dialogue between East Asian Buddhists and Catholics, are unusual precisely in respect of their separation into exclusivist lineages. Other forms of East Asian Buddhism have remained more inclusive, or eclectic. The appropriate balance between doctrine and practice, for example, is a central concern of Korean Buddhism, and the right relationship between Zen style meditation and the more devotional style of meditation found in Pure Land Buddhism (forms which are split into separate lineages in Japan) is important to Vietnamese Buddhism. Chinese, Korean, and Vietnamese Buddhist traditions are, on the whole, better prepared than most Japanese Buddhist traditions to enter into dialogue with the full range of Catholic doctrine and practice.

Theravada, the Buddhism of South Asia, has a single 'philosophy' or explanatory system, Abhidhamma (a word we might translate as 'advanced teaching'). Specialists in Abhidhamma are a match for Christian theologians in a way that virtuous but unscholarly monks, or random teachers of Insight Meditation, the abbreviated form of Theravada meditation practice popular in the West, are not. For example, an honest debate between Theravadin and Christian scholars could illuminate the vexed question of why systems which attribute the causes of events respectively to a Creator God and to interdependent arising (*paticca-samuppada*) are apparently incompatible, or at least irrelevant to each other.

The direction in which sophisticated dialogue between intellectual equals might go is indicated by John Keenan, whose *The Meaning of Christ: A Mahayana Theology*[21] is a fine example of what can happen when Buddhist, rather than Greco-Roman, philosophical ideas are allowed to interact with and inform the Christian message. Keenan's book goes a long way towards healing anonymous dualism in Christianity.[22]

Default Idolatry

Officially, once again, Christianity is bitterly opposed to idolatry, but in practice it gets stuck on images of God. We all know that 'really' God is not an old man in the sky, yet we speak of God as *Him* and blithely attribute human thoughts, emotions, and actions to 'him.' Perhaps we think that if we do not speak of God as *him* then the only other option would be to speak of God as *It*. All but the most radically feminist Christians display an immediate distaste for the image of God as female. It seems to bring up fears of paganism, perhaps because the Hebrew Bible generally reserves female imagery for the deities of 'the nations,' although there are a few passages in which female imagery is used for the God of Israel.[23] Buddhism can help us find a middle way by showing us how to assert the *existence* of an object or being while denying its *inherent existence*.

The Madhyamika explanatory system (or philosophy) of Mahayana Buddhism asserts the existence of a thing at the level of conventional truth. It then asks us to point out where *precisely* that object is. We find that although we can point to the object in general we cannot point to its essence, and the more specific we try to get in regard to the existence of the thing in space and time the less precise we can be. We are thus forced to assert that, in the ultimate sense, the thing does not exist. But this is not the end of the matter. Clearly there is something there, and what we have shown is not its non-existence but the absence of *inherent* existence, the emptiness (*shunyata*) or, as I prefer to translate, the transparency of the thing's existence. We are forced to return to the statement that the thing exists, but with the realization that it simultaneously does not exist. This is called the Middle Truth and is the final teaching on Emptiness or Transparency as the nature of reality.

This insight can be applied to Chritian notions of God by transforming the epistemological statements of Madhyamika to ontological statements suitable to Christian theology. The movement is from cataphatic to apophatic and back again.[24] First, we assert the existence of God, listing all his qualities according to standard cataphatic theology. Then we try to be as precise as possible about God's existence, locating God exactly in space and time. We find that the exercise is impossible, that the more precise we try to be the more absurd our search becomes, and we are forced to conclude that ultimately God does not exist. This is the position of negative or apophatic theology. But, again, this is not the end of the matter, for the Christian God is not merely an abstraction, a Cosmic Mind, but is incarnate as Jesus Christ, who is (or was while on earth) locatable in space and time. We thus return to the statement that God exists, but with the realization that God simultaneously does not exist. This is the standard Nicene Christology, that the divinity and the humanity are simultaneously present in Christ in the mode of co-inherence (Greek: *perichoresis*; Latin: *circumincessio*).[25] When we view God in this way we assert his existence but not as a solid or reified 'thing' or idol.

The feminist reader will have noticed that I have used the masculine pronoun for God. This was deliberate, but not because I wish to claim that God is male. Apophatically, God is supra-personal and so without gender, but cataphatically God is a person and must manifest gender or be relegated to a sub-personal object. Having liberated ourselves, by contact with Buddhism, from default idolatry in regard to the Christian God, we can allow God to have a fluid personality and a shifting or multidimensional gender. It is not a Buddhist, but a very Christian mystic, who is our guide here—Mother Julian of Norwich (c.1347-c.1420). In different passages of her *Showings* or *Revelation of Love* she calls God by male and female titles, and sometimes she unhesitatingly combines these antinomies in a single sentence: 'And thus I saw God enioyeth that is our fader, God enioyeth that he is moder, and God enioyeth that he is our very spouse, and our soule is his lovid wife.'[26]

Mother Julian was, I am sure she would be amused to discover, very postmodern. Or, we could say, she realized that God definitely exists but not inherently. God's existence is empty, it does not have, as the schoolmen mistakenly thought, *aseitas* or *quidditas*. Realizing this, we can be free to address God differently in different contexts. As sovereign of the universe, he is Lord. As revealed in what the Fathers called the Second Bible, the Book of nature, she is Mother. As devoted lover, he is male or she is female depending on the sex and the sexual preference of the devotee. As source of all, God is supra-personal Light. (At the end of Chapter 83, Mother Julian calls God 'our endless day.') What effect would it have on Catholic spirituality if the English liturgy were to be rewritten in this consciousness of God's multidimensionality?[27]

Universal Compassion

Christian compassion (*caritas*) is limited in a way that Buddhist compassion (*karuna*) is not. Although Christianity occasionally, especially in the Celtic tradition, reverences non-human life, it focuses almost exclusively on humans as creatures of God and the sole objects of God's love. Occasionally it has even sanctioned the destruction of non-human life on the basis of the argument that only humans have souls which can be redeemed. It is a straight line from this myopic view to the practice of factory farming and the lack of concern for, and the destruction of, the biosphere.[28]

Buddhism cannot make sense of this limitation. Any being which manifestly seeks pleasure and avoids pain is a *sattva*, a sentient being which can and, in time will, be reborn as any other sentient being, and which has, finally, the potential for attaining Buddhahood. Buddhist ethical conduct even extends to insentient things, since the emphasis is on the intention of the actor as much as on the effect the recipient of the action. If I slam a door without thinking about it, or, if I do think about it, say to myself, 'It's only a door, it can't feel anything' I am practicing callousness. Since the door is insentient it is not affected one way or another, but the next time I meet a sentient being I may find that I act in a callous manner, since I have built up a habit of callousness. The Vietnamese Buddhist monk Thich Nhat Hanh impressed Thomas Merton when he told him that his training included many years learning how to close a door.

Were Christians to learn from Buddhists to respect all sentient life and act towards inanimate objects as they would toward sentient beings, vexed questions such as abortion would be handled with greater wisdom, compassion, and sophistication. It would be realized that human abortion cannot be considered apart from the routine abortion of animals in factory farming, nor can it be separated from broader ecological or ecosophical[29] concerns of how we treat the environment as a whole.

Meditation

Perhaps the most obvious and immediate result of Christian dialogue with Buddhism is the revival of Christian meditation techniques. Christians are struck that Buddhists, at least those Buddhists who teach in the West, place so much emphasis on meditation. Most often, this dialogue could be described, in tennis terms, as 'Advantage: Buddhism.' The Christians capitulate and start sitting on *zafus* and ringing bells, imagining themselves to be Zen Buddhists. Some Christians are more aware of their own tradition and they are stimulated to look into their past and dust off their meditation manuals, coming up with quasi-Buddhist techniques such as Centering Prayer (once again, on a *zafu*, if you please).

The haphazard nature of this interchange should be brought to order. The variety of Christian and Buddhist meditation techniques should be classified according to content and goal, and they should then be matched, as far as possible, with each other. It will take some discussion to decide what are the main forms of meditation in each tradition, especially in Buddhism, where pan-Buddhist meditation practice is unusual. Theravadin, Tibetan (both Sutrayana and Vajrayana), T'ien-t'ai, Zen, and Pure Land seem to be the main candidates in Buddhism, and Benedictine, Dominican, Franciscan, Jesuit, and Sulpician the chief methods in Catholicism. It then could be that, for example, Soto Zen 'just sitting' (*shikantaza*) and Sulpician 'just looking' (*contemplatio*) might form a fruitful dyad, as also perhaps Tibetan liturgies involving chanting and visualization (*sadhana*) and Benedictine psalmody and the celebration of Mass (*opus dei*). All this needs much more careful thought than I can give it here. And, be it noted, if it turns out that matched dyads are difficult to identify, this will teach us something important about the difference between Buddhist and Christian meditation.

Monastic Interchange

The lifestyle of the Buddhist *bhikshu* and *bhikshuni* is sufficiently close to that of the Christian monk and nun that we have become accustomed to translating the two Buddhist terms by the two Christian terms, as if they were identical. There are, in fact, important differences, at the same time as there are remarkable similarities and resonances. In Buddhism, for instance, the Christian coenobium presided over by an abbot has not developed, but something clubby enough to be mistaken for it allows dialogue between *communitas* and *sangha* (the Buddhist monastic community) to take place. Again, by no means all those who are called, in English, Buddhist monks, are vowed to celibacy, yet their meditative traditions are sufficiently similar to that of Christian monks for this difference to be ignored in practice, as long as the value of celibacy itself is not the topic of discussion.

It was at the level of monastic exchange that Thomas Merton made perhaps his greatest contribution to interfaith dialogue. He felt most at ease with Buddhists when they were monastics. Although the difference in doctrine (especially, the belief or disbelief in the existence of God) are so extreme that the other's viewpoint may be unintelligle, monks and *bhikshus*, nuns and *bhikshunis*, recognize that, somehow, they are in the same line of business.

The dialogue between Buddhist and Christian moanstics is now, as stated above, a prominent feature of Catholic interfaith activity, and I do not have to do much more here than applaud it and wish it long life and continued growth. I would like, however, to repeat my call for the setting up of a double Buddhist-Christian monastery which would, over the long term, nurture the monastic interfaith dialogue at its most profound level, that of daily practice of the different traditions in the full consciousness of each other's presence.[30] This could support the intelligent, prayerful and meditative renewal of such key texts as the *Regula monachorum* and the *Vinaya Pitaka* (the basic Buddhist monastic regulations).

The insights gained from this renewal of the life of traditional monastics under vows could then be applied to wider questions of community. Monastic communities are pre-eminently 'families of choice,' and their experience and accumulated wisdom could be of great benefit to the formation and health of the many non-monastic families of choice that are gaining in popularity just as (strident voices to the contrary notwithstanding) biological families are becoming increasingly irrelevant.

Co-Inherent Consciousness

And now, our feature presentation…the transformation of the cosmos! A big task, but nothing less than is implied in the Christian vision of the New Jerusalem in Revelation 21 and the Buddhist goal of the end of all suffering forever.

Because nirvana is expressed in negative terms, as the end of suffering, or the emptying of *samsara* (cyclic existence) it is often mistaken for nihilism. Nihilism (called *ucchedavada* in Buddhism, the view that nothing at all exists), however, is only the other side of eternalism (*nityavada*, the view that permanent entities exist) or essentialism (*svabhavavada*, the view that there are self-existing entities isolated from the matrix of interdependent arising). Nihilism is still within the purview of dualistic mind, and is not, said the Buddha, the end of all suffering forever. Nirvana can also be described as bliss (*sukha*) but it is unalloyed bliss, never-ending and untainted by any suffering (*duhkha*) and it cannot be imagined as merely an absence of pain. In Mahayana Buddhism, nirvana is taught as coterminous with samsara—not as identical with it, but co-inherent with it. Vajrayana (Tantric Buddhism) gleefully calls nirvana Great Bliss (*mahasukha*) or the Diamond Realm (*Vajradhatu*), visualizing the co-inherence of samsara and nirvana as a glittering palace mandala.[31]

The transformed cosmos in Revelation 21 is called a city, but it is a very curious one. It is a cube, twelve thousand furlongs in length, breadth, and height. Its walls are diamond and the city is made 'of pure gold, like clear glass' (v. 18) – perhaps it is a kind of translucent gold that shines from within. The foundations are layers of twelve different kinds of gems and its twelve gates are each made from a single pearl. It is lit eternally from inside and 'nothing unclean may come into it' (v. 27). Curious, perhaps, but strangely familiar. It is a mandala, the Palace of the Triune God, protected from the impurities of the temporal world by its *vajra* fence.

The New Jerusalem does not stay in heaven, it 'come[s] down out of heaven from God' (Rev. 21.2) to replace the old earth, which 'had disappeared' (v. 1). If the Christian heaven is located elsewhere than earth, anonymous dualism has returned to our vision; but if the Christian heaven is identified with the earth as it is now, the Work of Christ is rendered vain. The new heaven and the new earth must be, as Charles Williams realized, simultaneously present, that is, co-inherent.[32] And this, of course, is precisely how Nagarjuna understands the relationship between samsara and nirvana: 'Nirvana's limit is the limit of samsara; not even the subtlest something is observed between them.'[33]

I have argued that co-inherence is the natural state of the evolved consciousness in both Christianity and Buddhism, and that in this consciousness, or super-consciousness, the dichotomy between absolute and relative is sublated, that is, contained and superseded, yet without being abolished. In this consciousness, the dualities between samsara and nirvana are sublated, without admixture or the dominance of one over the other; and, again, the opposites of the divine and human natures in Christ, as understood by the Council of Nicea, are sublated, without admixture or the dominance of one over the other.[34]

Now, I wish to go further and claim that, as the dialogue between Buddhism and Christianity becomes richer and more fruitful it will propel many Buddhists and Christians into this co-inherent consciousness. Christians and Buddhists would, then, no longer feel the need to identify themselves as Christians or Buddhists (or both or neither) for they would each severally live in both and both would live in them. More and more people are reporting multiple loyalties to different traditions, and Merton (slightly ahead of us as usual) may have been moving in this direction when, leaving for his fateful Asian journey, he told Brother David Steindl-Rast that he intended to become as good a Buddhist as he could.[35] If this occurs, the traditions will become co-inherent, sublating each other without admixture or the dominance of one over the other. The full co-inherence of Buddhism and Christianity might then become a model for the co-inherence of other, perhaps of all, religious traditions.[36] In that case, the dilemma of choosing between the contradictory activities of dialogue and proclamation will be solved, not by collapse into indifferentism or a triumphalist victory of one tradition over another, but by a sublation into co-inherence, in which each tradition subsists fully in itself, without confusion with another tradition, as Christians say is the case for the divine and human natures in Christ and Mahayana Buddhists say is the case for nirvana and samsara.

This consciousness, in which many absolutes co-inhere, in which we live in many absolutes and many absolutes live in us, may be the structure of the consciousness of certain major religious figures. Buddhists are as reluctant to speak of how Buddha's mind works as Christians are reticent about the mind of Christ, but it may be that the *structure* of their minds (the *content* of their minds may indeed be forever beyond our understanding) was (is) co-inherent.[37] If the noosphere (as Teilhard de Chardin called the planetary environment of ideas) evolves such that co-inherence becomes the norm rather than the rare attainment of a few great minds, it will, to all intents and purposes, be new, and it will need a new name. I suggest calling it a *polyverse of symperichoretic multiple absolutes*. It would be a *polyverse* because it is a meta-system of an indefinite number of universes, and it would contain *multiple*, or an indefinite number of, *absolutes* in the mode of *symperichoresis* or full co-inherence.[38] A cumbersome term, I fear, and, if co-inherent consciousness comes about, we may not need it, for the condition will be normal and obvious. If that state of consciousness is genuinely new, we cannot at the moment imagine what it would be like, but if it becomes the norm, we will marvel mightily about our ancestors who, we will tell our wide-eyed children, believed, despite all the evidence to the contrary, that there was only one universe and one absolute and that 'absolute' and 'relative' were eternally opposed fundamental givens of reality. We will then awaken to a greater spiritual richness and, I would hope, to a nobler humanity.

Notes

1. For a detailed study of this issue see my 'Fire on the Seven Storey Mountain: Why Are Catholics Looking East?', *Toward an Integrated Humanity: Thomas Merton's Journey* (ed. M. Basil Pennington, OCSO; Cistercian Studies Series, 103; Kalamazoo: Cistercian Publications, 1988), pp. 204-21.

2. For a discussion of the uneven relationship between D.T. Suzuki and Thomas Merton, in which it appears that Merton honestly tried to learn about Buddhism from Suzuki but Suzuki was not interested in, and even despised, Christianity, see my 'In Search of a Context for the Merton-Suzuki Dialogue', *The Merton Annual 6* (1993) pp. 76-91.

3. For discussion on the triumphalism of Zen missions to the west, and the 'other side' of D.T. Suzuki, see James W. Heisig and John C. Maraldo (eds.) *Rude Awakenings: Zen, the Kyoto School, and the Question of Nationalism* (Honolulu: University of Hawai'i Press, 1995).

4. A moving tribute to Merton by the Dalai Lama, who refers to himself as 'one of his Buddhist brothers', was delivered at the end of the July 1996 Buddhist-Christian retreat at Gethsemani Abbey. Donald W. Mitchell and James A. Wiseman OSB (eds.), *The Gethsemani Encounter* (New York: Continuum, 1998), pp. 260-61.

5. The account of the experience at Polunnaruwa is in Thomas Merton, *The Asian Journal of Thomas Merton* (ed. Naomi Burton *et al.*; New York: New Directions, 1973) pp. 233-36.

6. See, for example, such remarkably prescient books as Thomas Merton, *Mystics and Zen Masters* (New York: Farrar, Straus & Giroux, 1967) and *idem, Zen and the Birds of Appetite* (New York: New Directions, 1968).

7. καὶ ο μετὰ λόγου βι\σαντες, Χριστιανοί ε σι, κἄν ἄθεου ἐνομιαθήσαν. Justin, *1 Apol.*, 46 (Patrologia Graeca, v. 6, col. 397)

8. The interpretation of this apparently clear dictum has never been straight-forward. See Francis A Sullivan, SJ, *Salvation Outside the Church? Tracing the History of the Catholic Response* (Mahwah, NJ: Paulist Press, 1992) I am indebted to Professor Terrence Tilley of the University of Dayton for this reference.

9. 'When I go into those villages, the children do not give me the leisure (*no me dexavan*) to recite my Office, to eat or to sleep, until I have taught them some prayers.' *Epistolae Sancti Francisci Xaverii aliaque eius scripta* (ed. G. Schurhammer, SI and I. Wicki, SI; Rome: 1944), vol. I, p. 148, lines 21-23.

10. *Nostra ætate*. Section 2. *Interreligious Dialogue: The Official Teaching of the Catholic Church (1963-1995)* (ed. Fransesco Gioia; Boston: Paulist Books and Media, 1994), p. 38.

11. In Europe, the exchange has been largely between Benedictines and Japanese Buddhists, whereas in the USA the Tibetan Buddhists have been more prominent with, once again, Benedictines on the Christian side. For the European dialogue, see Mitchiko Ishigami-Iagolnitzer, *Dialogue interreligieux monastique Bouddhistes- Chrétiens au Japon at en Europe* (Paris: Sciences et Lettres, 1992). The exchange in the USA remains largely unstudied and information on it must be gleaned from the *Bulletin Monastic Interreligious Dialogue*, published at Gethsemani Abbey.

12. English text printed in Gioia, *Interreligious Dialogue*, p. 102. See also the extended discussion on the Secretariat for Non-Christian Religions document 'The Attitude of the Church toward Followers of Other Religions: Reflections and Orientation on Dialogue and Mission (May 10, 1984)', Gioia, *Interreligious Dialogue*, pp. 566-80, which reads as if it had been written by at least two different people (and, given what ones knows about how Vatican documents are produced, that may indeed be the case). The analytical index of *Interreligious Dialogue* rewards careful study.

13. 'Proclamation vs. Dialogue: Mixed Reactions to Pope's Call for Conversion of Asia', *National Catholic Reporter*, 3 December 1999.

14. Merton, *Asian Journal*, p. 343.

15. In addition to the articles already mentioned, see my Christian Perspective on Buddhist Liberation', in Claude Geffré and Mariasusai Dhavamony (eds.), *Buddhism and Christianity* (Concilium, 116; New York: Seabury Press, 1975), pp. 74-87. I build upon and modify this early work in 'Some Buddhist Contributions to Catholic Theology', a paper read at the conference on The Future of the American Church: From Dream to Reality to Vision: 25 Years after Vatican II, held in Washington, DC, September 1990. This paper remains at the moment unpublished.

16. Paul K. Knitter, 'Thomas Merton's Eastern Remedy for Christianity's "Anonymous Dualism"', *Cross Currents* 31.3 (Fall 1981) pp. 285-95.

17. For a critique of this situation and suggestions of how to move beyond it, see my 'Sense and Nonsense in Buddhist-Christian Intermonastic Dialogue', *Monastic Studies* 19 = Buddhist and Christian Monasticism (1991), pp. 11-22.

18. The neologism 'dharmologian' is suggested as the Buddhist counterpart of 'theologian,' but some scholars are comfortable with the phrase 'Buddhist theology' despite the absence in Buddhism of a God as recognized by Christianity. See the articles in Roger R. Jackson and John J. Makransky (eds.), *Buddhist Theology: Critical Reflections by Contemporary Buddhist Scholars* (Curzon Critical Studies in Buddhism; Richmond, Surry, UK: Curzon Press, 2000), including my 'Hermeneutics and Dharmology: Finding an American Buddhist Voice', pp. 95-107.

19. *Mūlamadhyamakakārikā* 13.8 (my translation)

20. Thubten Losel, 'Buddhist-Christian Dialogue—a Prolegomena [sic]', in M. Darrol Bryant and Frank Flinn (eds.), *Interreligious Doctrine: Voices from a New Frontier* (New York: Paragon House, 1989), pp. 191-97.

21. Maryknoll, NY: Orbis, 1989.

22. I have made some suggestions myself in 'Can Buddhism Validate the Truth of God Incarnate?' *Modern Theology* 3.4 (july 1987) pp. 333-43.

23. The Hebrew Bible commonly uses the mythologem of the Sky Father for the transcendent God of Israel and the mythologem of the Earth Mother for the gods (goddesses) of the nations. When these mythologems are taken literally they remove the Biblical God fom creation and produce another form of anonymous dualism. Christian mysticism is more this-worldly and can provide a corrective to the acosmicism of the theologians. See my 'The Christian Mystic as *paganus redevivus*: A Hermeneutical Suggestion', *The Merton Annual* 3 (1990), pp. 203-16.

24. For a more exended discussion of this movement see my 'Idolatry and Inherent Existence: The Golden Calf and the Wooden Buddha', in David Loy (ed.), *Healing Deconstruction: Postmodern Thought in Buddhism and Christianity* (Atlanta, GA: Scholars Press, 1996), pp. 11-31

25. Christology has come to prefer the term 'hypostatic union' to 'co-inherence' but that term strongly suggests only an ontological structure. I use the more neutral term co-inherence since it can relate to the ontology of Christology as well as to the epistemology of Madhyamika. Co-inherence can also be a translation of *communicato idiomatum*, which likewise resonates with Dharmological structures.

26. The opening sentence of Ch. 51. Julian of Norwich, *A Revelation of Love*, (ed. Marion Glascoe; Exeter: University of Exeter Press, 1993), p. 81.

27. For a more extended discussion see my 'The Androgynous Mysticism of Julian of Norwich', *Magistra* 1.1 (Summer 1995), pp. 55-71.

28. For the opposite view see the essays in Charles Birch, William Eakin, and Jay McDaniel (eds.), *Liberating Life: Contemporary Approaches to Ecological Theology* (Maryknoll, NY: Orbis Books, 1990) and in Albert

J. LaChance and John E. Carroll (eds.), *Embracing Earth: Catholic Approaches to Ecology* (Maryknoll, NY: Orbis Books, 1994). In 1999 the US and Canadian bishops issued a draft of an ecologically sensitive pastoral letter on the Columbia River and its resources. The final text is expected in 2000. *National Catholic Reporter* (4 June 1999), 'Restoring the Sacred in Nature'.

29. The neologism *ecosophy* has been suggested by Raimundo Panikkar.

30. See my 'The Dialogue of Silence: A Comparison of Buddhist and Christian Monasticism with a Practical Suggestion', in G.W. Houston (ed.), *The Cross and the Lotus: Christianity and Buddhism in Dialogue* (Delhi: Banarsidass, 1985), pp. 81-107.

31. In Buddhism, *mandala* has three basic meanings: (1) the space in which the Buddha sat to gain enlightenment (Sanskrit: *bodhimandala*; Japanese: *dojo*), and, by extension, any place of meditaitive practice; (2) the world seen as an ordered cosmos of beautiful things, offered to one's lama and all the Buddhas, Dharma Teachers, and so forth, of the past, present, and the future; (3) the palace of a deity. The last meaning is the one in question here. It is the commonest use of the word in English, but it is also the most commonly misunderstood. It is not merely a symmetrical diagram, as C.G. Jung thought: the diagram is the two-dimensional blueprint of the three-dimensional reality of the mandala.

32. Charles Williams, *The Descent of the Dove: A Short History of the Holy Spirit in the Church* (repr., Grand Rapids: Eerdmans, 1980 [1939]).

33. *Mūlamadhyamakakārikā* 25.20 (my translation).

34. I advanced this view in a major position article on which much of my later work has been based: 'The Mutual Fulfillment of Buddhism and Christianity in Co-inherent Superconsciousness', in Paul O. Ingram and Frederick J. Streng (eds.), *Buddhist-Christian Dialogue: Mutual Renewal and Transformation* (Honolulu: University of Hawai'i Press, 1986), pp. 115-36.

35. This phenomenon is beginning to be studied. Catherine Cornille of Leuven is preparing a collection of essays by a baker's dozen of scholars with the working title *The Challenges of Multiple Religious Belonging.*

36. See my 'The Coming of the Dialogian: A Transpersonal Approach to Interreligious Dialogue', *Dialogue and Alliance: A Journal of International Religious Foundation* 7.2 (Fall/Winter 1993), pp. 3-17.

37. There is not the space to demonstrate this here, but I have so often come across co-inherence in the description of spiritual or mystical experiences that I suspect that it is this structure, rather than a presumed common content, that is the long-sought universal feature of such states of consciousness.

38. I intend to discuss this more fully in 'Many Selves, Many Realities: The Implications of Heteronymy and the Plurality of Worlds Theory for Multiple Religious Belonging', submitted to *The Challenges of Multiple Religious Belonging*.

The Meeting of Strangers: Thomas Merton's Engagement with Latin America

Malgorzata Poks

From 1957, the year of Ernesto Cardenal's acceptance into the monastery of Gethsemani, the circle of Merton's Latin American contacts was growing rapidly. Though ill health eventually prevented Cardenal (Brother Lawrence) from being a professed Trappist and forced him to leave that demanding Order, both of these contemplative poets remained in close touch, exchanging letters and manuscripts; discussing poetry, politics, and spiritual matters; and collaborating on numerous publishing and translating projects. Thanks to this close friendship with Cardenal, Merton had the sense of becoming part of Nicaragua's intellectual movement.

In 1958 Merton was introduced to Cardenal's cousin, Pablo Antonio Cuadra (1912-2002), who had come to Gethsemani for a brief visit. The extensive correspondence between Merton and Cuadra that followed their initial encounter testifies to an instant mutual understanding and a panoply of shared concerns. The Trappist monk and poet was impressed by Cuadra's poems from his recent volume *El jaguar y la luna* (published in Managua in 1959) and began translating some of them for New Directions. Pioneer of a literary movement known as *la Vanguardia*, Cuadra combined his poetic vocation with those of a publisher and a Christian. He eagerly seized upon the opportunity of winning over the Trappist poet and spiritual master for "our other America."[1] Upon his return to Nicaragua, Cuadra set about spreading Merton's spiritual and poetic message "south of the border," where it was so much needed. Soon he would be sending Merton books and literary reviews to keep him updated on the work of many important poets of the Latin American continent.

In 1959, planning to launch the literary review *El pez y la serpiente,* Cuadra announced his intention to include something of Merton's work in each issue and asked the contemplative poet to become their "Maestro." "Be one of us," urged Cuadra in a letter.[2] The aim of the review whose logo pictured a fish (*pez*) encircled by a serpent (*serpiente*), symbolically uniting the Christian and Indian cultures was to explore Nicaragua's double heritage. It would serve to unite the voices of artists of both Americas in their Christian witness. Cuadra envisioned the journal as a rallying point for all intellectuals working towards a better world.[3] On January 4, 1960, Merton wrote to him: "I shall be delighted to collaborate in the wonderful work."[4] Soon he was sending scores of poems and essays for publication, translating Latin American poets and putting his friends from the "other" America in contact with James Laughlin (of New Directions) and other publishers in the United States. Merton's Latin American translations, accompanied by short biographical notes, were beginning to appear in the *Sewanee Review, Continuum,* and the annual *New Directions* anthologies.

In the meantime, Cardenal had left the Trappists and was temporarily staying in Mexico City with his former college professor, Nicaraguan priest and poet Angel Martínez Baigorri (1899-1971). There, with another compatriot, Ernesto Mejía Sanchez (1923-1985), he started working on a Spanish-language edition of Merton's selected poems. Translated by Cardenal and illustrated by the Nicaraguan-born artist Armando Morales (1927-), this was to be Merton's first collaborative volume, one that Merton thought might even surpass the original English version in artistic merit. About Morales' profoundly spiritual contribution to the work, Merton enthusiastically commented: "What luck, what grace, to collaborate with such a good artist so ready to understand the poems."[5] The understanding that was somewhat slow coming from readers in North America was instantaneous and complete in the other America. Little wonder that Merton's deeply cherished desire to prepare the advent of "the true America" through a concerted creative effort "of creators, of thinkers, of men of prayer"[6] struck a responsive chord among his Latin American acquaintances.

Frequent correspondence between Merton, Cuadra, and Cardenal, revolving mostly around translating and publishing projects, put Merton firmly in touch with the intellectual life of Central America, and before long he would be exchanging letters with new contacts. Angel Martínez was "impressed"[7] upon receiving Merton's letter with a copy of the latter's "Nativity Kerygma"; Mejía Sanchez was eager to see Merton's article on Pasternak ("The Pasternak Affair") published in Mexico. Soon the university press at Mexico's Universidad Nacional Autónoma would be issuing Spanish versions of Merton's poetry and poetic prose, and a literary supplement to *Mexico en la Cultura* would publish Cardenal's translation of Merton's "An Elegy for Ernest Hemingway."

For obvious reasons, politics was an area of concern in 1959, the year of both the Cuban revolution and the Nicaraguan insurrection against Luis Somosa Debayle. The news of the Cuban revolution was greeted by Merton with cautious optimism at first, for he viewed it as offering a chance for a new type of democracy to emerge, one that would represent a "third force" beyond the Gog-Magog alternative, the opposition between the two super-powers about which he had already written. But he soon grew discouraged when he saw how the fear of communism that characterized the US government and the institutional Church forced Castro actually to *choose* communism against Western imperialism, and so the chance was lost. The Nicaraguan insurrection, on the other hand, involved Merton more personally and more directly. Managua's outspoken newspaper *La Prensa*, dedicated to the service of truth and justice[8] and co-edited by Pablo Antonio Cuadra and Pedro Joaquin Chamorro, was suppressed by the Nicaraguan dictator. Cuadra managed to escape repercussions, but many insurgents, Chamorro included, were imprisoned and feared tortured. On July 4, 1959, Merton broke with his "bystander" status and wrote letters to the Nicaraguan president and the Organization of American States to intercede on behalf of these insurgents. His religious superiors were soon to forbid him to make any public statements on political issues, but he would find a way to circumvent the ban by writing personal letters with social and political content, true to his understanding of genuinely "Catholic" action. Over a hundred "Cold War Letters," bound together in a self-edited, mimeographed volume, testify to the scope of Merton's concern.[9]

In September 1961 Merton sent Cuadra a "statement of where I stand, morally, as a Christian writer,"[10] for inclusion in *El pez*. Although he later upbraided himself for the rashness of some of his opinions, "A Letter to Pablo Antonio Cuadra Concerning Giants" was an important event, and not only in Nicaragua. Republished in several other magazines (e.g., the influential *Sur* of Buenos Aires), Merton's open letter to Cuadra was widely read and discussed by Latin American intellectuals, many of whom were moved to write to the author. Cuadra himself called it "one of the great documents of our time."[11] Esther de Cáceres of Uruguay recognized Merton as the only living spiritual master in both Americas, and wrote about her admiration for his integrity as a writer and witness to truth.[12] The stir the article caused would be matched by the publication of *Emblems of a Season of Fury* (1963), the volume of poetry and prose that includes the letter "Concerning Giants"; Merton's translations of five Latin American poets, three of whom are Nicaraguans; and his original poem dedicated to Alfonso Cortés.

When *Emblems* appeared, Cardenal felt "honored" at being published in such a good company,[13] and Cuadra was enthusiastic about the whole volume. Stefan Baciu, a professor of Spanish and Portuguese languages at Washington University,[14] told Merton he was reading *Emblems* with profound emotion.[15] He had already sent Merton his article on César Vallejo, inscribing it with the words: *"A Thomas Merton, grande poeta, amigo de meu amigo Ernesto Cardenal."*[16]

Emblems testified to Merton's growing understanding of the "other" America. Its author was rapidly becoming a rallying point for an ever growing number of Latin American poets, publishers, and intellectuals, who sent Merton their work and busied themselves translating his, while also asking Merton to put them in touch with North American publishers, begging him to contribute to their little magazines, looking to him for spiritual guidance, and, above all, showering him with letters impatient for a reply and urging him to write more and more frequently. The contemplative Merton, ever more attracted to the solitary life of a hermit, could barely cope with the demand these requests put upon him, yet he felt they were an important, even if paradoxical, part of his vocation. The importance he attached to his correspondence with Latin American authors can be gleaned from his effort, beginning in the mid-sixties, to respond to them in Spanish rather than English, though this was much more difficult for him and put an extra demand on his already strained use of time.

Occasionally Merton felt ambivalent about certain magazines publishing his material, preferring not to be identified with their political affiliation. This was the case with the bilingual review *El Corno Emplumado,* or *The Plumed Horn.* Co-edited by Margaret Randall and her husband Sergio Mondragon and published in Mexico, the journal tended to be hostile to the Church, leftist, and sometimes artistically uneven. On January 28, 1963, reflecting on his involvement with *El Corno Emplumado*, Merton jotted down in his notebook: "I am to some extent in sympathy with them and some of their poets are fine but much of it is crass and gross."[17] So he decided to limit his contribution to poetry only, while allowing no private correspondence with Randall to be published. Half a year later he added, with concern for dialogue so typical of him: "Ambivalence about certain poetry magazines. I really think I have no business at all in *El Corno Emplumado*, but still I doubt, like good stuff from Cuba there, and communication must remain open —is this a delusion?"[18] Randall's next letter seemed to prove Merton right. Appreciating Merton's unique contemplative understanding of the world's problems, Randall was eager to discuss important social and political issues with him. Besides, her belief in the New Man of America bridge-builder, constructor of peace, and redeemer of the world coincided with Merton's deepest hopes in the dawning of the new American consciousness which would include both continents. Even though she was soon to see the New Man incarnated in the Cuban proletarian, Merton remained "part of the Corno family,"[19] even allowing Randall to publish more of his letters, which she regarded as "so relevant."[20]

Merton's Cuban contacts are a story in themselves. After the 1961 Bay of Pigs invasion, Merton received a letter from a Cuban refugee woman whose husband had participated in the landing and been captured by the Castro army. She was seeking spiritual guidance from Merton, and her letter initiated a two-year correspondence between them (1961-1963). Merton seemed the right person to whom to turn. In 1958 he had read Czeslaw Milosz's *The Captive Mind*, and the ensuing correspondence with the Polish poet, as well as Merton's involvement with "the Pasternak affair," made him familiar with "ascesis for survival under totalism."[21] This familiarity also explains his caution in contacting his Cuban poet-friends. Merton had no way of knowing whether his letters would even reach them. Mail was censored, and one had to be careful not to arouse the censors' suspicion by an opinion that might be interpreted as critical of the revolution and the new regime. Such a letter would almost certainly implicate the recipients as political subversives. By 1962 Merton had been in correspondence with "a whole little group of most charming people"[22] in Havana converging on Cintio Vitier (1921-), poet, novelist, essayist and literary critic. In addition to Vitier, the poetic circle consisted of his wife Fina Garcia Marruz (1923-), Eliseo Diego (1920-1993), Roberto Friol (1938-), and Octavio Smith (1921-1987). Along with José Lezama Lima (1910-1976) they constituted the core of the *Orígenes* group of Cuban writers. Having been cut off from the world by the Castro regime, this group was hungry for Merton's letters and friendship, his essays and poetry, immediately translating into Spanish everything he sent them. In their political and artistic isolation, these Christian writers depended on Merton's word as well as his contemplative silence to guide and strengthen them. In their letters to Merton they frequently expressed gratitude for his attempts to embrace the entire American hemisphere, and they thanked him for opening, by his work and the exchange of letters, a way of communication between Cuba and the rest of the hemisphere. Merton's own Cuban experience of 1940, which he recorded in *The Secular Journal* and which they apparently knew, allowed them to treat him as part of the spiritual life of Cuba.[23]

Emblems of a Season of Fury was received by this literary group as testimony to Merton's determination to listen to the stranger and to make his voice heard and understood in the larger world. "Charity listens to the voice of the stranger," Vitier wrote on October 4, 1963, unmistakably identifying the volume's "sophianic" leitmotif. Vitier proved to be not only an enthusiastic but also a perceptive and concerned reader of Merton's verse. The letter, along with the enclosed translations into Spanish of some recent verses by Merton especially close to his heart, moved the Gethsemani monk deeply and elicited this telling comment: ". . . the meeting of the strangers. I feel they have profoundly understood everything and I love them."[25] Some years later the Cuban poets meditated deeply on Merton's poem "With the World in My Bloodstream," likening its anguish to something expressed only by Vallejo in the Castilan language, and appreciating in Merton's painful honesty the absolute sincerity of a child. But, Vitier's letter of November 1966 cautiously continues, they could not help detecting something else there, something resembling bitterness and frustration at having chosen a way of life that seemed to permanently close off other choices.[24] They could not have known that this most famous Trappist of the century had just been in love with a woman and in crisis over his vocation.

In Merton's vocabulary, "the stranger" was synonymous with the monk-poet, that is, a person alienated or estranged from the prevailing technological culture of the Western world and from the death and violence that so often underpin it. Merton considered it essential for poets to maintain the attitude of a stranger with respect to the society they lived in, in order to preserve their freedom and innocence. Merton's sense of being "a bramble among the flowers"[26] in his own powerful, successful, and highly industrialized country had the additional advantage of making him feel close to "whole nations of strangers"[27] inhabiting the poorer regions of the world, Latin America in particular. When asked by the Venezuelan poet and publisher Ludovico Silva (1937-1988) to submit an essay describing his typical day for inclusion in an anthology consisting of similar contributions from other writers, Merton gave his essay the title "Day of a Stranger." Published in *Papeles* in 1966, this deeply contemplative essay presents Merton the hermit as free to be his own self beyond any collective illusions, and living in harmony with the natural world. In the silence of his hermitage, the voices of birds fuse with some other voices that "choose themselves" to be heard: these are the voices of poets and writers, which together create a "living balance of spirits."[28]

Among those voices, Ludovico Silva's was not the quietest. Author of *Boom!!! Poema*, he was as preoccupied with the imminent atomic cataclysm as was Merton. Silva's apocalyptic poem about the atomic destruction of the world is a visual shout, its pages dotted with exclamation marks and words written in capital letters. In its content it obviously resonates with Merton's meditation *Original Child Bomb* (1962); in its form it is a telling condemnation of the meaningless "magic of words," the sheer incommunicability of the language of escalation. The exclamation of the atomic apocalypse, Merton stated in a letter to Silva, must be counteracted with the "silent exclamation" of dissent.[29] Naturally, it was the stranger's dissent he had in mind. Silva's poem, published in 1966, was preceded by a prologue (*prológo*) written by Merton. Their joint publication was another reason for Merton to feel included in the Hispanic America's poetry scene.

Ludovico Silva, like a number of Merton's friends by correspondence, was impressed by the Trappist contemplative's knowledge of Latin American poetry[30] and struck by his mystical approach to faith and religion, which was so close to the Latin American heart. He invited Merton to collaborate with him and his friends, first on the magazine *Sol cuello cortado*, and then on *Papeles*, which he was just starting; for a time he even considered publishing a little Merton anthology in Spanish. Heir to the surrealist imagination, Silva was deeply interested in Merton's late poems, wanting to publish in Spanish *Cables to the Ace* and the "epic of madness,"[31] as Merton described *The Geography of Lograire*. Despite all the madness of history, in response to Silva's concern about the future of poetry Merton remarked: "My reaction is totally positive . . . the poets will triumph. We will triumph. God is with the poets. That is why I am especially happy to know that *Boom* has some success with those who know how to read."[32] It was Merton's acquaintance with Latin American poets and poetry that, to a large extent, warranted this optimism.

It is also symptomatic that, while claiming pan-American identity and Latin American sensibility, Merton should always have seen himself affiliated most closely with the Nicaraguan movement in poetry. Nicaragua was to him "a wonderful land which I love and which I inhabit in spirit. The land where I have many friends I have never seen."[33] In the mid-twentieth century Nicaragua was experiencing a massive outpouring of creative energy in the arts, and a poetic fervor was sweeping the country, testifying to the Nicaraguans' ardent search for authentic spiritual values and their longing for life, truth, and hope amid the wasteland of destitution and abusive politics. Symbolically placed at the center of the hemisphere, the country seemed predestined to be at the spearhead of a global movement toward a more lucid consciousness, which would loosen the grip of inauthentic, habitual patterns of thought, pious attitudes of shallow religiosity, and submission to corrupt power. The independence of Nicaraguan publishing from big institutions, literary movements, and the mass media was another inspiring and hopeful sign of intellectual freedom. Merton interpreted the Nicaraguan *sui generis* poetic revolution as the stirrings of a new consciousness, and the awakening of the New Man of America. Merton's Nicaraguan friends: Napolean Chow, Ernesto Cardenal, Pablo Antonio Cuadra, José Coronel Urtecho, Angel Martínez, Alfonso Cortés, and Ernesto Mejía Sanchez were a living proof that the Nicaraguan intellectual was committed to bringing about a real change of consciousness and life through literature as well as through participation in the democratic process.[34] At the time of the Second Vatican Council (1962-1965), Merton dared to believe that the Christian intellectual in Nicaragua, with his broadminded, far-ranging interests, was most predisposed to attain to the goal of the conciliar revolution, namely, to authentic catholicity understood as a truly catholic openness to the world, purged of the narrowly Catholic ideology, which had become merely one more crippling pattern of thought synonymous with European culture.

While the natural alliance of the arts, religion, and politics so characteristic of Latin American countries could bring the whole of Nicaragua closer together in the work for a common goal (the overthrow of the dictator in this particular case), it also carried a risk of its own: that of restricting the artists' creative freedom. Some of Merton's Nicaraguan contacts considered it their duty to turn their backs on Cuba in protest against its growing Stalinist absolutism. When Cardenal declared his and several other poets' determination to boycott the leading Cuban literary magazine *Ventana*, Merton kept encouraging them not to "adopt a policy of withdrawal" so as to avoid letting the magazine "fall completely into the hands of Communists."[35] The Gethsemani contemplative understood his Nicaraguan friends' legitimate apprehension of "guilt by association," but he feared that their protest would seal off the vital avenues of dialogue with the Communist "brother." It was the lay Christian intellectual, he thought, who was best predisposed to shoulder the burden of maintaining the dialogue. To Napolean Chow, a Nicaraguan poet actively involved in the Latin American Christian Democratic Movement, Merton confided in 1963, in the spirit of the recent papal encyclical (1961):

> Politics are of vital importance. The Catholic in Latin America who refuses a priori to have anything to do with politics of any kind, is doing more to destroy the faith than the Catholic who does not refuse, if necessary, to make common cause with the most radical elements.[36]

Chow had written Merton that the Hispanic Christian Democrats, following the social teachings of Jacques Maritain, were trying to unite all the South American countries, Cuba included, in working toward the common good. "If the Christians will not do politics," Chow contested, "others will do it for us."[37] Just as Christian intellectuals should not be afraid to cooperate with people of good will on both sides of the political divide, so poets should not limit their concerns only to "Christian poetry," he believed. In response Merton assured him of his "profound agreement," writing, "Keep sending *Ventana* . I feel that the work you [Christian Democrats] are doing is of great importance."[38]

But it was the Nicaraguans' love for the poor indigenous inhabitants of Ibero-America as well as their commitment to the contemplative dimension of life that was a constant cause for joy for the Trappist writer, and the chief unifying factor between him and his Nicaraguan friends. Contemplatives by nature, they were strangers *par excellence* in the modern world of hectic activism. The literary movement *la Vanguardia* that Pablo Antonio Cuadra had helped launch in 1927 was dedicated to recovering the indigenous, contemplative roots of the Nicaraguan culture, a concern to which Merton could not but wholeheartedly subscribe. Another founder of *la Vanguardia*, José Coronel Urtecho, had abandoned the busy world of urban centers and lived an almost eremitical life in the solitude of Rio San Juan, on the border of Costa Rica. There, as Cardenal reported in his letters,[39] he was reading the Rule of St. Benedict and studying the history of Hispanic America. Around the same time (1962), Ernesto Cardenal was studying theology at La Ceja seminary in Medellin, Columbia, visiting the Cuna Indians on San Blas Islands, and publishing articles about Indian spirituality. Both Cuadra and Cardenal made frequent retreats from their busy lives into the silence of Rio San Juan, where together with Coronel Urtecho they would read Merton's poetry and prose and discuss literature, spirituality and politics. They would also collaborate on various publishing projects involving Merton. Little wonder that Urtecho considered the Gethsemani Maestro a "mysterious link"[40] between them and credited Merton with helping Nicaraguan poets become the most united community of writers in all of Latin America. The communion of poets is a reality, he assured Merton on March 31, 1964, despite their dispersion in diverse places. Cuadra was based in Managua, Cortés was in a sanatorium, Padre Martínez and Carlos Martínez Rivas lived in Mexico, and Cardenal was studying in Colombia, and yet, said Urtecho, they felt united and considered themselves "Merton's disciples in Christ."[41]

In 1964 Cuadra, Cardenal, and Urtecho were busy translating works by Merton for a Latin American Merton Reader that the Rio San Juan poet was planning to publish. Urtecho was convinced it would be "a little book of great importance"[42] for Latin America, hoping it would address the tremendous need of his fellow Americans for the living experience of God. Merton kept sending Urtecho material to include in the anthology and found it moving that Urtecho should "respond to it so completely."[43] The author of *Emblems* rejoiced in this "generous and understanding" reader.[44] Every book or article he sent would be welcomed by Urtecho as "magnificent" or "profound," and Urtecho would thank Merton with a phrase used by the Nicaraguan poor upon receiving charity: *Dios se lo pague,* "God reward you."[45] Merton responded in kind, feeling a debtor to both Urtecho and Cardenal for making him part of a lively and comprehensive community of poets.[46] Though the Merton Reader was never published, the work on it brought the four poets closer together in a communion of minds, which Merton considered much more important than the end product.[47]

When, still in the same year of 1964, *La Prensa* dedicated a special section to Merton, with articles contributed by Cuadra and Urtecho, Merton felt he was really "engaged in the work in the literary movement which is so alive and so important in Nicaragua."[48] For Merton, his collaboration as a priest with lay Catholics in the literary sphere seemed to be a manifestation of true Catholic action, prophetically initiating a new era in the life of the Church. In a letter to Cuadra dated June 30, 1964, he expressed his belief that the real life of the Church was not in the hierarchy but in people who still knew how to listen and who were open to an exchange of ideas as opposed to a mere defense of a particular doctrine. "It would be wonderful to participate to some small extent in the beginnings of the awakening,"[49] he confided, referring to the dawning of the new, transcultural consciousness that he hoped would soon reach maturity. He may have participated in it more actively than he dared believe, and the Argentine Miguel Grinberg had a vital part to play in extending Merton's influence further south and to Latin Americans who might have felt disaffected with the Church.

A poet, publisher, and translator of North American poetry, editor of the literary review *Eco contemporáneo: Revista Inter-Americana,* Miguel Grinberg (1937-) first contacted Merton in 1963. In contrast to Merton's Nicaraguan friends, Grinberg never openly referred to religion in his letters; his religion was life. He had just founded an organization called Acción Interamericana. Presided over by Henry Miller, it was dedicated to promoting cultural exchange between both parts of the hemisphere. "My group is preparing literary revolt in Argentina," Grinberg declared pointblank in his first letter. "Are you interested?"[50] Merton was. The two men immediately found a common language. Merton's first contribution to Grinberg's inter-cultural initiative was an article "Answers on Art and Freedom," written in response to nine questions asked by readers of *Eco contemporáneo.* This was followed by Grinberg's request that Merton draft a message for the first inter-American encounter of the New Solidarity Movement of poets he had just launched. The meeting was to take place in Mexico City in February 1964. By that time Grinberg had already started two printing houses, the Angel Press and Poesia Ahora, with the objective of disseminating the new American poetry written in all the republics of the hemisphere. His literary revolt was assuming the shape of a full-blown revolution.

Merton's "Message to Poets" (1964) was one of his most important contributions to the realm of Latin American poetry. Although initially he automatically signed the "Message" with his monastic name (Father Louis), Merton decided to change the signature to Uncle Louis[51] in the essay's later versions, so as not to make anyone uncomfortable with his religious affiliation: there were non-Catholics and disaffected Catholics among its addressees. First read at the Mexico meeting of poets, and excerpted in *Américas* in April 1964, Merton's essay was on everybody's lips. To Miguel Grinberg it was "a prophetic anticipation of the things that were to develop."[52] The North American monk and poet realized that, despite the violence of Latin American politics and the threat of a global nuclear conflict, poets all over the southern continent were spontaneously affirming life and searching for signs of hope. They were the long anticipated New Men, and theirs was the only revolution capable of changing the world. "Violence changes nothing," Merton declared, "but love changes everything. We are stronger than the bomb."[53] The "we" of solidarity was already a pledge of victory. Poets-dervishes "mad with secret therapeutic love" were urged to enter the Herakleitan river of life to dance in it.[54] In his journal Merton wrote: "I think the *Nueva Solidaridad* is one of the most hopeful signs of life in the hemisphere."[55] Hispanic America seemed predestined to be the redeemer of the modern world.

When in March 1964 Grinberg visited Merton at Gethsemani, the latter could appreciate how profoundly they were in harmony. They spent two days together "exchanging ideas and addresses."[56] On the morning following their first encounter, Merton made copious notes from his guest's "remarkable"[57] "Message to the Cronopios," which Merton had just finished reading. There he was discovering resonances beyond expectation with his own way of thinking: he was struck by Grinberg's concept of poetry as "a proposition of solidarity with the weaker brothers" and by his definition of a poem as "an act of love," but above all by his belief that life itself is the ultimate poetic act.[58]

Some time later, in a pamphlet entitled "Poesia y revolución," Grinberg would call poets "total revolutionaries" and "new people" who sometimes live their poems instead of writing them.[59] The whole of Latin America, he claimed in the same essay, is straining towards the new beyond the merely novel. In a private letter, Grinberg assures Merton: "The revolution of the heart keeps growing and growing."[60] The letter closes with truly revolutionary greetings: "Joy and Tulips." Merton responds by affirming joy as "the sustenance of the New Man," and finishes the letter with a revolutionary challenge: "Down with importance. . . Up with the revolution of tulips."[61] In another letter Merton predicts: "The new consciousness will keep awakening. I know it."[62]

The encounter with Grinberg opened up to Merton the literary wealth of the Andean countries. His mind was filled with names of new writers—"people I must find out about like Julio Cortazar and Witold Gombrowicz"[63]–titles of new poetry magazines and new books to read. He was discovering Nicanor Parra and reading Peruvian poets. To the Buenos-Aires-born Alejandro Vignati (1934-), Merton wrote: "You are in Rio, you see other skies than I and hear different harmonies and rhythms, but we seek the same innocence."[64]

The Argentine Rafael Squirru (1925-) was another important discovery for Merton. In 1964 the Pan American Union published his book under the symptomatic title *The Challenge of the New Man*. Merton was reading it with a mounting conviction that the salvation of America and of the whole Western world depended on "hearing the voice of the new man who is rooted in the American earth. . . especially the earth of South America."[65] Moved to write to the author to express his gratitude, he assured Squirru of his dedication to the task of inter-American dialogue. "It seems to me that this little book represents a vitally important trend of thought,"[66] he stated. Merton hoped that it would generate some interest in things Latin American among readers in the United States, or at least challenge some existing stereotypes. The meager number of reliable publications on the "other" America available in North America was a depressing sign, and more Pan American Union books were badly needed. But the individual effort counted most in correcting this imbalance of interest. Merton's determination to become an expert in Hispanic America's literature and his-

tory was a case in point. "I must read, read, and read. It is my
vocation," he emphasized. But his understanding of the Latin
American literary and political scene was sufficient not to
downplay the possibility of all the creative energy of the continent being misdirected and misspent, so he added with exaspera-
tion: "They are looking for a Savior and will take *anyone* as one."[67]
Hence his expertise in Latin America was to serve a double purpose: on the one hand, it was to be a reparation for North American neglect; on the other, Merton was taking seriously his role of
maestro and spiritual guide for South American intellectuals. Ultimately, then, his hope was to help the whole hemispheric America
become a "great living unity."[68]

It was the Argentine feminist intellectual Victoria Ocampo
(1891-1979), writer and director of the literary review *Sur* and a
publishing house under the same name, who was for Merton a
living symbol of American unity. Envisioned as a bridge between
continents and peoples, her magazine and publishing house had
been disseminating the thought of outstanding writers from Europe and the Americas, and incorporating the wisdom of the Old
and the New World within the larger frame of a universal culture.
In an article for a commemorative volume of articles published by
Ocampo's friends, Merton honored her as the embodiment of
"America in the broad sense, the only sense, in which I am proud
to be numbered among Americans."[69]

Inter-American relations were also an issue in the epistolary
dialogue Merton maintained with Hernan Lavín Cerda (1939-), a
Chilean poet and writer of Marxist orientation, who contacted
Merton in 1965. Cerda considered the cooperation of poets and
the dissemination of new poetry written on both continents of the
hemisphere a matter of the greatest importance for American unity.
He asked Merton for names and addresses of interesting North
American poets, and, naturally, for material for inclusion in the
magazine *Punto Final* he was editing. Merton's "way of seeing the
world" as Latin Americans do, Cerda wrote in a letter, made him a
natural ally on the continent that "does not listen" to South
America.[70] In the same letter, while voicing his and his compatri-
ots' admiration for the people, values and culture of the United
States, Cerda complained that they felt betrayed by the American
government. "Our principal enemy is called the USA," he stated,
citing the history of US interventions in South America, the Monroe Doctrine, and the US government's Big Stick policy. Merton

agreed that North American civilization had become a "barbarity."[71] In 1967 the Chilean writer and publisher invited Merton to answer a set of questions on technology, politics, and society for his magazine. Merton embraced the invitation as an opportunity to reach his "brothers from Chile."[72] The result was "Answers for Hernan Lavín Cerda,"[73] which appeared in the form of an interview in the September issue of *Punto Final*. Merton must have found the concern for brotherhood that Cerda repeatedly expressed in his correspondence very moving, for he signed his letter of October 20, 1967, *"tu hermano lejano,"* "your distant brother."

This brotherhood was distant in spatial terms only. Forbidden by the abbot of Gethsemani to travel any distance away from his monastery, Merton had to content himself with spiritual solidarity with the New Men of America. But the distance melted on December 10, 1968. Ernesto Cardenal, having waited for more than a decade, could finally welcome his friend and spiritual master to the experimental monastic foundation he had launched in Nicaragua in 1966. "At last you have reached Solentiname" he wrote in his fine long poem "Death of Thomas Merton"[74] "you are here . . . and in all places"[75] because

> dying is not to leave the world
> but to dive into it
> to reach . . .
>   the *underground*
> out of this world's *Establishment.*[76]

After years of traveling vicariously throughout the world, Merton could finally arrive in the land he had so long inhabited in spirit.

Editor's Note: "Unpublished" letters by Merton are included here for scholarly use and are within "fair use" procedures.

Notes

1. Pablo Antonio Cuadra, letter to Merton, 1958. Unless noted otherwise, all references to letters to Merton are to unpublished material researched at the Thomas Merton Center, Bellarmine University, Louisville, KY.

2. Cuadra, letter to Merton, Dec. 1959.

3. Cuadra, letter to Merton, 22 Feb. 1961.

4. Thomas Merton, *The Courage for Truth: Letters to Writers*, ed. Christine Bochen (New York: Farrar, Straus & Giroux, 1993), p. 187.

5. Merton, letter to Cuadra, 8 Jan. 1959, *Courage for Truth*, p. 183.

6. Merton, letter to Cuadra, 4 Dec. 1958, *Courage for Truth*, pp. 182-83.

7. Cardenal reports it in his letter to Merton, 9 Aug. 1959.

8. "Al servicio de la verdad y la justicia" was its mission statement.

9. See Thomas Merton, *Cold War Letters*, eds. Christine M. Bochen and William H. Shannon (Maryknoll, NY: Orbis Books, 2006).

10. Merton, *Courage for Truth*, p. 189.

11. Cuadra, letter to Merton, Christmas 1961.

12. Cáceres, letter to Merton, 1961.

13. Cardenal, letter to Merton, 29 Feb. 1964.

14. In 1964 Stefan Baciu was forced to transfer to the University of Hawaii for political reasons.

15. Baciu, letter to Merton, 19 Nov. 1963.

16. "To Thomas Merton, great poet, a friend of my friend Ernesto Cardenal." This dedication, dated June 30, 1963, can be read on Merton's copy of Baciu's article "Cesar Vallejo, Poeta Comunista?" Thomas Merton Center, Bellarmine University, Louisville, KY.

17. Thomas Merton, *Turning Toward the World*, ed. Victor A. Kramer, journals, vol. 4, 1960-1963 (San Francisco: HarperCollins, 1997), p. 295.

18. Merton, *Turning Toward the World*, p. 345.

19. Randall, letter to Merton, 30 Mar. 1967.

20. Randall, letter to Merton, 31 May 1967.

21. Thomas Merton, "Pasternak's Letters to Georgian Friends," *The Literary Essays of Thomas Merton* (New York: New Directions, 1985), p. 88. The article was written in 1968, and first published in the *New Lazarus Review* in 1978.

22. Thomas Merton, *Dancing in the Water of Life: Seeking Peace in the Hermitage* (ed. Robert E. Daggy, journals, vol. 5, 1963-1965; San Francisco: Harper, 1997), p. 39.

23. Vittier, letter to Merton, 31 Dec. 1962.

24. Vitier, letter to Merton, 13 Nov. 1966.

25. Merton, *Dancing in the Water*, p. 39.

26. Merton, letter to Silva, 10 Apr. 1965, *Courage for Truth*, p. 224.

27. Robert E. Daggy, introduction, *Day of a Stranger*, by Thomas Merton (Salt Lake City: Gibbs M. Smith, 1981), p. 15.

28. Merton, *Day of a Stranger*, p. 35.

29. Merton, letter to Silva, 10 Apr. 1965, *Courage for Truth*, p. 225.

30. Silva, letter to Merton, 24 Apr. 1965.

31. Merton, letter to Silva, 19 May 1967, *Courage for Truth*, p. 231.

32. Merton, letter to Silva, 27 Apr. 1967, *Courage for Truth*, pp. 230-31.

33. Merton, letter to Urtecho, 17 Apr. 1964, *Courage for Truth*, p. 173.

34. In a letter to Merton, dated March 4, 1962, Cardenal speculated about the chances of Pedro Chamorro, "un Fidel Castro cristiano," win-

ning the next year's presidency. Chamorro's enormous popularity with the common people encouraged Cardenal to bet on Pablo Antonio Cuadra becoming the Minister of Culture in the future Chamorro-led government. Unfortunately, despite favorable prognosis, the election results were rigged and Anastasio Somosa, Jr. became Nicaragua's next president-tyrant, pledged to continue his father's and brother's line of military dictatorship, terror, and abuse of human rights, until, sparked off by the assassination of Pedro Chamorro in 1978, a full-blown Sandinista revolution would depose him from power. By an irony of fate, in 1979 Ernesto Cardenal would become the Sandinista government's Minister of Culture, estranged by politics from his friend and cousin Pablo Antonio Cuadra. But in the 1960s nothing foretold these dramatic changes or rifts within the movement.

35. Merton, letter to Cardenal, 29 May 1963, *Courage for Truth*, p. 140.

36. Merton, letter to Chow, 26 Dec. 1962, *Courage for Truth*, p. 170.

37. Chow, letter to Merton, 22 Apr. 1963.

38. Merton, letter to Chow, 14 May 1963, *Courage for Truth*, p. 171.

39. Cardenal, letter to Merton, 4 Mar. 1962.

40. Urtecho, letter to Merton, 31 Mar. 1964.

41. Urtecho, letter to Merton, 30 Apr. 1964.

42. Urtecho, letter to Merton, 31 Mar. 1964.

43. Merton, letter to Urtecho, 30 Jun. 1965, *Courage for Truth*, p. 175.

44. Merton, *Courage for Truth*, p. 175.

45. Urtecho, letter to Merton, 10 Jun. 1965.

46. Merton, letter to Urtecho, 17 Mar. 1966, *Courage for Truth*, p. 176.

47. Merton, letter to Urtecho, 15 Mar. 1964, *Courage for Truth*, p. 171.

48. Merton, letter to Cuadra, 28 Oct. 1964, *Courage for Truth*, p. 192.

49. Merton, *Courage for Truth*, p. 192.

50. Grinberg, letter to Merton, 5 May 1963.

51. Grinberg mentions this incident in his talk "Merton and the New World Kairos," given at the Fourth General Meeting of the International Thomas Merton Society in 1995. Recording available at the Thomas Merton Center, Bellarmine University, Louisville, Ky.

52. Grinberg, "Merton and the New World Kairos."

53. Merton, *Literary Essays*, p. 374.

54. Merton, *Literary Essays*, p. 374.

55. Merton, *Dancing in the* Water, p. 89.

56. Merton, *Dancing in the Water*, p. 89.

57. Merton, *Dancing in the Water* 87. Grinberg's "Mensaje a los Cronopios," distributed at the Mexican conference of poets, was published as "A Mis Hermanos de la Nueva Solidaridad" in the Buenos Aires journal *Primo* 2 (May-June 1964).

58. Merton, *Dancing in the Water*, p. 88.

59. Miguel Grinberg, "Poesia y revolución," Thomas Merton Center, Bellarmine University, Louisville, Ky. "Poesia y revolución" was later published in an Argentine literary magazine *Sol Calmo* 1 (Summer 1967/68).

60. Grinberg, letter to Merton, 26 Jul. 1964.

61. Merton, letter to Grinberg, 16 Aug. 1964, *Courage for Truth*, p. 200.

62. Merton, letter to Grinberg, 28 Oct. 1966, *Courage for Truth*, p. 204.

63. Merton, *Dancing in the Water*, p. 89.

64. Merton, *Courage for Truth*, p. 234.

65. Merton, letter to Cardenal, 12 Jul. 1964, *Courage for Truth*, p. 146.

66. Merton, letter to Squirru, 12 Jul. 1964, *Courage for Truth*, p. 232.

67. Merton, *Dancing in the Water*, p. 124.

68. Merton, letter to Cardenal, 1 Aug. 1963, *Courage for Truth*, p. 141.

69. "To Friends of Victoria Ocampo," published in Thomas Merton, *Seeds of Destruction* (New York: Farrar, 1964), pp. 283-84.

70. Cerda, letter to Merton, 7 Sept. 1965.

71. Merton, letter to Cerda, 6 Oct. 1965, *Courage for Truth*, p. 206.

72. Merton, letter to Cerda, 12 Aug. 1967, *Courage for Truth*, p. 206.

73. Thomas Merton, "Answer for Hernan Lavín Cerda," *The Merton Annual*, 2 (1989), pp. 3-12.

74. Ernesto Cardenal, *Marilyn Monroe and Other Poems*, trans. Robert Pring-Mill (London: Search, 1975), p. 133.

75. Cardenal, *Marilyn Monroe*, p. 134.

76. Cardenal, *Marilyn Monroe*, p. 130.

Sacred Play:
Thomas Merton's *Cables to the Ace*

Robert Leigh Davis

Thomas Merton's *Cables to the Ace* is the first of two book-length poems written at St. Mary of Carmel, the Gethsemani hermitage where Merton lived from August 1965 until his death in 1968. In his essay, "Merton's Hermitage," Belden Lane argues that Merton's writing became more subversive and playful after the move to St. Mary of Carmel. The hermitage was a place where the unconscious could be "unhoused," Lane argues, a place that invited Merton to give up the need to "be someone, to nurture his artificial persona as ideal monk and renowned writer. . . . He began to play the fool more creatively than ever, and to make mistakes which would free him from the weight of a contrived self he had nurtured so long."[1]

The author of *Cables to the Ace* is certainly not afraid to "play the fool." Composed in spontaneous verse paragraphs Merton calls "cantos," *Cables* challenges most everything we know about how to write (and read) a poem—including the idea that poetry should progress from start to finish. The 88 cantos of *Cables* can be shuffled like a deck of cards—one sense of the "ace" in its title. Readers may enter the poem almost anywhere—reading from back to front or from the middle out—as if "plot" is less important than experiencing the poem from all sides, like a montage or cubist painting. Merton scatters quotations across the book like handfuls of seed. He even moves back and forth between French and English. He slips in and out of the subversive "anti-language" he had used for years in his correspondence with his friend, Bob Lax— a language of parody, ambiguity, and word-play which Merton called "macaronic" writing.[2] The poem rotates through dozens of voices and perspectives—sometimes straight-ahead first person, sometimes a disembodied omniscience disconnected from any particular character or context. It changes moods: playful, angry, surreal, apocalyptic. It changes genres: from lyric poetry to science fiction, from film and radio scripts to parodies of advertising and news broadcasts, from a quote by Meister Eckhart—"No man can see God except . . . through folly"—to something Merton picked up from *Esquire* magazine.[3] In the course of writing *Cables* he had asked his friend, W.H. Ferry, to mail him some "good, gaudy, noisy *ad* material," and Ferry had sent him, among other things, copies of *Playboy, Fortune,* and *Esquire.* Merton wrote back to say, in effect, enough is enough: "for petesake [sic] no tearsheets from Playboy. . . . It was all I could take. Am still retching. Weak stomach. Getting old. Too long in the woods. Can't handle Esq. Old gut won't hold it."[4]

"Playing the fool" means many things to Merton. It suggests a deeper capacity for risk and emotional intimacy—a self unhoused and unguarded. It marks his interest in new styles of experimental poetry: from the Latin American surrealism of Nicanor Parra to the spontaneous playfulness of the Beats. "My head is a boney guitar," the Beat poet, Bob Kaufman, writes, "strung with tongues, plucked by fingers and nails."[5] In German, as Merton knew, the word for holy—"selig"—is the same as the word for silly, and playing the fool allowed Merton to deflate pomposity and religious self-righteousness, including his own, and explore a style of writing that was more like prayer: attentive, limber, tuned like a boney guitar to the eccentric rhythms of God.[6]

But there is another meaning to the foolishness of *Cables,* as we will see. Playing the fool is a response to *power* for Merton and an intervention in a mass culture that left him sick at heart: "It was all I could take. Am still retching." This kind of play acts like a Brechtian "alienation effect" within Merton's poetry: it causes us to question social conventions we would otherwise take for granted and reveals toxic or sinister aspects of everyday life so grooved into our cultural unconscious we barely notice they are there.[7] "The right fragrance," a voice whispers in the poem, "is so right it is not noticed."[8] The foolishness of *Cables* makes us notice. Merton defamiliarizes the "right fragrance" (or voice or gesture or perspective). He demythologizes social constructs that seem so natural and inevitable that we do not think of them as "constructs" at all, not something we learn but something we are, and so beyond the reach of conscious thought and revision.

Not noticing, however, is deadly. Merton peoples his poem with a host of characters who are being extinguished by subtle manipulations of power—half-conscious, often child-like "trainees" who are learning cultural scripts that are killing them.[9]

Merton's concern for these "fatal children"—for *us*—is moral and spiritual as well as literary.[10] The play Merton has in mind is not the ethically neutral "free play" of Derridean deconstruction but something closer in spirit to the wise fools of Zen Buddhism or the holy folly of Meister Eckhart or the sacred play of Thoreau's *Walden*: didactic play, play with an urgent moral and spiritual purpose, the kind of play that might save one's life.

Quiet Desperation

As he pulls back the veil to reveal the toxic effect of social norms, Merton follows the lead of nineteenth-century American romantics like Henry David Thoreau, another heart-sick hermit diagnosing his country's spiritual malady from a one-room cabin in the woods. "The mass of men lead lives of quiet desperation," Thoreau writes, in one of the most famous sentences of American literature. "What is called resignation is confirmed desperation. From the desperate city you go into the desperate country, and have to console yourself with the bravery of minks and muskrats."[11] He should know. By the time he started *Walden*, Thoreau was out of work, grieving the death of his brother, John, and experiencing at Walden Pond the first stirrings of the tuberculosis that would eventually end his life. And so: "The mass of men lead lives of quiet desperation." But what Thoreau goes on to say is equally important: "There is no *play* in them."[12] He means, of course, no joy, no delight in the adventure of living. But he also means "play" like the play of a hinge: looseness, flex, bend. More than frivolity or quirkiness, play serves a moral purpose in *Walden*: it promotes spiritual growth by loosening rigid or compulsive habits and opening the spiritual seeker to experimentation and change. Play is the antidote to desperate thought. It is associated for Thoreau with nimbleness, looseness, suppleness, the ability to change course, the ability to change the paradigm. Thoreau thinks of it almost in physical terms: as a light-handed athleticism of mind constantly adapting to new perspectives and revising fixed assumptions in the light of fresh experience.

Merton liked to joke that he set off to the woods "with Thoreau in one pocket" and "St. John of the Cross in another."[13] Merton dips into Thoreau's transcendentalism from time to time in *Cables*— which he calls "Swimming in Walden Pond"—and uses the figure of the "nubile swimmer" to evoke the athleticism of Thoreau's limber mind and the capacity for play so important to the spiritual vision of *Walden*.[14]   But *Cables* is no transcendental poem.   The cubistic proliferation of voices and narrators in *Cables* operates without a consistent or privileged center.   It is hard at times to know which voice is actually "Thomas Merton," and the poet shows little interest in the adaptive but ultimately unified self of nineteenth-century romanticism.   In this sense, Thoreau is less important as a stylistic and philosophical model for *Cables* than any number of modern and postmodern writers—from Pound and Joyce to Bob Dylan and Allen Ginsberg. What is important, however, is Thoreau's understanding of the moral function of literature: how it inculcates a notion of the good in people and intervenes in the moral crisis of a culture. As Stephen John Mack points out, the idea that literature has a moral (rather than purely aesthetic) function has a long tradition in Western criticism, beginning with Aristotle.[15]   Unlike Aristotle, however, Merton and Thoreau do not see that purpose in terms of edifying *models*: aesthetically pleasing pictures of the good life or good person (which comes off as just another kind of salesmanship in *Cables*). What matters instead is the writer's ability to defamiliarize cultural constructs that permeate the life of a society and shape the subjectivity and needs of its people—constructs, both Merton and Thoreau stress, which serve the historical interests of power.[16] Literature of course is one of those constructs, and Merton uses the cranky voice of the Prologue in *Cables*—an "author" giving advice and instructions to his readers—to de-mystify literary power and make the book's designs on us still more apparent. Although neither writer would phrase it quite this way, literature serves a moral purpose by making *ideology* visible and helping readers glimpse compulsive and unconscious norms—Thoreau's "quiet desperation"—obscured by habit, tradition, indifference, or routine. These norms comprise what Merton calls the "habit frequency" of American culture—a set of ready-made scripts that play like a radio station in the minds of his characters.[17] Disrupting that frequency— by expanding the band-width of his poem to include dozens of other voices, messages, communications, "cables"—Merton introduces sacred elements of literary and spiritual play.[18]

As a single instance of this larger concern, consider Merton's description of the air-conditioned waiting room in Canto 41 of *Cables*, a place where the desperation is so quiet you have to lean in to hear it:

Approved prospect of chairs with visitors to the hero. Temperature is just comfortable for a variety of skins. It is with our skins here that we see each other all around and feel together. We are not overheated, we smell good and we remain smooth. No skin needs to be absolutely private for all are quiet, clean, and cool. The right fragrance is so right it is not noticed. The cool of the whole area is like that of a quiet car and presences. No one is really ailing and no one is quite that tired. See the pictures however for someone elsewhere who is really tired. Hear the sound of the music for someone who is relaxed (with an undercurrent of annoyance). She is glad to be sitting down with her limbs as if her long legs were really hers and really bare. This year the women all worry about their skirts. But she is well arranged. Whether they walk or sit they manage to be well arranged. In any case all is springlike with the scent of very present young women which with all our skin we recognize. Nothing is really private yet each remains alone and each pretends to read a magazine. But each one still smuggles a secret personal question across the frontiers of everybody: the skin of the body and the presence of the scent and the general arrangement. Nothing is out of place or disapproved. One by one each skin will visit the hero.[19]

By the end of the scene, human beings are merely "skin"—so dissociated and numb that they experience themselves in pieces, as body parts. The Dick-and-Jane plainness of the passage—"see the pictures," "hear the music"—conveys Merton's insight that what is happening in the waiting room is a kind of cultural "primer"— an elementary grammar in how to think and feel. And the primary lesson of that grammar is the anatomy of *cool*: "all are quiet, clean, and cool."[20]   Marshall McLuhan said famously that television was a "cool medium"—meaning that it levels individuality and eccentricity downward, toward a toneless common denominator, the white-noise hum of whatever happens to be on.[21] Merton captures that tonelessness in the prose: "In any case all is springlike with the scent of very present young women which with all our skin we recognize." *What scent?* one wonders. *Whose skin? Who's speaking?* The writing floats free of any concrete referent—a "disembodied voice, seemingly in a cloud"—and Merton allows the poetic "spring" to drain out of the line to make us experience the loss of sharper accents or deeper feelings.[22]

There are many images of hell in *Cables*, and this is one of them: not Milton's "overheated" hell of demons and brimstone, but something cooler, more bureaucratic. The torments are so subtle that no one really notices they're being *pithed* in that room, de-souled, even when they stop feeling their legs. This vision of hell is close to what Henry Miller called "the air-conditioned nightmare"—an antiseptic America scoured clean of lust, hunger, fatigue, illness. "We will make you into an air-conditioned wishing well," Merton writes in Canto 43, parodying the voice of American advertising: "Afloat or abroad we will decorate your / Favorite place with monograms of daring souls / And instant specialists of flavor charm and grace / To win you baroque lawns / And crystal suitings / For your (day off) *Samedi du plaisir*."[23] This is life re-presented as an *Esquire* ad. No one smells bad. No one feels much of anything, except a vague waiting-for-Godot annoyance. The old words of Plato or Jesus flatten into advertising copy. "Grace" is a brand name. "Daring Souls" is the corporate monogram on a brand of lawn furniture. Fear doesn't go away in this happy-place fantasy. It turns inward, becoming an undertone just below the bland surface, "a secret personal question" no one is willing to share for fear of upsetting the "general arrangement."[24]

Merton responds to the desperation of the waiting room by introducing elements of randomness and surrealism into the "general arrangement" of the poem. In one of his notebooks, Merton wrote that the essential quality distinguishing poetry from prose was that poetry was "useless"[25]—that is, unbound by workaday norms. Poetry is language "on vacation": "The poet has not announced these mosaics on purpose," the narrator declares in the Prologue. "Furthermore he has changed his address and his poetics are on vacation."[26] In this mood, Merton tried dozens of sound and thought experiments in his writing—visual poems (which look like what they describe), found poems, spontaneous poems—to loosen the strictures of high art and make it dip below the conscious, cerebral surface. In this period, Merton read and translated the Spanish surrealists Rafael Alberti, Alfonso Cortes, and Nicanor Parra. Parra visited Merton at Gethsemani in the spring of 1966, and Merton adapted what he called the "nonsense" of Parra's *Poems & Antipoems* to his own writing in *Cables* and *The Geography of Lograire*.[27] During this period, Merton also read the Beat Generation poets—whom he called the "esoteric American pontiffs of the day"[28]—and may have modeled the "fatal children" of *Cables* on the "angel-headed hipsters" of Allen Ginsberg's *Howl*, spiritual seekers who are also being pithed by American culture— "present[ing] themselves on the granite steps of the madhouse with shaven heads and harlequin speech of suicide, demanding instantaneous lobotomy."[29]   Like Parra, Alberti, and Ginsberg, Merton sought to release poetry from the dominant rules of academic formalism and recover its ancient roots in dream, vision, and the unconscious—the secret undercurrents of the psyche denied by the waiting-room primer of cool.   "[T]he peculiar chaotic intensity" of the Spanish surrealists, Merton wrote in an essay on Rafael Alberti,

> results from a rich profusion of unconscious images jarring against one another in creative dissonances and dream-like shock effects with a result quite different from the dry, deadpan parade of objects (and "objective correlatives") with which we have become familiar (and perhaps so exhausted) in English and American verse.[30]

The prime figure in the other—formalist and academic—stream of modern poetry, T.S. Eliot, who of course coined the term "objective correlative," makes a brief appearance in *Cables*, stumbles across Eve shopping for "naked fruit" in Merton's version of Ginsberg's California supermarket, and is so spooked he has to look away: "Eve moves: golden Mother of baroque lights. She visits a natural supermarket of naked fruits. . . . T.S. Eliot is vexed and cannot look."[31]   Risking the disdain of Eliot-inspired academic formalists—which *Cables*, by the way, received in spades—Merton turns to the "dream-like shock effects" of surrealism as a liberating alternative to objectivity and formal control.[32]   And he discovered an unlikely source for this project in the poetry and lyrics of Bob Dylan.

Lynn Szabo notes that Merton's friend, Ed Rice, had sent recordings of Dylan to Merton in the hopes that he would review them for *Jubilee*. In a notebook, Merton writes that "Dylan sees life as a mosaic of unrelated [and] superficial images—clashing in a ludicrous entertainment that has its own special significance."[33]   Whether or not Dylan "sees life as a mosaic," Merton certainly did. And Merton's description of Dylan's writing—"ludicrous entertainment that has its own special significance"—could stand as a motto for *Cables*. In a topsy-turvy world where "sanity" was no impediment to the barbarism of the Nazis (an argument Merton poses in his essay on Adolf Eichmann) and where being well-adjusted constitutes a kind of spiritual death (as in the waiting-room scene of Canto 41), the madness of the outsider may yet lead us home. In that sort of world, a Christian poet may discover in the "ludicrous" (from *ludus*: game or play) an alternative to the psychopathology of everyday life Merton found movingly revealed in Dylan.

When Dylan asks, "where have you been, my blue-eyed son?"—as he does in the 1963 song, "Hard Rain"—the child/prophet answers in a series of surrealistic images that don't "mean" in the way popular songs are supposed to mean—at least not in the how-much-is-that-doggie-in-the-window style American audiences had cherished a few years earlier:

> Oh, where have you been, my blue-eyed son?
> Oh, what did you see, my darling young one?
> I saw a newborn baby with wild wolves all around it,
> I saw a highway of diamonds with nobody on it,
> I saw a black branch with blood that kept drippin',
> I saw a room full of men with their hammers a-bleedin',
> I saw a white ladder all covered with water,
> I saw ten thousand talkers whose tongues were all broken,
> I saw guns and sharp swords in the hands of young children,
> And it's a hard, and it's a hard, it's a hard, it's a hard,
> And it's a hard rain's a-gonna fall.[34]

For the generation coming of age during the Vietnam War, the Patti Page puppy-songs could well seem insane while the bleeding branches and hammers of "Hard Rain" were nothing if not real. Like many of the songs in *The Freewheelin' Bob Dylan*, "Hard Rain" is a study of progressive trauma. The damage in "Hard Rain" spreads out from the physical body of the sufferer to transform and mutilate everyday things—ladders, hammers, weather, trees: "I saw a black branch with blood that kept drippin'." It is not that Dylan's prophet/son cannot see or show the physical suffering of the children, and so projects that wounding onto innocent landscapes. Rather Dylan suggests how trauma ripples out from individual victims to change the way they experience the world, as if trees (as well as children) can bleed and hammers (as well as bodies) be wounded. Indeed Dylan suggests that the tools one might use to repair the "real," those bleeding hammers, are just as damaged as everything else.

The problem for the children in "Hard Rain" is that they feel too much. The damage keeps spreading. The problem for the children in *Cables* is that they do not feel at all, mouthing ad slogans to mask private distress and substituting media stereotypes, as Ross Labrie has argued, for original, idiomatic experience.[35] Like many writers in the 1960s, Merton felt that language had been cheapened and debased by American mass media, its edges ground down by advertising, television, politics, and most especially by the Vietnam War—which created ingenious new ways of *not* showing the suffering children and bleeding trees: *pacification, free-fire zones, protective reactions, collateral damage.*

What results from this debasement is a slippery, only half-true media-talk Merton calls "the monogag":

> For a nominal fee one can confide in a cryphone
> With sobs of champagne
> Or return from sudden sport to address
> The monogag
> The telefake
> The base undertones of the confessional speaker
> Advising trainees
> Through cloistered earphones.[36]

Sometimes we hear the "monogag" by itself in *Cables*, as a newscast or advertisement. Sometimes a media voice is positioned against older discourses in the poem: the voices of Plato, Christ, Eckhart, Blake—often presented as "(Plato)" in the soft whisper of the parentheses. And if it is a competition, the media voice is winning: using up the good words—*grace, daring, cloistered, confessional*—drowning out competing discourses or relegating them to parenthetical margins. And worst of all, translating the intimate language of subjectivity and spirit into the same impersonal dialect: "You wake and wonder / Whose case history you composed / As your confessions are filed / In the dialect / Of bureaux and electrons."[37]

There is a great deal at stake here. The confessional programs humming through media cables are not a distraction from the real,

Merton suggests. Rather they produce and organize the real, blueprinting in people the deep pattern of feelings and fears that constitute humanness in a particular time and place: what it means to be a woman, a man, a poet, a Christian. In this sense, the "base undertones" of television and advertising represent a novitiate for "cloistered" "trainees"—a rigorous pedagogy in a certain kind of cultural gospel.[38] The undertones are *base* not because they are venal or crass—or at least not only in that sense—but because they are so *basic*, so fundamental to a certain way of experiencing the world. Despite the apparent plurality of voices in this media pedagogy, what we hear, Merton suggests, is basically the same chorus, the same half-hearted "monogag." And it's *gagging* the trainees—choking them, making them sick at heart—like Allen Ginsberg's angelheaded hipsters or Bob Dylan's blue-eyed son.

For Dylan, such language is broken: "I saw ten thousand talkers whose tongues were all broken." And the alternative is a different kind of music and a different kind of poetry, something jarring and surrealistic and decidedly un-pretty. An antipoem. An anti-pop-song. This is 1968, after all. The year of the Tet Offensive, Dr. King's assassination, the race riots in Newark, Watts, and Detroit. When Jimi Hendrix played "The Star-Spangled Banner" at Woodstock, he turned it into a wailing, Stratocaster guitar scream. *Cables to the Ace* is like Merton's guitar scream, the antipoetic jeremiad of a Catholic mystic writing experimental poetry in a 20x20 cinder-block room in rural Kentucky—and yet absolutely tuned in to the hard-rock bass line of American culture. That is how *Cables* begins, with Merton hearing power guitar chords through the high-tension wires of a suspension bridge:

> Edifying cables can be made musical if played and sung by full-armed societies doomed to an electric war. A heavy imperturbable beat ... With the unending vroom vroom vroom of the guitars we will all learn a new kind of obstinacy, together with massive lessons of irony and refusal.[39]

Bob Kaufman heard guitars in his head. Merton hears guitars in the wind, in the wires of a bridge, in the "vroom vroom vroom" of an "electric"—that is, massively televised—"war." And the guitars are all telling him the same thing: a hard rain's a gonna fall.

Merton's response in *Cables* is to offer a "new kind of obstinacy" to the waiting-room primer of cool.[40] The poem, therefore, is a massive counter-lesson of "irony and refusal" that turns loose dozens of outlaw voices—still present but so faint one can barely hear them: sobs, whispers, nursery rhymes, a bird song, a door-bell, the sound of someone being called back to consciousness ("Bernstein! Can you still hear me? Are you conscious?"), the sound of "ten thousand crickets in the deep wet hay of the field," the "Nine even strokes" of the Gethsemani bell calling the monks to prayer.[41] When T.S. Eliot hears the nine strokes of the church bell at Saint Mary Woolnoth in *The Waste Land*, it is just more noise, more of the Babel of the Unreal City, and a reminder of how far we have fallen. It feels a little like death: "And each man fixed his eyes before his feet. / Flowed up the hill and down King William Street, / To where Saint Mary Woolnoth kept the hours / With a dead sound on the final stroke of nine."[42] When Merton hears the church bells at Gethsemani, it's a nine-beat canticle of morning. It is Thoreau's chanticleer delivering a wake-up call to a barely conscious America: *Can you still hear me? Are you conscious?*

Running the Vote Backwards

The surrealistic derangements of poetry may not be so "useless" after all. It may well take a certain kind of poetic violence to jar the mother-wit free and help us return to our senses, as Thoreau would say—in part, because the "senses" are not given but *made*, rehearsed through cultural primers so intimate and invisible we barely notice them. Most of the time the cultural primer is so naturally and inevitably a part of our identity—so *us*—that we do not think of it as cultural at all. The problem is not that we hear one monogag or see one telefake. We see thousands of them—until we do not see them any more: "The right fragrance is so right it is not noticed."[43] Finally the scents and images feel natural, a part of what we might now call the cultural unconscious. So that our bodies are no longer our own, and we stop feeling our legs. So that other ways of being in the world look foolish, "ludicrous"— which is to say, holy.

To recover this holiness, Merton turns back the clock and appeals to states of memory and imagination existing *just before* the slogans and stereotypes took hold:

> What do you teach me
> Mama my cow?
> (My delicate forefathers
> Wink in their sleep)

"Seek advancement
Then as now
And never learn to weep!"

What do you want of me
Mama my wit
(While the water runs
And the world spins)
"All the successful
Ride in their Buicks
And grow double chins"

What do you seek of me
Mama my ocean
(While the fire sleeps
In well baked mud)
"Take your shotgun
And put it in the bank
For money is blood."[44]

In contrast to the totalizing language of the monogag, Merton makes us hear, almost simultaneously, two different voices: something aggressive and contemporary: "seek advancement," "never learn to weep," put blood money "in the bank." And something just behind that voice, an earlier discourse of nursery rhymes ("Mama my cow") and childhood dreams ("While the water runs / And the world spins"). It is hard not to gender the two voices: a father tongue that's rule-bound and prescriptive, concerned with banks and Buicks. And a mother tongue that is playful, sleepy, funny, a little surrealistic. The father tongue uses exclamation points. The mother tongue does not care much about punctuation one way or the other but is partial to the parentheses with its sly whispers: "(While the fire sleeps / In well baked mud)." The father tongue lays down the law. It issues "bare-faced literal commands." It calls the reader, "Buster." It does not like a lot of backtalk. The mother tongue is all backtalk. You ask questions in the mother tongue: "What do you want of me?" You dream in the mother tongue: "Mama my ocean." You tell jokes in the mother tongue: "My delicate forefathers / Wink in their sleep." Merton's point is that you know the mother tongue when you hear it. This other, earlier way of thinking and feeling is back there—not lost, just layered over with all sorts of slogans and instructions: "seek advancement," "never learn to weep." And the poem serves as a kind of catechism leading us back to the place just under "their song": "My vow," the poet tells us, "is the silence under their song."[45]

"Their song," as it happens, is a gender pedagogy in very specific sexual roles. How to be a man: seek advancement, never learn to weep. How to be a woman: wait for the hero, worry about your skirt. To challenge this ideology, Merton shows it being formed. He takes us back to the "trainee" level of consciousness and has us listen to the "base undertones of the confessional speaker / Advising trainees / Through cloistered earphones." At this early stage, the "base undertones" may still sound a little phony, a little *truthy*, and the trainees may be open to other ways of being in the world. Once the program is complete, however, and the trainees start talking like the Marlboro Man—"I will get up and go to Marble country / Where . . . all the cowboys look for fortunate slogans / Among horses' asses"—the game's pretty much up. They cannot tell an ad slogan from a horse's ass.[46]

Merton calls this cultural re-wind—"run[ning] the vote backwards"—a phrase that emerges in Canto 66, one of the pivotal scenes of the poem as a whole:

> Oh yes it is intelligence
> That makes the bubble and weather of "Yes"
> To which the self says "No."
>
> Science when the air is right says "Yes"
> And all the bubbles in the head repeat "Yes"
> Even the corpuscles romp "Yes"
>
> But lowdown
> At the bottom of deep water
> Deeper than Anna Livia Plurabelle
> Or any other river
> Some nameless rebel
> A Mister Houdini or somebody with fingers
> Slips the technical knots
> Pops the bubbles in the head
> Runs the vote backwards
> And turns the bloody cooler
> All the way
> OFF.[47]

Running the tape backwards is a dream of artistic and spiritual innocence shared by many writers—especially in the midst of war. In *Slaughterhouse-Five*, for instance, Kurt Vonnegut shows a deeply traumatized Billy Pilgrim becoming "unstuck in time."[48] As Billy watches a late-night movie about American bombers during World War Two, he sees the film in reverse. He watches American bombers open their bomb bay doors and miraculously shrink the fires on the ground and suck flame and bomb fragments back into metal canisters in the bellies of the planes. He watches German fighter planes draw bullets out of the bodies of some of the American crewmen. As the film continues, he sees the American bombers fly backwards in formation to bases in England where women unload and disassemble the canisters and re-bury the raw, innocent minerals in the earth. Vonnegut lets the tape continue rewinding in Billy's mind, long after the film is over. Billy watches the American fliers turn in their uniforms and become high school students again. He watches Hitler turn back into a baby. As the rewind continues, Billy watches the world roll back through countless centuries until it reaches "two perfect people named Adam and Eve."[49] Merton allows his poem to follow the same course and register the same longing: for the Garden, for Eve shopping for "naked fruits," and for our earliest memories of "Mama my ocean," when the fires of war still slept "In well baked mud."[50]

But why run the *vote* backwards—rather than the *tape* backwards, as Vonnegut does? Merton's phrasing stresses the crucial role of *consent* in this cultural process. Unlike Billy Pilgrim, who denies the possibility of free will in order to protect himself from the terrors of the war, Merton insists on free choice, even in the midst of one of his most searching examinations of social control. We may not have personally ordered the "Deathloving Jacks" to drop napalm and incendiary high-explosives on Vietnam.[51] But the social and economic choices *we're making here and now*, Merton stresses, support that terror, profit from it, and give it meaning. Gethsemani Monastery is less than twenty miles from Fort Knox, Kentucky, and Merton could hear the pounding of the Fort Knox guns during morning prayer. Belden Lane describes how Merton "watched with horror as huge SAC bombers flew over the hermitage, no more than 150 feet above the trees."[52] In Merton's view, there is no "Walden Pond" in 1968, no place of withdrawal and isolation where one can choose *not* to participate. What we buy, wear, read, watch; how we spend time, energy, and money; most of all, what we notice or refuse to notice, the human gift of visibility and attention: these are "votes" in Merton's ethical vocabulary. They are ways of saying "yes" or "no" to all sorts of political and economic commitments that seem, at first, to have nothing to do with an Asian war thousands of miles away. It is never just a "Buick," for Merton. In a time of war, disease, and famine—which is to say, all human time—it is blood-money in the bank. And changing that vote, running it backwards, is a profoundly ethical act.

But we need help with this refusal. The lonely "self" saying "no" at the beginning of Canto 66 is immediately swamped by a tide of votes going the other way. At the point in *Cables* when the air-conditioning is just about "right" and everything, it seems, is saying the same thing—yes, yes, yes—a "nameless rebel" emerges to burst the "bubble" and roll back the vote.[53] That rebel is Merton's most important image of limber thinking in *Cables*: a figure of fluidity and spiritual grace who comes from a watery medium below language, a place deeper than primers and poems, deeper even than Anna Livia Plurabelle, the dream river of James Joyce's *Finnegans Wake*.[54] Below what Thoreau calls "the mud and slush of opinion, and prejudice, and tradition, and delusion, and appearance";[55] below the base undertones of the monogag and the ten-thousand talkers whose tongues are all broken—below all that, a deep-water savior pulls off a spiritual escape. That figure, it seems, is Christ. But Christ in disguise as fish or fin (*Finnegans Wake*); Christ as the culmination of Merton's many of images of water, rivers, rain, and ocean. But also Christ as "Mister Houdini," a spiritual escape artist who slips the knots of language and culture and turns off the "bloody cooler"—a phrase that also evokes the horrors of the death camps.

This scene, like many in *Cables*, evokes Merton's dread of patterning and control—a theme that emerges with great force in American writing during the 1950s and '60s: from *Catcher in the Rye* to *Catch 22*. But Merton is less fatalistic about the scope of that control than many. At times, *Cables* evokes a science fiction dystopia of human life as *wiring*: cultural stereotypes wet-ported into us by cryphones and the telefake, ad slogans playing in our heads on the "habit frequency."[56] Even the flights of birds follow scripted circuits: "We learn by the cables of orioles."[57] But there are other messages in the air, Merton shows, cables of play, intimacy, solitude, and deep memory. Just below the cultural monotone, we can still pick up other frequencies: the nine strokes of the Gethsemani bell, the songs of birds and children, a choir of ten-thousand crickets whose tongues are not broken. And that spontaneous poetry can lead us back, as if by fragile threads, to a sacred source Merton calls the "ace of songs" and the "ace of freedoms"—a life-affirming divine oneness (an "ace") that clears the noxious head-bubbles, loosens the tricky knots of culture and language, and turns the air-conditioned nightmare all the way OFF.[58]

If this is a resurrection rather than a burial—*Finnegans Wake*—it is an Easter moment that emerges when life is nearly wrung out in *Cables*. George Kilcourse points out that the "ace" in a deck of cards is both high and low, and that if Christ is the "ace of freedoms" in *Cables*, he is the self-emptying savior "who … identifies with the wounded and seemingly bankrupt moments of human life."[59]   At just such a moment in the poem—when life is "lowdown," "At the bottom"—Merton allows us to glimpse a sudden upwelling of presence and power that picks up speed with the rapid-fire verbs—slips, pops, runs, turns—before coming to a complete, capitalized stop: OFF.[60]   And then silence. The white space at the end of the stanza seems, at that moment, rinsed and charged, like the sky after a storm. When the poet tries to pick up the thread in the next canto and codify the experience into a "model" or "imperative," a theology of spiritual liberation, speech fails him and he turns away like a discouraged T.S. Eliot:

> This is how to
> This is with imperatives
> I mean models
> If you act
> Act HOW.[61]

The capitalized words of the two cantos form both halves of a dialogue: OFF, HOW. The goal of *Cables* seems clear enough: rage against the machine with every bit of love and lore you can get your hands on: nursery rhymes, bird songs, Dylan songs. Whatever fragments of mother-wit are left to rouse an America entertaining itself to death. But the exact HOW is a little tricky. Especially is this so for a culture that specializes in vacuuming up live instances of dissent and turning them into new marketing campaigns for its corporate gospel of cool. In a culture like that, the prophet/poet has to enter a place *below* language: "the silence

under their song," the place "where speech / Is trying to go."
Because that's where Christ is: "lowdown," in the "deep water."[62]

And that's about all Merton will say about it. No religious
doctrine emerges from the Anna Livia Plurabelle scene. There are
no "imperatives / I mean models."[63] No twelve-step program for
spiritual growth available in a limited time offer: "For a dollar
ninety-nine you will have immortal longings here on the front
porch. You will become as slim and lovely as our own hypnotic
phlogiston toothpaste."[64] Merton refuses to take that bait. He
leaves the meaning of the episode open and slightly off-center—
Christ as Houdini?—in order to preserve a realm of imagination
and play where Christ may not always look like "himself."

This is one of the ironies of the Easter story and part of the
counter-lesson of Merton's Christianity. When Merton names
Christ directly in Canto 80 and allows us to witness his return to
the garden, a sleepy disciple—one of many half-conscious
"Bernsteins" in *Cables*—mistakes him for the moon:

> Slowly, slowly
> Comes Christ through the garden
> Speaking to the sacred trees
> Their branches bear his light
> Without harm . . .
>
> Slowly slowly
> Christ rises on the cornfields
> It is only the harvest moon
> The disciple
> Turns over in his sleep
> And murmurs:
> "My regret!"[65]

Rolling the tape back to the garden, Merton pictures Christ's appearance as a return to innocence for all the fatal children—
Ginsberg's hipsters, Vonnegut's Billy Pilgrim, Dylan's blue-eyed
son. The trees are no longer bleeding in the Easter garden, as they
are in "Hard Rain." They are sacred and alive, bearing Christ's
light "without harm." At least to some. To the half-conscious disciple, however, Christ's light could just as easily be "the harvest
moon." Or rather *"only* the harvest moon"—as the disciple looks
out at a landscape which seems to be stripped of the divine.

When Christ appears at the empty tomb in St. John's gospel, Mary Magdalene doesn't recognize him at first, mistaking him not for the moon but for the gardener—or as Merton's disciple would say, "only the gardener." When Christ calls Mary by name, however, the scene shifts for her, the tumblers drop, and she sees Christ, as if for the first time. The shift from gardener to Christ in the Easter scene evokes, for me, the puzzle pictures of childhood: stairs that seem to go up, then down, then up again. A picture of a vase that becomes a picture of two people kissing. Once you get the hang of it, you can keep sliding back and forth between the images. But you cannot force the shift. It has nothing to do with control or will power. In fact, if you seek it, Merton says, "you do not find it. If you stop seeking, it is there."[66] The pleasure of the puzzle is the jump in the image—the sudden "it is there"—when the picture changes from one thing to another. But to experience the shift, we have to "misunderstand" the vase—the subtitle of *Cables* is "familiar liturgies of misunderstanding"—in the same way Mary must misunderstand the gardener and the sleepy disciple must misunderstand the harvest moon. Such thinking is *familiar*, because we do it all the time, seeing and re-seeing a hundred times a day. It is a *liturgy* because such limberness is sacred, a ludicrous gospel of playfulness and surprise. "No man can see God," Eckhart says, "except . . . through folly."[67]

This, ultimately, is the blessing of *Cables* and Merton's prayer for a quietly desperate world: more play, more folly, more of what he calls the "inventions of unprecedented laughter"[68]—the good deep belly laugh we get when the tumblers shift and the head-bubbles clear and we see, for a moment, the stairs ascending or the lovers kissing or the face of Christ in disguise.[69]

Notes

1. Belden Lane, "Merton's Hermitage: Bachelard, Domestic Space, and Spiritual Transformation," *Spiritus: A Journal of Christian Spirituality* 4: 2 (Fall 2004), p. 125. For other accounts of creative and spiritual play in Merton, see Michael Mott, *The Seven Mountains of Thomas Merton* (Boston: Houghton Mifflin, 1984), p. 460; and Belden Lane, "Merton as Zen Clown," *Theology Today*: 46: 3 (October 1989), pp. 256-68. For Merton's reflections on how Trappist discipline and liturgy constitute forms of sacred play, see *The Intimate Merton: His Life from His Journals*, ed. Patrick Hart and Jonathan Montaldo (New York: HarperCollins, 1999), p. 29.

2. Quoted in Lane, "Zen Clown," p. 264.

3. Thomas Merton, *Cables to the Ace: Or, Familiar Liturgies of Misunderstanding* (New York: New Directions, 1968), p. 28.

4. Quoted in Ross Labrie, *The Art of Thomas Merton* (Fort Worth: Texas Christian University Press, 1979), p. 138.

5. Bob Kaufman, *Cranial Guitar* (Minneapolis: Coffee House Press, 1996), p. 82.

6. For an analysis of the influence of the Beat Generation writers on *Cables*, see Claire Hoertz Badaracco, "The Influence of 'Beat' Generation Poetry on the Work of Thomas Merton," *The Merton Annual* 15 (2002), pp. 121-35.

7. Derived in part from the Russian Formalists' concept of "defamiliarization," Brecht's *Verfremdungseffekt* or *V-effekt* disrupts an audience's passivity. Making the artifice of the play as high-profile as possible—through disruptive commentaries, jarring scene shifts, and sudden outbursts of song—Brecht encourages his audience to see through the illusions of the play and recover self-conscious critical distance—a goal Merton shares with Brecht. On the alienation effect in Brecht, see Chris Baldick, *The Concise Oxford Dictionary of Literary Terms* (New York: Oxford University Press, 1990), pp. 4-5.

8. Merton, *Cables to the Ace*, p. 28.

9. Merton, *Cables to the Ace*, p. 24.

10. Merton, *Cables to the Ace*, p. 11.

11. Henry David Thoreau, *Walden and Other Writings* (New York: The Modern Library, 1950), p. 7.

12. Thoreau, *Walden* , p. 7.

13. Quoted in Lane, "Zen Clown," p. 30.

14. Merton, *Cables to the Ace*, pp. 51, 23.

15. Stephen John Mack, *The Pragmatic Whitman: Reimagining American Democracy* (Iowa City: University of Iowa Press, 2002), p. 139.

16. In his review of Roland Barthes' *Writing Degree Zero*, Merton describes the political purpose of literature this way: "[The writer] does something to society not by pushing against its structures—which are none of his business—but by changing the tune of its language and shifting the perspectives which depend on the ways words are arranged. He systematically de-mythologizes literature." Thomas Merton, *The Literary Essays of Thomas Merton*, ed. Brother Patrick Hart (New York: New Directions, 1981), p. 144. Despite the either-or phrasing, Merton intervenes in the social crises of his culture in *both* ways: "pushing against its structures" in countless works of political and social advocacy in the 1960s as well as "shifting the perspectives" through the kaleidoscopic anti-language of poems like *Cables to the Ace* and *The Geography of Lograire*. For an analysis of how the postmodern language experiments of *Geog-*

raphy support a theology of empowerment and liberation, see Bradford
T. Stull, *Religious Dialectics of Pain and Imagination* (Albany: State University of New York Press, 1994), pp. 61-94.

17. Merton, *Cables to the Ace*, p. 13.

18. For theories of literary and cultural play that emphasize change, as Merton does, and stress the power of play to unsettle fixed or dogmatic systems of control, see Johan Huizinga, *Homo Ludens: A Study of the Play Element in Culture*, trans. R. F. C. Hull (London: Paladin, 1970); Roger Caillois, *Man, Play and Games*, trans. Meyer Barash (London: Thames and Hudson, 1962); Jürgen Moltmann, *Theology of Play*, trans. Reinhard Ulrich (New York: Harper and Row, 1972); James S. Hans, *The Play of the World* (Amherst: University of Massachusetts Press, 1981); and Brian Edwards, *Theories of Play and Postmodern Fiction* (New York: Garland Publishing, 1998).

19. Merton, *Cables to the Ace*, pp. 28-29.

20. Merton, *Cables to the Ace*, p. 28.

21. For a reference of McLuhan's influence on *Cables*, see George Woodcock, *Thomas Merton, Monk and Poet: A Critical Study* (New York: Farrar, Straus, Giroux, 1978), p. 175.

22. Merton, *Cables to the Ace*, pp. 28, 6.

23. Merton, *Cables to the Ace*, p. 30.

24. Merton, *Cables to the Ace*, pp. 28, 29.

25. Quoted in Labrie, *The Art of Thomas Merton*, p. 110.

26. Merton, *Cables to the Ace*, p. 1.

27. Thomas Merton, *The Asian Journal of Thomas Merton* (New York: New Directions, 1973), pp. 118, 178.

28. Quoted in Labrie, *The Art of Thomas Merton*, 110.

29. Allen Ginsberg, *Howl and Other Poems* (San Francisco: City Lights, 1974), p. 22.

30. Merton, *Literary Essays*, pp. 313-14.

31. Merton, *Cables to the Ace*, p. 27. In March, 1948, just after *Figures for an Apocalypse* was published, James Laughlin sent Merton's first three collections of poetry to T. S. Eliot, hoping for a favorable review. Eliot wrote back saying that Merton composed too much and revised too little, a remark so devastating it led Merton to consider giving up poetry altogether . See Mott, *The Seven Mountains of Thomas Merton*, p. 242. For Merton's response to the spirituality of Eliot's *Four Quartets*, see Merton, *Literary Essays*, p. 314.

32. Merton, *Literary Essays*, p. 313.

33. Quoted in Lynn Szabo, "'Hiding the Ace of Freedoms': Discovering the Way(s) of Peace in Thomas Merton's *Cables to the Ace*," *The Merton Annual* 15 (2002), p. 107.

34. Bob Dylan, *Lyrics: 1962-2001* (New York: Simon and Schuster, 2004), p. 59.

35. Labrie, *The Art of Thomas Merton*, p. 136.

36. Merton, *Cables to the Ace*, p. 24.

37. Merton, *Cables to the Ace*, p. 14.

38. Merton, *Cables to the Ace*, p. 24.

39. Merton, *Cables to the Ace*, p. 2.

40. Merton, *Cables to the Ace*, p. 2.

41. Merton, *Cables to the Ace*, pp. 18, 6, 7.

42. T. S. Eliot, *The Waste Land and Other Poems* (New York: Harcourt, Brace and World, 1962), p. 31.

43. Merton, *Cables to the Ace*, p. 28.

44. Merton, *Cables to the Ace*, pp. 6-7.

45. Merton, *Cables to the Ace*, pp. 43, 1, 6. My thinking here has been influenced by Ursula LeGuin's 1986 Commencement Address at Bryn Mawr College, quoted in Jane Tompkins, "Me and My Shadow," in *The Intimate Critique: Autobiographical Literary Criticism*, ed. Diane P. Freedman, Olivia Frey, and Frances Murphy Zauhar (Durham: Duke University Press, 1993), p. 29.

46. Merton, *Cables to the Ace*, pp. 24, 40.

47. Merton, *Cables to the Ace*, p. 42.

48. Kurt Vonnegut, Jr., *Slaughterhouse-Five: Or, The Children's Crusade* (New York: Delacorte Press/Seymour Lawrence, 1969), p. 22.

49. Vonnegut, *Slaughterhouse-Five*, p. 72.

50. Merton, *Cables to the Ace*, pp. 27, 7.

51. Merton, *Cables to the Ace*, p. 43.

52. Lane, "Merton's Hermitage," p. 133.

53. Merton, *Cables to the Ace*, p. 42.

54. Anna Livia Plurabelle is the mother-source in *Finnegans Wake*— the free-flowing matrix of all waters and a profound image of the sacred for Joyce: "In the name of Anna, the All-Maziful, the bringer of plurabilities, halloed be her eve, her singtime sung, her rills be run, unhemmed as they are uneven." James Joyce, *Finnegans Wake* (New York: Penguin Press, 1976), p. 104. Merton references Anna Livia Plurabelle not only in this canto but earlier in the "Mama my ocean" of the child's pre-conscious dreams and develops a similar set of associations among water, swimming, and the sacred.

55. Thoreau, *Walden*, p. 88.

56. Merton, *Cables to the Ace*, p. 13.

57. Merton, *Cables to the Ace*, p. 60.

58. Merton, *Cables to the Ace*, pp. 59, 60.

59. George Kilcourse, Jr., *Ace of Freedoms: Thomas Merton's Christ* (Notre Dame: University of Notre Dame Press, 1993), p. 178.

60. Merton, *Cables to the Ace*, p. 42.

61. Merton, *Cables to the Ace*, p. 42.

62. Merton, *Cables to the Ace*, pp. 6, 10, 42.

63. Merton, *Cables to the Ace*, p. 42.

64. Merton, *Cables to the Ace*, p. 60.

65. Merton, *Cables to the Ace*, p. 55.

66. Merton, *Cables to the Ace*, p. 58.

67. Merton, *Cables to the Ace*, p. 28.

68. Merton, *Cables to the Ace*, p. 35.

69. I like to thank a number of friends and colleagues who read earlier versions of this essay: Jon Barber, James Fitzpatrick Smith, Alison Tyner Davis, George Kilcourse, Ross Labrie, and Mike Wilcox. The research for this essay was partially funded by a grant from the Faculty Endowment Board of Wittenberg University.

An Interview with Fr. Kilian McDonnell, O.S.B.
February 11, 2005

Conducted and edited by Victor A. Kramer*

I

Kramer: My idea is to talk about vocation and the religious life of the Church during the period which paralleled Merton's entry into the monastic life. Then we will try to fit the famous Fr. Louis into the mix. But that is not as important as beginning to understand your family and background and how your religious vocation fits in here.

What we want to do is to let you develop a picture of your life and vocation during the past many decades.

McDonnell: I come from a family of eight children, seven boys and one girl. I am the fourth from the oldest. We were a lower middle-class family—never really poor and certainly never well off. When I came to college, I would not have been able to go to college had I not been studying for the priesthood. My parents simply did not have the money.

Kramer: Did you go to a public school?

McDonnell: I went to a public school through high school. I did not attend a Catholic school until I came here as a freshman in college.

---

*These interviews (this one and the following, both conducted at the Abbey of St. John's, Collegeville, February, 2005) reveal much about the nature of religious vocation during the era of Merton's life. Along with providing new information about Merton, it is hoped that their inclusion in *The Merton Annual* will also provide insight into the nature of religious vocation in the twentieth-century and may encourage scholars to interview other persons who were Merton's contemporaries, not so much to uncover material just about Thomas Merton, but rather to document the wider life of the Church during the periods both before and after Vatican II.

While Merton is perhaps the best known religious of his era, it is also quite valuable to be reminded of the many hundreds, indeed thousands, of vocations which contributed to the development of the Church during this time of change. (V.A.K.)

Kramer: So you came to St. John's in what year?

McDonnell: 1940.

Kramer: What do you remember about St. John's in 1940?

McDonnell: It was a quite different place as you can suspect. It was very much a pre-Vatican II monastery. There were no women on the faculty. Almost all the professors were monks. The monks wore their habits more often. The students went to Mass daily. So life was less open and more ordered. St. John's was already a national center of theology and beginning to be so for the arts. It was a center of not only a liturgical movement but also a rural life movement, a farm movement.

Kramer: If you think back to your family life then coming to St. John's, did you find it a kind of surprise, a different way of life?

McDonnell: Yes, it was a different way of life. I grew up in a very small town with one thousand people. St. John's represented cosmopolitan [life]. There were possibilities and opportunities that were not available to me in Velva, North Dakota.

Kramer: So you came already with the idea in mind that you had a religious vocation.

McDonnell: Yes. I came with that idea.

Kramer: But you were not necessarily planning to be a Benedictine?

McDonnell: No, I was not. I was planning to be a diocesan priest. But my vocation came about this way: in my family at the beginning of Lent, everybody gave up something. When I was in high school—probably a sophomore or freshman—I said, "I'm not going to give up movies for Lent." Then I thought instead of giving something up, why not do something like go to Mass every day. So I started to going to Mass every day. When the end of Lent came, I kind of liked it. And so I kept on doing it. For a young man to go to Mass every day in Velva, North Dakota, was highly suspicious! So the pastor came to visit my parents. He said I had been coming to Mass every day and he thought I had a vocation to the priesthood. My parents said they wanted to talk to me first. Several days later, my parents cornered me and asked, "Is it true?" I said, "What is this? Can't a guy go to Mass without you shipping him off to seminary?" I said I did not have any intention of joining the priesthood.

But I kept thinking about it and began praying actually, praying that I receive a vocation. Then I had a rather strong calling. I was going to a public school. The Catholic Church was extremely small. We were a very small minority in a Protestant village. I decided that in order to protect my vocation, I would not go to dances. But giving up dances was a big, big sacrifice because I loved to dance. And I was pretty good too! So that kind of cut me off. Also I would not date. Perhaps if I had socialized more at that age, it would have been better for me.

But I retained my vocation and the Bishop came. This was Bishop Muench, Aloysius Muench. He became an apostolic delegate to Germany after the War and then a Cardinal. He came to my town on a confirmation tour. Pastor arranged for me to see the Bishop. He asked me about my vocation. I said I wanted to be a priest. He then asked what kind of priest. I said, "I don't know. I don't know any religious order. But I kind of suspect that is what I want to be." He said, "You go to St. John's and study for the diocese of Fargo until you make up your mind. We'll take care of your expense." So I went to St. John's, and I liked what I saw. I liked it very much. But I was torn between the Dominicans and the Benedictines. I had as my spiritual director, the Novice Master.

Kramer: Who was the Novice Master?

McDonnell: Basil Stegmann. I talked to him about the Dominicans and Benedictines and finally decided to be Dominican.

Kramer: How old were you at this point?

McDonnell: I was a junior in college.

Kramer: Did you live in the monastery?

McDonnell: No, I lived in the dormitory.

Kramer: So, no dancing?

McDonnell: No! No dancing. That was hard. But when the ducks went over in the fall, I would go duck hunting. I was a great duck hunter and enjoyed being outdoors. That was hard too to give up. So I went off to the Dominicans after my junior year.

Kramer: Was that 1942 or 1943?

McDonnell: That was 1943. I loved the Dominicans. But I got sick. I think it was from standing on a flagstone floor when it was cold.

Kramer: Which Dominican friary did you attend?

McDonnell: It was in River Forest, Chicago.

Kramer: So you were there in 1944 and 1945?

McDonnell: Yes. 1944 and 45. But I did not finish the Novitiate. I wanted to finish it. I loved the life. But I became ill and I had to go to the doctor. I decided I would not leave on my own. If they threw me out, I would go. But I was not going to leave of my own free will.

Kramer: Why did you want to be a Dominican?

McDonnell: I was interested in preaching. I loved the community life. I just wanted to stay. Finally after about seven months, the Novice Master told me they could not give me vows and I would have to leave. It broke my heart.

Kramer: So you were in Chicago, and it was 1944.

McDonnell: Pardon me. It was 1943 when I left for the Dominicans. So it was now 1944. I left the Dominicans in 1944. I had an invitation to work in a school for the deaf in the Bronx. So I went there. But first I went to St. Thomas Seminary in Denver. The only reason I went was because it was wartime, and it was not proper to be wandering around if one was not in the Army. I had gone to the draft board in my county in North Dakota. I said, "I'm home. My health is bad. I'm a priesthood student. I'm a 4-A because I'm a seminarian. But as soon as I get my health, I'm going back." I hoped that that would take care of it. But the draft board did not seem impressed. When I came home the pastor said, "Don't stay in Velva. Go to some seminary. Just get out." So I went to St. Thomas Seminary in Denver. I received my 4-A designation by mail. I went to the Rector who sent me to the Archdiocese lawyer. The lawyer said, "If you're in bad health, you won't pass the exam. So take it and we'll go from there." So I took the exam and I flunked it! Then I did not have to be in the seminary. So I went out to the Bronx to work at the school for the deaf.

Kramer: Was it a religious institution?

McDonnell: Yes. It was run by the Viatorians. I was there for about six months. The work I was doing was mostly as the night watchman. But being up all night was not a good idea for somebody trying to get back on his feet. I had a chance to go to Mount

Manresa on Staten Island, which is a Jesuit Retreat House. I worked there for about six months.

Kramer: How old were you then?

McDonnell: It was 1945. So I was about twenty-five. After working there for six months, I went home to Power, Montana. My parents had moved back to Montana. So I got on the train, which passed right through here [St. John's]. I stopped to say hello to friends here. I also saw Basil Stegmann. We talked about what happened. I told him I loved it, I really wanted to stay and that it broke my heart to leave. He said, "Why don't you apply here?" I said, "Would they take a broken-down reject?" He said to apply. So I did, and I was accepted by the monastic community at St. John's on the Feast of St. Dominic.

Kramer: During these years, were you thinking much about the Benedictine Order or the Benedictine Rule?

McDonnell: I was here, and I liked it here. That is all I knew.

II

Kramer: So your relationship to St. John's basically started over again and your vocation took a new twist.

McDonnell: Yes. It started over.

Kramer: So you started as a novice. Was the Novice Master the same person?

McDonnell: It was Basil. I had had a very, very difficult Novitiate. The reason it was difficult was because we got up at 4:10 a.m. That is early. And we did not get breakfast until about 6:30 or 7:00. That nearly killed me. I was not completely healthy, and it was just very tough. I was not sick, just a weakened state.

Kramer: So the routine still at that time at St. John's was going into the Church many times a day. So you would go for the evening hours at 4:30 or so. When was the community Mass?

McDonnell: Mass was in the mornings. It was after Sext, I think— after five of the liturgical hours.

Kramer: It really was a rigorous life because these guys were also all teaching or working.

McDonnell: Yes, it was rigorous, but I loved it. During the Novitiate, my physical strength went down.

Kramer: Did a novice at that point sleep in the dormitory with others?

McDonnell: Yes, we did. There were about twelve novices with me. That was not a hardship to me. Because I had such a difficult time—Basil really wanted me to stay and he did everything he could. I was just so exhausted.

Kramer: How long was the Novitiate?

McDonnell: One year.

Kramer: Then you made temporary vows?

McDonnell: I made vows under a special arrangement. According to our constitutions, if the community accepts me for temporary vows, then the community cannot reject me at solemn vows for health reasons. So if they accept me, they are taking a risk. Father Basil wrote out a document that said if my health is not better by the time of solemn vows, I will not hold the community to its obligations. So I said, "Where do I sign?" And I signed it gladly. When it came time for solemn vows, my health was worse. When my application came up in the Chapter, this was an issue. Basil wanted me to stay. An older monk got up in Chapter and said, "That document is immoral and uncanonical. And it has no force." So the community said, "Ok, he's in."

Kramer: Then what was your job?

McDonnell: I was still a student. I finished as a student in 1951. I was ready for ordination then. But my health continued to deteriorate. By then I was in very bad shape—having a major problem keeping up with everything. They gave me a private room. There was a bed and a chair, and that is all. I was not in the lap of luxury!

But I was ordained. I had to spend a lot of time resting. They decided to put me in a parish because they thought a parish might be easier for me. So I went for three years at Hastings. I got better, a little better. But it was desperately hard. I was having to say three Masses without any food. That was really hard.

Kramer: Were you in Hastings by yourself?

McDonnell: No. I was an assistant. After three years, I changed from Hastings to Detroit Lakes. When I got to Detroit Lakes I saw that the job would be not only beyond my physical strength, but way beyond. But I said to myself, "Do the best you can." So I did not say anything to my superiors.

Kramer: How long were you there?

McDonnell: I was there for one year. After the year I was supposed to go to school in the summer at Notre Dame. When I got on the train to go back to Notre Dame, I collapsed in Minneapolis. I did not say anything to the monastery and stayed there for about four or five days. Then I went to Notre Dame to start classes. I lasted three or four days before I was in the hospital. But there was nothing wrong with me. I had just spent all my capital. If you spend all your capital, you have nothing to build on. So I was in the hospital for a week. I went back to classes again and only lasted about three days. Then I was back in the hospital.

My brother who was a pilot flew down and got me and brought me to Minneapolis. I rested there for a week then I told St. John's what had happened. I went back to St. John's and stayed in the infirmary for a month. Gradually, over the next thirty years I got better, but it was a struggle.

Kramer: I know what you are talking about. You just run out of energy. But your religious life has been built. You had a good foundation, and you had found a good place here. So then you had already begun your work as a religious. What about those earliest years? What was satisfying about that work?

McDonnell: I loved preaching. I liked being in the parish, but I like being here at St. John's better. I was effective as a young priest.

Kramer: When did you start having an interest in non-Catholic religions?

McDonnell: Growing up in Velva, North Dakota, I was surrounded by Protestants. Very few of my friends were Catholic. At the end of the 1950s, ecumenism was on the horizon. The Theology Department met to decide whether or not they should teach Protestant theology to our undergraduate students. I was teaching religion in the theology department. I said I was against it because we did not have enough time to teach them Catholic theology. Why should we take the little time we have and teach Protestant theology? But I lost the vote. They said, "If we're going to do this, we should have someone really trained to do it." They looked around and said, "Kilian, you're the one."

Kramer: But you voted against it.

McDonnell: Yes. I voted against it. I went to the Abbot and said, "They want me to go on for Protestant theology. I think I can get a grant for this."

Kramer: Roughly, when did you get permission to write this grant proposal?

McDonnell: It was the late 1950s. I wrote out a two-page application and sent it to ten foundations. Eight said no. Two said yes. The first that said yes was the Butler family from St. Paul. But because my health was bad, the Abbot said it was not a good idea for me to go to Europe, which is where I wanted to go to study Protestant theology. So I went to Ottawa for a year. I had a very difficult time in Ottawa because I was still not back on my feet.

Kramer: What kind of program did Ottawa have?

McDonnell: It did not have a Protestant program. It was Catholic, but it was good. I got through the year and received the Licentiate. Then I went to Europe for three or four years at various universities—Trier, Tübingen, Münster, Heidelberg and Paderborn.

Kramer: Did you have any contact with Benedictine monasteries in Europe?

McDonnell: No.

Kramer: So you went from university to university listening to lectures.

McDonnell: Yes. And I did my thesis on John Calvin, the Church and the Eucharist.

Kramer: And this became a book?

McDonnell: Yes, published by Princeton University Press.

Kramer: Then you came back and had this idea about the Ecumenical Institute which has now existed for over four decades. The Butler family was in the background. What would you say about the religious life during this same period? You were studying and thinking about teaching Protestant religion at roughly the same time that Vatican II came along. So you came back here and all of the sudden the Church was a different church.

McDonnell: It was a different church. But I was part of the change. I was not exterior to it. I did not find the change difficult. I found it exhilarating. And I found my studies in Calvin exhilarating also.

III

Kramer: So all of the sudden, it was possible for a Catholic priest and professor to talk about Protestant theology. It was not forbidden. Indeed, it might even be good.

You also became editor of *Sponsa Regis*. How did that happen?

McDonnell: I became editor of *Sponsa Regis* before I went to Europe. When I was in Europe, there was another monk who was my assistant. He became the editor during that time.

Kramer: When you were editor, you had lots of manuscripts coming across your desk. And somehow you ended up with some Thomas Merton manuscripts. Then you corresponded some with Merton.

McDonnell: I corresponded with him, but my most substantial contact with him had nothing to do with *Sponsa Regis*. It had to do with a book he wrote on the Eucharist, *The Living Bread*. I was given that book to review. *The Living Bread*, from what I can remember, was unlike his other books in that it was a more formal presentation of the Eucharist—rather than the kind of reflective nature of his other writings. The formal writing Merton was not prepared to do. He was not educationally prepared.

Kramer: You are right. He wrote a book in 1951 called the *The Ascent to Truth* which was a systematic theological study using Aquinas to look at St. John of the Cross. He himself was not satisfied with that book. Then this book about the Eucharist came later, and it is the same type of book.

McDonnell: Yes. So I panned the book. Then my book review appeared in *Worship* [*Orate Fratres*] magazine. Two weeks after it appeared, Merton came to St. John's for a seminar. I was sitting alone in the refectory eating breakfast. He came down and sat right across the table facing me. This was not a meeting I wanted because of the review. I pushed the coffee and bread over and kept my head down. Finally, Fr. Louis says, "Can we talk?" I said, "Sure." So we talked. It was very nice.

We established contact. He was here for two weeks. During those days, I had other contacts with him.

At one point he asked me for a boat. So I got him a boat. One afternoon, he went out into the Bay. He was out there two or three hours and came back dripping wet. I said, "What happened?"

He said, "I was leaning over the boat looking into the water. It was so clear. I could see the fish and the seaweed. It was so blue and beautiful. I wanted to be a part of it, so I just jumped in."

Kramer: That is a great story. Did other people see him?

McDonnell: I do not think so. It was during the time he had had the confrontation or meeting with Zilboorg. He later said if I was in the area of Gethsemani, I should visit him. I said I would like to do that. He left. I then went to Ottawa. When I was at Ottawa, I asked for permission to go to Gethsemani during Christmas. I was given permission.

On the way down, I stopped at Mt. Saviour monastery in Elmira, New York. There was a Brother there who had been a novice under Merton at Gethsemani. He had left there and entered Elmira. When he heard I was going to Gethsemani, he asked if I would take a letter to Fr. Louis for him. I said, "Sure." So he wrote a letter and gave it to me. I went on my way to Gethsemani.

Kramer: This would have been around 1957 or 1958, before you went to Europe.

McDonnell: Yes. After I got to Gethsemani, Fr. Louis came to my room and we visited. I said I had the letter for him. But he did not take it. I asked if I had done something wrong. He said no, but he could not receive "secret letters." According to the rules, he was right. And he would not take it. So I asked him what he wanted me to do with it. He said I could read it out loud. So I opened it and read it.

It basically said, "Dear Fr. Louis, I thought I would drop you a note since Fr. Kilian is here and is going to Gethsemani. I want you to know how much I appreciated all you did for me while I was a novice. You really helped me find my Benedictine vocation, and I am very happy here at Elmira. I'm in my third year of theology, and I work in the garden and in the kitchen. Again, many thanks for all you did for me. Fraternally, Br. ...."

So then I still had the letter, and I asked what I should do with it. He said, "Eat it." I am sure it was in jest. At some point he took me out to his little hermitage.

Kramer: The tool shed—St. Anne's.

McDonnell: Yes. So we talked and talked. It was great. We talked about theology, ecumenism, and Europe. After some time I left for Germany. I kept up the correspondence with him for a while but had to give it up. I was doing doctoral studies.

Kramer: Have you read much of Merton? Have you looked at the poetry?

McDonnell: I have read a little. I cannot say a lot. I have looked at the poetry. We have a collection of all his poetry, which is a mean thing to do because some of it he surely would not want published.

Kramer: Yes. It is 1,048 pages.

McDonnell: Yes! Only an enemy would do that. But some of the poetry is lovely. He really had a gift.

Kramer: The early stuff is very intense and ambitious. The later stuff is kind of oblique and purposefully anti-poetic. There is a lot of nice stuff along the way. Do you think Merton's work has lasting value?

McDonnell: Oh yes. I think it does. He is a major spiritual writer. He is here to stay for sure.

Kramer: Have you looked at the journals?

McDonnell: I have. And I have one upstairs. I enjoy it. One thing he does that is very important—and it is a weakness in Catholicism. It is not to say that it does not belong to our tradition. You can find it in our tradition. But it is not a prominent feature; that is, the personal moment in faith. That is where Merton is strong. Because we do not get it from other places, we get it there.

Kramer: That is a very good point.

McDonnell: It is one of the things I learned from the Pentecostals. That is their area of strength. The whole evangelical arena asks, "Have you received Jesus as your personal savior?" So it is that personal element which I think will give him a permanent place, together with his honesty.

Kramer: I happened to be reading *Weavings* for March-April, 2005. And I found two of your poems: "A Place to Hide: Light Off" and "A Place to Hide: Light On." My question is, what is going on in these poems?

McDonnell: Well, something is going on in those two poems. They are two states—a person who has been in the religious life for a long time and endures—light off, which is more of the permanent state, or the usual state. You are fighting to escape from formalism. And you are trying to get back to the personal moment of faith. The only way to do that is to make faith a personal endeavor and to use the scriptures in a personal way. I can use Merton in that way also. He is very helpful that way. I do not want to talk about the "Dark Night of the Soul," but it is something like that. You are left without the slightest interest in things religious.

Kramer: Yes. And that is hard. It is very hard. I just threw these two poems into the discussion because I think Merton had to deal with the same thing. Early, Merton had certain concepts about the Church. And, early, he had certain concepts about the poems. He said himself that he did not like aspects of *The Seven Storey Mountain*, but he was not going to revise it. At the same time, there is a considerable shift as he moves from the 1930s to '40s to '50s to '60s. There is something going on which has to do with his own life and spiritual life. I think that is what is really good about what he is able to do. That is what Catholics need to learn about their own spiritual life, that their own personal life can be part of that spiritual life. It seems to me that so many Catholics are back in the 1930s hoping the priest will provide them whatever they need.

McDonnell: "Light On" represents not the usual but a rare moment when God does not abandon you, and he opens the door an inch.

Kramer: To go back to Merton for a minute, why do you think some readers, some Catholics seem to be afraid of Thomas Merton? Did you hear about the new catechism that the Bishops were doing? They had a draft and a section on Merton but they pulled it because they said he would be too difficult for people to understand. They substituted Elizabeth Seton because they said they needed women. So Merton is not in this draft of the new American Catechism.

McDonnell: Mother Seton is fine, and they need a woman. But to leave Merton out shows that Bishops do not think they can handle Merton in the space allotted or they are trying to protect the poor, dumb laity.

Kramer: That is true. That is absolutely right.

McDonnell: Another reason why Merton will endure is that, unlike Mother Seton, Merton was a cosmopolitan person. He had been immersed in the secular culture. So he comes out of that culture. He knows it well and he has this seeking of God in a contemplative context. That is very attractive. The other thing is that there is no sham. He never covers up his faults.

Kramer: Right. That is the whole purpose of the journals. This last batch of questions—Did you meet him? Did he have a sense of humor? You have already answered the questions.

We could ask many other questions regarding your work and people like yourself and Merton and Vatican II as a dividing line. A lot of people are very disappointed and frustrated with some changes in the Church. I think you can look at Vatican II and all those changes as very valuable.

I was speaking with Sr. Shaun O'Meara of St. Ben's Monastery yesterday. She was talking about how so many people are disappointed that there are not sisters to work in the schools. Well, lay people can work in the schools. It was never the sisters' job to work exclusively in schools anyway. So it is not that we are in some kind of crisis. We are in a moment of opportunity. I think the work that you have done with the Collegeville Institute for Ecumenical and Cultural Research is a perfect example of that. What is interesting is that you were given sufficient latitude in your vocation to do the work you have accomplished.

An Interview with Fr. Raymond Pedrizetti, O.S.B.
February 12, 2005

*Conducted and edited by Victor A. Kramer**

I

Kramer: What I would like to do first is to ask you to provide information about your choice to become a religious, your childhood, and your family. What size family did you come from and what do you remember about your early Catholicism?

Pedrizetti: I had two brothers and one sister. It was a more or less pious Catholic family. My father is Italian. My mother is Irish. That combination raised some eyebrows, but it worked out well.

Kramer: Where were you born?

Pedrizetti: I was born in Duluth, Minnesota in 1930.

Kramer: What do you remember about your early years and when you first started school?

Pedrizetti: I went to school in a Catholic parish run by Benedictine nuns at St. Scholastica in Duluth. What I remember mostly is running around doing things and enjoying sports, and having a congenial neighborhood to live in. There were a number of good-size families and kids my age to play with. It was during the Depres-

---

*These interviews (this one and the preceeding, both conducted at the Abbey of St. John's, Collegeville, February, 2005) reveal much about the nature of religious vocation during the era of Merton's life. Along with providing new information about Merton, it is hoped that their inclusion in *The Merton Annual* will also provide insight into the nature of religious vocation in the twentieth-century and may encourage scholars to interview other persons who were Merton's contemporaries, not so much to uncover material just about Thomas Merton, but rather to document the wider life of the Church during the periods both before and after Vatican II.

While Merton is perhaps the best known religious of his era, it is also quite valuable to be reminded of the many hundreds, indeed thousands, of vocations which contributed to the development of the Church during this time of change. (V.A.K.)

sion, so we created our own fun and played games and did not feel deprived too much because we did not have anything to compare it with, of course.

Kramer: What did your father do?

Pedrizetti: My dad worked for the City Water and Gas Department. He repaired water and gas facilities and so on and later became a supervisor. He started out as a meter reader. Before I was born, I think he was a sales person in a department store.

Kramer: When you think back on the religious atmosphere in your school and home, is there anything that stands out?

Pedrizetti: Well, what stands out in retrospect is that we took religion for granted. We were taught by nuns and were expected in school to show up for weekday Mass frequently. And that was a given part of the schedule. Some activities revolved around the Church. The Assistant Pastor would play sports with us, for example. Things like that were taken for granted.

Kramer: When did you consciously begin to think about the possibility of perhaps a religious vocation?

Pedrizetti: In the middle of my year in the seventh grade, a good friend of mine was killed in a car accident. I remember being shocked—I was a pallbearer—by seeing a dead body for the first time, and all that goes with that. I am sure that was the incident that tripped my thinking about the possibility of a religious life. And by the time I reached the middle of the 8th grade, I had asked about going to St. John's Preparatory School with the possibility of becoming a priest. Through the Assistant Pastor at my parish who had studied theology here and knew the place, I began my first year of high school at St. John's.

Kramer: What year was that?

Pedrizetti: 1944.

Kramer: What building was the Prep School in?

Pedrizetti: This was during World War II. There were only five college graduates in my first year of prep school. The Prep School was the predominant institution at the time. Everything took place more or less in the quadrangle buildings.

Kramer: So you were here for those four years. Then did you continue at St. John's?

Pedrizetti: I continued for two years at college. My classmates then entered the Novitiate here. I entered the Novitiate at Spencer, Massachusetts.

II

Kramer: So you entered a Cistercian monastery? That was fairly unusual wasn't it?

Pedrizetti: I was a Trappist novice for a year and a half after my sophomore year of college.

Kramer: What was Spencer like at that point?

Pedrizetti: It was a very interesting situation. I received my acceptance papers the day the monastery that was originally in Rhode Island burnt down. So I wrote back and asked if I should still come at the end of the school year. This occurred in the spring sometime. They said to come. They were relocated in an old C.C.C. camp in Chepachet, Rhode Island. The Novitiate program was set up there at that C.C.C. camp. Among the rest of the community, some were at the camp and some were at the new location at Spencer.

Kramer: How many people were there as novices at the camp?

Pedrizetti: There were two novitiates and about twenty or thirty people. We commuted back and forth between Spencer and Chepachet which was about an hour's trip. We worked to help build and modify the buildings at Spencer in preparation for the whole community to move there.

Kramer: So there were already buildings there?

Pedrizetti: There were buildings there. It was originally a large dairy farm. There were several buildings already there. One was reformed into a chapel.

Kramer: So what stands out in your memory from those years?

Pedrizetti: It was a very intense time. I had become interested in the Trappists rather than the Benedictines during my first two years at college at St. John's. I sought advice and decided to give it a try and went there after my sophomore year. This was the first time I had been without an academic program to follow. So I read up and prayed about the development of the spiritual life.

Thomas Merton['s books] began to appear during this time.

Kramer: Merton had already become known, and you had read him?

Pedrizetti: I read the usual works—*The Seven Storey Mountain*.

Kramer: Then in 1949, did you read *Seeds of Contemplation*?

Pedrizetti: I read it somewhere along the way. I cannot remember exactly when.

Kramer: So he was someone whom you were aware of?

Pedrizetti: Very much so. In fact, we had a visitation by Dom James Fox during the time I was there in the novitiate. He made some remarks about Merton. I do not remember exactly what he said, but the point is that he was already well known.

Kramer: Right, he was ordained in 1949. And already by 1951 he was assuming the role of Master of Scholastics which was very fast work.

Pedrizetti: Yes. That was the year I was in the novitiate. 1950, or 51.

Kramer: So you stayed a year and a half. You must have felt there were many good things there. But you decided to come back here. How did you decide that?

Pedrizetti: In the middle of that year my health began to give away a little. I sought some advice and, for various reasons, it was decided that it would be better for me to leave. I wanted to stay around and keep at it for a while longer. But the writing was on the wall so I said, "Ok, I'll go."

Kramer: And you were only twenty or twenty-one? So then what did you do?

Pedrizetti: Yes. I came back here and finished college. I managed to do that in a full senior year, then a summer program. I took a few courses at what was eventually UMD in Duluth, University of Minnesota in Duluth. Then I took my senior year of college here. Then I thought about entering here and decided to go ahead and do that.

Kramer: So when you entered St. John's, you in effect had to start the novitiate over?

Pedrizetti: Yes. I spent two and one half years in the novitiate.

Kramer: Was there someone at that time who served as novice master?

Pedrizetti: We entered by classes rather than just any old time. I entered with twelve others on July 11, 1953. The Novice Master was Fr. Cosmas Dahlheimer. The associate Novice Master who sorted out our jobs and things like that was a young cleric who has been a classmate of mine in school. But by then those who I had studied with in prep school were a year ahead of me.

Kramer: So you did a year of novitiate and you continued....

Pedrizetti: I continued on and took four years of theology and was ordained in 1958.

Kramer: And had you started teaching by then?

Pedrizetti: I started teaching right after ordination.

Kramer: During your years of religious formation you had regular conferences with your novice master? How was that done at that point?

Pedrizetti: There were regular conferences in the program. We were isolated from the rest of the community. It was a rather strict sort of existence.

Kramer: Did you go to choir with the community?

Pedrizetti: Yes, we went to choir with the community. We did not eat with them because we were the permanent waiters! So we usually ate before or right after. That was standard procedure.

Kramer: Did you have a spiritual director in addition to a novice master?

Pedrizetti: Not in the novitiate. We had a confessor. There were half a dozen or more that were recommended—priests in the monastery. We could choose anybody, but it was recommended to choose one of those priests.

Kramer: So, during that time when you were preparing for ordination, what seemed to be most valuable for you in developing your vocation and moving toward ordination?

Pedrizetti: Well, I discovered philosophy when I was in the Trappist [monastery] which was rather odd. But before that time, I was mostly interested in sports and making money and doing things. The intellectual life did not mean much to me at all until I was in the Trappist novitiate. So when I came back it was great fun to study philosophy which was what I was doing to finish college.

Kramer: Were you reading Aquinas? What were you reading?

Pedrizetti: I was reading ancient Greek philosophy as well as medieval philosophy. In those days Aquinas was pretty well the theological standard. So my interests in philosophy dove-tailed with much of my theological work.

Kramer: Do you remember a particular moment in your religious life when you were absolutely sure that you would stay and that you were certain that this was it; and that you did not have any doubts about continuing?

Pedrizetti: I cannot recall a particular moment, but there was an atmosphere that grew and suggested I fit well with this life and with possibilities of teaching and with the Benedictine Rule and its application here. So it gradually grew on me. I suppose there was one day when I said, "Well, it is perfectly obvious that I belong here."

Kramer: How is the Benedictine Rule important for you?

Pedrizetti: It gives me a framework within which to make decisions. The major vows of poverty, chastity and obedience provide a particular framework in which you make decisions by and how you are going to live your life. And it gives meaning on a daily basis, the daily horarium.

Kramer: Are there particular persons who seemed to be of special value to you during your period of formation?

Pedrizetti: My confessor—I held onto him right until I was ordained and shortly after actually. I always received good advice from him. There were a few of my teachers in philosophy and history who were members of the monastic community who were people I looked up to and could call upon to ask questions.

Kramer: Whom in philosophy do you remember?

Pedrizetti: Well, I remember Fr. Ernest Keltzer very much and Eleutherius Winance who was actually a Benedictine from another community. But he was one of those charismatic kinds of people for many of us and I got a lot of ideas from him.

Kramer: Would you want to say something about your work as a religious? You are the Prior now. And what other kinds of religious jobs have you had over the years?

Pedrizetti: When I was ordained my major job was teaching. I started out teaching Classics actually. Much of my graduate school training was in Classics. I started teaching Latin and Greek. But then the Vatican Council came along and Latin and Greek were no longer all that important for seminary training. So it was suggested to me to switch into philosophy, which I did. And I spent about thirty years teaching philosophy and enjoyed it quite a bit. I had an opportunity to read and think about a lot of things and discuss a lot of ideas that I was learning about and familiar with.

Kramer: Did you write in this area?

Pedrizetti: The only thing I wrote at that time was book reviews. But I did a lot of collecting of ideas. I have files full of stuff but have not published much.

Kramer: I saw an article in *Sponsa Regis* with Pedrizetti's name on it. But your name in religion was Anselm.

Pedrizetti: Yes, Anselm.

Kramer: So I saw something in *Sponsa Regis* by Anselm Pedrizetti, but I cannot remember the title.

Pedrizetti: Well, I wrote several articles for that.

Kramer: What kind of articles were those?

Pedrizetti: Oh, pious articles about religious life.

Kramer: Pious articles…what to do to be holy! So if you think about where you were in the 1950s and 1960s and where we are now, would you like to comment about any changes in the religious life? I mean this house itself is so different from when you first came.

Pedrizetti: When I first came it was a pre-Vatican Council regime. Since that time, just in terms of the architecture and the Church building itself, it sort of symbolizes the vast changes that took place. What is now the Great Hall was the former Church. It was the very traditional style with choir stalls on either side of the sanctuary. In the new Church the layout of the Church itself is an indication of the vast changes that have taken place.

Kramer: To leap all the way into the present moment, you still have people who come and are novices. The religious life still exists. Are people motivated to be religious for the same kind of reasons? In other words, it was pretty clear that if you became a monk in the 1950s or 1960s, you would probably end up teaching. Now it would not be so definite.

Pedrizetti: In my time, if you were going to teach, it probably meant that you were going to become a priest. That is not the case anymore. The academic life and the priesthood are not as important in the minds of younger people as they were. That is part of what was taken for granted in my time. If you were smart enough to get through college you were smart enough to be a priest. So if you had the talent the assumption was that is where you would go. But now we have people with Ph.D.'s who have no interest in becoming priests and never did. So this emphasizes that the religious life itself is of more importance than the pastoral work as priests and even teaching in some instances.

Kramer: But there was a time where people were not examined so carefully for the priesthood. They were not tested or encouraged to think long and hard. And in some ways I think it might have been easier to get into monasteries. Thomas Merton wrote an article about the neurotic personality in the monastery. I guess he wrote the article because he had been serving as Master of Scholastics and then as Novice Master, and he had been dealing with some pretty "special cases." My guess is that you would not have as many problematic men in a novitiate or monastery now because you are much more careful about who you admit.

Pedrizetti: I should have mentioned that one of my major jobs that absorbed a lot of time and did not give me a chance to get much writing done was living in the dormitory and working with students. Then I became Cleric Master right through the Vatican Council period.

Kramer: What does the Cleric Master do?

Pedrizetti: In those days a cleric was between the novitiate and ordination. At the beginning of the Vatican Council, there were about 70 or 75 clerics who came here. We had a theology program that attracted many from other places. Three or four years later at the end of Vatican Council that group had been reduced to 25. So there was vast turmoil and change just during the time of my first job as an administrator. Since that time the priesthood and academic life are less important than they were.

III

Kramer: Years earlier St. John's set up a Summer Workshop on Psychology and the Monastic Life. When did that begin?

Pedrizetti: It was during the time I was studying theology. It would have been in the mid- to late 1950s.

Kramer: And it ran for almost 20 years?

Pedrizetti: Something like that. I was on the support staff for the mental health workshops. And the whole point of them was to have a dialogue running between psychology and theology or spirituality.

Kramer: So how many men would come to these workshops?

Pedrizetti: Well they restricted the numbers. Maybe 40. Each week they had a team of people—two psychiatrists who gave talks and four who led discussion groups of maybe ten or twelve each.

Kramer: Would the topic change from year to year?

Pedrizetti: Yes. Merton came to one of those of mental health weeks and ran into Gregory Zilboorg and had an interesting battle, part of which I witnessed.

Kramer: So you were there and you watched Gregory Zilboorg "perform." He was rather well known at that point.

Pedrizetti: He was very famous within the psychoanalytic movement because he had been a student of Freud.

Kramer: Can you describe him? Do you remember him?

Pedrizetti: He was the stereotypical image that you have of an intellectual: sort of rotund wearing a tweed coat and smoking a pipe. I do not know if he actually smoked a pipe but he should have if he did not.

Kramer: Did he come more than one summer?

Pedrizetti: Oh yes. He came often.

Kramer: But he was not Catholic? Was he Jewish?

Pedrizetti: He was Jewish, I think, but converted to Catholicism.

Kramer: So he came several summers. Then one summer Merton came with his Abbot?

Pedrizetti: I am a bit confused about that. There were possibly two occasions when Merton was here. One was for a workshop on psychology and theology. Later on, there were workshops on spirituality set up for those "in charge" in monasteries and religious life.

Kramer: That would have been when he was Novice Master, I suppose—after 1955. So what did you see happen between Merton and Zilboorg?

Pedrizetti: Mostly that they disagreed. They tried to be polite. But the battle was over a manuscript that Merton wrote about psychology and theology. And Zilboorg said it was nonsense, at least the psychology part of it. And basically Zilboorg's message was "Stay in your own field. Don't mess around with mine."

Kramer: That manuscript, "The Neurotic Personality in the Monastic Life," was published in *The Merton Annual*, Vol. 4 (pp. 3-19).

Pedrizetti: Right.

Kramer: So they were polite, but they disagreed.

Pedrizetti: Yes.

Kramer: Did you watch anything else about Merton?

Pedrizetti: On another occasion I sat in on a conversation between Merton and a classmate of mine whom Merton knew or was in academic or intellectual contact with.

Kramer: Who was that?

Pedrizetti: James Kritzeck. He went on to become an expert on Near Eastern languages. He was from St. Cloud. I sat in on their conversation. And it was a relaxed, interesting conversation where Merton was just chatting with this other fellow. I had arranged the meeting so they let me sit in and watch. They talked for at least an hour. My impression of Merton in that instance was amiable. He just seemed like an ordinary guy. He was this great important person who traveled around the world and was known everywhere. He was sitting in this office and just being an ordinary American person.

Kramer: I think often that is what people report: that he could focus in on a conversation and be totally with that conversation and not in any way pretentious or self-conscious. Have you ever visited Cistercian monasteries since you left Spencer?

Pedrizetti: One year I went to a conference on Merton and Maritain. It was in Louisville. I went to Gethsemani also to look around. But that was after Merton had died.

Kramer: Yes. I think that conference was in 1980, or so. I think I went to the same conference.

Pedrizetti: One of the participants was a priest who I mentioned had taught me philosophy. He was from another Abbey. He was from Claremont, California. He is still alive. And Raimundo Pannikar was there.

Kramer: Bob Lax was there, but did not talk much.

Pedrizetti: But my visit was just one of those tours of the Abbey. I saw Merton's grave and so on.

Kramer: Gethsemani had been renovated. So you saw the Church with its nice white walls and beautiful yellow and black glass. They really cleaned that building out. It had filled up over the years. There are photographs of it. At Merton's ordination it is all Baroque imitation!

So you had some contact with Merton. Did you read much of Merton?

Pedrizetti: Oh yes. I read the usual stuff.

Kramer: Have you looked at any of the Journals?

Pedrizetti: I only picked up a few last summer. There is a nun in Duluth, Minnesota who has an extensive Merton collection. I went to visit her once and realized that was my old parish where I grew up. And the actual room where she has all those materials is the very room where I spent the 7th and 8th grade.

Kramer: That is something! I am aware of her because she has gone to the International Thomas Merton Society meetings. So she has a good collection. The Journals are interesting because he was keeping a journal before he entered Gethsemani.

Pedrizetti: Oh, his personal journals.

Kramer: Yes. They are now edited and published and there are seven volumes. Of course, *The Sign of Jonas* (1953) comes from his journals and *Conjectures of a Guilty Bystander* (1966) is re-worked material from the journals. But they were finally published in seven volumes, which can give you a good sense of the development of his life. Although there are moments where he does not keep a journal—1942 to 1946, there is not much. He loved to write.

I wanted to talk with you because I feel the changes in the religious life during this period—and Merton experienced many of these changes also—but he did not live past 1968—make a lot of people nervous. Merton makes a lot of people nervous too because the assumption is that he was not a good monk or Catholic or Christian. I think that is probably not true, but if you stand back from people like yourself or like Thomas Merton who lived through this period of fantastic change in the Church and you see where we are now, some would be pessimistic I think. Some are really afraid that the old Church is gone. I do not feel that way. I feel that we are in a moment of opportunity. I wonder what you feel when you think about these completely different ways of structuring Church and spirituality and education and so on. Do you feel optimistic?

Pedrizetti: Well, I do not feel optimistic. But I do not feel pessimistic either. I think that we have a long way to go with the upheaval that has taken place on the level of spirituality with the ecumenical movement and the theological nuances that are complex and interesting but also difficult for it to impact our culture.

I think the basic strains of monasticism indicated by the vows are still valued by everybody. The ways they are practically worked out are much different. People entering religious life these days are much more highly educated and much more mature at least in the sense of having a variety of experience before they enter. So they have a lot of questions. At times one gets the feeling that we are just floating with a lot of ideas but no solid structure to put them into.

Kramer: I sometimes think it is similar in a parish structure where earlier the assumption was old Fr. So-and-so or Monsignor So-and-so would answer all the questions. Now in a large parish with two or three thousand families, the pastor is surrounded by people with all their questions, ideas and projects. And this would be almost too much to manage.

Pedrizetti: Yes, that would be impossible to manage. As a result, large parishes have begun to use others besides the pastor to handle those sorts of concerns.

Kramer: Have you been involved in activities here at St. John's that fall under the general rubric of liturgical renewal?

Pedrizetti: That has been a part of my life. I have an interesting perspective because I taught Latin and Greek for about five years before going into philosophy. So I know enough about Latin so that I can understand the liturgy in Latin and enjoy it. I think the Gregorian chant and things like that are treasures that we should not just dump entirely. But at the same time there is a lot of new stuff that is very interesting.

Kramer: When you came and first walked into the choir, everything was in Latin. And, now, the only time you would hear Latin would be on a Feast Day where you have a special reason for singing a hymn.

Pedrizetti: I am on the liturgy committee in the monastery. It is a committee mostly of people who are trained in liturgy and teach it in the graduate school. But we discuss things like where to put the Presider's chair in the sanctuary during weekday Mass. It does not excite your interest too much.

Kramer: The liturgy here is very clean. It is very carefully structured, and it gives you a feeling of wholeness. So often when you wander into a Mass in a parish, you may or may not be surprised at this accretion and that accretion, and this or that prayer and so on. What is so nice about coming to the Office or Sunday Mass here is that it is very carefully thought through.

Pedrizetti: Fortunately we have had for a long time at least two or three people who are trained in liturgy. So we can first avoid a lot of egregious errors and mistakes in how we perform the liturgy, and, secondly, we offer a lot to the people who are interested in creating and constructing a form of communal prayer that is meaningful for us today.

In the early days when it was all in Latin, a monk was sort of in a world apart because prayer was in Latin rather than English. And people did not participate like they do now. They just observed. This, to me, is an indication of the difficulty with monasticism. In St. Benedict's time, monasticism was a kind of protest against the reigning culture. But now the effort is to make monasticism a part of culture and at the same time retain something that is distinctive about it so it is recognizable for what it is.

Kramer: That is a big challenge. But it is very valuable. I think St. John's has a wonderful history doing exactly that.

Are there other things you would like to say?

Pedrizetti: You asked the question about the future. Am I optimistic, and I said not really. But I think that monasticism and religious life in some form will continue. I do not know a lot about Eastern thought, but one of my favorite authors is Fr. Martin Cyril D'Arcy. He was the person I read who helped me to undergo the transitions that I had to experience in coming back from the Trappists and getting into community life here. He has a book on the spirituality of the East and West. He points out that we in the West should be more concerned, as Merton was, about the experience of spirituality that seems to be almost pervasive in the East.

Kramer: Yes. And it is a personal experience that people live. This is what people are beginning to learn in the West: you can have both formal liturgy and a personal spirituality.

Pedrizetti: That is what I was looking for in the Trappists. And I retained my interest in that sort of thing. But on the social level there does not seem to be much interest in the West about this way of life. It strikes me that the future of monasticism will be connected to the development of this kind of spirit.

Kramer: I think there is something lacking in American culture which also has to do with the need for the contemplative. But Americans are so busy, successful and content that they do not even know that they have any need for the contemplative. In the East, it is more a part of how everyone lives, or at least it was until the Chinese and Japanese wanted automobiles just like the rest of us.

"Living and Learning with Merton for Decades": An Interview with Victor A. Kramer, Editor

Conducted and edited by Glenn Crider

I

Crider: How did you become interested in Thomas Merton?

Kramer: That is a very slowly developing story, a story which has been in process for the better part of fifty years. It finally took flight in 1972. I can remember reading Merton that summer, in Austria. We were in Graz and my first book, on James Agee, was finished. At that time I had a contract to do a book about Merton which led to many other things later. In a sense, I've now been living with Merton for three or four decades.

Crider: Can you remember when you first actually read Thomas Merton?

Kramer: Yes. I was an undergraduate at St. Edward's in Austin, Texas and in the spring of 1958 I bought a Dell 25-cent paperback of *Seeds of Contemplation* in the St. Ed's book store. To me, at the time, Merton's book seemed good pious advice. I didn't read *Seeds* carefully. I put it on the shelf with Thomas à Kempis's *Imitation of Christ*. Both writers seemed to possess a 1950s Catholic stamp of approval, and I must admit they did not make much of an impression on that young innocent reader. He was too busy with too many other things—courses, books, girls, dreams. I certainly did not then go out and read *The Seven Storey Mountain*. I avoided that book until 1972.

Crider: So if that first book remained on the shelf, how long did it take before you took it down?

Kramer: Oh, maybe a decade in terms of careful reading. Actually in 1966 I was given a copy of *Raids on the Unspeakable* by one of my teaching assistants at Marquette, Kaye Duncan. That was a beautifully printed book. I enjoyed Merton's abstract drawings. And by the early 1970s, as I have suggested, I was doing some serious thinking about Merton. He had begun to seem like a critic of American culture to me. I now have learned that as so he is also a critic of all Western civilization.

Crider: What does that mean?

Kramer: I had written a lot about James Agee and was teaching American literature. I was in a position where I was then looking for a twentieth-century author, comparable perhaps to Agee, but little recognized, yet someone who was important as a non-fiction writer and observer of culture. Someone I might "use" as a research topic.

Crider: What do you mean by "observer of culture"?

Kramer: I mean that in European and American literature we have a variety of writers who combine analysis of culture along with a spiritual strain. By 1972 I had taught several non-fiction courses. Early writers like Jonathan Edwards, transcendental writers including Emerson and Thoreau, and writers of the twentieth century such as Henry Adams, William Carlos Williams, Ralph Ellison, interested me because they were asking questions about the self and the wider culture. Today Wendell Berry is part of this group.

Crider: But your first Merton "project" was a Twayne's United States Authors Series book.

Kramer: Yes.

Crider: Well, that is a standard format, right?

Kramer: Actually, there is a great deal of latitude in the requirements for that series. I was free to structure the book as I wished. I chose to emphasize the fact that Merton was a writer who was also a monk, and a monk who profited greatly from his writing. If I ever revise the expanded second version of that study, the book entitled *Thomas Merton, Monk and Artist*, I could use Merton's Journals and correspondence now available, to make my points in much more detail.

Crider: What is your point?

Kramer: That Thomas Merton was very much an adopted American writer, but as a Christian monk formed in the Benedictine and Cistercian tradition the spiritual aspects always were dominant in his view.

Crider: Could you define "spiritual aspects"?

Kramer: I mean Merton's seeking of God and the mystery of that quest. What has become increasingly significant to me is that in life—all lives—there are only a relatively small and limited number of pivotal and life-changing events. For Merton his conversion and baptism changed everything. That simple decision is an example we can all learn from.

Crider: Changed everything?

Kramer: Yes. What I have come to understand now is that what I earlier wrote about Merton (1972-1982) was to focus upon his accomplishments as a writer, monk, novice master, etc. What I have become increasingly aware of is that all these things—important as they may be—are "after the fact." There is, to use a Gerard Manley Hopkins phrase, "a hidden deep-down" thing which was for him always much more important which then caused an overflow into his well-known accomplishments as a spiritual, and then as a celebrity, writer.

Crider: So would you say there is a vital aspect of Merton which must remain hidden?

Kramer: Yes, but you can triangulate on this by looking at his poems and books and collecting stories about the monk-writer.

Crider: Could you tell a story which you think reveals an essential fact about Merton?

Kramer: Yes. I remember something John Foley (who was a Holy Cross priest in Atlanta in the early 1970s) told me. Merton, that lover of words and monk, was confident about himself, and while he had many doubts about his vocation, he was also confident he was in the right place. This is an early 1960s or late 1950s story: John Foley remembered once running into Thomas Merton (Father Louis) as he was on his way out the monastery garden going to Louisville on some errand. Merton was wearing a black business suit, probably taken off a rack in a common room. It did not seem to fit him very well. He winked at Foley, and said "I look just like a bishop, don't I." Of course the point is he did not, yet could at the same time joke about it.

Crider: I have another way of asking my basic question. Why did you want to write a book about Merton?

Kramer: I did so because I knew he was a significant American writer of prose, not just a "Catholic" writer. All the while I was in graduate school and then in my earliest years teaching I kept returning to American non-fiction prose. I loved teaching a Non-Fiction Prose course at Marquette (1966-1969). Also thirty years later when I could chose a Lecture Course for the University of Heidelberg when I returned to Germany as a Senior Fulbright lecturer, I did another survey course on Non-Fiction. Our earliest writers—Puritans like Cotton Mather, thinkers like Jonathan Edwards, ponderers like Emerson and Thoreau. Then writers like Henry Adams, Ralph Ellison, James Baldwin, Wendell Berry, all of whom have all contributed to the flow of our deepening spiritual awareness by questioning what it means to live. Merton is surely part of this pattern and to me his continuing value is that his questioning is itself a model from which we learn.

I sensed Merton was part of this undertow and so when I did that Twayne United States Authors Series book about him I sought to study his work like I had James Agee's writing and through my study of *Let Us Now Praise Famous Men*, because, of course, I knew there had to be much more there.

Crider: Why, after that first book, did you decide to continue writing about Thomas Merton?

Kramer: One thing led to another. Part of it clearly was the pleasure of meeting many monks at Gethsemani; then Conyers; and at other monasteries; a string of articles; then the clear realization that Merton was important to me as a person. Going to the Abbey of Gethsemani, which I visited first in 1973, helped as did the many subsequent visits. Getting to know some of the monks was a real grace.

II

Crider: Is it correct that you did some oral history work about Merton?

Kramer: Yes. Beginning in 1980 some nineteen monks, or friends, of Merton were included. Many of these "archival" interviews have been published in journals, or revised for *The Merton Annual*. My wife, Dr. Dewey Weiss Kramer, and I also did a second oral history of the monk-founders of Gethsemani's first daughter-house, Conyers in 1982-83.

Crider: When did the idea for *The Merton Annual* develop?

Kramer: It grew out of work for A.M.S. Press (New York) while I was editing the Georgia State University "Literary Studies Series" (1987-1997). As that series was planned, I also discussed the possibility of a yearly publication for Merton-related studies which would publish lengthy pieces.

Crider: How did establishing of *The Merton Annual* evolve?

Kramer: It began with the encouragement of Gabe Hornstein, publisher of A.M.S. He agreed to do the first five volumes. Our second series (Vols. 6-10) was published by Liturgical Press. It was at that time that George Kilcourse and Michael Downey came on as editors. At that time we thought that *The Merton Annual* could sprout interests and connections beyond just Merton studies with inclusion of related parallel studies. The Abbey Center at Gethsemani, a discussion group designed to bring monastics and like-minded people together, sponsored conferences during those years (1992-1994) and our Vol. 6 reflects this influence. Yet the fact is the *Annual* has remained pretty well focused on just Merton's work and on his influence, with only a few forays into other territories. That says a lot about Merton's appeal.

Crider: Will you comment about the various "batches" of *Merton Annuals* and how they might be distinguished from one another?

Kramer: The first group of hardbacks (Volumes 1-5) contains many fairly long monographs. From the start we always included an interview of someone who knew, or was influenced by, Merton and we also used an "unpublished" or "obscurely published" Merton piece.

Volumes 6-10 rotated editors for successive volumes. That had some good and bad features. With volumes 11-16, we had only two editors. Sometimes it encouraged an editor to think of a book as "his" volume. Since Fons Vitae assumed publishing, beginning with volume 17, we have witnessed a much healthier pattern develop. I have edited each volume, but also many other persons have done the Bibliographic essays, have been responsible for the sub-sections of papers which grew out of the I.T.M.S. meetings, conducted interviews, etc.

Crider: What can you say about the future of *The Merton Annual*?

Kramer: I believe that the relationship with the International Thomas Merton Society which has agreed to sponsor this publication during the next five years bodes well for the future. We have selected, expanded and revised some I.T.M.S. papers in the *Annual* from volume 3 forward, but year after year the tie between the *Annual* and I.T.M.S. has grown.

III

Crider: What does Merton mean to you now that you have lived with him for five or so decades?

Kramer: I think an autobiographical volume might well be written on that subject. I would have to think about Merton as classic; Merton's work as writer; the true facts of his vocation; my own slow learning about the traditions of monasticism; also, then integration of all this with my own life and the beauty of many friendships with people I have come to know through Merton circles; and now, doing retreats on Merton as well as academic work. It is fun today (in 2007) to look forward to teaching still another graduate course on "Merton as Spiritual Master" in 2009.

Crider: Has Merton affected your "scholarly" interests and your own writing?

Kramer: I can say that I have been very "lucky" when I have chosen to concentrate upon various subjects in American studies. To me, however, it is all of a piece: My thinking and reading about literary theory, ethnic literature, contemporary poetry and fiction has all been in terms of honoring says, James Agee, "the dignity of actuality."

Merton always did this too. And with increasing focus my present work with Walker Percy builds, I hope, the same way.

Crider: Do you see Merton as a valuable asset for today's spiritual seeker?

Kramer: He is a very valuable figure which most Catholics and many of the Hierarchy do not appreciate. Quite a bit like Henri Nouwen, but monastic; a far more complicated figure than Fulton J. Sheen, and a far more complex figure than the meditative poet Mary Oliver. For Merton, as I have said, the poetry, the meditations, the journals are overflow, not anywhere near the essence of his life or contribution. Nevertheless, through these items we glimpse what he glimpsed of the wonder of God.

Crider: What is the best thing you can suggest about studying Merton?

Kramer: I believe Merton's primary gift to today's readers and to our culture is that he saw the value of monasticism and embraced it. He wants his reader to seek the essential. "Not resting until we rest in God," he assures us of the importance of prayer in the same way as does St. Augustine. Fully committed to serving and seeking God, once he discerned this was the way to be a saint—he was like St. Ignatius. My Merton is, I guess, like a modern melding of these different saints' earnestness and talents. Once converted, he is focused, honest, and true. I think it is from that focus—honesty and intensity—that we learn.

Crider: I think what distinguishes Merton in an important way is his commitment to the monastic life. Commitment is complex in nature, and our cunning tendency to avoid commitment often eludes us. Merton's life and work shows us both the joy and difficulty he experienced as he continued to commit to his vocation. Underneath Merton's commitment, I see an on-going, intentional turning, or evolving. This is a challenging position to assume much less remain in. You just commented that once Merton converted, he was focused, honest and true. What specifically do you think enabled Merton to commit in the way that he did?

Kramer: He learned that life, love and learning within a Benedictine framework is a process. Once one knows this, then the commitment as a Christian is never static. As process, the dynamic of becoming a saint keeps changing. Think of a giant kaleidoscope with all kinds of fundamental, yet always different patterns, to be enjoyed and affirmed.

Crider: And what do you think hinders others from committing in a way that Merton did? Put another way, what do you think keeps people from living an authentic life that is open to ongoing and revolutionary change and transformation?

Kramer: At the base is our Western sense of individualism. Deeply seated is our culture's ill-founded rationalization that we should, or worse can, control our lives. Merton learned to celebrate the mystery of living in community, and as the sense of mystery deepened, his understanding of Church and community opened up. His life endorsed the wonder of an ever-changing world to be celebrated. For many today, who seem to be driven by their own narrow desires, or who apparently are afraid to admit to much mystery, life remains a narrow matter of limited and fixed choices which seem to allow such persons to build a private portfolio without regard to others. In so much of what Merton observed and celebrated it becomes most fundamentally a matter of sharing in the goodness of creation and praising God's gifts.

WEEK OF A STRANGER:
Thomas Merton Bibliographic Review 2006

Donald Grayston

While I was working on this review-essay of works by and about Merton published in 2006, I had the pleasure of spending a week on Savary Island, a little chunk of paradise accessible only by water taxi and float plane from the coast of British Columbia near Powell River and Lund. I was by myself in a cabin belonging to a friend: one main floor with a sleeping loft, a propane stove and refrigerator, running water but no electricity. The cabin —Iniswood Cottage, to give it its proper name—has a deck on which I could sit on sunny days, and a wood-stove/fireplace for cool mornings and evenings. Many times I saw deer, on one occasion two together, grazing peacefully in the salal less than a dozen feet from where I was sitting, and, perhaps because no hunting is permitted on the island, quite content to come close, occasionally turning to look—no, to gaze: deer are natural contemplatives—at me. Of course when I came home, I wanted to re-read the section ("Poetry of the Forest") in George Kilcourse's *Ace of Freedoms: Thomas Merton's Christ* in which he reflects on the deer as symbol for Merton of the shy inner self which the contemplative unavoidably encounters in the hermitage.[1] I affirm here in print that, contrary to my children's teasing, not only do I not think I am Thomas Merton, I am not even *trying* to be Thomas Merton! But it didn't take me more than an hour after my arrival to recognize that I had been given the gift of a brief taste of quasi-eremitical living. Of course I knew from the day I got there that I would be leaving at the end of the week, and that necessarily relativized the impact of the experience; whereas Merton, when he embarked on his time as a hermit, had no way of knowing how long he would so continue. Even so, staying in the cabin, I knew in my own way and in this brief time the truth of Belden Lane's characterization of Merton's hermitage years: that on my own in the cabin, on the island, I had no need to "be someone," no need to nurture the outer or social self.[2] In the hermitage, similarly, rather than having any need to "be someone," the hermit has time and opportunity to open himself/

herself to "a deeper personal authenticity," to give love and solitude a chance to "test each other," and to relinquish illusions which
in a communal context might easily and unconsciously be sustained.[3] As someone with no need that week to be anybody in
particular, I walked, I went to the beach, I sat in front of the fire, I
prepared my own food and did my own dishes (nirvana =
samsara), and I read some of the books I mention in this review.
Experientially, my week there picked up on another major theme
in Merton: the recovery of paradise. It was a very fine time.

*

I began my reading there by looking at, that is, by appreciating the
visual as well as the textual quality of Roger Lipsey's *Angelic Mistakes*,[4] a beautiful book (the recipient of the 2007 ITMS Book Prize)
which explores Merton's work in the sixties as calligrapher and
printmaker, most of which he undertook during his hermitage
years (1965-68). The book is divided into three distinct sections:
the first is Lipsey's description of Merton as artist, and in particular, how his artistic efforts colored and expressed the spiritual path
of his time as hermit; the second presents a portfolio of reproduc-
tions of 34 of Merton's drawings, calligraphies and prints from
that time, beside each of which Lipsey has placed one or more
apposite quotations from Merton; the third offers an account of
friends and colleagues "crucial to the development of Merton's
art in the 1960s"[5]—D.T. Suzuki, Jacques Maritain, Victor Hammer,
Ad Reinhardt and Ulfert Wilke, as well as a discussion of another
spiritual son of Suzuki, John Cage, and an account of the exhibitions of Merton's art. The book concludes with a very interesting
appendix in which three printmakers, at Lipsey's request, recount
their reconstruction of Merton's printmaking technique.[6]

Angelic Mistakes (the name comes from a list of sardonic de-
scriptors of his pieces in a letter from Merton to Jim Forest in 1966[7])
is the "first extensive exploration of Thomas Merton's visual art of
the 1960s. In those years … Merton had matured into the radiant,
questioning, profound human being whose writings reach out to
this day with undimmed appeal."[8] Merton toyed with whether to
describe his drawings and prints from this time as "edifying" or
"disedifying,"[9] because there was "no obvious bridge between his
art and the values and traditions of the Catholic Church"[10] of which
he was a solemnly professed monk. Lipsey says that Merton's later
art, moving beyond the institutionally ecclesial, had located itself

in an "ecumenical, cross-cultural terrain," which he characterizes under the headings of "Kyoto" and "Lower Manhattan."[11] By these rubrics Lipsey means to suggest that Zen, which has a long tradition of the practice of calligraphy among its practitioners, and American abstract expressionism were two chief contexts or conceptual framings for Merton's art.

Critical to the production of these pieces in Merton's last years was the hermitage itself, which was also his artist's studio: "Had there been no hermitage," says Lipsey, "there would probably have been no art."[12] The hermitage provided Merton with the autonomous space in which he could make artistic correlations "between marks on paper and the marks in [his] mind and heart."[13] His art-making was for Merton spiritual practice, involving mind, heart and hand; it was *contemplative* art, a following of the heart's path through pen, brush, found objects and paper. The two pieces which I found most engaging were 23, entitled by Lipsey "The three doors (they are one door)," a phrase which readers of Merton will recognize from the *Asian Journal*, and 33—"That is what it means to be a Christian," part of a less-well-known passage from *Conjectures*.[14] In both instances I found myself pulled into the images as one is pulled into an icon, conscious that I was looking at marks on paper that were indeed marks of both mind and heart.

The community of Merton readers and scholars has great reason to be grateful that a critic of Roger Lipsey's breadth and depth of experience turned his attention to this long-neglected portion of Merton's *oeuvre*. Donna Kristoff, in her review of this book in *The Merton Seasonal*, acknowledges Lipsey's high standing as an art critic, and expresses her appreciation of the portion of Merton's art on which he concentrates; but she also expresses a reservation in regard to his comparative neglect of Merton's immersion in the Christian-mystical and prophetic aspects of his personhood.[15] She also takes issue with Lipsey's equation (in the book's subtitle) of the word "art" with visual art. I concur with her latter point; but on the former, I am inclined to stand with Christopher Pramuk's understanding of Merton's "unknown and unseen Christ" as illuminative of Merton's spirituality of this period (see below on Pramuk).

In the fall of 1964, Lipsey also tells us, Merton began to explore photography, an interest which continued active until his death.

Charting the points of contact between his work with brush and ink and his work with the camera exceeds the scope of [*Angelic Mistakes*], but that project would be well worth the time of a historian of photography. When Merton damaged the simple camera he was using in September 1964, it was repaired and returned to him. "Darling camera," he recorded in his journal, "so glad to have you back!"[16]

No single such work on photography comparable in scope to Lipsey's on Merton's late art of other kinds has yet, it is true, been brought forth. However, the wittily-entitled article ("Late Developer: Thomas Merton's Discovery of Photography as a Medium for His Contemplative Vision") by British theologian and photographer Philip Richter, makes a substantial theoretical beginning.[17] Richter's article tackles no less formidable a theoretician than Susan Sontag, whose *On Photography* asserts that the taking of photographs is an aggressive act, an act of predation, appropriation and objectification.[18] Allied to her viewpoint is that of Peter Osborne, who characterizes the photographic gaze as potentially imperial or colonizing.[19] But Sontag's claims, Richter counters, "are massively generalized. What she claims may be true of some photography, at some times, by some people, but these are not necessarily essential features of the medium."[20]

A predatory or voyeuristic photographer will tend to promote the kind of photography that Sontag critiques, and a voyeuristic society (one thinks of the paparazzi and their harassment of celebrities) will encourage this; but the camera can also be the instrument of a respectful, indeed contemplative relationship. For Merton, he says, taking photographs, so far from being predatory or voyeuristic, was a form of meditation, a way in which Christ could develop Merton's life "into Himself like a photograph"[21]— and I find it interesting that Richter found this last quotation in *New Seeds of Contemplation*, published in 1962, two years before Merton began the serious practice of photography. To take a contemplative photograph was for Merton a way of acknowledging the *haecceitas*, the "thisness" or inscape of that which is being photographed.[22] Like the Shakers, the sublimity of whose crafting Merton admired, he tried in his photography to be "attuned to the music intoned in each being by God the Creator and by the Lord Jesus,"[23] a comment which evokes his use of the word *consonantia* in "Day of a Stranger," that "one central tonic note that is unheard and unuttered,"[24] and yet which contains all things in their specificity, their thisness. Richter's article is very rich; perhaps it could be the germ of the larger work that Lipsey has called for.

*

I turn now to Merton's own writings, which continue, almost four decades after his death, to be published: "he, being dead, yet speaketh" (Hebrews 11.4, KJV). The *pièce de resistance* in 2006, literally—Gerry McFlynn, of Pax Christi UK, hails Merton as a "theologian of resistance"[25]—was the publication of *Cold War Letters* (Maryknoll, NY: Orbis), edited by Christine M. Bochen and William H. Shannon (a happy collaboration, given that Christine Bochen is the current holder of the William H. Shannon Chair in Catholic Studies at Nazareth College, Rochester, NY), with a Foreword by James W. Douglass. In his preface, William Shannon points to what he has earlier called "The Year of the Cold War Letters," the time between October 1961 and October 1962.[26] James Douglass, in his foreword, calls it "probably the most dangerous year in history."[27] Valerie Flessati, like McFlynn a member of Pax Christi UK, recalls the terror of that time.

> In 1961 the Cold War between East and West became exceedingly dangerous, and nuclear war was a real and frightening possibility. In April a CIA-backed attempt by Cuban exiles to invade Cuba and overthrow Castro had failed. In August the Berlin Wall was constructed. In December President Kennedy sent troops—for the first time openly—to Vietnam. The Cuban missile crisis occurred in October the following year, and the world held its breath for a week during the standoff between Kennedy and Krushchev [sic]. ... [It] was an apocalyptic time.[28]

Merton believed that he had a responsibility, both spiritual and civic, to speak out against the possibility of nuclear war, which he saw, as did many others, as the greatest threat to the continuance of human existence. (In our own time, when the threat of global warming looms so large, this point may be contested, without in any way diminishing the nuclear threat or Merton's response to it.) He began to write articles, most notably "The Root of War is Fear," essentially a chapter from *New Seeds of Contemplation* which was published in the October 1961 issue of *The Catholic Worker*.[29] At the same time, he was sharing his deep concern in letters to friends, and soon decided to put together a collection of these letters, which he himself called "The Cold War Letters." Following— ironically as a patriotic American—in the Russian *samizdat* tradition, he circulated mimeographed copies of the letters, first in a shorter edition of 49 letters (late spring 1962), later in a longer edition of 111 letters (January 1963), written to 81 recipients in nine countries. Shannon makes the point that the writing of the letters was not in response to the prohibition from the Abbot General of the Cistercian Order, Dom Gabriel Sortais, of which he only learned on April 26, 1962, to publish on matters of war and peace—a most unmonastic topic, in Dom Gabriel's view—but was part of his thinking as early as October 1961.[30] Merton's own preface gives trenchant expression to his purpose in writing, collecting and privately ("not for publication," he says on the original title page) distributing the letters.

> The letters form part of no plot. They incite to no riot, they suggest no disloyalty to government, they are not pandering to the destructive machinations of revolutionaries or foreign foes. They are nothing more than the expression of loyal but unpopular opinion, of democratic opposition to what seem to be irresponsible trends.[31]

Then why is he writing them? Because of his conviction

> ...that the United States, in the Cold War, are [sic] in grave danger of ceasing to be what they claim to be: the home of liberty, where justice is defended with free speech ... and where responsibility is sustained by a deep foundation of ethics. In actual fact it would seem that during the Cold War ... this country has become frankly a warfare state built on affluence, a power structure in which the interests of big business, the obsessions of the military, and the phobias of political extremists both dominate and dictate our national policy.
>   ... [T]he majority opinion in the United States is now a highly oversimplified and mythical view of the world divided into two camps: that of darkness (our enemies) and that of light (ourselves). ... In consequence of this, everything the enemy does is diabolical and everything we do is angelic. ... It follows that we have a divinely given mission to destroy this hellish monster and any steps we take to do so are innocent and even holy.[32]

Reading these words, the interval between their writing and the present collapses: Merton is speaking to us now. Quite apart from the time-bound specifics of the letters themselves, Merton's underlying prophetic awareness of how human beings and governments act when in the grip of fear speaks as directly to the epoch of Iraq and the so-called "war on terror" as it did to the epoch of Vietnam and the Cold War. Over against the demonization of "the other," he places his own incarnational and contemplative humanism (the letters also include his thoughts on literature, ecumenism, interfaith dialogue and mysticism) which envisions, as Christine Bochen says in her introduction, "a world in which social and political actions are informed by regard for the dignity of the human person rather than by pragmatism and power-seeking and by a commitment to non-violence rather than recourse to armed conflict."[33]

War is at root a spiritual problem, in Merton's thought, and therefore required—requires—a spiritual resolution. This would/will involve *metanoia, teshuvah*, repentance, conversion, a change of heart, a spiritual transformation, commitment to the practice of non-violence. That his Church was largely passive in response to the crisis of the time he regarded as scandalous, as a matter for the utmost dismay. So Merton spoke out through these letters as a Christian, as a Catholic, as a monk, yes, and also as a citizen and as a human being. James Douglass says that the *Cold War Letters* represented Merton "at his best, writing to us at our collective worst."[34] Again James Douglass:

> We were the cold in the Cold War, just as we are the terror in the War on Terror. We are also God's faith and hope—the Creator's reasons for putting us on this planet, God's faith in each of us, with the hope that we would choose finally to embody the love from which we came.[35]

Readers of Thomas Merton stand very much in debt to Christine Bochen and William Shannon for making available to all of us in this book the faith, hope and love with which these letters of Merton's plead, thunder and whisper across the years.

The second major publication of Merton's thought in 2006 could hardly be more different from the *Cold War Letters*; and yet it comes out of the same contemplative and monastic humanism foundational to all of Merton's thought. This is Patrick O'Connell's exquisite editing of the second volume in Cistercian Publications'

Monastic Wisdom Series, *Pre-Benedictine Monasticism: Initiation into the Monastic Tradition 2*, pref. Sidney H. Griffith (Kalamazoo, MI: Cistercian Publications). It is an outstanding piece of scholarly recovery, masterfully edited and introduced, which has released to us the typed or mimeographed notes for Merton's lectures to the novices at Gethsemani between January 1963 and August 1965 from their longtime obscurity as part of the "Collected Essays" previously available only at the Merton Center and at the abbey. In his preface, Sidney Griffith frames the value of the work thus:

> One of Thomas Merton's most enduring gifts to the Church sprang from his ability to read deeply in the abundant and multifaceted literature of her spiritual and mystical heritage and to give expression to the wisdom he found there in communicable, modern American English.[36]

This extensive reading included not only secondary sources in English, but as the footnotes reveal, in French, Italian and German, as well as many primary sources in Latin. Merton mined the entire Christian tradition of monasticism, East and West, for the gold it would yield up; although I have to say that he passed along some of the dross as well, perhaps because all things monastic—the profound and the bizarre, the healthy and the pathological—were of interest to him. There is, in fact, a somewhat undigested character to much of the material. In this regard, I found it instructive that in his comparison of the written lectures with the taped record of what Merton actually said in presenting his material, O'Connell points out that in the actual conferences Merton "tends to omit material that is of more scholarly than practical interest,"[37] and "to highlight the applicability of the material to his students."[38] Not having myself listened to any of these taped conferences, I am trusting that these omissions included the reference to Eusebius of Chalcis, who said his prayers in a dry well while wearing 250 pounds of chains, or the admonition of the *Collectio Monastica* to young monks not to scratch themselves while others were looking.[39] Knowing what we now do about what was happening in Merton's life at the time of the delivery of these conferences and in the hermitage years which followed, it is not hard to catch an echo of Merton's inner conversations with himself in comments such as his highlighting of the warning of Ammonas, successor to St. Anthony as abbot of Pispir, not to succumb "to a seemingly productive busyness that is actually 'excessive and inopportune work'";[40] or the thought he takes from Philoxenos, that "the cenobite who wishes to go and live in a cell"—for which we may read "hermitage"—"... must first prove himself perfectly obedient in community."[41] Again, when he quotes Rabbula, bishop of Edessa in the fifth century, as a critic of monasteries which involve themselves in *"much business and many exterior relations,"* we are reminded of his longstanding irritation with the growth at Gethsemani "of large-scale and business-like cenobitic development,"[42] and we can hear, if we will, the unremitting noise of the cheese factory. Again one wonders if after Merton's time in 1966 with the nurse, M, his mind returned to the quotation he took from the *Admonitio ad filium spiritualem*: "he who touches the flesh of a woman does not escape without harm to his soul";[43] and the frequent condemnations from some of the ancient writers of music and laughter are impossible to reconcile with the monk whose sense of humor was legendary, and who listened to Bob Dylan on his turntable in the hermitage. I have no doubt whatever that at the end of his life Merton would have readily admitted the inapplicability of many such ancient prohibitions and admonitions to the life of contemporary monastics.

At the same time, I recognize that Merton was giving his novices an initiation into the monastic *tradition*: and in that tradition, as in the Christian tradition generally, there is gold and dross, wheat and chaff. He recognized that although historically continuous with that long tradition of monastic experience, the form and the forms of monastic life needed to change in his own time and the future, from the institutional (cf. his comments on Pachomius[44]) to the familial, from obedience to fraternal dialogue, from a strict cenobitism to one that supports the hermit life as well, from an attitude which elevates monastic virginity above marriage instead of seeing them as complementary, and from a spirituality which negates and degrades the body to a spirituality in which body and soul embrace one another in the Spirit.

Having referred mostly to dross, let me now speak of the gold. He warmly commends the Pachomian emphasis on scripture, the "strong belief that the words of Scripture are addressed directly and personally to each monk, who is now *living in the time of the fulfillment of the word of God*."[45] He takes manifest delight in his reading of the Spanish nun and proto-pilgrim Egeria (whom he calls "Aetheria"), from which he took the inspiration to write his essay "From Pilgrimage to Crusade."[46] He powerfully interprets "the insights of Philoxenos for a contemporary audience,"[47] making a connection between the monastic tradition and contemporary cultural critique by his linking of Philoxenos and the Theater of the Absurd.[48] Still with Philoxenos, Merton explores his deeply scriptural theological paradigms of the desert and of paradise, challenging his hearers then and his readers now with the flat assertion that "there is no way to the Promised Land but through the desert."[49] He gives major attention to Ephrem the Syrian, particularly to his *Hymns on Paradise*. *"We spend our lives making our own key* [italics Merton's] to the door of paradise. Each one has to have his own key. In our lives, the door 'seeks us,' smiles on us," says Merton, and quotes from one of Ephrem's hymns.

> Door of discernment, it measures those who enter
> Wisely making itself small or great according to its judgement
> Fitting the stature of each ....[50]

Behind these lines, of course, is "Christ's own statement, 'I am the door'" (John 10.7, 9); and from here it is but a short step to Merton's magnificent meditation on the three doors —which are one door— during his retreat at the Mim Tea Estate.[51]

A particular gift to me in this book was the revelation of the origin of Merton's dedication in *The Seven Storey Mountain*: *Christo vero regi*. Previously I had thought it might have been inspired by the representation of Christ the King in the sanctuary of Corpus Christi, the church in New York in which Merton was conditionally baptized in 1938. I now realize it is a quotation from the Latin original of the prologue to the *Rule* of St. Benedict, which invites the reader to renounce his own will in order to fight "for the true king, Christ."[52] What a feast was enjoyed by those who started as novices on the Benedictine path in its Trappist-Cistercian form and were privileged, as this book so thoroughly attests, to be initiated into the monastic tradition by one so deeply acquainted with it.

Two further items conclude our survey of the publication of Merton's own words. The first is *An Invitation to the Contemplative Life*, edited by Wayne Simsic (Ijamsville, MD: The Word Among Us Press), already known to many as the author of *Praying with Thomas Merton* (Winona, MN: St. Mary's Press, 1994). After a brief introduction, there follow ten chapters on basic themes in Merton: freedom, contemplation, the true self, the person of Christ, the prayer of the heart, solitude and silence, nature, community, work and social concern. Each chapter consists of an introductory page from Simsic, followed by a dozen or so pages of paragraphs from Merton, many well-known, others less well-known. Like the little book by James Martin, SJ, and the booklets from the Merton Institute for Contemplative Living on which I comment at the end of the survey, this is the kind of book that one may confidently give to someone who asks for an introduction to Merton. John P. Collins, in his review, offers this summary comment:

> ... with the publication of this small volume we have some of the best of the Merton canon regarding the contemplative life which can guide our daily meditations whether [they] take place within a monastic enclosure, a suburban home, a rural farmhouse or in an urban condominium ....[53]

The second such item of interest is the transcription of a conference, in highly colloquial language, which Merton gave to the novices on June 10, 1964, in response to the civil rights protests then going on in Birmingham, Alabama.[54] The book in which it appears is an anthology of public statements from the religious sector about the civil rights movement. In it Merton uses the "ten commandments" given to non-violent protestors as a checklist for the examination of conscience in the monastery: monks, he asserts, cannot be content to be less intentional in the pursuit of their vocation than activists outside the monastery in their pursuit of gospel justice. The editors, in their introduction to the transcription, refer to his use, common for the time, of exclusive language, but follow this with the very pertinent comment that "[T]he inclusivity of his message in this lecture rises above the exclusivity of his language."[55]

*

As we survey the critical studies of Merton, once again, as with Lipsey and Richter, we find a rich harvest. From Poland comes *Spirituality and Metaphor: The Poetics and Poetry of Thomas Merton* (Opole: Uniwersytet Opolski), by Waclaw Grzybowski. Malgorzata Poks, Grzybowski's fellow-countrywoman, has already given us a very substantial and thorough review in *The Merton Seasonal*,[56] on which I would be hard put to improve. The nub of Grzybowski's linking of spirituality and metaphor, as she says, comes from Merton's conviction ... that the Scholastic concept of God as Pure Being is consonant with William Blake's poetic vision of [God as] the source and ground of life. Contrary to the Platonizing St. Augustine,... Blake intuited beauty in the Particular, which intuition seems to parallel Aquinas's concept of *claritas*—the glory of form ... shining through matter according to the degree of likeness between an individual created being and the uncreated Pure Being which in-forms everything.[57]

Reading this comment immediately evokes for me Hopkins' emphasis on the uniqueness of inscape which Merton so strongly shares and puts forward in the poetic prose of *Seeds of Contemplation*, and, later, in *New Seeds*.

The forms and individual characters of living and growing things and of inanimate things and of animals and flowers and all nature, constitute their holiness in the sight of God.

Their inscape is their sanctity.

The special clumsy beauty of this particular colt on this April day in this field under these clouds is a holiness consecrated to God by His own Art, and it declares the glory of God.

The pale flowers of the dogwood outside this window are saints....

This leaf has its own texture and its own pattern of veins and its own holy shape ....[58]

Poks commends Grzybowski's placing of Merton's poetry of the forties and fifties in its larger American context through comparisons with Robert Lowell and T.S. Eliot; stylistically, he asserts, Merton reached a place of originality and maturity in *The Strange Islands* (New York: New Directions, 1957), a style "informed by Asian spirituality and sapiential awareness, purged from verbosity and excesses of vision."[59] However, says Poks, although Grzybowski "skillfully documents this shift, [he] does not seem to approve of it, as if this new Merton voice was spoiling the underlying thesis of his work: that spiritual poetry must be based on a rising movement of metaphor."[60] At this point, Poks takes the gloves off, and again I cannot improve on her words.

... the work's fault line can be spotted ... in Grzybowski's somewhat narrow definition of spirituality. ... The moment he shuts spirituality within strict Roman Catholic orthodoxy, he is bound to misconstrue Merton's more mature poetics. Had he read Merton's journals … he would have understood that *The Seven Storey Mountain* type of spirituality he builds his arguments on is what Merton came to reject in the nineteen-fifties. Already by 1958, the year of the Fourth and Walnut illumination, Merton was prepared to see religious dogmatism as destructive of an authentic monastic experience and gradually started to believe that a monk had to become an "anti-monk" to qualify as a genuine seeker.[61]

As an "anti-monk" writing poetry, of course, Merton had to become an anti-poet and write anti-poetry: and this takes us to his poetry of the sixties, *Cables* and *Lograire*, as well as to his "empathetic renderings of the anti-poetry of Nicanor Parra,"[62] as Poks points out. Essentially her critique is that while Grzybowski deals well, theologically and Christologically, with Merton's early poetry, and while she acknowledges that his book is "a thorough piece of criticism, handsomely edited, erudite and argued with passion,"[63] he fails, she asserts, to present a theoretical framework equal to the different character of his late poems. To her critique I will only add the comment that the work is marred by a very large number of mistakes and misspellings.

William Apel has given us a very different kind of book in his *Signs of Peace: The Interfaith Letters of Thomas Merton* (Maryknoll, NY: Orbis). The book is a testimonial to Merton's desire, indeed, sense of vocation, to *unite in himself* [64] Catholics from many centuries and ethnicities, other Christians and the other great religious traditions of the planet. Given his vow of stability, it was through correspondence with members of other traditions that he most often acted on this aspiration, carrying on what Apel calls a "ministry of letters."[65] Apel's aim in putting the book together was "to explore the importance of this correspondence for Merton's life and thought, and to examine the lessons these interfaith letters have to teach us today in the unfinished business of achieving mutual respect and appreciation for one another within the world's great religions."[66]

He does this in nine chapters, each one focused on one of Merton's correspondents: Muslim Abdul Aziz, Hindu Amiya Chakravarty, Confucian-Buddhist-Taoist-Catholic John Wu, Jewish Abraham Joshua Heschel, Zen Buddhist D.T. Suzuki, Baptist Glenn Hinson, Vietnamese Buddhist Thich Nhat Hanh, Quaker June Yungblut, and Dona Luisa Coomaraswamy—a Roman Catholic with Jewish origins and a syncretistic perspective derived at least in part from the influence of her husband, Ananda. In each chapter Apel begins with a reflection on the lesson or virtue which he sees most prominently evident in a particular correspondence (in the Merton-Abdul Aziz correspondence, for example, "blessing"; in the Merton-Hinson letters, "openness"), follows this with a discussion of the character of the correspondence, and concludes with a letter from Merton to his friend. The book ends with a postscript on hope, which is the gift above all which Apel has received from his study of Merton.

Christopher Pramuk's fine and generally balanced review[67] of this book salutes the author for his "clear, resoundingly urgent, and elegantly demonstrated"[68] thesis: that we need to pay attention to those spiritual pioneers who serve the entire human community as signs or sacraments of peace, to the lessons we can learn from them and to their virtues that we can emulate. He also celebrates the way Apel has in each instance provided "the historical and spiritual context for understanding [the] exchange"[69] between Merton and each chosen correspondent. However, he faults Apel for the same reason that George Kilcourse, in *Ace of Freedoms*, faulted Merton's practice of interfaith dialogue—for what he sees as a one-sided emphasis on religious experience, and a general unwillingness to engage issues of theology or doctrine,[70] as well as for his "penchant for romantic flight and over-simplification."[71] Pramuk contrasts the spiritual kinship between Merton and Heschel, for example, around their shared "mystical-prophetic" sense of the Bible as the Word of God, with the Suzuki-Merton relationship, in which God *qua* God does not figure. Thus his questions:

> ... is it really the case—as Merton intimates in the Suzuki letters, and Apel uncritically agrees—that "his Zen Buddhist friend saw Christianity, in its essence, more clearly than many Christians"? Is the "essence" of the gospel really "a Zen-like commitment to 'direct experience,' unmediated by preconceived structures"? Or is not Christianity's essence much closer, both in doctrine *and* experience, to Heschel's mystical-prophetic account of a personal God's headlong pursuit of human beings? ... In short, how do we reconcile the fact that Merton experienced such a deep kinship with Heschel *and* Suzuki, Abdul Aziz *and* Thich Nhat Hanh?[72]

Pramuk acknowledges that it would be unfair to expect Apel to resolve the theological questions, particularly questions related to the Christian understandings of creation and incarnation, in terms of Apel's stated purpose in writing the book. But he charges Apel, as Kilcourse did Merton, with dismissing

> theology and doctrine as abstract, authoritarian, and divisive, while celebrating religious "experience" as pure, concrete, democratizing, and unifying... [and thereby exacerbating] the now rather tired dichotomy between doctrine and experience, theology and spirituality, tradition and mysticism.[73]

I can see Pramuk's point; but I have to question whether it is fair to fault Apel for exacerbating a dichotomy which has been with us for millennia and promises to be with us for centuries (at least) to come. Merton was ready to talk theology with those who wanted to talk theology with him (although in his later years it was well-known that he would excuse himself from discussions of scholasticism), and to talk experience with those who wanted to talk experience. It was his empathetic disposition, about which I have written elsewhere,[74] which moved him regularly into a stance of intense dialogical identification with his correspondents and interlocutors. As Rowan Williams comments, "so much of his...correspondence [has a] 'ventriloquial' character: he speaks uncannily with the voice of [whomever] he is writing to, from Sufi scholar to teenage girl."[75] Merton was, in other words, a man of many voices, including his experiential and theological voices, which were complementary rather than dichotomized; the analogy with the many languages with which he was conversant works for me here.

Pramuk does say that Merton at his best worked hard at recognizing and resisting "the overdrawn split between doctrine and mystical experience,"[76] and concludes by maintaining that yes, "the real Merton" is to be found in his interfaith letters, but not only there. In reading Pramuk's review, however, I think I overhear the sound of an ecclesial axe being ground, unnecessarily in my view. In Merton's hands the comparable sword of spiritual/experiential and theological discernment (cf. Hebrews 4.12) was already very sharp, perhaps even as sharp as the cleaver belonging to Prince Wen Hui's cook,[77] although Merton did not choose to use it in every instance.[78]

Still with Christopher Pramuk, I confess to a sense of real excitement as I read and re-read his "'*Hagia Sophia*: The Unknown and Unseen Christ of Thomas Merton," published in *Cistercian Studies Quarterly*.[79] He begins by asking how, in the "social turbulence and epistemological fragmentation of the 1960s,"[80] and with a bow to Yeats, the center held for Merton, or, alternatively, how Merton was able to hold his center in such a time; and here is the nub of his response to his own question, a response which he explores from many angles in the article: "... the center held for Merton because he never ceased deepening his understanding of Christ at the heart of the Christian tradition, nor his daily adherence as a monk to Christian faith and praxis."[81] From this starting-point, Pramuk presents the features of Merton's mature Christology, specifically its view of Christ "as Wisdom of God, the 'unknown and unseen' Sophia, in whom the cosmos is created and sustained."[82] It was through this aspect of his Christology, Pramuk suggests, that Merton was able, in interfaith dialogue, "to affirm the other *as other*," "to say 'yes' to *everyone*,"[83] not as a systematic theologian, but as a theologian of *theologia*, a spiritual theologian. It is puzzling to me that in this discussion, Pramuk registers no discomfort with Merton's experiential approach (such as he did in the Apel review), his "attention to religious *experience* more than verbal formulas, to divine *presence* and *light* more than revealed names," acknowledging that this "facilitated his uncanny ability to connect deeply with practitioners of other religious traditions."[84]

What Pramuk calls a first step in his project of assessing Merton's Christological thinking is an examination of *The New Man* (New York: Farrar, Straus and Cudahy, 1961), particularly in regard to its theological anthropology. It was written, he points out, as his journals of the years preceding bear out, at "the high point of his immersion in Russian mystical theology."[85] He focuses particularly on chapter 6, "The Second Adam," which concerns the origin and re-creation of the human race in Christ, the Christ who is not only "the fulfillment of creation but also ... its source and beginning."[86] This provides Merton with a "basis for an all-encompassing Christian inclusivism, the ground for an openness and dialogue that positively expects to encounter Christ, the light and Wisdom of God, hidden in the stranger."[87] In Merton's view, in other words, if and when Christians contemplate the unity of the human race, they can see it in the Second Adam, through whose incarnation and reclaiming of an alienated humanity all human beings, ontologically and spiritually, are already one—as he memorably and very simply said in his informal talk in Calcutta in 1968: "My dear brothers, we are already one."[88] If I understand what Merton is saying here, it is not that he is imposing an identity of the "anonymous Christian" variety on the religious other, but rather that—*as a Christian*—he sees himself as one with all other human beings by virtue of their shared membership in the human race. Everyone, and not only the Christians, are "walking around, shining like the sun."[89] The recognition that, together, we are Adam, and that together, we are Christ, forms the basis of his theological (and intra-Christian) anthropology. We come to the experience of this, of course, through contemplation, as Merton presents it, as the experience, in God, of oneness beyond all the dualities, including Christ and ourselves, seen as dual. Here Pramuk touches on the promise of his title with a long quotation from a letter of 1959 from Merton to D.T. Suzuki. "The Christ we seek," says Merton,

> is within us, in our inmost self, is our inmost self, and yet infinitely transcends ourselves. ... Christ Himself is in us as unknown and unseen. We follow him, we find Him (it is like the cow-catching pictures[90]) and then He must vanish and we must go along without Him at our side. Why? Because He is even closer than that. *He is ourself.* Oh my dear Dr. Suzuki, I know you will understand this so well ....[91]

It was the language of Wisdom, of Sophia, which in Pramuk's view enabled Merton so to express his experience of Christ to his Zen Buddhist friend, one of his prime religious "others." Then comes a crunch: while acknowledging the power of this for Merton, Pramuk asks if a sophianic Christology can "find a foothold in the imagination of ordinary Christians in our time."[92] Only, he answers himself, "to the degree [to which] it finds some reference in analogous experiences of transfiguration, light, resurrection, or presence."[93] This comment returns us to the interfaith conversation, in which mystic speaks to mystic "outside of a historical and chronological framework and inside a sapiential, aesthetic, or liturgical mode of rationality."[94]

Another strand of Pramuk's discussion which I find puzzling is the question of how he sees Merton's overarching position as a practitioner of interfaith dialogue: does he see Merton as an inclusivist or a pluralist? In one comment already quoted, he speaks of Merton's "all-encompassing Christian inclusivism."⁹⁵ In another place, he lists Merton together with Rahner, von Balthasar, the authors of the documents of Vatican II and Benedict XVI in *Dominus Iesus* as all offering different approaches to inclusivism.⁹⁶

Earlier he had said that the present time, in its postmodern character, is one in which "a thousand voices proclaim, not a few quite credibly, that there really is *no center* and that to posit a center into which all things converge is to perpetuate a 'totalizing' myth that can only lead to more violence."⁹⁷ One of these credible voices is that of Jesuit scholar Roger Haight, who asserts that it "is impossible in postmodern culture to think that one ... religion can claim to inhabit the center into which all others are to be drawn,"⁹⁸ that the time of the theological meta-narrative is over. Interestingly, and in somewhat the same vein, yet as if he wanted at some level to push the question away himself, Pramuk asks in a long footnote whether the time has not come to move beyond inclusivism into a pluralist mode "of learning from non-Christians as such... in all their luminous distinctness."⁹⁹ He then challenges those who would follow this risky path by saying that if the Christian, in turning to the other in dialogue and openness, is rooting this in the biblical revelation, "then perhaps the question becomes this: which biblical symbols are most able to affirm the other ... *as other*; [and] which symbols lend positive theological support to pluralism *de jure*?"¹⁰⁰ It seems to me, although Pramuk does not say so, that Merton has answered this question for him through his exploration of the New Adam and Sophia, which, "unknown and unseen" in the mind and heart, indeed the body and soul of the contemplative, constitute a mystical and non-coercive center for the Christian practitioner of dialogue. Again Pramuk asks: "Are we so grounded in Christ's Resurrection that we may risk 'going along without Him at our side,' allowing him to 'vanish,' in a manner of speaking, even from our theology?"¹⁰¹ In alluding thus to Merton's statement in his letter to Suzuki, is he not characterizing Merton as just such a pluralist, simultaneously grounded in Christian scripture and its symbols and ready to risk even the disappearance of the name of Christ from his theology, indeed, ready in dialogue to risk the disappearance of theology (in its propositional forms) as such? I leave it to other readers of Merton to help Pramuk and myself with the resolution of these questions, and I look forward to further studies of Merton from this very promising writer.

The nature of contemplation provides the link between this last article and the next: Ross Labrie, now president of the Thomas Merton Society of Canada, has given us a fine study of this topic in "Contemplation and Action in Thomas Merton," published in *Christianity and Literature*.[102] Contemplation as Merton conceived it and as Labrie describes it is an experiential and intuitive awareness of God beyond our own thoughts, feelings and conceptualizations through which one can come "to see oneself as one is seen through the eyes of God."[103] This of course is the personal dimension of contemplation, which, as one comes to know oneself, is found to stand beside the social dimension, whereby

> one's fellow human beings ... are seen not abstractly as an institution might see them but rather as distinct persons, each valued by God and thus deserving of care and justice, a justice that, for Merton, encompassed even the ecological integrity of the earth as the divinely created cradle of life.[104]

Contemplation in this social dimension, if I understand Labrie here, comes under the rubric of *active* contemplation, the experiencing of God in the continuing events of daily life in which one is related to others to whom one gives oneself in love. Merton also speaks of *natural* contemplation, which is a consciousness of the presence of God in prayer and in the world simply valued for itself. Finally, Merton hoped for the experience of *infused* contemplation, in which, beyond the simple consciousness of God's presence, one's soul can be "permeated by the presence of God ... [in] the very center of one's being."[105] To receive the gift of infused contemplation, one would need to be passively disposed to it, a consistently passive disposition which "Merton believed was unattainable within the active state of creative composition,"[106] activity which would short-circuit the journey into God. There is no way to tell, as Labrie correctly asserts, to what extent such infused contemplation was a reality in Merton's life, "since such experience would by its very nature have been ineffable."[107] However, after some struggle early in his monastic life on the relation of contemplation and action, Merton concluded not only that they did not contradict each other, but that they were complementary to each other. This was not all that easy for Merton at first, because he experienced a tension due to the time and energy he gave to his writing rather than to his prayer. But by the late 1950s and early 1960s, Merton had concluded not only that they were not in competition, but that they were necessary to each other for the sake of balance in the life of the contemplative, and because of the necessary relation of the contemplative to the life of the larger world—which Merton first thought he had left behind when he entered the monastery, only to realize in maturity that he was in the world and the world was in him, even as he was in God and God in him. Contemplation then became *his way of being in the world as well as in the monastery*, an orientation by which the Cold War and his opposition to it, the features of the natural environment in which he lived and his relations with other people, were given their proper proportion and their proper relatedness: it functioned for him as "the secret 'stabilizer' and 'compass' of the Christian life."[108] Merton was moving towards this integrative understanding as early as 1952, when he wrote the exquisite and lyrical "Fire Watch, July 4, 1952,"[109] as Labrie points out; and he surely reached a very deep experience—at once active, natural and infused?—when he visited the great statues of the Buddha at Polonnaruwa nine days before his death.[110] In the decade or so before his death, through his reading and reflection in the areas of Buddhism, as well as Heidegger's phenomenology and existentialism, he had come, as Labrie deftly summarizes it, to a place in which these intuitive modalities could resolve whatever leftover tension there might have been between contemplation and action "by allowing one to see *being* as an intermediate and unifying space in which thought and action, subject and object, were ontologically unified."[111] By the end of his life as an active contemplative, then, Merton had learned, simply, *to be*.

The last article I consider here is Michael Kreyling's "A Good Monk is Hard to Find: Thomas Merton, Flannery O'Connor, the American Catholic Writer, and the Cold War," published in 2006 as a chapter in a book of presentations at an earlier conference on O'Connor.[112] O'Connor, who like Merton had Robert Giroux as an editor, was, again like Merton, "a cold-war writer as well as a Catholic and southern one,"[113] if indeed Kentucky is in the South, which is arguable. Giroux, according to Kreyling, observed a "mutual curiosity and admiration between the monk and [O'Connor],"[114] both of whom were committed to the integration of their religious perspectives into their literary texts. Kreyling uses Merton as a foil for his critique of O'Connor, and concludes that for "a Catholic writer who claimed the certainty of the absolute, O'Connor's cultural politics proved stronger"[115] (she resented, for example, Dorothy Day coming to Georgia in support of local activists) than Merton's. There is some carelessness with dates in the article: Kreyling says that Merton was not baptized until a few years after reading Huxley (Merton read Huxley in 1937, and was baptized one year later, 1938, at Corpus Christi), and that he entered Gethsemani in 1942 rather than 1941.

*

Our year of grace 2006 also gave us two collections from British sources. The first of these is *Making Peace in the Post-Christian Era*,[116] which by its title is manifestly a follow-up to the publication in 2004 of Merton's *Peace in the Post-Christian Era* (PPCE).[117] It collects three papers, by Valerie Flessati, Gerry McFlynn and Anthony Maggs, all active in Pax Christi UK, originally presented in November 2005 at a day conference in London organized and co-sponsored by Pax Christi and the Thomas Merton Society of Great Britain and Ireland to explore the contemporary implications of Merton's long-delayed book. As the introduction comments, the conference was organized because its sponsors believed that "Merton provides wisdom and sustenance for twenty-first century Christians who want to recover the peace message of the gospel."[118] Valerie Flessati's paper, "Thomas Merton and Pax Christi," describes their connection. While many Merton readers on this side of the Atlantic wondered over the years what had happened with the typescript of PPCE, there rested in the Pax Christi archives in London an original copy, sent by Merton in the summer of 1962 to Charles Thompson, then editor of the *PAX Bulletin*. Merton worked during Vatican II (1962-65) with Pax Christi and with Archbishop Thomas Roberts, SJ, formerly archbishop of Bombay/Mumbai, in lobbying bishops at the Council to include in the documents that were to be published as representing the official position of the Roman Catholic Church on issues of war and peace sufficient statements of opposition to specific aspects of warmaking as well as safeguards for the individual conscience in a time when the Church was clearly not ready to challenge the continuance of war itself as an instrument of national/international policy. Valerie Flessati summarizes their contribution.

> Although they did not achieve everything they hoped for, *Gaudium et Spes* (the *Pastoral Constitution on the Church in the World of Today*) included crucial points about the

unacceptability of indiscriminate warfare and the right of the individual conscience to refuse participation in war. This, in Merton, and Roberts' view, was more important than the condemnation of any particular weapons' system. The weapons might change, but Catholics would have the freedom to make conscientious judgements.[119]

Her article concludes with the estimation that this historical moment saw Pax Christi at its best,

> working with the worldwide network of those concerned that the voice of the Church should be prophetic and clear. Thomas Merton was the still point at the centre of all this activity, the wise man on the mountain, a hermit, yet in touch with all those striving to make the Church's witness to peace a reality in the post-Christian era.[120]

In the second article, "Merton Today: No Guilty Bystander," by Gerry McFlynn, Merton is characterized, as aforementioned, in a phrase which I soberly expect to see in a book title one of these days, as a "theologian of resistance."[121] In giving him this sobriquet, McFlynn places him beside Dorothy Day, the Berrigans and their followers. McFlynn sees the theology of resistance as the principled grounding of Dorothy Day's Christian anarchism, with Day contributing her long-held and steely convictions to the resistance movements of the 1960s. Like her, the Berrigans chose their actions of resistance less from any expectation that they would compel governments to change their minds or that they would generate a mass movement in support "than for their power to give existential expression to a spirituality of personal resistance and disaffiliation."[122] The word "disaffiliation" there is a very strong one; yet the insanity, hypocrisy, indeed the cold willingness of "our side"—on behalf of which Merton and the others felt the calling to exercise their responsibility as citizens—to risk the future of the planet and the human race through a readiness to use nuclear weapons, moved them to withdraw their assent to such actions of their government and indeed their nation. That their work remains unfinished was forcefully brought home to me as I worked on this review in an email which I received from a friend that describes the danger to which the planet remains subject through the continued operability of the "launch-on-warning" systems still functioning in the militaries of the United States and Russia.[123] Merton saw then, as Gerry McFlynn would have us all see now, that to live out a theology and spirituality of resistance—resistance to racism, injustice, violence, "and all the other trappings of empire"[124]—was the only way, given the times in which we live, to offer hope, reassurance and meaning to a world in which all three are in short supply. As always, contemplation is the foundation of this spirituality: its basis for Merton is his conviction of "the sacredness of human life based upon his own contemplative experience of the presence of God as the still point of each person's true self."[125] Even though there is no longer a Cold War (although the recent posturings of the United States and Russia in regard to missile "defence" are strongly evocative of that period), Merton's thinking as applied to the so-called "war on terror" remains "bang up to date."[126] The third article, by Anthony Maggs, "The Voice from the Hermitage: Thomas Merton's Contribution to Peace,"[127] covers much the same ground in terms of Maggs' own experience. I note that Maggs regards Rowan Williams as one of Merton's spiritual heirs in the area of peacemaking. Certainly, as archbishop of Canterbury, he could, if he would, give Merton a bully pulpit as prophet of peace and theologian of resistance in our own time.

The second set of papers comes from the Sixth General Meeting of the Thomas Merton Society of Great Britain and Ireland, held in March 2006 at Merton's old school, Oakham, just five months after the Pax Christi symposium. Called *Beyond the Shadow and the Disguise*,[128] it includes the three plenary addresses from that conference, by Monica Weis, Paul Pearson and Kathleen Deignan, with a foreword by A.M. Allchin.

The title, to which each of the speakers responded, comes from the highly-charged passage in the *Asian Journal* in which Merton records his unexpected response to the great and ancient statues of the Buddha in Sri Lanka.

> Surely, with Mahabalipuram and Polonnaruwa my Asian pilgrimage has come clear and purified itself. I mean, I know and have seen what I was obscurely looking for. I don't know what else remains but I have now seen and have pierced through the surface and have got beyond the shadow and the disguise.[129]

Monica Weis's paper is called "The Birds Ask: 'Is it time to be?':
Thomas Merton's Moments of Spiritual Awakening." Her thesis is that Merton's "deeply-embedded love of nature not only nour-

ished—but also evoked"[130] many of his moments of awakening. At school at Oakham he took advantage of nearby Brooke Hill, simply to be there in a place of closeness to the earth. At Gethsemani, he reveled in the opportunities for natural contemplation which the woods and the knobs and the wildlife afforded him: among other examples, she notes his observation of the killing of a starling by a hawk on February 10, 1950, and how it directed his mind to the dedication required for the deepening of spiritual practice: "... that hawk is to be studied by ... contemplatives because he knows his business. I wish I knew my business as well as he does his."[131]

Later he comes to the writing of the passage from which Weis takes her title, the rich passage in *Conjectures* in which Merton reflects on the *point vierge* of the day, "the genesis of day, that moment of creation repeated daily all over our planet."[132]   She later interprets the *point vierge* as "the moment of poise when anything is possible,"[133] a moment experienced not only in the diurnal awakening of the planet, but, as Merton expands on it in his reflections[134] on the Louisville epiphany, a moment to experience the mercy of God "within each human being."[135] Her paper is a celebration of the *dailyness* of Merton's integration of his own participation in creation.

Paul Pearson's paper is "Beyond the Shadow and the Disguise: Thomas Merton's Embrace of *Logos*." Merton, he says, was drawn, even before his conversion to Roman Catholicism, to the concept of the *logos*, understood as the Word of God uttered at creation ("Let there be light") which is also the uttering of God's own Name within each of us, sustaining us in being and ready to speak in God's time, in silence, symbol or insight. A number of times he draws on the thought of Clement of Alexandria, selections from whose *Protreptikos* Merton published in 1962, particularly in relation to his emphasis on the *logos*. Merton described Clement in words equally applicable to himself—a regular habit of his if one thinks of his description of Clement in company with his celebration of that other mischievous hermit, Chuang Tzu, and his characterization of the "fully integrated" person in his review of Reza Arasteh's book, *Final Integration in the Adult Personality*.[136] Clement, he says, was "a man of unlimited comprehension and compassion who did not fear to seek elements of truth wherever they could be found."[137] It is a comment which is highly revelatory, of course, of Merton's own spiritual aspirations, as were his comments about Chuang Tzu and the "fully integrated" person. Pearson also points to how Merton found an *"epiphany of logoi"* in the handicrafts and furniture of the Shakers, and in their buildings, which in their balance and proportion revealed the *logos* of the places where they were built, something very important in the siting of the early Cistercian abbeys.[138] Like Clement he listened for the Word of God in his reading of the many poets he read (Pearson mentions Rilke in particular), and, whether so named or not, in his conversations with representatives of other faiths. As Clement in his time, so Merton in his, public intellectuals both, they offered to their contemporaries a Christian humanism ready to search for " elements of truth wherever they could be found."

The third paper at the conference, by Kathleen Deignan, is called "Within the Shadow and the Disguise: Thomas Merton's Sacramental Vision." Her focus is on Merton's "vividly incarnational sensibility," his "vibrant sacramental spirituality," a sensibility of apophasis and iconoclasm, a sensibility which took him, finally, "beyond the shadow and the disguise."[139] Paradoxically, however, and in keeping with her conviction that Christianity is fundamentally kataphatic, she asserts that Merton's apophatic orientation "bore fruit in a more vibrant and vivid kataphatic sensibility, the restoration of perception—a sacramental vision of the startling immediacy of an ever-incarnating divinity at once revealed and concealed in creation as mercy and love."[140]

It is kataphasis that leads to sacramentality, and Merton, says Deignan, "was a sacramentalist from birth,"[141] both genetically, she avers, and by his parents' tutoring him in the sacramentality of contemplation of nature, "in the art of beholding."[142] This bore particular fruit on his visit to Rome in 1933, aged 18, when he was dazzled by the mosaics in the great basilicas, an experience which awakened the Christ-consciousness which remained with him for the rest of his life. Ultimately, as a hermit, he found himself, ecologically, sharing his daily office of praise with the "huge chorus of living beings … choirs of millions and millions of jumping and flying and creeping things."[143]

This was also the time when he learned to appreciate the Celtic saints and writers with whom he shared a sense of the communion of human with animal and plant, rock and fish that would take him through the thin places to the Presence, to paradise recovered. This ecological consciousness also had a prophetic side for Merton, as he inveighed against human irresponsibility and

destructiveness vis-à-vis the creation. It remains highly appropriate then, that in his penultimate sacramental experience at
Polonnaruwa, he took off his shoes in reverence, to walk barefoot
one last time on God's earth.[144]

*

Now to biography. Kudos first of all to Millie Harford for suggesting to her husband James that he write a book on three great friends,
two of whom, Ed Rice and Bob Lax, he had known personally for
almost fifty years, the third, Merton, whom he knew through his
writings and the place he held in the hearts of Rice and Lax. The
book is *Merton and Friends: A Joint Biography of Thomas Merton, Robert Lax, and Edward Rice*,[145] and I have to say that I inhaled it. In
fact, I felt, for the first time since I have started to read Merton,
now a practice of more than fifty years, a sense of envy. Why could
I not have been born at a time and under the circumstances to
permit me to go to Columbia, work on the *Jester*, and so on? (I do
know the answer to that!) All three were simultaneously on a journey with God and with each other, heading (not in a straight line)
in the direction of the true self. The response that the three hermits
on the island give to the bishop in Tolstoy's marvelous story, when
he asked them how they prayed, comes to mind in this regard:
"Three are we, three are ye; Lord, have mercy upon us!"   Three
hermits? Merton tried to be a hermit, but the record on his attempt
is a mixed one. Lax, in fact, was more of a hermit than Merton, for
much longer, and Rice simply spent a lot of time on his own. As
Harford comments: "Rice once told me that he thought Lax had
the life of solitude that Merton really wished for."[146] Another iconic
image comes to mind, from Chinese religious art, the figures of
Confucius, Lao Tzu and the Buddha, standing together and smiling out at the viewer of the painting, scroll or mural—three friends,
so alike and so different, "exemplary in their friendships with one
another over decades."[147] The book is a contemporary *De amicitia*,
a celebration of a magnificent set of friendships, as well as a perceptive study of American Roman Catholic life over the greater
part of the 20th century. Harford gives us Merton and Rice unvar-
nished; Lax, in his sweetness of soul, has never needed varnish-
ing. Solidly researched, it also gathers up memories from Harford's
friendship with Lax and Rice, many of them generated from his
many years of involvement on the editorial board of *Jubilee* magazine, published from 1953 to 1967, and tellingly subtitled *A Maga-*

zine of the Church and Her People. (A personal memory here: I became a *Jubilee* reader in the sixties, and it was a small ad in *Jubilee*,
perhaps in 1964 or so, that moved me to order a vinyl recording of
the music of Taizé, which brought me to tears when I first played
it, as it continues to do whenever I am fortunate enough to go
there. The encouragement of quality in the liturgical arts was in
fact a notable commitment of the magazine.) Rice (baptismal spon-
sor/godfather to both Merton and Lax) was the editor, Lax a "rov-
ing" editor, and Merton a major and substantial contributor. All
three as Columbia undergraduates had worked on *Jester*,
Columbia's humor magazine; and there is a sense, as Rice commented, in which *Jubilee* was "a kind of extension of *Jester*."[148] In
the years before Vatican II, it pointed forward to all the major issues with which the Council would struggle, and it played a major role in preparing American Catholics for the changes that the
Council would bring. But alas (a word which Harford finds occasion to use frequently, alas!), always produced on a shoestring, it
ran out of money and ceased publication in 1967. After this, Rice
continued to work as writer and photographer, Lax found his *métier*
in minimalist poetry and his hermitage on one or other of the Greek
islands, and Merton, with the one year left to him, continued with
his unique living out of the monastic and eremitical journey at
Gethsemani.

Harford, before and after his chapter on their collaboration on
Jubilee, chronicles the effects on all of them of World War II, their
literary triumphs, their experience at a distance of Vatican II, their
romantic gains and losses, their exploration of Eastern religions
and their opposition to the Vietnam War (these last three of greater
substance for Rice and Merton than for Lax). Merton dies in 1968,
decades before the other two; Lax responds with a one-word tele-
gram to Gethsemani: "Sad."[149] The book finishes with a celebration of their later literary accomplishments, with a look at what
Harford calls "the Merton Movement"—not a happy term, in my
view—and with a consideration of their legacy. Mary Anne Rivera,
in her review of the book, commends Harford for the "thought-
provoking answers"[150] he provides in his reflection of their impact
on American Catholics and society in general, but I have to say
that I find it hard to agree with this assessment. Certainly I can
only agree that Merton has had a major impact on Christian spirituality, both within and beyond the Roman Catholic Church; and
that all three nourished the process of *aggiornamento* before, dur-

ing and after the Council. But Harford's frame of reference—their impact on a troubled Catholicism—is too narrow. Lax's influence is almost entirely literary; Rice's *corpus, Jubilee* excepted, is more historical and literary as well as more religious than ecclesial; and Merton's impact extends well beyond American Catholicism—which indeed, as Harford recounts in his treatment of Merton's non-appearance in the new American Catholic catechism, which he rightly describes as "bizarre,"[151] has a somewhat conflicted view of him.

There are other weaknesses in the book: there is, for example, no reference in the chapter on Vatican II to what was surely Merton's major contribution, his collaboration with Abraham Joshua Heschel on *Nostra Aetate*, a story well told in *Merton and Judaism*.[152] Interesting also though the first-person material on *Jubilee* is, there were times when Harford's presentation of it seemed to me to be out of proportion with the main subject, the friendship of the three. There were also more errors in the book than a careful editor should have let through: it is the Thomas Merton Society of Canada (I confess to conflict of interest here) and not the International Thomas Merton Society, that organizes the "excursions"—better, pilgrimages—to Merton-related locations (x); there is no chapter of the ITMS at Oakham (7)—it is rather the location of a number of conferences/general meetings organized by the Thomas Merton Society of Great Britain and Ireland; the L'Eau Vive retreat house at Soisy-sur-Seine, now, if the web is to be believed, a psychiatric hospital, is more likely to have been associated with Madame de Pompadour than Madame Pompidou (85-86); the L'Arche community, founded by Jean Vanier, serves both women and men with developmental disabilities, not just men (86); contrary to the statement that it is "Swiss monks who brewed Grande Chartreuse" (104), it is French hermits who *distill* Chartreuse (not Grande Chartreuse, the name of the monastery) liqueur; the term "Dog Rib" refers not to a region of the Northwest Territories of Canada, but to a native people or First Nation who live there (123); it is unhelpfully reductionistic to describe Islam as merely an "offshoot" of Judaism and Christianity—although this is Rice's error, not Harford's (168); for "Nam" in reference to Indian bread we should, I would think, read "naan" (231); for "Mahablipuran" (234, again Rice's error), we should read Mahabalipuram (now Mamallapuram); and although the Friedsam Library at St Bonaventure's does have *a* Merton archive, surely *the* Merton archive is the one at the Merton Center at Bellarmine University in Louisville (265). Most curious of all is the inclusion of this sentence—"I am not giving in to an ingenuous, admiring expression of friendship when I rank Merton with the Fathers of the Early Church and those of the Middle Ages" (217)—in an excerpt from an undated document written by Rice, and summing up Rice's sense of Merton's importance, when in fact it is a statement from Jean Leclercq's introduction to Merton's *Contemplation in a World of Action*.[153] Liking the book as much as I do, I hope that there will be a second edition in which these and other *errata* might be corrected.

Having thus indulged my copy-editor *manqué* identity, let me conclude with further appreciation. A part of the book which I found of particular interest was the description (207-14) of the writing and impact of Rice's *The Man in the Sycamore Tree*,[154] not least because it was this tendentious and very personal book which in 1972 reanimated my interest in Merton, first established when I read *The Seven Storey Mountain*. As Harford states,

> some Merton devotees, as well as Gethsemani colleagues, felt that it was impulsively written, published opportunistically, and gave erroneous impressions of the monk's disposition toward his future, seeming to imply that he was headed for Buddhism.[155]

John Eudes Bamberger, for example, longtime colleague of Merton, and later abbot of the Genesee, now, like Merton at the end, a hermit, was very critical, taking particular exception to Rice's characterization of Merton, which tilted in his view too far towards Buddhism. He also objected to Rice's take on Merton's relationship with his longtime abbot, James Fox. Similarly, Mark Van Doren and Jim Forest found it unbalanced. His Columbia peers, on the other hand, found Rice's "blunt, candid style"[156] very appropriate.

And what does "opportunistically" mean, if not simply that it came out before other biographies of various kinds? My own sense of the book, thirty-five years after first reading it, is that it was a very personal, and yes, idiosyncratic, presentation of his understanding of and grieving for a very close friend, indeed, his godchild, and written with a strong dollop of the zaniness he and Merton had shared. It was surely never intended to be a biography in any sense official or definitive, such as Michael Mott's *The Seven Mountains of Thomas Merton*, with its 2311 endnotes.[157] In the undated ms. on Merton to which I have already referred, Rice shows that he is capable of giving a much more sober assessment of his friend, which I am grateful to Harford for discovering and sharing with us.

Thomas Merton summed up an era. If one wishes to know where the Western world was in the second half of the twentieth century, Thomas Merton

> offers considerable enlightenment. He showed us our spiritual potential in the midst of our secular endeavors. He made holiness equivalent with a life that seeks to be whole, honest and free. He taught us that it was possible to be truly religious without being formally religious. He proved that contemplation could occur in the throes of restlessness and that it was permissible to be fully human.
>
> Merton was part of the great Catholic tradition and yet seemed not to be confined by it. ... Thomas Merton never left us. The journey goes on.[158]

But let Robert Lax, speaking, I would say, for Merton and Rice as well as for himself, have the last word: "Where There's an Oy, There's a Vey."[159]

The second major biographical work of the year is Joan C. McDonald's *Tom Merton: A Personal Biography*, published by Marquette University Press. Clearly it is a labor of love, with the author feeling personally indebted to Merton: "When I was lost in the liturgical and philosophical changes being considered in the Church [during and after Vatican II], he found me. I will be eternally in his debt."[160] She presents the book as

> the first biography of Merton that combines the details of his diaries with other circumstances of his life that have been published in a number of different places. I have chosen to title the book with his original name, Tom, to emphasize the personal approach I have taken ....[161]

Alas (Harford's continuing influence!), I find myself hard pressed to offer a generally positive assessment of the book. Although the book contains many statements the authenticity of which I wondered about, there are no references either to primary or secondary sources which would enable me to give context to her assertions. More difficult for me, as a reader familiar with the range of Merton's styles of writing, were the extensive passages in which she wrote in Merton's own voice. These I found painful to read, particularly a conversation between Merton and Dom James, in which she imagines Dom James, about to retire as abbot, coming during a rainstorm to see Merton in his hermitage and to seek his counsel on the possibility of his retirement.[162] I also found the narrative excessively sequential, lacking in integration and contextualization. Nor does she quote from Merton himself at times when one would expect a substantial quotation, as for example in her reference to the Louisville epiphany, given with no part of Merton's memorable account of it (224). Beyond this, the frequency of erroneous statements and misspellings undermine the seasoned Merton reader's confidence in the rest of her text. She says, for example, that Merton never explained the meaning of the curious phrase spoken, as it were, by God, in the last line of the SSM: *"That you may become the brother of God and learn to know the Christ of the burnt men."*[163] She calls these words a prophecy, and clearly she uses the word, in the sense of prediction, to make a connection to the burning of Merton's body by the fan at the time of his death. But in a journal entry of August 26, 1949, he does explain its meaning.

> I know well the burnt faces of the Prophets and the Evangelists, transformed by the white-hot dangerous presence of inspiration, for they looked at God as into a furnace .... They are the "burnt men" in the last line of *The Seven Storey Mountain*.[164]

She also asserts that Merton never referred to his practice of donating blood; but again he does, in *Conjectures*.[165] Some other errors: Merton's birthplace in Prades is not built on the ruins of the abbey of St. Michel de Cuxa, which still stands at a distance of some three kilometers from the house (28); it's very unlikely that Merton, as McDonald claims, would have attended the Catholic parish church of Montauban, given that he was a Protestant child at a Protestant school (46); Maud Grierson was Merton's father's aunt, not his sister (50); Merton was not forced into a ditch by Nazis in Italy, but in Germany (60, 101);[166] the New Testament which Merton was reading in Rome was part of the Vulgate Bible he had bought, not a NT furnished by the *pensione* (63);[167] he became an American citizen in 1951, not 1954 (71—she does give the correct date on 179); his baptism at Corpus Christi was "conditional," not "provisional" (85); Gerard Manley Hopkins had never been an Anglican priest (86); God is not "contained" in the Eucharistic wafer (111); City Lights is in San Francisco, not Santa Barbara (251); Eldridge Cleaver's notable book is *Soul on Ice*, not *Sand on Ice* (272); Merton always called his parents Mother and Father, not "Ruth" (338) or "Owen" (343, in passages where the author writes in Merton's voice); for "Chimary" read "Chimay" (379); for "embassy" read "high commission"—because India and Canada are both Commonwealth countries, the terms high commission and high commissioner are used instead of embassy and ambassador (415); and for "Samut Praharn" read "Samut Prakan"—the place of Merton's death (432). I salute Joan McDonald for the depth of her feeling for Merton, and for the substantial research and travel she undertook in the book's writing; but I cannot recommend it as a fully reliable biography of Merton.

*

And now to Merton for the multitudes. I would be rich today if I had a nickel for every occasion that someone has asked me to recommend a starter book on Thomas Merton.

Currently I recommend William Shannon's *Thomas Merton: An Introduction* (Cincinnati, OH: St Anthony Messenger Press, 2005), and/or the Cunningham or Bochen anthologies. In this review, the Simsic book would certainly qualify, as would James Martin's very readable *Becoming Who You Are: Insights on the True Self from Thomas Merton and Other Saints* (Mahwah, NJ: Hidden Spring, 2006)—with the notation that the word "saint" as applied to Thomas Merton is a tendentious one in a time when he has been deliberately excluded from a catechism. Perhaps the use of the term could be supported by the memorable dialogue between Merton and Lax in the SSM (237-38), although Merton would certainly have shelved it towards the end of his life, when through Zen, to his personal satisfaction, he had deconstructed so many of his early assumptions. Beyond these single volumes, however, the year 2006 saw the beginning publication of an ambitious and potentially far-reaching project, an eight-booklet series entitled *Bridges to Contemplative Living,* all edited by Jonathan Montaldo and Robert G. Toth, each booklet 64 pages long. The first two of these are *Entering the School of Your Experience* and *Becoming Who You Already Are* (Notre Dame, IN: Ave Maria Press, 2006). The next four booklets (*Living Your Deepest Desires, Discovering the Hidden Ground of Love, Traveling Your Road to Joy* and *Writing Yourself Into the Book of Life,* together with a Leader's Guide, have been published since; the last two (*Adjusting Your Life's Vision* and *Seeing That Paradise Begins Now*) remain to be published. The series is a project of the Merton

Institute for Contemplative Living, formerly the Merton Foundation, which describes each booklet as

> a small group resource ideally suited for groups with four to ten members. A tool for spiritual development, *Bridges* invites participants on a journey toward spiritual transformation and a more contemplative, peace-filled life. Using Merton's writings as a starting point, each session seeks to mine the life experience and spiritual depths of those who use it.[168]

The introduction to each booklet includes definitions of what the editors mean by "contemplative living" and "contemplative dialogue," a brief biographical note on Merton's life and importance, suggestions for the use of the booklet, a section entitled "Eight Principles for Entering Into Contemplative Dialogue," and a list of additional resources. This is followed by eight session outlines, each of which includes an opening reflection from the Psalms, an introduction to the texts, a passage from Merton, a second passage from another writer ("Another Voice"), a set of questions for reflection and discussion, and suggestions for closing the session with prayer or quiet reflection. The first session in the first booklet, for example, "Contemplative Living," begins with Psalm 91:2-3, 5-6. Then comes the introduction to the texts, which does not address the specific texts which follow, but rather offers suggestions of how to approach them. The Merton text comes from *New Seeds of Contemplation,* and the second text from Pema Chodron's *Start Where You Are* (full bibliographical information on all the readings, together with biographical sketches of their authors, is found at the end of the booklet: other authors whose writings are used in this first booklet include Karen Armstrong, Wilkie Au, Pierre-Marie Delfieux, Paul Evdokimov, Abraham Heschel, Rainer Maria Rilke and Eckhart Tolle). The questions are contemplative, evocative and spacious—open-ended and thoughtful. The level of writing and the choice of texts is suitable for almost any group of adults, even older teenagers; each session is manageable both in terms of challenge and of time (90–120 minutes), if the setting is a parish or congregational one, or a retreat, a student group, a Merton chapter or study group, or even if the booklet is used by an individual.

I would describe the ethos of the booklets as both simple and profound, both gentle and challenging. Manifestly the booklets, without ignoring Merton's earlier life, resonate most strongly with the perspectives of the transcultural pioneer whom he had become in his later years. The inclusion of passages from writers from beyond the Christian tradition also testifies to Merton's global inclusiveness, his recognition that Christians live in a very big world, in which through shared respect and a consistent contemplative perspective they can build bridges of understanding, communication and even communion. Michael Brennan's thorough and highly laudatory review salutes the editors for having found "a dynamic way to present Thomas Merton's writings,"[169] an assessment with which I would entirely concur. The huge volume and unsystematic character of the Merton corpus has often intimidated or defeated the beginning reader; the faithful use of these booklets, contrariwise, is much more likely both to whet the appetites of their users for further knowledge of Merton, as well as, even more importantly, giving them guidance on how to set out on the contemplative path. I plan to use them myself in a variety of settings, and I hope that they will be very widely used. Brennan helpfully notes[170] that the Leader's Guide and a "Series Sampler" which includes the full text of sessions one and six of the first booklet can be downloaded (from www.avemariapress.com). In terms of reaching out in the spirit and perspective of Merton to engage people on a grassroots level, this is probably the most significant undertaking ever mounted.

Less likely to be widely popular, but no less worthy in its own genre, and capable of touching through its elegant *consonantia* those among us to whom music speaks more directly than words, is the CD "Sweet Irrational Worship: The Niles-Merton Songs," Opus 171 and Opus 172; words by Thomas Merton, music by John Jacob Niles, and sung by baritone Chad Runyon accompanied by pianist Jacqueline Chew. The text comprises 22 poems of Merton, including such well-known pieces as "For My Brother: Reported Missing in Action, 1943," and "Love Winter When the Plant Says Nothing." Of these, parts of 12 of the songs can be heard on any computer with an mp3 feature (at http://cdbaby.com/cd/runyonchew). In her review, Monica Weis, herself an accomplished musician, and someone to whose musical discernment I willingly defer, acknowledges that these are "eclectic art songs, difficult to perform, and requiring careful attention from both artist and audience."[171] At the same time, she describes it as "well-crafted and splendidly interpreted ... not just technically proficient [but] intelligently musical, doing justice to the creative vision of both Niles and Merton."[172]

*

And so to conclude, with an attempt to see through a glass, darkly, at what might lie ahead for this feature of the *Annual*. The running bibliographies in the *Seasonal* contain a number of items in languages other than English. I would commend to the new editors of *The Merton Annual* the thought that this review might be expanded to include reviews of the more significant of these, recognizing that this would require the recruitment of reviewers conversant with the languages so represented. Recognizing also that the greater part of Merton scholarship appears in English, I would want to see as many as possible of these items translated into English or indeed, published in the original English out of which they may have been translated for appearance in another language. In particular I register the hope that there will soon appear an English counterpart of *Thomas Merton: Solitudine e Communione*, a collection of the papers (surely all written originally in English) presented by Bonnie Thurston, Donald Allchin, Jim Forest, Lawrence Cunningham, Paul Pearson and Rowan Williams at the conference held at the ecumenical monastic community at Bose, in Italy, in October 2004.[173] Some space might also be given to publications in which Merton's influence is strongly manifest, such as *A Monastic Vision for the 21st Century: Where Do We Go From Here?*[174] In my view this is a book that would probably not have been written without Merton's life and witness, as in fact the dedication ("In grateful memory of Thomas Merton, whose prophetic vision embraced monasticism in all its expressions.") testifies; and doubtless there are others.

*

Another year, then, 2006, of a renewed access to some of Merton's own words, and a year in which we may celebrate the ingathering of an ample sheaf of Merton studies as well as the publication of a number of items the intention of which is the communication of his legacy to broader audiences and readerships. Let Ed Rice conclude for us.

> Merton was part of the great Catholic tradition and yet seemed not to be confined by it. ... Thomas Merton never left us. The journey goes on.[175]

Notes

1. George Kilcourse, *Ace of Freedoms: Thomas Merton's Christ* (Notre Dame, IN: University of Notre Dame Press, 1993), pp. 76-87.

2. Belden Lane, "Merton's Hermitage: Bachelard, Domestic Space, and Spiritual Transformation," in *Spiritus* 4 (2004), pp. 123-50.

3. Lane, p. 139, p. 140, p. 142.

4. Roger Lipsey, *Angelic Mistakes: The Art of Thomas Merton*, Foreword by Paul M. Pearson (New Seeds/Shambala: Boston and London, 2006).

5. Lipsey, p. 133.

6. Lipsey, pp. 167-73.

7. Lipsey, p. 3.

8. Lipsey, p. 3.

9. Lipsey, p. 8.

10. Lipsey, p. 8.

11. Lipsey, p. 9.

12. Lipsey, p. 19. Lipsey also summarizes his understanding of the hermitage and Merton's art in "'How I pray is breathe': Thomas Merton in the Hermitage Years," in *Parabola* 31.1 (Spring 2006), pp. 16-22.

13. Lipsey, p. 19.

14. *The Asian Journal of Thomas Merton*, ed. Naomi Burton, Patrick Hart and James Laughlin, consulting ed. Amiya Chakravarty (New York: New Directions, 1973), pp. 153-55, quoted in Lipsey, p. 106, the image appearing on p. 107; and *Conjectures of a Guilty Bystander* (Garden City, NY: Doubleday, 1966), p. 199, quoted in Lipsey, p. 126, the image appearing on p. 127.

15. "Signatures of Someone Not Around," *The Merton Seasonal* 31.2 (Summer 2006), pp. 30-32.

16. Lipsey, p. 29.

17. *Spiritus* 6 (2006), pp. 195-212. Other approaches to Merton's photography include those of Deba Prasad Patnaik, Paul Quenon, Anthony Bannon, Marilyn Sunderman, John Howard Griffin and Paul Pearson, all cited in the article's notes; and in J. S. Porter, *Spirit Book Word: An Inquiry into Literature and Spirituality* (Toronto: Novalis, 2001), p. 187. Richter's article is available online at http://www.press.jhu.edu/journals/spiritus/

18. Quoted in Richter, pp. 195-96.

19. Richter, p. 197.

20. Richter, p. 199.

21. Richter, p. 202.

22. Richter, p. 203; cf. chapter 5 of *New Seeds of Contemplation* (New York: New Directions, 1961), "Things in their Identity," in which Merton expands on the *thisness* of a colt, a dogwood tree, a leaf, a lake, a mountain (pp. 30-31).

23. From Merton's introduction to Edward Deming Andrews and Faith Andrews, *Religion in Wood: A Book of Shaker Furniture* (Bloomington, IN: Indiana University Press, 1973) ix, reprinted in Thomas Merton, *Seek-*

ing Paradise: The Spirit of the Shakers, ed. and introd. Paul M. Pearson (Maryknoll, NY: Orbis, 2003), pp. 72-89 (see p. 78).

24. Thomas Merton, "Day of a Stranger," in Lawrence S. Cunningham, ed., *Thomas Merton: Spiritual Master* (New York: Paulist Press, 1992), p. 222.

25. "Merton Today: No Guilty Bystander," in *Making Peace in the Post-Christian Era*
(London: Pax Christi, 2006), p. 12.

26. CWL, xix; *Silent Lamp: The Thomas Merton Story* (New York: Crossroad, 1992), pp. 209-24.

27. CWL, p. xi.

28. "Thomas Merton and Pax Christi," in *Making Peace in the Post-Christian Era*, p. 3. For "Krushchev" read "Kruschchev."

29. CWL, p. xix.

30. CWL, p. xxi.

31. CWL, p. 3.

32. CWL, pp. 4-5.

33. CWL, p. xxix.

34. CWL, p. xvi.

35. CWL, p. xvii.

36. PBM, p. vii.

37. PBM, p. liii.

38. PBM, p. lv.

39. PBM, p. 230; p. 269.

40. PBM, p. xxxiv, p. 195.

41. PBM, p. 298.

42. PBM, p. 277.

43. PBM, p. 142.

44. PBM, pp. 72-114. See also note 174, below, and my related comments.

45. PBM, p. 77.

46. PBM, xxix-xxxii, pp. 169-87; "From Pilgrimage to Crusade," in *Mystics and Zen Masters* (New York: Dell, 1967), pp. 91-112.

47. PBM, p. xlvii, a reference to Merton's essay "Rain and the Rhinoceros," *Raids on the Unspeakable* (New York: New Directions, 1966), p. 23.

48. PBM, p. xlviii.

49. PBM, p. xlvi; cf. p. 304.

50. "Trois hymnes" 38 (2.2), in PBM, p. 261.

51. *Asian Journal*, pp. 153-55. See also note 14, above.

52. PBM, p. 139.

53. John P. Collins, "A Guide to Full Integration," *The Merton Seasonal* 31.4 (Winter 2006), pp. 24-26.

54. "Some points from the Birmingham Nonviolence Movement," in Davis W. Houck and David E. Dixon, eds., *Rhetoric, Religion, and the Civil Rights Movement 1954-1965*

(Waco, TX: Baylor UP, 2006), pp. 743-52.

55. "Some points," p. 744.

56. "Jacob's Ladder with a Few Missing Rungs," *The Merton Seasonal* 32.1 (Spring 2007), pp. 32-35.

57. Poks, p. 32.

58. From "Things in their identity," chapter 2 of *Seeds of Contemplation* (Norfolk, CT: New Directions, 1949), p. 25. In the parallel passage in *New Seeds* (see also note 22, above), to the statement in *Seeds*, "Their inscape is their sanctity," Merton adds, "It is the imprint of His wisdom and His reality in them"; he also deletes the word "Art," and replaces it with "creative wisdom" (p. 30).

59. Poks, p. 34.

60. Poks, p. 34.

61. Poks, p. 34.

62. Poks, p. 35.

63. Poks, p. 35.

64. Cf. his well-known statements on this in *Conjectures*, p. 12 and p. 129. In this regard, I find it curious that James Harford (see notes 145 and following, below) says that Merton's comments seem arrogant in what he saw as its implication that what Merton undertook personally in ecumenism and interfaith dialogue was crucial to the success of their cause (Harford, p. 95). To me it seems that he was simply modeling a specific and contemplative way of contributing to Christian and human unity.

65. Apel, p. 1.

66. Apel, p. xvii.

67. "A Vocation of Unity," *The Merton Seasonal* 32.1 (Spring 2007), pp. 28-31.

68. Pramuk, p. 28.

69. Pramuk, p. 29.

70. Pramuk, p. 28; Kilcourse, pp. 217-19, quoted in Pramuk.

71. Pramuk, p. 29.

72. Pramuk, p. 30; the internal quotations are from Apel, p. 93.

73. Pramuk, p. 30.

74. "Thomas Merton, the Holocaust, and the Eclipse of Difference," in Beatrice Bruteau, ed., *Merton and Judaism: Recognition, Repentance and Renewal/Holiness in Words*, Foreword by Victor A. Kramer (Louisville: Fons Vitae, 2003), pp. 83-103; see also, in the same volume, Karl A. Plank, "An Open Letter to Donald Grayston," pp. 105-08.

75. "The Courage not to Abstain from Speaking: Monasticism, Culture and the Modern World in the Public Interventions of a Disturbing Monk," *The Merton Journal* 12.1 (Eastertide 2005), p. 17.

76. Pramuk, p. 30.

77. "Cutting up an Ox," in Thomas Merton, *The Way of Chuang Tzu* (New York: New Directions, 1965), pp. 45-47.

78. For the way in which Merton holds together the experiential and theological voices, there is in my view no better example than "A Christian Looks at Zen," originally published as a preface to John C. H. Wu's *The Golden Age of Zen*, then rpt. in *Zen and the Birds of Appetite* (New York: New Directions, 1968), pp. 33-58, and in Cunningham, pp. 399-420.

79. CSQ 41.2 (2006), pp. 167-92; hereafter UUC. The article, for the most part very engaging and indeed provocative, does, however, sag a little in the middle, in its explication of *The New Man*, particularly in section 2.3, on the natural-supernatural distinction in Merton's late utilization of scholasticism.

80. UUC, p. 168.

81. UUC, p. 168.

82. UUC, p. 168.

83. UUC, p. 168, p. 167.

84. UUC, p. 169. I note here Pramuk's use of the word "uncanny," cognate with "uncannily," used by Rowan Williams; see note 75, above.

85. UUC, p. 170.

86. UUC, p. 173.

87. UUC, p. 175. See also Pramuk, p. 180, for further references to "the stranger."

88. AJ, p. 308, quoted in UUC, p. 181.

89. *Conjectures*, p. 157.

90. Sometimes called the "ox-herding pictures," or the "ten bulls." See "Ten Bulls," in Paul Reps, *Zen Flesh, Zen Bones: A Collection of Zen and Pre-Zen Writings* (Garden City, NY: Doubleday, n.d.), pp. 131-55.

91. Merton to Suzuki, in *The Hidden Ground of Love*, p. 564, quoted in UUC, p. 184. This evokes for me the aphorism often quoted by Carl Jung: *Vocatus aut non vocatus, Deus aderit*—"called or not called, God will be there"; or perhaps in this context we should translate *vocatus* as "named."

92. UUC, p. 187.

93. UUC, p. 189.

94. UUC, p. 189.

95. See note 87, above.

96. UUC, p. 190, note 55.

97. UUC, p. 171.

98. In *Jesus Symbol of God* (Maryknoll, NY: Orbis, 1999), p. 333, quoted in UUC, pp. 187-88.

99. UUC, p. 190, note 55.

100. UUC, p. 190, note 55.

101. UUC, p. 191.

102. Vol. 55, No. 4 (Summer 2006), pp. 475-92.

103. Labrie, p. 477.

104. Labrie, p. 477.

105. Labrie, p. 479.

106. Labrie, p. 486.

107. Labrie, p. 487.

108. Labrie, p. 482.

109. In *The Sign of Jonas* (Garden City, NY: Doubleday, 1953), pp. 339-52; cf. Labrie, pp. 487-89.

110. AJ, 230-36; cf. Labrie, p. 489.

111. Labrie, p. 491.

112. Jan Nordby Gretlund and Karl-Heinz Westarp, eds., *Flannery O'Connor's Radical Reality* (Columbia, SC: University of South Carolina Press), pp. 1-17.

113. Kreyling, p. 2.

114. Kreyling, p. 3.

115. Kreyling, p. 16.

116. Valerie Flessati et al., *Making Peace in the Post-Christian Era* (London: Pax Christi, 2006).

117. Ed. and introd. Patricia A. Burton, foreword Jim Forest (Maryknoll, NY: Orbis, 2004).

118. *Making Peace*, p. 1.

119. *Making Peace*, p. 8.

120. *Making Peace*, p. 8.

121. *Making Peace*, p. 12; see also note 25, above.

122. *Making Peace*, p. 15.

123. Ron Rosenbaum, "The Return of the Doomsday Machine? Please don't count on me to save the world again," posted August 31, 2007, in *Slate Magazine*: http://www.slate.com/id/2173108/

124. *Making Peace*, p. 15.

125. *Making Peace*, p. 17.

126. *Making Peace*, p. 18.

127. *Making Peace*, pp. 25-36.

128. Stratton-on-the-Fosse, Somerset, UK: Thomas Merton Society of Great Britain and Ireland, 2006.

129. AJ, pp. 235-36.

130. *Beyond the Shadow and the Disguise*, pp. 12-13.

131. *Entering the Silence: Becoming a Monk and Writer*, The Journals of Thomas Merton, v. 2, ed. Jonathan Montaldo (San Francisco: HarperSanFrancisco, 1996), p. 408, quoted in *Beyond the Shadow and the Disguise*, p. 16.

132. *Conjectures*, pp. 131-32; *Beyond the Shadow and the Disguise*, p. 18.

133. *Beyond the Shadow and the Disguise*, p. 21.

134. *Conjectures*, p. 158.

135. *Beyond the Shadow and the Disguise*, p. 22.

136. Leiden: E. J. Brill, 1965. The encomium on "the man who has attained final integration" may be found in Merton's article, "Final Integration: Toward a Monastic Therapy," in Rob Baker and Gray Henry, eds., *Merton and Sufism: The Untold Story, A Complete Compendium* (Louisville: Fons Vitae, 1999), p. 272.

137. From his introduction to his *Clement of Alexandra: Selections from the Protreptikos* (New York: New Directions, 1962), p. 3, quoted in *Beyond the Shadow and the Disguise*, p. 29.

138. *Beyond the Shadow and the Disguise*, pp. 32-33.

139. *Beyond the Shadow and the Disguise*, p. 45.

140. *Beyond the Shadow and the Disguise*, p. 47.

141. *Beyond the Shadow and the Disguise*, p. 48.

142. *Beyond the Shadow and the Disguise*, p. 48.

143. *The Sign of Jonas*, p. 360, quoted in *Beyond the Shadow and the Disguise*, p. 53.

144.. Two corrections: for "Santa Prudenza" (p. 50) read Santa Pudenziana, and for "Jaques Maritan" (p. 51), read Jacques Maritain.

145. New York and London: Continuum, 2006.

146. Harford, p. 219.

147. Harford, p. vii.

148. Harford, p. 98.

149. Harford, p. 193.

150. "Communication Leads to Communion," *The Merton Seasonal* 31.4 (Winter 2006), p. 29.

151. Harford, p. 290.

152. Bruteau, *Merton and Judaism*, chs. 10-13.

153. *Contemplation in a World of Action* (Garden City, NY: Doubleday, 1973), p. xviii.

154. New York: Doubleday, 1970.

155. Harford, p. 207.

156. Harford, p. 211.

157. Boston: Houghton Mifflin, 1984. Mott makes only a very brief reference (pp. 533-34) to Rice's book.

158. Harford, pp. 216-17.

159. Harford, p. 100.

160. McDonald, p. 12.

161. McDonald, p. 11.

162. McDonald, pp. 366-69.

163. McDonald, p. 14; SSM, p. 423.

164. Thomas Merton, *Entering the Silence*, ed. Jonathan Montaldo (San Francisco: HarperSanFrancisco, 1966), p. 362. I am grateful to Paul Pearson for his help in locating this quotation for me.

165. *Conjectures*, p. 310.

166. Mott, pp. 61-62.

167. SSM, p. 110.

168. From the Institute website, www.mertoninstitute.org

169. "Merton as Contemplative Catalyst," *The Merton Seasonal* 31.3 (Fall 2006), p. 29.

170. Brennan, p. 29.

171. "Merton Set to Music," *The Merton Seasonal* 31.3 (Fall 2006), p. 31.

172. Weis, p. 31.

173. *Thomas Merton: Solitudine e Communione. Atti del Convegno Internazionale di Spiritualità, Bose, 9-10 Ottobre 2004, a Cura della Communità di Bose* (Magnano: Edizioni Qiqajon, 2006). Only the preface by Enzo Bianchi, prior of Bose, would need to be translated for the book to be published in English.

174. Ed. Patrick Hart, introd. Bernardo Olivera (Kalamazoo, MI: Cistercian Publications, 2006). Monastic Wisdom Series Number Eight.

175. Harford, p. 217.

Reviews*

MERTON, Thomas. *Cold War Letters,* eds. Christine M. Bochen and William H. Shannon. Foreword by James W. Douglass (Maryknoll: Orbis, 2006), pp. xxxiv + 206. ISBN 13: 978-1-57075-662-7 (paperback). $16.00.

The appearance of this volume more than forty years after Merton wrote the letters requires some explanation. During the year October 1961–October 1962 Merton wrote a number of articles and a book manuscript in which he spoke out against war and for peace.

* Editor's Note:

These sixteen reviews divide into four categories. The first category consists of three texts by Thomas Merton:

1) *Cold War Letters*

2) *Signs of Peace*

3) *Pre-Benedictine Monasticism: Initiation into the Monastic Tradition Pre-Benedictine Monasticism*

The second category consists of texts about Merton:

1) *Merton and Friends: A Joint Biography of Thomas Merton, Robert Lax, and Edward Rice*

2) *Angelic Mistakes: The Art of Thomas Merton*

The third category emphasizes the importance of community as a conduit of faith development:

1) *Creating a Human World: A New Psychological and Religious Anthropology in Dialogue with Freud, Heidegger and Kierkegaard*

2) *Spirituality and Mysticism: A Global View*

3) *We Walk the Path Together: Learning from Thich Nhat Hanh & Meister Eckhart*

4) *Contemplation in Action*

5) *Great Mystics & Social Justice, Walking on the Two Feet of Love*

The final category focuses on spiritual direction and culture:

1) *Transforming Heart and Mind: Learning from the Mystic*

2) *Chanting the Psalms: A Practical Guide with Instructional CD*

3) *A Monk's Alphabet: Moments of Stillness in a Turning World*

4) *The Discerning Heart: Exploring the Christian Path*

5) *Waking Up to What You Do: A Zen Practice for Meeting Every Situation with Intelligence and Compassion*

6) *Portraits of Grace, Images and Words from the Monastery of the Holy Spirit*

[GC]

Merton's awakening to a prophetic vocation of prayer and writing for the abolition of war and creation of cultures of peace arose from his vocation as monk and writer. Grounded in a deep appreciation of God's presence within him and all persons, Merton believed that his faith could not serve "merely as a happiness pill. It has to be the Cross and the Resurrection of Christ" (#3, p. 13).

By April 1962, Merton's superiors forbade him to publish on the subject of war. In obedience, he took up other writing projects; as a result, the book did not appear in his lifetime.[1] However, Merton recognized that the threat humanity faced required that he continue to work for the abolition of war as a monk and writer. He prayed. He published a few articles under pseudonyms or in obscure publications. He wrote letters to his wide circle of friends and contacts and then selected, had mimeographed and disseminated forty-nine Cold War Letters in April 1962, increased to a total of one hundred and eleven in January 1963, marked, "strictly confidential. Not for publication." This allowed Merton both to comply with the ban, and to be heard in relation to war and peace.[2]

What did Merton want to say to his correspondents? In her introduction, Christine Bochen summarizes his message: "Simply put war is the most critical issue of our day and we need, with all the resources available to us, to work to abolish war and build peace" (p. xxvi). In Merton's words, "The issue is too serious. This is purely and simply the crucifixion over again. Those who think there can be a just cause for measures that gravely risk leading to the destruction of the entire human race are in the most dangerous illusion, and if they are Christian they are purely and simply arming themselves with hammer and nails to crucify and deny Christ" (#1, p. 10).

Living physically apart from the world, Merton urged those "in the world" to understand the forces producing a "Cold War mentality," notably propaganda and technology. He urged correspondents not succumb to a "progressive deadening of conscience" (#19, p. 48) but rather to live more simply (#12, p. 33) and to seek an inner transformation (#25, p. 59).

Believing that there is that of God in every person, Merton supported peaceful exchanges with the so-called enemy and even sought some way to participate in a "peace hostage exchange" (#111, p. 193). He encouraged "non-violent and civil-disobedience movements" but warned that such movements must be disciplined rather than a form of rebellious "beatnik nonconformism" (#52, p. 106).

A generation of peace activists inspired by Merton in the sixties widened the scope of Christian non-violence. Does Merton have anything to say today? Crucially, Merton reminds us that when atomic bombs fell on Hiroshima and Nagasaki, the problem of seeking and keeping world peace ceased to be a social concern among many; it became the dominant problem not simply for Merton (who penned some of these letters amidst the Cuban missile crisis) and his generation, but also for ours. Failure to solve it means the end of seekers and solutions. Britain, China, France, India, Israel, Pakistan, Russia and the United States possess arsenals of nuclear weapons. North Korea, Iran and others may join the nuclear club. There are other dangers: highly carcinogenic plutonium is a health risk; enriched uranium may become accessible to nuclear terrorists.

Readers today may draw wisdom from Merton's faith, trusting God not to make us infallible but to protect us from serious error. As Merton counseled, let us listen to God and try to avoid illusions about the nature of "this great moral and spiritual challenge" (#90, p. 161). Though these letters have previously been accessible in the five volumes of Merton's letters, under the general editorship of William H. Shannon, reading this book tells us what politicians, the media and others do not (#88, p. 155). Along with the suppressed book and anthologies of Merton's social essays,[3] it is a great benefit to have the letters in a single volume, with an appendix providing biographical information about the original recipients of the *Cold War Letters*.

Merton's message to readers still governed by those who can annihilate the enemy remains remarkably relevant. I trust that publication of this collection will inspire desperately needed witness against war and for peace.

Notes

1 Thomas Merton, *Peace in the Post-Christian Era*, ed. Patricia A. Burton (Maryknoll: Orbis, 2004).

2 Thirty-five letters, most of them from *Cold War Letters*, were included in Part III, "Letters in a Time of Crisis," in *Seeds of Destruction* (New York: Farrar, Straus, Giroux, 1964), pp. 237-328.

3 Thomas Merton, *Passion for Peace: The Social Essays*, ed. William H. Shannon (New York: Crossroad, 1997).

Paul R. Dekar

APEL, William, *Signs of Peace: The Interfaith Letters of Thomas Merton*. Foreword by Paul M. Pearson (Maryknoll: Orbis, 2006), pp. xxi + 202. ISBN 13: 978-1-57075-681-8 (paperback). $19.00.

In an icon over my desk, Thomas Merton, portrayed wearing the Cistercian cowl, sits in a Zen position. With great serenity, Merton unites two spiritual trajectories. With his raised right hand he seems to recall Jesus saying in a number of contexts, "do not be afraid" or "peace be with you."[1] With his left hand pointed down, Merton seems to recall the Buddha saying, "Be mindful." On the back of the icon, an inscription observes that Merton pointed a way forward in this time of profound cultural change, and danger.

As William Apel states in his preface, Thomas Merton corresponded with people around the world, especially during the last years of his life, a period when four books on Asian religions appeared: *Gandhi on Non-Violence* (1965), *The Way of Chuang Tzu* (1965), *Mystics and Zen Masters* (1967), *Zen and the Birds of Appetite* (1968) plus the *Asian Journal* (1973). Merton's approach to dialogue was experiential rather than dogmatic, as suggested in a passage in *Conjectures of a Guilty Bystander*:

> If I can unite *in myself* the thought and the devotion of Eastern and Western Christendom, the Greek and the Latin Fathers, the Russians with the Spanish mystics, I can prepare in myself the reunion of divided Christians. From that secret and unspoken unity in myself can eventually come a visible and manifest unity of all Christians.... We must contain all divided worlds in ourselves and transcend them in Christ.[2]

Merton saw his study of the world's religions and his engagement with a great variety of people as a contribution in the direction of world peace and unity. He received correspondents at the Abbey of Gethsemani; he visited some elsewhere, whether in New York City—Daisetz T. Suzuki (1964)—or in Asia (1968). Most, however, he never met. As a spiritual discipline he encouraged his interfaith friends to embrace others, that they too might unite in themselves and experience in their own lives all that is best and most true in the numerous spiritual traditions, "a kind of arduous and unthanked pioneering."[3]

After an introductory chapter on Merton's life of letters, Apel organizes his book around a cluster correspondents chosen for the depth and variety of their religious experiences: Abdul Aziz (Muslim), Amiya Chakravarty (Hindu), John Wu (Chinese),

Abraham Heschel (Jew), D. T. Suzuki (Buddhist), Glenn Hinson (Protestant Christian), Thich Nhat Hahn (Buddhist), June Yungblut (Religious Society of Friends) and Dona Luisa Coomaraswamy (Roman Catholic with Jewish origins). Each chapter introduces the friend, a theme specific to each individual and the text of a significant letter by Merton to that individual. Notes and bibliography guide readers to such literature as Rob Baker and Gray Henry, eds., *Merton and Sufism* (1999), Beatrice Bruteau, ed., *Merton and Judaism* (2003) or Robert H. King, *Thomas Merton and Thich Nhat Hanh* (2003).

For twenty-first-century persons of faith, Apel has lifted up the most urgent contribution, perhaps, of Merton, who wrote,

> If I had no choice about the age in which I was to live, I nevertheless have a choice about the attitude I take and about the way and the extent of my participation in its living ongoing events. To choose the world is not then merely a pious admission that the world is acceptable because it comes from the hand of God. It is first of all an acceptance of a task and a vocation in the world, in history and in time. In my time, which is the present. To choose the world is to choose to do the work I am capable of doing, in collaboration with my brother [and sister], to make the world better, more free, more just, more livable, more human. And it has now become transparently obvious that mere automatic "rejection of the world" and "contempt for the world" is in fact not a choice but the evasion of choice. [Those] who pretend [they] can turn [their] back on Auschwitz or Viet Nam [or Iraq, Darfur …] and act as if they were not there [are] simply bluffing.[4]

Providing an excellent introduction to interfaith pioneers, Apel has written a satisfying book. Each chapter stands on its own and can be read separately, for example, by a study group. My main source of disappointment is the absence of letters by Merton's correspondents, a strength of volumes edited by Mary Tardiff, *At Home in the World: The Letters of Thomas Merton and Rosemary Radford Ruether* (1995), Robert Faggen, *Striving towards Being: the Letters of Thomas Merton and Czeslaw Milosz* (1997); and Patrick Hart, *Survival or Prophecy?: The Letters of Thomas Merton and Jean Leclercq* (2002).

Notes

1. Mark 5: 36 (healing of Jairus' daughter) or John 20:19 (Jesus to disciples after the resurrection); on Merton and fear as a source of war, "The Root of War is Fear," originally published in *The Catholic Worker*, October 1961. A version appeared as Chapter 16 of *New Seeds of Contemplation* (New York: New Directions, 1962).

2. Thomas Merton, *Conjectures of a Guilty Bystander* (Garden City, NY: Doubleday, 1966), p. 12.

3. William H. Shannon, ed., *The Hidden Ground of Love: The Letters of Thomas Merton on Religious Experience and Social Concerns* (New York: Farrar, Straus, Giroux, 1985), p. 126; letter to Dona Luisa Coomeraswamy, January 13, 1961.

4. Thomas Merton, *Contemplation in a World of Action* (New York: Doubleday, 1971), p 149.

Paul R. Dekar

MERTON, Thomas, *Pre-Benedictine Monasticism: Initiation into the Monastic Tradition* 2. Edited with an Introduction by Patrick F. O'Connell. Preface by Sidney H. Griffith. Monastic Wisdom Series 9 (Kalamazoo, Michigan: Cistercian Publications, 2006), pp. lxix + 391. ISBN 0-87907-073-0 (paperback). $24.95.

Pre-Benedictine Monasticism represents a renewed attempt on the part of Thomas Merton to introduce monastic novices to the riches of ancient monastic spirituality. These notes are the basis for two lecture series that Merton gave to a newly combined novitiate of lay brothers and choir monks from early 1963 until August 15, 1965, five days before leaving for the hermitage. Compared to the previously published *Cassian and the Fathers*, which contains Merton's notes for lectures delivered on the same topic from 1955 to 1962,[1] these lecture series are chronologically more focused and culturally more diverse. Merton limits himself to the fourth through sixth centuries, and his coverage of Syriac monasticism constitutes half of the course. The Preface by Sidney H. Griffith, one of today's premier scholars of Syriac Christianity and of Ephrem in particular, helps the reader understand just how pioneering Merton's interest in the Syriac tradition was for the mid-1960s.

As with *Cassian and the Fathers*, Patrick F. O'Connell has expertly edited and annotated Merton's lecture notes. O'Connell's helpful Introduction of fifty-nine pages discusses the historical context of the lecture series. They were originally conceived as a account of the Latin sources that directly influenced the *Rule of St.*

Benedict, but developed in the course of their writing into a survey of monastic writers, both western and eastern, who lived before the composition of the *Rule* (traditionally dated ca. 540). O'Connell traces the writing of the two lecture series through Merton's comments in his letters and his journals, summarizing the main topics of the lectures in the process. He discusses how Merton's written notes compare with his oral delivery (recordings of all but one of them exist), noting Merton's use of humor, his commentary on current events, and his interest in making the material relevant for the monks of his monastery. Appendix B (pp. 359–362) is a table of correspondences between the written lecture series and the recordings. The Introduction concludes with a discussion of the textual witnesses for *Pre-Benedictine Monasticism*, and in Appendix A (pp. 339–358) O'Connell has supplied textual notes. Once again, he is to be commended for his meticulous attention to detail in the editing of this text.

As I said in my review of *Cassian and the Fathers*, scholars and others interested in the thought and personality of Merton will find in this book a hitherto largely inaccessible aspect of the man which complements and at times contrasts with the "public" Merton found in his works written for publication, the "interpersonal" Merton revealed in his letters, and the "intimate" Merton unveiled in his recently-published journals. This work thus constitutes a unique perspective for those engaged in the retrieval of Merton's ideas and in the reconstruction of his monastic and personal identity. Yet as this book is published in Cistercian Publications' Monastic Wisdom Series, in this review I would like to answer the following question, as suggested by the subtitle: would it be any good for initiating monastic novices or others into the monastic tradition? A reply to this question requires looking at the two lecture series in some detail.

Merton's first lecture series begins with a statement of its purpose: to help his students gain a deeper understanding of *The Rule of Benedict* by situating him in his historical context (p. 4). Merton seeks to disabuse his students of the then-prevailing notion of Benedict's uniqueness. Rather, Merton wants his students to appreciate how much Benedict is indebted to the preceding monastic tradition. As mentioned earlier, Merton does not stick to this plan, but goes where his enthusiasm takes him. The first lecture series then deals with Greek and Latin sources: Paulinus of Nola (pp. 10–13), Martin of Tours (pp. 13–17), Antony (pp. 17–24),

Rufinus (pp. 24–40), John Cassian (pp. 40–72), Pachomian monasticism (pp. 72–123), Basil of Caesarea (pp. 123–151), Roman monasticism in Palestine (pp. 151–169), and Egeria (pp. 169–187), and has two appendices.

The brief sketches of Paulinus of Nola and Martin of Tours focus more on their lives than their monastic doctrine. Merton then turns to Antony. Unlike in *Cassian and the Fathers* (pp. 31–39), where Merton's treatment of Antony's doctrine depends solely on the *Life of Antony*, here Merton discusses Antony's apophthegmata as "the best, simplest, most authentic resumé of Antonian spirituality" (p. 20). Unfortunately, his treatment of these apophthegmata is a mere summary of their themes without much commentary. So while Merton's recognition that one cannot rely solely on Athanasius's *Life of Antony* to understand the historical Antony and his teaching is a step in the right direction, his failure to discuss his sayings in any detail, as well as the letters of Antony—today widely accepted as authentic, though such was not the case in Merton's time—compromises the effectiveness of this section for today's audience. Because of Merton's brevity here, his discussion of the *Life* is more successful in *Cassian and the Fathers* to which the informed reader may go.

Merton next turns to Rufinus and John Cassian. In his section on the former, he focuses primarily on Rufinus's translation of the *Historia Monachorum*. Merton emphasizes Rufinus's role in the transmission of Greek monastic teaching into Latin, then discusses at length the *Historia Monachorum* as "one of the main sources of Antonian spirituality" (p. 28). He gives a good summary of the monastic doctrine in the Prologue and in Chapter 1, on John of Lycopolis, then discusses select chapters of interest to him. Merton's discussion of this important text is unfortunately based on the derivative Latin version of Rufinus (which differs significantly at times from the original Greek), so those interested in the original Greek version will have to look elsewhere. Nonetheless, this lengthy discussion of the work of the under-appreciated Rufinus is valuable. Merton's section on Cassian (pp. 40–72) nicely complements his extensive treatment in *Cassian and the Fathers* because he had recently come across Salvatore Marsili's book that compared Evagrius of Pontus and Cassian. This results in a fresh treatment of *Conferences* 1, 3, 9, 10, and 14 informed by Marsili's scholarship.

Though Merton had discussed Pachomius and Pachomian monasticism in *Cassian and the Fathers* (pp. 39–45), his treatment here is far better. In his earlier treatment, Merton was limited to using Jerome's Latin translation of the Pachomian rules. Here he avails himself of recent scholarship on Pachomius done by Louis Lefort and Heinrich Bacht. Merton tries to counter the view that Pachomian monasticism represents a "purer" strand of Egyptian monasticism opposed to the Antonian strand (i.e. Origenist-Evagrian). Merton provides an excellent summary of Pachomian spirituality (pp. 80–94) and the coenobitic ideal of Pachomius and its operation (pp. 94–107). While Merton annoyingly keeps insisting that Pachomian monasticism is not opposed to eremiticism— a concern foreign to the sources—on the whole these two sections provide an excellent synthesis of many Pachomian notions and practices. His section on Pachomian monasticism includes summaries of and commentary upon of the *Vita Pachomii* (pp. 107–114) and the *Doctrina Orsiesii* (pp. 114–118), and concludes with a section of Shenoute, whom Merton views as "the outstanding figure of *late* Pachomian monachism" (p. 120). While Merton relies solely on secondary scholarship in this discussion, it is remarkable that he includes this still-understudied figure at all.

Merton next turns to Basil of Caesarea, whom he had treated only briefly in *Cassian and the Fathers* (pp. 45–51). Merton's lengthier discussion here is far superior. He begins by judiciously discussing Basil's life, his notion of a monastic "rule," and the influence of Eustathius of Sebasteia upon him (pp. 123–129). Merton here offers an insightful interpretation of Basil's well-known censure of hermits (p. 128). Merton then comments on a number of "Basilian" texts (while all of these were viewed in antiquity as authored by Basil, modern scholarship has judged that some of them are not by him): *Letter* 2 to Gregory Nazianzen (pp. 129–133), the *Sermo Asceticus* (pp. 133–137), the *Admonition to a Spiritual Son* (pp. 137–145),[2] and the *Asceticon* (pp. 145–151).[3] Each of these is an excellent summary and discussion of the main points of these texts, though perhaps Merton's choices for discussion are at times idiosyncratic.

The next section, on Roman monasticism in Palestine, is more satisfying than a similar section in *Cassian and the Fathers* (pp. 60–69). He briefly describes the monasticism of Jerome and Paula at Bethlehem, and that of the two Melanias on the Mount of Olives (pp. 152–156). Merton then considers some texts. He provides an outline of the *Life of St. Melania the Younger* (pp. 156–159) and summarizes Jerome's controversy with Vigilantius, who had impugned monks (pp. 159–162), concluding the latter by saying: "Jerome argues like a Kentucky politician" (p. 162)! This section concludes with a nice discussion of Jerome's monastic ideas (pp. 162–169).

What comes next is without parallel in *Cassian and the Fathers*: an interesting discussion of the *Pilgrimage of Egeria*. Merton reviews the scholarship concerning the actual name of the author of this text (still a much-disputed question) and summarizes the biblical character of her spirituality, her understanding of pilgrimage, and her view of monks. He then runs through her descriptions of the monks she encounters. While most of this is a mere list of details, it concludes with a scholarly discussion of the term "apotactites," one of Egeria's names for monks (pp. 184–187). Merton has chosen to discuss this text, which he admits has scanty substantial monastic doctrine, because it provides a picture of ancient monasticism "somewhat different" (p. 187) than the patterns already discussed in Egypt and Palestine.

The first appendix to the first lecture series (pp. 188–190) is a collection of ancient monastic texts on liturgical chant that reveal the diversity of opinion on the topic. When commenting on Diadochos's view, Merton reveals his own: "This is a saner and more moderate view, which holds that *chant is sometimes very useful and good* but does not simply equate spiritual prayer with good singing" (p. 190). The second appendix (pp. 191–208) deals with Ammonas, the disciple of Antony. Ammonas was a recent discovery of Merton's (cf. O'Connell's introduction, pp. xxxii–xxxv), and his enthusiasm for Ammonas is evident in his discussion. Ammonas remains an understudied figure, and Merton's treatment is an excellent introduction to the texts attributed to him.

In the first lecture series, while Merton's treatment of individual *figures* may at times be deficient and outdated in light of more recent scholarship, on the whole his discussion of particular *texts* is very good. Merton was a careful and insightful reader of ancient monastic literature, and had the rare ability to digest the main themes of any text and re-express them succinctly. This is the great value of first lecture series in *Pre-Benedictine Monasticism*. Coupled with his critical engagement with some of the best monastic scholarship of his day, Merton's consideration of the many classic monastic texts that he discusses remains a valuable introduction to these texts. A reader of ancient monastic literature would be well served by taking Merton as initial guide through the texts he discusses.

We turn now to the second lecture series, on Syriac monasticism. Merton's treatment of Mesopotamian and Syrian monasticism in *Cassian and the Fathers* was less than satisfying, being little more than a list of names. Furthermore, Merton viewed Syrian monasticism as defective for its extremism, betraying an implicit comparison to the "norms" of the desert fathers or Benedictine monasticism that does not obtain historically. It was apparently Merton's recent reading of the scholarship of Arthur Vööbus that led him to re-evaluate the Syriac tradition. The discussion of Syriac monasticism begins with a review of Syriac Christianity: its influences, its origins, its early figures, movements, and literature (pp. 213–219), for which Merton is entirely dependent on Vööbus, whose views were subject to debate in the 1960s, and remain so today. Better sketch-introductions to Syriac Christianity than Merton's are plentiful today. Next Merton deals with Theodoret (pp. 219–231), Aphrahat (pp. 232–241), Ephrem (pp. 242–274), Syrian monastic rules (pp. 275–279), and Philoxenus of Mabbug (pp. 279–325), and concludes with five brief appendices.

Merton first summarizes several of the more interesting chapters of Theodoret's *Religious History*, occasionally adding a comment or two about ascetic practices, prayer, and the coenobitic life (pp. 219–229), then provides a résumé of Theodoret's monastic doctrine, based on the scholarship of Pierre Canivet and A. J. Festugière (pp. 229–231). All in all, this section is a mere recounting of details and largely derivative. This same holds true for the section on Aphrahat, where Merton heavily depends on the scholarship of Irénée Hausherr for his introduction (pp. 232–234). Then Merton launches into a long summary of Aphrahat's sixth *Demonstration*, entitled *On Monks* (pp. 234–241), but without much commentary. In his treatments of Theodoret and Aphrahat, Merton, very dependent on others' scholarship, seems not to have thought too deeply about what he read, content to summarize rather than analyze.

The same trend continues when Merton comes to discuss Ephrem, where he depends upon the scholarship of Edmund Beck and others. After a brief introduction (pp. 242–244), Merton summarizes Ephrem's doctrine under nine headings (pp. 244–257): (1) church, (2) nature (here Merton summarizes the *Memre on the Blessing of the Table*, pp. 245–249), (3) the world, (4) faith, (5) prayer, (6) fasting and watching, (7) virginity and monasticism, (8) devotion to Mary, and (9) miscellaneous topics. The fifth through seventh items receive the most attention, reflective as they are of Merton's own interests. Merton then intends to look at some of Ephrem's themes by examining particular writings in more detail, but winds up merely summarizing their contents. First, he discusses the *Hymns on Paradise* (pp. 259–267). Here one finds a surprising section in which Merton compares the doctrine of the *Hymns on Paradise* to Origen's doctrine of creation, drawing on the work of Vladimir Lossky. Next Merton summarizes a text attributed to Ephrem in the Ethiopian tradition, but which Merton admits is misattributed. He nonetheless discusses it because it deals with monastic formation and hermits (pp. 267–271). Finally, Merton summarizes Ephrem's *Hymns on Virginity* (pp. 271–274) and concludes by citing a prayer attributed to Ephrem by Alcuin of York (p. 274). In dealing with Ephrem, Merton appears to engage very little with his thought and the treatment of him is haphazard.

After a brief summary of Syrian monastic rules and their themes (pp. 275–279), Merton turns to Philoxenus of Mabbug. He begins by summarizing Philoxenus's life, works, homilies, and doctrine, drawing from Eugène Lemoine's introduction to his translation (pp. 279–284). Merton then discusses his homilies and letters, not sequentially but thematically (pp. 284–); here for the first time when discussing the Syriac material he really seems engaged by it.

Merton is at his best when he discusses Philoxenus, showing himself analytical and insightful. Notable are the sections on simplicity (pp. 289–294), silence (p. 295), the vocation to the desert (pp. 298–309), and fornication (pp. 320–325). In discussing Philoxenus's teaching on gluttony and temperance (pp. 309–318), Merton strangely adds texts from Pachomius on asceticism (pp. 318–320).

Following upon the excellent treatment of Philoxenus, Merton concludes the second lecture series with five appendices. The first concerns itself with the identity, writings, and teaching of the Abbot Mark cited in the *Philokalia* (pp. 325–329); the second and third with, respectively, the Palestinian monks Theodosius (pp. 329–331) and John the Hesychast (pp. 331–333); the fourth with the Ethiopian church and its monasticism (pp. 333–335); and the fifth with the prayer of Cyrillonas (pp. 335–337). Each of these appendices appear to be more or less notes taken by Merton in the course of reading recent scholarship.

Indeed, the entire second lecture series, with the exception of the section on Philoxenus, has the character of reading notes rather than lecture notes. A reader interested in mere summaries—albeit at times quite idiosyncratic—of the main works of the Syriac figures discussed by Merton will not be disappointed. But the reader who would take the second lecture series as his or her first-time guide through these writers and their texts could do better by reading more recent scholarship. For, unlike in the first lecture series, Merton's typical insightfulness and ability to digest the main themes of any text and re-express them succinctly is not evident (excepting the treatment of Philoxenus). This seems to be due to the fact that Merton was encountering these texts for the first time and had yet to digest them, whereas he had reflected on the texts discussed in the first lecture series for many years. In conclusion, then, to anyone interested in being initiated into the riches of the monastic tradition, I would recommend the entire first lecture series, especially the sections from Rufinus and Cassian onward, but only the section on Philoxenus from the second lecture series. These sections contain much that is valuable and helpful for understanding the ancient monastic tradition. Accordingly, Merton's *Pre-Benedictine Monasticism* constitutes another fine addition to Cistercian Publications' new Monastic Wisdom Series.

Notes

1. Thomas Merton, *Cassian and the Fathers: Initiation into the Monastic Tradition*. Edited with an Introduction by Patrick F. O'Connell. Foreword by Patrick Hart, OCSO. Preface by Columba Stewart, OSB. Monastic Wisdom Series 1 (Kalamazoo, Michigan: Cistercian Publications, 2005). See my review in *The Merton Annual* 19 (2006), pp. 400–7.

2. O'Connell has omitted listing the recent translation of this important text: Robert Rivers and Harry Hagan, "The *Admonitio ad Filium Spiritualem*: Introduction and Translation," *American Benedictine Review* 53.2 (2002), pp. 121–46.

3. There is a new translation of the *Asceticon* not mentioned by O'Connell: Anna Silvas, *The Ascetikon of St. Basil the Great* (Oxford: Oxford University Press, 2005).

Mark DelCogliano

HARFORD, James, *Merton & Friends: A Joint Biography of Thomas Merton, Robert Lax, and Edward Rice* (New York: Continuum, 2006), pp. 336. ISBN 13: 978-0-8264-1869-2 (hardcover). $35.95.

The task of writing a joint biography for three close friends whose very productive lives were intertwined for thirty years is one that requires a serious effort to organize a wealth of information from published and unpublished documents in addition to that obtained from numerous personal interviews. James Harford was a friend of both Edward Rice and Robert Lax, and he and his wife Millie had spent much time with them over many years. At Millie's suggestion in 1997, Harford decided to write this biography of Rice, Lax, and their friend Thomas Merton.

Harford starts by recalling his own memories and recording those of Millie along with the memories of their four children who had spent much time with Rice and Lax. The book chronicles salient information that depicts highlights of their lives by presenting their major life-decisions, selected communications among the three, as well as others, and their major accomplishments. Thus, the text is heavily punctuated with many direct quotation, letters from friends and others, as well as poems.

As a close friend of both Lax and Rice, Harford had first-hand experiences with each to accompany the volumes of materials that he possessed or found in archives. His personal experiences and knowledge of the two men provide the reader with much detail that captures the essence of their two personalities. The strength of Harford's discussion of Thomas Merton is that he was able to embellish information about Merton with memories of Rice and Lax about his early years.

Rice was born to Catholic parents on October 23, 1918, and as a youth he aspired to be an artist but was discouraged by his mother who wanted him to prepare for a medical career. While in college, he pursued his own interests and took classes in French and German; studio classes in drawing and painting; history of art courses that included ancient, medieval, and Renaissance art; also English subjects – eighteenth-century Restoration drama, biography, advanced composition, and literature after the death of Shakespeare.[1]

Rice became a brilliant writer. His list of twenty published books reflects a wide array of interests. The college courses he took and his subsequent travels were certainly instrumental in spawning multiple pursuits that showed up throughout his life.

As the only Catholic among the three, he was asked to serve in a special way as a sponsor to his two best friends. Merton, who was a Protestant, and Lax, a Jew, both went through a lengthy period of spiritual discernment. On November 16, 1938 Merton was baptized and received his first communion. Rice was godfather.[2]

Once again, on December 18, 1943, Rice was call to serve as godfather, this time for Lax, who was likewise converting to Catholicism. Lax was baptized at the same church as Merton, St. Ignatius of Loyola Church in New York. Before Lax's baptism, Fr. O'Pray "...wondered if he knew enough about Catholicism to take the sacrament."[3] Lax told him that he had been reading St. Thomas, St. Augustine, and St. John of the Cross. This convinced Fr. O'Pray.

Each of the three men possessed unique gifts that supported many noteworthy accomplishments. All three were extremely creative: Rice was an illustrator, photographer, writer, magazine editor and publisher. From 1953 to 1967 he edited and published *Jubilee* magazine, using a small staff, with assistance from Merton and Lax. *Jubilee* won several awards and was widely acclaimed for airing salient issues facing Catholics. It addressed problems that still confront the Church: "abortion, birth control, race relations, celibacy, the status of women, lay participation, government policy toward the poor, the Third World, environmental degradation, ecumenism."[4]

The focus of *Jubilee* had a core agenda that permeated the individual thinking and concerns of Merton, Lax, and Rice. In each of their contributions, there were signs of these concerns. Merton, in particular, wrote a great deal about many of the issues.

Mary Anne Rivera[5] cited Rice commenting about *Jubilee* in *The Merton Seasonal: A Quarterly Review*. Rice stated that the magazine was "a significant force in the awakening of the American Catholic Church to a wider world in the post-war and Vatican II period."[6] Rivera elaborated further in her doctoral dissertation:

> *Jubilee* chronicled the changing styles of Christian life and thought for a universal Church. By highlighting the image of the Church as the Mystical Body of Christ, it emphasized the concrete social, political, and cultural responsibilities of the whole Church, and encouraged its active and critical engagement in society and culture.[7]

Nearly forty years later in a personal interview with Harford, Lax reflected what he felt was the importance of *Jubilee*.

> *Jubilee* was lively, creative and beautiful, and that's something that a lot of, particularly religious magazines, never thought of being – I really think that's why it made such an impact.

Rice wouldn't let an issue go out unless it was beautiful – and so it got good reviews, won prizes, not because its point of view was so liberal or progressive. I think it's because people felt, "It's a magazine for the greater glory of God." That was what impressed me about Rice so much right from the beginning – in *Jester* and everything else [Rice, Merton, and Lax were staff members of the Columbia University humor magazine]. He might not be able to give you a lecture on why this figure here, that photo there, he just knew – like having absolute pitch.[8]

Both Merton and Lax provided impressive support for the magazine. "Merton was a constant promoter of the magazine, sometimes exaggerating Rice's privations as publisher in his exhortations to get his friends and correspondents to subscribe."[9] Moreover, Merton wrote numerous articles for *Jubilee* and was instrumental in mobilizing many acclaimed writers for the magazine. In the early years, Lax worked as a text editor. His subsequent letters to Rice provided much personal encouragement for the magazine, and he did write a few articles and published some poetry in *Jubilee*. Throughout its life *Jubilee* was beleaguered by financial stress notwithstanding fifteen years of successful publishing. In 1967, publication of the magazine was permanently suspended and the magazine folded due to the financial strain.

After Merton's death, Rice wrote *The Man in the Sycamore Tree*, a biography of Merton. The book caused concern because some felt that Rice was too frank in his descriptions of Merton's life. After Merton died in 1968, many viewed him as a man with a halo. These perceptions were contrary to Rice's candor that described him with the same drives and temptations of every man, while his accomplishments were extraordinary. This frankness was not well accepted by some critics. However, Rice continued to write, and

In 1973 he edited a book on contemporary Indian yogis, swamis, and gurus (*Temple of the Phallic King*), and in 1974 Doubleday published *John Frum He Come*, an account of a cargo cult in the South Pacific, a subject that had been of interest to Merton [as exemplified in *The Geography of Lograire*].

The resumé he sent to potential publishers, written in the third person with a dollop of mischief, recapped his language capabilities:

Athough he has been accused of being "only semi-bilingual," Edward Rice, as the result of a classical education and some fifteen years experience in wandering about five continents can carry on macaronic[10] conversations not only in his native dialect (which he speaks with fluency) but French, Spanish, Italian, Portuguese, German, Russian, Hindu and Urdu, and even classical and medieval Latin. He has survived a week in Damascus on five words of Arabic, and reports that the words nem and iggen solve all problems in Hungarian. He can read the street signs in Hellenic, Cyrillic and Devanagari, and scientific summaries in Inter-Lingua.

Also, for "young adults" he wrote about growing up in a Third World country *(Mother India's Children* [Pantheon, 1971]); the religions of Judaism, Christianity, Islam, Hinduism, and Buddhism *(Five Great Religions* [Four Winds Press, 1973]), and his personal view of India's great river (*The Ganges* [Four Winds, 1974]). The latter two had some of Rice's most striking photos of the Indian people, and the Ganges book had absorbing asides on history, archeology, and geology.

All of that writing was prelude to some seven years of work in the 1980s—after an even longer period of travel in Asia and Africa—on the creation of what would become, in 1990, his *magnum opus*—the life of Captain Sir Richard Francis Burton.[11]

After many years suffering from Parkinson's disease, Rice died on August 18, 2001 at the age of 82.

Lax was born in 1915 and died in Olean, New York on September 26, 2000. He was regarded as an experimental poet. His writings were characterized by broken phrases, enjambments, and by one or two words per line. Lax moved to Greece in 1962 and spent the rest of his life as a contemplative hermit writing poetry. In 1965 he was living on the island of Kalymnos. Why Greece? Lax said, "... i feel that the landscape here is properly classical, properly stripped of all that is not essential, all that is not universal. it is ready-made for abstraction and for concrete, exact, particular abstraction."[12]

Lax was repulsed by much of the world's preoccupation with material interests. He valued a simple life, with only the essentials that he needed to live. Living on a small Greek island for many years was the way he chose to live such a life of simplicity as a solitary contemplative who wrote poetry.

There have been many tributes written to Bob Lax that not only praise his poetry but also his intellectual integrity and professional honesty. Harford cites C. K. Williams'[13] eloquent analysis of Lax's poems.

> And he will not use degraded spiritual terminology to describe himself or his work any more than he will allow it or any semblance of it in that work. "Black and white," not "good or evil" or "life and death."
>
> The integrity of Lax's spiritual attempt is awesome. A renunciation, a series of renunciations, of falsehood, of sham, of any sort of pretence – even of relative "meaning" or traditional verbal music. It is an asceticism, and, like any such, may be misinterpreted as a mere system or aesthetic, but it is important to recognize how inspiring the task he has set for himself can be for us.[14]

Lax's earliest publications were in the *New Yorker* in 1940. The four published poems in seven months were without precedent at the magazine.[15] One of Lax's greatest achievements was the book of poems, *Circus of the Sun*. This book of poems metaphorically compared the circus to Creation.[16]

Like Lax, Merton went through an early period of spiritual searching. He craved asceticism. He was unhappy with his writing and blamed Catholics for wars.[17] He had considered becoming a priest for a long time, yet his attempt to enter the Franciscan Order was unsuccessful. Later, he made a Holy Week retreat at the Trappist Abbey of Gethsemani and was led to pursue a monastic life there. He entered the order as a postulant on December 10, 1941 and was ordained a priest on May 26, 1949.[18] A few months before Merton's ordination *The Seven Storey Mountain* was published. In an interview with Harford, Rice stated, "A lot of Catholics were struck emotionally by Merton's book and his ordination. I think Merton started a whole new movement and that he is still the most significant religious figure in the world today. He told the Church to bug off. He was thinking and writing about what was important."[19]

Merton spent many years studying and writing about mysticism. This period produced numerous publications on Christianity and Oriental mysticism. In 1951, he wrote about Christian mysticism in *The Ascent to Truth*. In this book, Harford cited Merton as saying, "The human race is facing the greatest crisis in its history, because religion itself is being weighed in the balance. The present unrest in five continents, with everyone fearful of being destroyed, has brought many men to their knees."[20] Today, this comment seems still to resonate and takes on great relevancy.

Harford reports that Merton's interest in mysticism led him in pursuit of an opportunity possibly to conduct retreats at Cistercian monasteries in Indonesia and Hong Kong. In May of 1968, he got permission to make the trip. Through friends, it was arranged for him to meet the Dalai Lama. In Dharamsala, he had three meetings on consecutive days with the Dalai Lama.[21] In the Dalai Lama's autobiography, his comments about Merton were very endearing: "I could see he was a truly humble and deeply spiritual man. This was the first time that I had been struck by such a feeling of spirituality in anyone who professed Christianity."[22]

Merton died on December 10, 1968 in Bangkok, Thailand from an accident in his room. Nearly all of his years at Gethsemani had been spent writing. He was a prolific writer and during his life published over 50 books, a couple thousand articles, papers, and poems. Merton's profound spiritual knowledge provided a platform for him to write. In a review of William H. Shannon's book, *Silent Lamp: The Thomas Merton Story*, Lawrence S. Cunningham said, "Merton's only peer . . . would be C.S. Lewis."[23]

Notes

1. James Harford, *Merton and Friends: A Joint Biography of Thomas Merton, Robert Lax and Edward Rice* (New York: Continuum, 2006), p. 15.

2. Harford, p. 23.

3. Harford, p. 55.

4. Harford, p. 118.

5. Mary Anne Rivera, *Jubilee Magazine and the Development of a Vatican II Ecclesiology* (Doctoral Dissertation, McAnulty College and Graduate School of Liberal Arts, Duquesne University, 2004), p. 14.

6. "Starting a Magazine: A Guide for the Courageous – The Short Happy Life of *Jubilee*," *The Merton Seasonal: A Quarterly Review*, 24 (Spring 1999), pp. 3-7.

7. Rivera, p. 14.

8. Harford, pp. 118-19.

9. Harford, p. 101.

10. Two or more languages jumbled together.

11. Harford, pp. 226-227.
12. Harford, p. 199.
13. C. K. Williams, in *ABC's of Robert Lax* (Exeter: Stride [Small Print Publication], 1999), p. 183.
14. Cited in Harford, p. 280.
15. Harford, p. 36.
16. Robert Lax web site: http://edge.net/~dphillip/Lax.html.
17. Harford, p. 49.
18. Harford, p.72.
19. Harford, pp. 98-99.
20. Cited in Harford, pp. 165-166 [Merton, *The Ascent to Truth* (New York: Harcourt Brace, 1951), p. 3.]
21. Harford, p. 180.
22. Cited in Harford, p. 191 [*The Autobiography of the Dalai Lama* (New York: Harper Perennial, 1991), p. 189.].
23. Lawrence S. Cunningham, *Silent Lamp: The Thomas Merton Story by William H. Shannon*—Book Review. *Commonweal* (February 12, 1993), p. 24.
Paul A. Montello

LIPSEY, Roger. *Angelic Mistakes: The Art of Thomas Merton.* Foreword by Paul M. Pearson (Boston & London: New Seeds, 2006), pp. 197 with Index. ISBN 1-59030-313-X. $26.95.

This book includes a bibliography of Merton's "Journals" and "Correspondence" (p. 187), documents apparently consulted by the author, along with other sections listing "Books" and "Books and Articles about Merton" (15 citations) as well as a list of "Other Sources" (42), yet this is a somewhat eclectic list. There are also often detailed notes (pp. 175-186). Thus, it seems this is a study researched in earnest. It is unique. It is a valuable study, yet somewhat limited in its focus.

The peculiarity of Lipsey's approaches to "Angelic Mistakes" is that it is a highly reverent genuflection to Merton's idiosyncratic late abstract "art" and print-making, yet is, therefore, by no means a book about "The Art of Thomas Merton," as its subtitle suggests. It is a beautifully printed book and it does provide valuable and suggestive (perhaps not always verifiably true) insights into Merton's "art," while Lipsey's exclusiveness might be a bit dangerous. So little is here finally included. The large numbers of extant photographs and enormous body of drawings, as well as the experiments in calligraphy and image-making are here in no way completely assessed. What is here will stimulate more research.

Further, while it may be controversial to say so, this study seems to attempt to make more of Merton's fun with making images than he himself might have understood. The commentary which he did include in *Raids on the Unspeakable* could here be more carefully digested (see pp. 8, 29, 45, etc. as indexed). That essay is included here at pp. 60-61.

To say as Lipsey does here that Merton's "distance from the symbols and traditions of the church explains why very few authors from within the church itself, and there have been many interested in Merton, have found their way to Merton's later art" (p. 9) is most likely misleading because for many it is dubious if what is often chosen here as "art" is so. A fellow acquaintance, an art historian who studied this book (someone who was in fact a novice of Merton) declined to review this volume and said in explanation: "I just couldn't do this to Merton..." meaning, perhaps, honest criticism of Merton's experiments as "Art" would raise too many valid questions about Merton's aspirations and accomplishments. Merton's relative isolation from art and Zen circles are explained here as if, for example, the 1964 meeting with D.T. Suzuki really allowed "two distinguished and largely separate lives [to] knot just here" (p. 11).

Lipsey finally argues that nothing in Merton's life or interests could be found to lead it seems "...inexorably, nonnegotiably to the serious practice of abstract art" (p. 19). This could be, but in Merton's own words "life moves on inexorably towards crisis and mystery" (*Turning Toward the World*, August 16, 1961) and thus we might argue Merton's enjoyment in making images was merely part of the whole sweep of his career shaped in the knowledge of the art of his parents, by his love of visual art already described in *The Seven Storey Mountain*, and throughout his journals which in this study are not really absorbed very well.

In fact, the language used in this intriguing study sometimes seems to betray Lipsey's assumptions rather than the reality of Merton's craft and "art." Lipsey, for example, mentions that Merton published "extended excerpts from his journal under the title *Conjectures of a Guilty Bystander*" (p. 23), yet if one studies that artistic reworking of the raw journals, it is impossible to call this "excerpts."

There are, it must be stressed, many quite stimulating ideas in the work of Lipsey. 1964 was an extraordinary year of flowering for Merton. And clearly, Lipsey's discoveries of the fact of "prints" rather than "brushwork" (p. 35) is quite important. Yet while some of this work by Merton is truly beautiful, or even arresting, the insistence that it is art is what remains a bit mysterious: "'signatures of someone who is not around'" (p. 43).

Pages 43-55 which speculate about the "Portfolio Images" are of greatest interest, yet when we view the images (p. 62) we are still in uncharted territory. Why all these words on the verso page? If what Merton himself has said is important—

> The only dream a man seriously has when he takes a brush in his hand and drops it into ink is to reveal a new sign that can continue to stand by itself and to exist in its own right, transcending all logical implication

—then we just do not need all these carefully chosen and maybe even irrelevant words. This method seems to me to be a real, confusing, even unnecessary, addition to a book which might best allow Merton's work to remain a mystery.

Many things are of interest in this rather special volume: the portfolio pages (pp. 62-129), the core of the book, are beautifully produced: a title (from Merton); some wonderful quotes; and on the recto page a very good quality reproduction of the selected image by Merton, yet, of course, quite mysteriously linked back to the chosen words.

Much is of implied value in these juxtapositions. Then "Three Studies," additional essays, follow, on 1) "Friends," 2) on "Unlikely Peers," ("most of the abstract expressionists were Merton's age peers," p. 155); and 3) "Exhibitions." Ultimately, and I suppose that Lipsey might agree, more questions are raised than given.

It should be stressed that the commentary which precedes the "Portfolio" shows Lipsey sometimes making insightful, even daring connections between and among points of intersection, or near misses, in Merton's life. Sometimes startling, and often grandiose in their assertions, these imaginative comments lay claim to territory which is of interest in our triangulation on Merton's enjoyment as he played with brush and/or folded paper.

The three additional essays which follow the Portfolio are quite ambitious and highly speculative. On friends and artistic influence; the Zeitgeist; and the actual "Exhibitions" of some of Merton's often ironic work, Lipsey gets us thinking, or gets us to move toward un-thinking.

All together, all this material will prove to be of value for future interpreters, maybe not so much of Merton's "art" but of his spirit. That too is the conclusion, it seems to me, of the final piece of work included here, the "reconstruction" of Merton's experimental technique, not in print-making but in the making of images which are (of course) not really images (pp. 167-173).

This book is highly speculative, and perhaps one might argue exactly what is needed at this juncture to begin to appreciate the mystery of Merton's ever-developing monastic journey—that journey is clearly reflected in his love of art, abstract drawings, calligraphies and as he put it once "blobs of ink" (p. 14).

Anthony Feuerstein

CARRERE, E. Daniel, *Creating a Human World: A New Psychology and Religious Anthropology in Dialogue with Freud, Heidegger, and Kierkegaard* (Scranton: University of Scranton Press, 2006), pp. x – 273. ISBN: 1-58966-116-8 (hardcover); 1-58966-122-2 (paperback). $30.00.

Guided by Freud, Heidegger and Kierkegaard, Daniel Carrere delivers a rigorous exploration of the human psyche and its inherent tendency to beset itself against that which is life-giving. Carrere proposes a 'new anthropology' that hopes in the human potential to coexist in an open, molten state, thereby freeing oneself (and humanity) from that which is illusory, defensive and, ultimately, fatal. *Creating a Human World*'s interdisciplinary character will likely appeal to a broad audience, both lay and professional. Due to some technical language, however, those at least familiar with Freud (in particular), Heidegger and Kierkegaard will be at an advantage. Carrere's focus on modes of being and living on both individual and collective levels, grounds his study amid theoretical and clinical investigations of Freud's monolithic *Eros* and *Thanatos* drives, Heidegger's *Dasein*, and Kierkegaard's pseudonymous works and journals.

In his Prologue, Carrere states, "This essay addresses the conundrum of how a person or group moves from a closed, defensive existence to a life that is open and sharing, not only tolerating otherness but celebrating others … it explores the crisis of being human." Carrere proceeds to ask whether one's very presence jeopardizes the presence of another and how nevertheless a shared, human world might be possible. As Freud, Heidegger and

Kierkegaard form the psychological, philosophical and religious basis (respectively) of Carrere's anthropological foundation, (Christian) scriptural themes of Exodus, kenosis and incarnation provide the means by which Carrere's vision of a shared, human world materializes. Part of what makes *Creating a Human World* appealing is its potential to stimulate needed discussion in philosophical, psychological and religious domains concerned with both theoretical and practical problems of self-knowledge and self-preservation as well as faith and reason.

Carrere's religious anthropology also lends itself to dialogue with cultural theories and theology such as that proposed by Kathryn Tanner, Professor of Theology at the University of Chicago's Divinity School. In her *Theories of Culture: A New Agenda for Theology,*[1] Tanner explores both the term "culture" and its varied theoretical and practical implications for the sake of better identifying a culture that enjoys freedom. The underlying challenge of Tanner's cultural exploration involves knowing what freedom is and what freedom looks like. Tanner operates under the assumption that theology is a form of cultural activity, or simply a human activity. Following epistemological assumptions of postmodern anthropology, Tanner's basic argument denies an *a priori* set of practices and standard of correctness in relation to "doing theology" in *any* sense. This means that no individual, institution or theory can characterize, prescribe, or even (perhaps) predict the immediate and distant future of "doing theology" because the (true) meaning of Christian practice unfolds as it occurs. So one constructs or understands meaning and purpose in the moment, so to speak. Tanner addresses the potential value of Christian identity and practice that holds diversity and disagreement as its defining characteristic as a religious community. Seeking to clarify and articulate the true nature of discipleship, Tanner says the freedom to follow God's dynamic Word is at stake. Tanner emphasizes her thematic point that being Christian hinges on discomfort with diversity in theological judgments. She argues this point because, ultimately, she sees it as inherent to being Christian. Engaging Tanner with Carrere's later chapters, which focus on interacting with the world in a new and shared fashion, will prove fruitful.

The following points are significant for both theoretical and practical purposes, for they bring to the fore certain philosophical assumptions, religious beliefs, and notions of the self that arguably result from the human mind's tendency to perpetuate an illusory, defense-filled existence rather than an open, vulnerable one that truly 'rests in God's presence.' To become clear about this point of Carrere's study is to say that the stakes are high if one takes seriously his proposed psychological and religious anthropology. In fact, in order to create the human world that Carrere proposes, one, I believe, must be willing to seriously challenge, if not let go of, several traditionally and preciously held beliefs about God, self and our world.

At the top of this list rests variegated Christian notions of "eternal life" and Otherness, revealing a checkered history that on occasion shows a sober approach and interpretation of such enigmatic themes. The New Testament's perceived attention to eternal life made possible through Christ (Otherness) is not without justification, however. But the challenge is identifying the nature of such justification. Whereas Kant's Copernican revolution severed the "ontological" link between humanity and the divine, the Kantian claim that we are neither suspended from heaven nor anchored on earth underwent fundamental revisions by Freud, Barth and Wittgenstein and their collective yet disparate criticisms of modern rationality. In his "Third Introduction" to the *Römerbrief*, Barth states:

> It seems to me impossible to set the Spirit of Christ—the veritable subject matter of the Epistle—over against other spirits ... Rather it is for us to perceive and to make clear that the whole is placed under the KRISIS of the Spirit of Christ. ...The Spirit of Christ is not a vantage point from which a ceaseless correction of Paul—or of anyone else—may be exercised schoolmaster wise. No human word, no word of Paul, is absolute truth... But what does the relativity of all human speech mean? Does relativity mean ambiguity? Assuredly it does. But how can I demonstrate it better than by employing the whole of my energy to disclose the nature of this ambiguity? ... It is precisely the hidden things, inaccessible to sense perception, that are displayed by the Spirit of God.[2]

From a Freudian perspective, one cannot underestimate the mind's cunning denial of Barth's point that God eludes human apprehension. For biblical examples, Genesis, Job and Ecclesiastes also emphasize the human tendency to 'become gods' by identifying

oneself with God, but history shows that we have a terribly difficult time with exegesis and its appropriation. Freud reminds us
of this problem of navigation by prescribing the culprit as a dis-
eased conscience. Wittgenstein urges us to at least look at the difficulty (of being human) by realizing the groundlessness of our
beliefs. Yet the religious tendency to cling to certainty in its countless shapes and forms persists. The paradox is that this particular
(human) tendency undercuts one's ability to understand the point
of Barth's "Spirit of Christ."

Chapter 10 of Carrere's study—"Beginning Anew: Envoi &
Cross-Cultural Entrée"—discusses the process of becoming an
authentic individual who is concerned both in the world and with
others. Heidegger's *Being and Time* and the work of Ananda
Coomaraswamy infuse Carrere's anthropology with four key elements: 1) self-emptying; 2) death (or Kierkegaard's "dying away
from") issuing in a deeper, 3) more integrated self that concur-
rently 4) opens to the broader world of others and otherness (p.
180). With its focus on sexuality and its traumas, Freud's *Beyond
the Pleasure Principle* offers bare sobriety to this process of becoming authentic, which is difficult, serious and full of risks, yet it also
potentially yields unparalleled freedom and joy. Carrere's Exodus drive emphasizes Freud's point of risking the unknown and
the new, which "…elicits periods of inscrutable pain as one inhab-
its emotional and mental states that are difficult to endure. Intense sorrow is sustained for all that must be left behind: a former
world and a former self, or parts of a self, that are irretrievably
lost" (p. 171).

Carrere challenges our affinity for certainty—or, better, our
comfort in exchanging the harshness of reality for an illusory one
that believes in particular certainties—by emphasizing the need
to embrace our humanity as well as our literal world, or earth.
Such an embrace, if actualized, would be a radical process with
life-changing effects. Yet the question of how one might create a
particular human world broods throughout Carrere's study, which
connects the thought of Freud, Kierkegaard and Heidegger (as
presented by Carrere) to the complex reality of our entangled
world. This particular tangled connection shows the collective
and individual potential of humanity, but it also reveals a chasm
between Carrere's world and our actual world.

Carrere's focus on the human dilemma of self-deception and
self-preservation shows a tacit connection to a rich lineage of mod-

ern philosophical and religious thought that casts a wide net, often perceived in part as the "Modernity Problem."[3] The complexity and magnitude of our human situation shows itself throughout this alleged problem.

Carrere offers a way to better understand our human situation that emphasizes our spiritual predicament brought on by inherent tendencies to construct illusions of safety, power, and achievement. True freedom and joy are at stake in recognizing and understanding how we tend to entrap ourselves in countless ways.

Notes

1. Kathryn Tanner, *Theories of Culture: A New Agenda for Theology* (Minneapolis: Fortress Press, 1997).
2. Karl Barth, *The Epistle to the Romans*, trans., Edwyn C. Hoskins (London: Oxford University Press, 1953), pp. 17-20.
3. See Robert Pippin's *Modernism as a Philosophical Problem*, 2nd edition (Malden, MA: Blackwell Publishers, 1999).

Glenn Crider

WISEMAN, James A., *Spirituality and Mysticism: A Global View* (Maryknoll, NY: Orbis, 2006), pp. xiv + 242. ISBN 1-57075-656-2. $20.00 (paperback).

As the subtitle indicates, this volume seeks to provide a broader perspective on its subject than many other surveys of Christian spirituality and mysticism (which, despite the more generic main title, is its exclusive focus). Part of the new "Theology in Global Perspective Series" from Orbis, it includes discussions of East Asian, African and Latin American spiritual traditions along with the more familiar chronological path from the Holy Land through the Egyptian deserts and Asia Minor into Europe and North America; it also is particularly careful to include the insights of women writers and practitioners throughout Christian history. Its author, James Wiseman, Benedictine monk, Catholic University professor and co-editor of the widely used anthology of Christian mystical texts *Light from Light*, is a wise and trustworthy guide to both the familiar and the less familiar ways in which the Gospel has been proclaimed and lived out across vast expanses of both space and time.

After a very helpful introductory chapter providing a concise history and clear contemporary definitions of both "spirituality" and "mysticism," drawing on the work of Sandra Schneiders, Bernard McGinn and others, along with a brief treatment of the methodology for studying spirituality based on Bernard Lonergan, Wiseman provides six largely chronological chapters examining key figures and movements in the development of Christian life from the New Testament period through the Reformation and its heirs. Chapter Two, on "Biblical Spirituality," briefly touches on the contributions of the Pentateuch, the psalms and the prophets from the "First Testament," and highlights the Pauline vision of living "in Christ" and the centrality of the communal matrix for the Christian life in the New Testament; the chapter also includes a look at the story of the sacrifice of Isaac (Gen. 22) from pre-modern (allegorical: Origen), modern (historical/critical: B. Vawter) and post-modern (feminist: P. Trible) perspectives to provide an overview of different methods of scriptural interpretation. Chapter Three focuses on the martyrs and other early witnesses to Christ, with particular attention to more familiar sources such as the *Didache*, Ignatius of Antioch, Clement of Alexandria and Origen, but also to early Syriac and Armenian texts such as the *Odes of Solomon* and the prayers of Gregory the Illuminator, along with a discussion of *The Martyrdom of Perpetua and Felicity*. The fourth chapter, on early monasticism, is probably the most traditional, focusing on Antony and Pachomius, the *Apophthegmata*, Basil, John Cassian and Benedict, though Wiseman highlights the presence of mothers and well as fathers in the desert, and notes the current scholarly questioning of the traditional attribution of the *Life of Benedict* to Gregory the Great. Consideration of the Patristic Era in Chapter Five includes expected discussions of Gregory of Nyssa, the first great master of the apophatic way, in the East and Augustine, model of both introspective and ecclesial spirituality, in the West, but also links the former with his sister Macrina, who exercised a deep spiritual influence both on Gregory, her biographer, and on their brother Basil; the Greek tradition is also represented by John Chrysostom, who exemplifies both the practical and the prophetic dimensions of Christian spirituality, but the chapter also includes significant treatment of early Syriac Christianity, represented by the poet Ephrem and the pastoral instruction of *The Book of Steps*, and briefer looks at early Christian life in Ethiopia and Nubia along with (stretching the chronological boundaries, along with the literal meaning, of the period rather far) the ninth-century Frankish noblewoman Dhuoda, author of a manual of instruction for her son (to which, Wiseman speculates, he may not have paid much heed). The various movements of spiritual renewal from the twelfth through the fourteenth centuries are discussed in Chapter Six: the Cistercians and St. Bernard; the mendicants and Dominic, Francis and Clare; the Beguines along with Meister Eckhart; the great English visionary Julian of Norwich; and the hesychasts of the Eastern Church, Symeon the New Theologian (d. 1042 – the earliest figure in the chapter) and Gregory Palamas (preceded by a brief discussion of the centrality of icons for oriental Christian spiritual life). The seventh chapter, on the Reformation, looks at Lutheran, Calvinist and Anglican spirituality among the Protestants and at Ignatius Loyola and Teresa of Avila as models of Catholic reform; for all but Calvin, modern representatives of each tradition are profiled, bring the reader up to the contemporary period: Dietrich Bonhoeffer for Lutheranism, Evelyn Underhill for Anglicanism, Karl Rahner for Ignatian spirituality and Thérèse of Lisieux for the Carmelites.

The remaining three chapters consider how Christian spirituality has developed in Asia, Africa and the Americas, respectively, with the major focus on contemporary representatives of each region. In Chapter Eight, after a brief look at the pioneering missionary efforts of the Jesuits Matteo Ricci in China, Roberto de Nobili in India and Alexandre de Rhodes in Vietnam, Wiseman considers the inculturation of Christianity in India by Abhishiktananda (Henri Le Saux) and Bede Griffiths, at the indigenous Japanese Christian spiritualities of the Lutheran theologian Katoh Kitamori and the Catholic novelist Shusaku Endo, and at the "prophetic, integral, contemplative and paschal" (180) spirituality of Filipino Benedictine theologian and prioress Mary John Manzanan (the first of the figures discussed who is still living). The chapter on African Christian spirituality follows a brief look at African Traditional Religion with a discussion of liturgical inculturation, particularly the development of the Zairean eucharistic rite, and profiles of the Catholic Archbishop Bakole we Ilunga of Zaire, a prophetic critic of the corruption and injustices in his country, and of the better-known Anglican Archbishop of South Africa, Desmond Tutu, winner of the Nobel Peace Prize for his resistance to apartheid and later the head of his nation's Truth and Reconciliation Commission; the chapter concludes with a brief survey of the development of independent Christian churches that draw upon traditional African spiritual beliefs and practices. The final chapter considers both the development of liberation theology and spirituality in Latin America, exemplified by the work of the Peruvian Gustavo Gutierrez, and the appearance of feminist, womanist (African-American) and *mujerista* (Latina) spirituality in the United States, followed by a look at the prominence of affective spirituality in the American context, represented early in its history by Jonathan Edwards and the Great Awakening and more recently by the rise of Pentecostal spirituality, which has become a global phenomenon in recent decades.

Chapter Ten, and the book as a whole, concludes with a profile of Thomas Merton, who had been briefly mentioned in the opening chapter as exemplifying a holistic vision of spiritual growth that focuses on continuities rather than distinctions among various stages (10), and as mining the resources of fiction for spiritual insight (13). The discussion of Merton in the final chapter highlights his efforts to reveal the contemplative dimension of every person's life, present beneath the surface of even the most ordinary events and circumstances. Wiseman draws on the hawk and starling scene from *The Sign of Jonas*, the Fourth and Walnut epiphany from *Conjectures of a Guilty Bystander*, and comments on Zen awareness from *Zen and the Birds of Appetite* to illustrate Merton's understanding and experience of contemplation (229-31). He goes on to point out that Merton's continuing influence is also due to his modeling of the openness to other religious traditions mandated by the Second Vatican Council, and to his insistence that "an authentic contemplative life necessarily includes an effective concern for all the great issues that confront people throughout the world in our time" (231), such as those raised by the various figures discussed in the three final chapters. Thus Wiseman's closing words to the chapter and the book present Merton as a model for what the volume as a whole intends to accomplish: "Because his vision knew no national or racial boundaries, it is fitting that this section on Thomas Merton conclude our book's presentation of Christian spirituality in *global* perspective" (231).

Spirituality and Mysticism is a wonderful book in many ways. The writing is crisp and accessible, the overarching perspective and the breadth and depth of vision are impressive, the reflection questions and suggestions for further reading appended to each chapter are helpful and to the point. The author knows the material well and communicates it in a way that is both academic without being pedantic and inspiring without being cloying. It is a book that will provide new information and insights even for those already well grounded in the history and theory of Christian spirituality, without overwhelming readers less familiar with the field. The author's ability to extend the customary boundaries of his topic is admirable and models the global consciousness that is essential for the present and future of Christian life.

Yet the book, perhaps inevitably, is not completely satisfying. As the author himself realizes and notes on more than one occasion, given the number of pages evidently allotted to him as part of the "Theology in Global Perspective" series, to include new regions and figures requires omitting others, resulting in gaps that are sometimes noticeable and disconcerting. A survey of Christian spirituality and mysticism that includes no discussion of Pseudo-Dionysius from the Patristic Era, or of Bonaventure from the Medieval Period, or of John of the Cross from the early Modern Age, among others (Wiseman plays no favorites: John Ruusbroec, whom he himself translated for the Classics of Western Spirituality series, is also absent), occasions a certain disappointment, as the author himself acknowledges (xiv). Likewise complete omission of the Celtic spiritual tradition, and a half-sentence on *The Way of a Pilgrim*, along with brief mention of the great iconographer Andrei Rublev, allotted to the long and rich Russian tradition, leave the "globe" of the global perspective with some blank spots. Even the sections on the non-European traditions may find the reader wishing for more. The Indian section is represented only by transplanted Europeans; an indigenous Indian Christian such as the early twentieth-century holy man Sadhu Sundar Singh (whose work has been republished recently in the Orbis Modern Spiritual Masters series), or perhaps Anthony de Mello, would have been an appropriate addition. Another Filipino, such as Bishop Francisco Claver, or the contemporary Redemptorist Karl Gaspar, who was imprisoned under the Marcos regime, would have complemented the discussion of Mary John Manzanan. The Japanese novelist Shusako Endo is somewhat of an anomaly as the only fiction writer in the entire book, and is represented by a single novel; the illuminating discussion of *Silence* could perhaps have been supplemented by some mention of a later novel such as *The Samurai*, which ends with a martyrdom rather than an apparent apostasy, or the pilgrimage novel *Deep River*; or perhaps the atomic bomb survivor Dr. Takashi Nagai, whose *Bells of Nagasaki* testifies to his own prophetic witness for peace, could have been profiled instead. Discussing Latin and North American spirituality in the same chapter provides an interesting and unusual perspective on the latter, but following the discussion of liberation theology in the south immediately with consideration of various forms of feminism in the north provides a somewhat abrupt introduction to North American spirituality, which is accorded rather spotty treatment: the single spiritual "movement" to receive attention, the affective revivalist/Pentecostal tradition, might have been balanced by a look at the prophetic spirituality of Martin Luther King and the movement he led, or by the contemplative activism of Dorothy Day and the Catholic Worker, which would complement the discussion of Merton as well; and Canada might well have been represented by Jean Vanier and the L'Arche movement.

These comments merely indicate that it is unfortunate that Wiseman was not allowed another hundred pages – or more – to fill in some of the gaps that the present account unavoidably contains. No doubt he would have provided just as insightful a commentary on missing figures and traditions as he has on those he chose to include. But what *Spirituality and Mysticism: A Global View* does contain certainly rewards the reader with a perceptive and enlightening encounter with many of the ways in which the Christian life has been lived out in diverse ages and places. If it is not the only book to read on its topic, it is certainly one that should not be overlooked.

Patrick F. O'Connell

PIERCE, Brian J., *We Walk the Path Together: Learning from Thich Nhat Hanh & Meister Eckhart* (Maryknoll, NY: Orbis Books, 2005), pp. 202. ISBN 13:978-1-57075-613-9. $18.00.

Thomas Merton and Thich Nhat Hanh met once, and then for only a few hours, yet in that brief meeting at Gethsemani Abbey in the spring of 1966 they established a deep spiritual connection. The young Vietnamese Buddhist monk had recently arrived in the United States at the invitation of the Fellowship of Reconciliation to speak against the war. He was at the time virtually unknown outside of his native country, yet so taken was Merton with him that he wrote a moving tribute entitled "Nhat Hanh Is My Brother" to introduce this monk to the American public.

Thich Nhat Hahn would need no such introduction today. Among Westerners, he is probably the best known Buddhist aside from the Dalai Lama. An exile from his own country for nearly forty years, he has lectured and given retreats throughout the world, published over thirty books in English, and at the age of eighty continues to provide leadership to three Buddhist communities he helped to found—two in the United States and one in France. While still regarded as a leading advocate for peace, he is now better known for teaching a readily accessible form of contemplation called "mindfulness practice." He also continues to engage in interfaith dialogue.

In *We Walk the Path Together*, Brian Pierce takes up the challenge of interfaith dialogue by bringing together in an imaginative and thoughtful way the teachings of Thich Nhat Hanh and the fourteenth-century Christian mystic Meister Eckhart (along with other Christian and Buddhist thinkers). For Pierce this dialogue is no mere academic exercise, but an integral part of his spiritual journey. Thich Nhat Hahn, or Thay as he prefers to call him, is not just one conversational partner among others, but his primary companion and guide on the journey. A Dominican friar by vocation, Fr. Brian has not only studied the writings of this Buddhist monk; he has adopted his principal form of spiritual practice. "What Thay has done with the practice of mindfulness," he writes, "is to show us how every moment of life is a sacramental moment—a moment in time that unites us with eternity, with the ultimate dimension of life" (p. 73).

As a Christian, Pierce feels he has benefited enormously from · the teachings of Buddhists like Thich Nhat Hanh and the Dalai Lama. He finds comparable expressions of spiritual truth in his own tradition, but nothing like the practical instruction which they provide. He notes especially the importance given to breath. "Through contemplative meditation and the practice of mindful breathing, we remain grounded in the present moment, in the presence of God, and are liberated from the shackles of fear" (p. 38). He has attended several Buddhist retreats, including one led by Thich Nhat Hanh at his Deer Park monastery in the winter of 2004. These experiences, he believes, have given him greater access to his own contemplative tradition, and in particular to the writings of Meister Eckhart, one of the most controversial members of his religious order.

Theologians of the Church have had difficulty knowing how to place Eckhart. His orthodoxy was seriously questioned during his lifetime, yet he was never condemned as a heretic. He was regarded as a brilliant teacher and a charismatic preacher with a wide popular following, even though his paradoxical mode of expression often bordered on the incomprehensible. In our own time, he has perhaps received more attention from non-Christian scholars, such as D. T. Suzuki, than from Christian scholars—one reason being that he is regarded as a "mystic" and therefore beyond rational understanding. Drawing on his own contemplative experience and the teachings of Thich Nhat Hanh, Brian Pierce offers a valuable corrective. He shows how Eckhart, while remaining within the Christian tradition, is able to access a non-dualistic form of spirituality more commonly associated with Asian religions.

The language which Christians and Buddhists use to speak of Ultimate Reality is markedly different. Yet there are some striking similarities, especially among the mystics of these two traditions. Meister Eckhart and Thich Nhat Hanh make creative use of the symbols of their respective traditions to express the inexpressible mystery—the union of the human and the divine, the presence of the holy in the whole of creation, the fundamental interrelatedness of all beings. Brian Pierce is at his best in exploring the similarities and differences in their ways of expressing this mystery. While realizing that no language is fully adequate to represent what is ultimately beyond our comprehension, he is more than ready to learn from their attempts.

A prime instance is the chapter entitled "Mindfulness and the Eternal Now," in which he brings Nhat Hanh's signature approach to contemplative practice to bear on Eckhart's characteristic theme of the immediacy of God. He compares a sign posted in the Buddhist's retreat center in California, reading "The Kingdom of God is either now or never," with the Christian mystic's insistence that "There is but one Now." Eternity for both men is not some distant prospect: it is a present reality fully available to us at any given moment. It is, moreover, a reality best found within oneself. "Whatever one's spiritual path," Pierce feels, the spiritual journey is a "journey home," to the true self (p. 23).

His approach throughout the book is irenic—more drawn to similarities than differences. His style is perhaps too much inclined toward the homiletical and not sufficiently analytical, but his message is certainly timely. It is summed up in this statement: "Though our paths vary and the what or Who by which we name the ultimate dimension of reality is understood differently in the various traditions, we all gain from listening to one another's music and sharing the fruits of one another's table" (p. 59). This viewpoint is much needed in the present day; it is one Thomas Merton would have endorsed.

Robert H. King

ROHR, Richard and Friends, *Contemplation in Action* (New York: Crossroad Publishing Company, 2006), pp. 157. ISBN 0-8245-2388-1 (paperback). $14.95.

Ash Wednesday, about noon. An unseasonably cold morning surrenders finally to a pale sun and for a moment, the gray skies and earth and faces reflect the light. We stood together, residents and visitors, we North Americans, the "aliens," poised to step into the season of reflection leading to the light of the Resurrection. What expectation of transformation might Rosy, holding my right hand, have for the immense sorrow in her life? Her teenage son died six months ago in a flash flood in the neighboring colonia. Or Concha, on my left, who buried an infant daughter, only girl among sons? Both women work and live with their families on a reclaimed garbage dump outside the city of Juarez, Mexico. Both women, two among many, embraced us as sisters and brothers, offering a place at their table and a hand to walk, briefly, the path of their daily lives.

Contemplation in Action, a recent work authored by Franciscan Father Richard Rohr and friends, cites Micah 6:8 on the book's cover. The authors, Daniel Berrigan, Sr., Christine Schenk, Aaron Froehlich, Edwina Gately and Walter Wink, Paula D'Arcy and Thomas Keating among others, explore what it means to "act justly, love tenderly and walk humbly with God" in the course of their lives and work. Rohr speaks of the "second gaze" of compassion and a "third way" of seeing in the first two chapters. Others entitled "Eyes That See," "My Integration," "Thoughts on Psalm 23," "The Duty of Confrontation," "Who, Me Tired?" and "A Clandestine Christian" are eight of twenty-three richly diverse essays attesting to the collective range of personal experience and prophetic wisdom found in these pages.

Rohr's Center for Action and Contemplation in Albuquerque, New Mexico, supports a new reformation, from the inside, encouraging actions of justice rooted in prayer in the spirit of the gospels, with a new appreciation for, and cooperation with, other denominations, religions and cultures (taken from the Center's mission statement). The Center's logo is a cross inscribed within an oval, but the cross ends in an arrow point on the left horizontally, and at the bottom vertically, powerfully and simply illustrating that truth comes from the bottom and from the margins. Rohr's personal charism is to model the balance of action and contemplation in his own life, in the life of the Center and at Stillpoint guesthouse. For nine days in February 2007, I lived a life of simplicity and prayer at that Center, with the central time spent in Juarez: a body, soul and spirit experience in the necessity of that balance. I found that I was not only out of my comfort zone physically, but also intellectually. My primary recourse of reasoning through unfamiliar circumstances was just not possible.

Edwina Gately says in the book, "I used to think that following Jesus was all rather noble and exciting and that if one really got on with it and flung oneself into the arena of Justice and Mission, one might well emerge shrouded in light and ecstasy" (p. 59). Most of us, if honest, probably agree. Following three days of preparation— simple communal living, prayer, guest speakers on conscientious consumption, sustainable living, fair trade and globalization, even diet—we drove to the border between two countries, two worlds. We stopped at the fence separating "us" from "them" and I stood with my camera, feet rooted, and recorded the faces of children who ran to inspect us through thick chain links, against a background of homes made of scrap that came ever so close to the boundary. By only moving my arms and changing the direction of my gaze, my camera captured all of El Paso, Texas; the teeming downtown area close to the Rio Grande, and the large, beautifully landscaped homes in the hills looking directly at the crowded streets, factories encompassing entire blocks, and barren earth across the river. Many of the men and women we were to meet work long hours in these factories, "maquilladoras" yet live on top of the poorly disguised refuse of all. Their homes, in view of the El Paso hills, are scattered along makeshift roads, constructed of concrete block and plywood, mattress springs and pieces of corrugated metal. In places, underground methane fires leak toxic smoke in spirals surrounding the homes, and dead dogs in varying stages of decay are usually smelled before being seen. The bone-dry earth has no color, no life left in it; human traffic and southwestern breezes continually reveal layer upon layer of debris.

Rohr says that, "the human mind will always try to name, categorize, fix, control and insure all its experiences" (p. 80). Further in the book, M. Basil Pennington reminds us that, "This is the construct of the false self. It is made up of what I have, what I do and what others think of me" (p. 88). There was for me, formed in a culture idolizing productivity and possession, no way to categorize, much less fix or control this reality. Yet believing that justice demands some response, I knew that the presence of each member of this small group was meant to be a catalyst in some way, compelled to confrontation, not solution.

Thomas Keating's essay confirms that, "The duty of confrontation is a hard one…(it) never works if it comes out of a feeling of anger" (114, 115). How are we to confront injustice of this scale with equanimity? As we learned in the days prior to our time in Juarez, the contributing factors are multiple and convoluted, the players multinational. Frederica Carney asks herself if she is ready for "a different journey, one that goes into the desert of humility and contrition, of Love and Forgiveness, into a new language beyond 'my' roles, beyond my need to fix situations and relationships.

We are born with a bottomless sense of inadequacy. Augustine named it original sin" (p. 137). In Justine Buisson's words,

> For all of us, the first step is to become conscious of the evil of our time, to look it in the eye and call it by its real name. Will we be uncomfortable, misunderstood, decried? Certainly, but didn't Jesus call us blessed in advance for standing up for what is right and naming what is wrong? In the morass of evil around us, we need to keep faith with the great mystery trying to understand itself—through us. This, I think, is what it means to be human and to show others that they are called to be human, too, as children of God (p. 102).

"Love alone can change people. This is the great confrontation that no one can resist," emphasizes Keating (p. 116).

In the chapter, "A Passage through India," Rohr recounts time spent in Calcutta with Mother Teresa's sisters, confirming that, "God calls us, uses us, transforms us, often in spite of ourselves. I have come to call it the Great Mercy" (p. 121). On the streets of the world's most densely populated city, in the face of extreme poverty, he found an unexpected ease and openness in the people. And in the sisters:

...that amazing and rare combination of utter groundedness and constant risk-taking that characterizes the true Gospel...these women wasted no time in fixing, controlling, or even needing to understand what is wrong with others. Instead, they put all their time and energy into letting God change them. From that transformed place, they serve and carry the pain of the world, which they are convinced is the pain of God. (p. 124)

With God's grace, we may come to understand what the sisters, the mystics and contemplatives know to be the only way to live in our world, learning in the silence that, "Our lives are usable for God. We need not be effective, but only transparent and vulnerable. God takes it all from there...we are all partial images slowly coming into focus, to the degree we allow and filter the Light and Love of God" (p. 134). In terms perhaps more accessible to the paradox of our daily struggle for justice, mercy and love, "...action is the ongoing good and the needed school, but the concluding lesson is always a contemplative seeing and being" (p. 130).

Aaron Froehlich's essay, "Eyes That See," was written following a trip from Albuquerque to Israel and the West Bank. The conclusion of his essay expresses the foundational premise of this book, and serves as a fitting summary to my experience of contemplation in action in Juarez:

Since then, my struggle to understand and communicate my experience has continued...It's not my place to search for the "solution" or to lead anyone else there either; my call is to be faithful to God's ongoing incarnation in my life, and to walk forward with a growing commitment to see with new eyes and live with greater integrity (p. 58).

Catherine Crosby

RAKOCZY, Susan, *Great Mystics & Social Justice, Walking on the Two Feet of Love* (Mahwah, NJ: Paulist Press, 2006), pp. 217. ISBN 0-8091-4307-0 (paperback). $18.95.

How can we meaningfully live out our Christian vocation in a world plagued by war, economic hegemony, ecological destruction and other structural evils? For Sister Susan Rakoczy, the answer lies in the example of the great Christian mystics whose lives of deep prayer lead to outward lives of love toward others and efforts to bring about justice and peace. Rakoczy should be commended for calling us all to consider the tie between love of God and love of neighbor in her new book, *Great Mystics and Social Justice, Walking on the Two Feet of Love.* She addresses the tension between contemplation and action by urging us to consider the testimony of the mystics that neither is sufficient without the other. Her personal experience, as a theologian, academic and spiritual director, actively engaged in working for justice as a white, woman religious in South Africa, qualifies her to speak on the subject of love of God and neighbor and the necessary link between prayer and working toward a more just and equitable society.

Rakoczy's thesis is "That the writings of the mystics have important things to say to contemporary Christians as they seek to integrate prayer and commitment to justice and peace."[1] She accepts William James' view that mysticism is not reserved for the rarified few, but is open to all and is the core of all religious experience.[2] This permits her to profile some who have not traditionally been acclaimed as mystics by devoting a chapter to the biblical account of Martha and Mary, and another chapter to four men who worked toward abolishing apartheid in South Africa: Nelson Mandela, Beyers Naudé, Anglican Archbishop Desmond Tutu and Catholic Archbishop Denis Hurley. The backbone of the book is a brief life history and selected insights from the writings of Catherine of Siena, Ignatius of Loyola, Evelyn Underhill, Dorothy Day and Thomas Merton.

The theme of this work is taken from the writings of Catherine of Siena—the two feet of love represent love of God and love of neighbor. Rakoczy sees love of God and love of neighbor as one love. For her, loving God is necessarily loving neighbor and loving neighbor is necessarily loving God. Somehow these loves should or will grow together, and if one is present so must be the other. She observes: "It does not matter which conversion happens first: to a deeper faith commitment in Jesus the Christ or an awakening to the imperative to labor for a just and peaceful society. Growth in both must continue apace."[3] Rakoczy's book challenges the reader to question himself, his church community and the Church at large as to why the love of neighbor that motivates both social justice and the desire for peace is not more evident in our world. The mystics she explores begin from profound experiences of God that over time fundamentally alter their way of seeing and engaging with themselves and with their worlds. Reading the testimonies of these mystics, in whose lives both love of God and love of neighbor grow and find meaningful expression, one is struck with the fact that the love of God and love of neighbor do not seem to grow equally in the life of the average Christian.

Rakoczy does not define social justice or offer us a clear distinction between it and the virtue of charity. Her assumption that love of God will automatically translate into love of neighbor for the average Christian is a significant and perhaps unbridgeable leap; assuming love of neighbor will automatically translate into a commitment to justice and peace is a quantum leap she fails to acknowledge. Consumed by the endeavor to live out her faith in the struggle for social justice, she might overlook the possibility that many Christians, particularly in the United States, think in individualistic rather than communal terms. While most Americans acknowledge that individual piety and acts of charity are fundamental to Christianity, many do not connect Christianity with a social justice imperative.

The mystics, like world-class chefs, show us what a perfect soufflé or a flaky puff pastry could look like but do not give us a step-by-step recipe. Those who have tried to raise social consciousness and incite action within Christian faith communities must often wonder what missing ingredients or yet-to-be mastered techniques might yield better results. What is it about the mystic's relationship with God that brings about a different relationship with neighbor that both motivates and emboldens him or her to work for a more just and peaceful society? If mysticism is open to all, why aren't more Christians experiencing the love of God and love of neighbor of which the mystics write?

Rakoczy's book showcases the mystics' insights that love of God and neighbor are inseparable but stops short of connecting their experiences to those of mainstream Christians so the reader might follow the path to transformed consciousness.

One mystic who profoundly connects mystical insights and experiences with mainstream Christianity and encourages the everyday Christian to follow the path to transformed consciousness and a social justice imperative, is Thomas Merton. Rakoczy describes Merton's progression from one who seeks solitude as an escape from the world to one who appreciates the true objective of Christian solitude and contemplation—encountering the truth which must then be spoken boldly and prophetically. Rakoczy paints the "before" and "after" pictures of Merton's personal journey and spirituality and devotes considerable space to his commitment to peace and nonviolence, but readers who appreciate Merton might wish for more. She never invites the reader into the kitchen, to continue the culinary analogy, to learn how Merton breaks the eggs and chops up the raw ingredients in order to help the reader connect the contemplative experience with love of neighbor and a commitment to justice.

Merton's writings openly describe the journey by which the Christian detaches from the false self and pseudo-Christianity and enters into the kind of experience that will result in an awakened social conscience. Merton boldly proclaims Christianity as it is commonly practiced as "scarcely Christian," resulting in "darkness" from which many "good people and souls of prayer suffer these days." He denounces the Christianity "we have subtly substituted for the will of God and for true Christian tradition" as a practice "of individualism, of greed, of cruelty, of injustice, which hides behind specious maxims and encourages a kind of spiritual quietism."[4] Merton attributes "a sense of righteousness and complacent satisfaction in the midst of the most shocking injustices and crimes" to collective narcissism.[5] He decries the well-fed man who "entertain[s] the most laudable sentiments of love for his neighbor, while ignoring the fact that his brother is struggling to solve insoluble and tragic problems."[6]

According to Merton, the antidote to this for all Christians is a serious daily commitment to contemplation and solitude, in which one finds freedom from the commotion of the world, detachment from the false self, oneness with the true self within and thereby oneness with God and others.[7] Like Merton, many Christian mystics emphasize detachment from the world as necessary in order to apprehend the ground of being in which all are one: the Mystery of Life, Love, Truth and Mercy. Discovering one's true self for Merton is discovering the great Mystery in whose image and likeness the soul is fashioned. Into a brilliant light that is read by the confounded senses as darkness, the mystic enters not simply with his mind but his entire being, and is transformed in God.[8] As one persists in the life of interior prayer, one becomes increasingly aware of the presence and action of the Holy Spirit in all things, and individual goal orientation is replaced by "an obedient and cooperative submission to grace."[9] Thereby the will of the individual is conformed to the will of God. Merton has much to say to contemporary Christians about love of God and love of neighbor and living these out in the struggle for social justice. To Merton, Christian vocation is not a choice between the contemplative life and the active life, but an entering into contemplation and solitude in order to find Truth and the will to live out of Truth – God's will. Getting the inward experience right, allowing God full access to one's being in silence, naturally leads one into expressing that experience outwardly in love of neighbor and a commitment to a more just and peaceful society.

Rakoczy's book urges us to wrestle seriously with the witness of the Christian mystics. Their prophetic voices challenge us not to be comfortable with a private piety that is not expressed in love of neighbor and a commitment to justice and peace. Merton's writings, in particular, can help Christians make the connection between mystical experience and social justice in the concrete particulars of their own lives.

Notes

1. Rakoczy, Susan, *Great Mystics and Social Justice, Walking on the Two Feet of Love* (Mahwah, NJ: Paulist Press, 2006), p. 11.

2. Rakoczy, p. 8.

3. Rakoczy, p. 4.

4. Merton, Thomas, *Cold War Letters*, ed. Christine M. Bochen and William H. Shannon (Maryknoll, NY: Orbis Books, 2006), p. 64.

5. Merton, Thomas, *Love and Living* (New York: Farrar, Straus, Giroux, 1979), p. 147.

6. Merton, p. 138.

7. Givey, David W, *The Social Thought of Thomas Merton, The Way of Nonviolence and Peace for the Future* (Chicago: Franciscan Herald Press, 1983), p. 32.

8. Merton, Thomas, *The Ascent to Truth* (New York: Harcourt, Brace, 1951), p. 261.

9. Merton, Thomas, *Contemplative Prayer* (New York: Herder and Herder, 1969), p. 49.

Martha Gross

BORYS, Jr., Peter N., *Transforming Heart and Mind: Learning from the Mystics* (Mahwah, NJ: Paulist Press, 2006), pp. 208. ISBN 0-8091-4336-4 (paperback). $19.95.

In 1921 the English writer, Evelyn Underhill, published *The Life of the Spirit and the Life of Today* in which she attempted to bring to bear the classic experience of the spiritual life and mysticism on the conclusions of modern psychology. It was a pioneering work in a subject area still very much in its infancy. The last half-century has seen marked developments in psychology, increased accessibility of mystical literature, and a proliferation of theological writing. It is the intent of Peter Borys, an attorney and Christian spiritual writer, to synthesize insights in these three areas and to bring them into conversation with each other. His aim is a practical one—to use these developments in order to support transformation which is at the heart of Christian life. A subordinate theme is his focus on healing, especially of childhood wounds, and its role in one's overall transformation as a Christian.

In his initial overview, Borys sets out the classic pattern of the Christian journey and its modifications by various mystical writers. He then explores the nature of the human person as articulated by Augustine and Thomas Aquinas, giving particular emphasis to human wounding in early life experience, the emotions in child development, and the impact of trauma on human life. In a chapter on theology, philosophy and psychology of transformation in Christ, he relies heavily on the insights of Bonaventure, Gabriel Marcel, Edith Stein and Bernard Lonergan. In Part Two of this volume he explores how the Christian lives the faith journey of transformation in Christ especially through prayer and liturgy. He sees self-restoration and renewal through the purgative way and suffering as a pathway to union with God.

Although an earnest and wide-ranging volume, Borys' work is limited in four ways. First, in some brief two hundred pages he attempts to take on three distinct knowledge areas—mysticism, theology and psychology. His scope is so all-inclusive that the exploration of any one thinker suffers. Second, his selection of mystics, theologians, and psychologists is very eclectic and idiosyncratic. These are Borys' favorite thinkers, but he does not convince the reader they should be the reader's own. Third, the language and conceptualization of the book does not invite in the reader. This is a book about Borys' spiritual journey, and although he tries to universalize it, I for one felt like an outsider.   Finally, totally missing in this book is any indication that service to others or entering into their suffering has any meaning for the spiritual life or Christian transformation.   This is the story of one good man's journey lived independently of others. The first commandment is explored in this book, but not the second.

Dana Greene

BOURGEAULT, Cynthia. *Chanting the Psalms: A Practical Guide with Instructional CD* (Boston: New Seeds Books, Shambhala Publications, Inc., 2006), pp-xv-275. ISBN-13: 978-1-59030-257-6 (hbk). ISBN-20: 1-59030-257-5. CD, Tracks 1-39, Total running time: 53:58. US$ 18.95, CAN $24.95.

I.

Contemplative prayer, once the prerogative of cloistered monasticism, has broken out of those confines and is now practiced worldwide by tens of thousands, through simplified methods such as Centering Prayer (furthered by, for example , the Cistercians Thomas Keating and Basil Pennington, and indeed by Bourgeault's own excellent recent investigations of the same. But **chanting** the **psalms** still seems esoteric to Christian seekers. Bourgeault wants to see this change and offers her book as a way of furthering that change.

Chanting the Psalms: A Practical Guide . . . might well have used as its sub-title the title of the author's previous book—a guide to *Inner Awakening*. [1]   For the insights she offers into the role of music-making in the journey of the spiritual life are nothing less than that, i.e. a guide to using our voices to bring us into the awareness and the presence of the Numinous. This is an imminently "practical" book, both in the word's meaning of "useable" and in the sense of spiritual *"praxis."*

Bourgeault admits head-on two major problems associated with psalmody in our era: first, that of the psalms themselves as suitable Christian prayer; and second, the almost exclusive identification of psalmody with Gregorian chant, and this chant's suitability for contemporary life and worship. Her considerations take both problems seriously, are beautifully nuanced, and able both to affirm the tradition and offer fruitful alternatives.

Why are the psalms so important, she queries? Her answer, an excellent *apologia* for the psalms as prayer, spread over several places in the text, is one of the valuable aspects of the book, a strong endorsement for their continuing validity as foundational Christian prayer. "For Christians on a path of inner transformation, the psalms have traditionally been a non-negotiable cornerstone. . . . For two thousand years they have been the backbone of the monastic program of spiritual awakening (x)." All our spiritual heroes have chanted them, from Cassian and Benedict in the fifth century to Thomas Merton and Joan Chittister in the twentieth, not to mention Jesus himself in the first. The author's pursuit of the "why?" is perhaps the most important and original contribution of this volume, namely its explanation of how "[t]he psalms have an intentional and effective part to play in fine-tuning the instrument of spiritual transformation—that is, *you* (x)." The book provides practical and specific ways of how **anyone** can gain access to this fine-tuning, to the "hidden wisdom in psalmody that makes sense of the practice [of chanting] itself" and which in so doing also "pulls a lot of the other elements in the Christian contemplative path together (xi)."

Already in the fifth-century the contemplative master Cassian had noted that the psalms carry within themselves "all the feelings of which human nature is capable" (15). Drawing on the psychological insights of later spiritual teachers such as Thomas Keating (of *Centering Prayer* and *Contemplative Outreach*), Bourgeault explains what intimacy with such a "vast cornucopia of personal experience" can do for us "when we introduce the psalms into our consciousness—and even more so into our *unconscious*—through a practice of contemplative psalmody." "They begin to create a safe spiritual container for recognizing and processing those dark shadows within ourselves, those places we'd prefer not to think about (43)."

II.

A consideration of the tri-partite structure of the volume reveals the author's method. I will describe briefly the three parts to whet readers' appetite. I shall, however, dwell more fully on certain aspects which either are truly original or/and which I consider of special value for those on the spiritual journey.

Bourgeault structures her work in three parts, each quite different, with different purposes, all equally valuable and practical in a different way. **Part One** I find profoundly important—theoretical, yet personal in the sense of offering insight into ourselves

386 The Merton Annual 20 (2007)

as physical, psychological, spiritual beings. And it answers a question long pondered by students of monasticism, namely: what is it about the Benedictine (monastic) life, or spirituality, or way, that is so attractive, so powerful. Or put another way: why is the *Rule of St. Benedict* so important? Wherein lies its transformative influence or power? The way Bourgeault's volume addresses this problem qualifies it as required reading for those interested in Benedictine spirituality. This is the author's truly original contribution, which I will return to shortly.

Part Two is quite "practical" in the more usual sense of the word, though again it is also related to *praxis*, explaining ways of actually chanting, but also with an excellent introductory foray into music as self-discovery (in Chapter 7, "Finding Your Own Voice") [2] and concluding with workable suggestions for integrating chanting into one's personal prayer life. The author's presentation of Gregorian notation is as clear an explanation as I have seen of both the intricacies of this medium and of its strength and essence.

Part Three presents "Creative Adaptations", ways in which those on the spiritual journey in various Christian traditions have already responded to the need for sung celebration of the Divine with adaptation to contemporary life-styles. The chapters on Taize, Iona, and Gouzes chant and Songs of the Presence invite and encourage the reader to join the chorus! Although Bourgeault warns her readers not to start a chanting practice if they don't intend to persevere, this chapter's material offers "practical" ways in which occasional chanting can in fact be used for specific situations. Further, the impressive number and diversity of the various chanting communities it describes is a sign of the great interest in this *praxis* and provides proof that chanting is by no means an "esoteric" or "medieval" oddity foreign to life lived within the twenty-first century.

III.

Both Parts Two and Three offer excellent material in "how to" develop a praxis of chant as personal prayer. But Part one's exploration of the essence of psalmody is so important that I will devote most of the following part of the review to these insights, in the hope (shared by the author) that my readers will sense the potential of a careful reading of the volume for their own spiritual and mental growth. Even if one still balks at **chanting**, the copious insights into the wisdom/transformative power/essence of the psalms and of the office (with its coordination of antiphons) will deepen anyone's communication with this body of sacred texts.

Christian psalmody differs from most chant traditions, which rely on repetition of a single mantra or phrase, by flooding the mind with images and emotions. It requires "compassionate engagement" with **meanings**. Yet though more "mental" than other traditions, contemplative psalmody is "a total immersion program" for "awakening the *unitive imagination*(49)." Bourgeault defines "unitive imagination" as a kind of full-spectrum "thinking with the heart" which goes beyond mere linear knowing, by engaging the faculties of intuition, sensitivity, creativity, and conscience lying deep within the psyche (49f). Christianity is a religion of the **"unitive" Word** which does not yield itself up easily to a linear, or cause-and-effect thought process. Bourgeault offers the quite cogent illustrations of this fact with reference to elements in the Christian tradition which at the **literal** level may not make clear sense— the Virgin Birth or the mystical body of Christ—but to the awakened unitive imagination "become precise road maps of the path of inner transformation (50)." This movement beyond the literal, she points out, was the whole goal of the spiritual journey for much of early Christian tradition.

Benedict did not have access to such terms as "archetypal unconscious" and "unitive awakening" in the sixth century, but his "school for the Lord's service" was essentially a systematic method for the awakening of the unitive imagination (50)." And the qualitative and quantitative focus of his school was psalmody. Benedictine monasticism refined the training of the unitive imagination to a high art, but the same potential lies in all of us. The cultivation of psalmody can help anyone to live a more focused life in the spirit.

Discussion of the very original—and most important aspects of the "hidden wisdom of psalmody" comes early, in Chapter 3 of Part One. As mentioned above, it could well be basic reading for all persons interested in an essentially spiritual way of life inspired by St. Benedict. Proceeding from the observation that the religious tradition based upon Benedict's *Rule* seems to have no actual spiritual *praxis*, in distinction to **all** other religious traditions, which offer "elaborate training in breathing, meditation, stimulation of the inner body through conscious vibrations, strengthening the power of conscious attention." Bourgeault reexamines the tradition. What is the "actual technology of transformation"? Her perceptive answer is that such a rigorous training **does** indeed exist, "lurking, just below the surface, in the Divine Office." "The esoteric training is accomplished in the choir, with Gregorian chant as the premiere vessel for the actual rearrangement of conscious perception (29)."

The author supports her thesis with a clear presentation of the four basic transformative principles underlying all sacred chanting. And again, as the volume's sub-title promises, she presents them as elements which we today can also work with toward a more focused, awakened life. In many traditions, she suggests, chanting is "fundamentally a deep immersion experience in the creative power of the university." The chanter makes music with the four basic chanting elements of which the earth was fashioned and through which all spiritual transformation take place—**breath**; **tone** or vibration when voice is added to breath; **intentionality** or meaning of words, especially important in Christianity where conscious attention and consent to the meaning of a passage is crucial; and **community**, listening to one another and adjusting to one another (32-34).

* * * * * *

Rounding out the good points of *Chanting* are its comprehensive index of topics, a glossary of technical terms, an extensive bibliography of primary and secondary sources, and its very listenable CD of chant examples. The CD contains chanting by the author herself and her groups, as well as examples from other communities, and its emphasis is always practical, do-able, and sincere.

IV.

I conclude with a personal witness to the practical effectiveness of this volume's offerings. At our regular bi-monthly gathering of Benedictine oblates, I presented an overview of *Chanting* as part of our educational program. I asked those present if they would be willing to try out the author's suggestions, using the familiar opening of the Benedictine office: "O God, come to my assistance, O Lord make haste to help me" as our chant text. I asked them first to find their own point of resonance and to feel their body resonate, simply by singing a tone, then adding the words "O God." We then chanted these sentences together for several minutes, using the simple Anglican tone Bougeault suggests. That was the extent of my plan for the group, and I expected to conclude the session with some discussion of their reaction. But when after the minutes of chanting I gave a gentle signal to cease, ready for reactions, we experienced instead an additional several minutes of profound meditative silence. The experimental chanting had indeed drawn the neophyte chanters into a different, deeper realm. And when we did discuss the "experiment," the predominant reaction was appreciation.

This volume can make anyone want to jump into the practice of chant. But it offers much, much more than directions for chanting. Anyone serious about becoming more aware of the presence of the Divine in their life can profit greatly from reading it, considering its insights, and applying many of its suggestions, even apart from an actual chanting practice.

Further, there are so many echoes of Benedict's *Rule* and so many probing references to and subtle meditations on foundational aspects of the Benedictine "way" in this volume that it might serve as required formation reading for monastics and oblates within the Benedictine tradition. For instance, Bourgeault's recognition that "thinking with the heart" is what psalmody furthers, constitutes a valuable gloss on Benedict's invitation to his daughters and sons to "listen with the ear of your heart" and to make such heart-listening the basic attitude of their lives.

Notes:

1. Cynthia Bourgeault, *Centering Prayer and Inner Awakening*. Cambridge, Mass.: Cowley Publications, 2004. The author has a richly diverse background of spiritual traditions and *praxis*. Her first-hand experience of eastern as well as western practices provides solid foundation for her discussion of the contemplative path. She is a hermit, an Episcopal priest, a medievalist, and a musicologist.

2. Bourgeault's discussion of the role our **voice** plays within our existence (in Ch. 3 and 7, pp. 33 and 75-78) will probably be quite new to most readers, and also most certainly mind-opening. One of the "hidden" truths long known and long lost to most Christians, her presentation shares much with the insights offered by study of the Aramaic Gospels (e.g. Douglas-Klotz, *Prayers of the Cosmos*) and the theology of twelfth-century Hildegard of Bingen's recognition of the Eucharistic/Incarnational essence of singing. "[T]rue voice is closely intertwined with true self . . . ." Our true singing voice is intimately connected to our authentic self, and "this authentic self is nothing less than the glory of God written in you as your *being . . . .(76-77)*"

3. An endnote on endnotes: One of the pleasures of this volume are its endnotes, several of which amount to mini-discourses on important topics. Bourgeault has the gift of focusing in on the essential elements of complex issues, such as the Cistercian (Trappist) method of transformation (pp. 214-215) and her characterization of the Celtic, Wisdom-oriented spirituality contrasted with the Roman style of Catholic Christianity (p. 229). She also includes extensive bibliographical references for further exploration as well as results of personal experience of the topics under discussion.

Dewey W. Kramer

DRISCOLL, Jeremy, *A Monk's Alphabet: Moments of Stillness in a Turning World* (Boston: New Seeds, 2006), pp. 210. ISBN-10: 1-59030-3733-3. (Hardcover) $19.95.

One must search far and wide in monastic writing to find a book such as this—one that speaks not *about* monasticism, but *out of* monasticism as a daily experience—a book of a monk going about being a monk—albeit in some circumstances outside a monastery. We accompany the fertile and subtle mind of Jeremy Driscoll inside his monastery of Mt. Angel in Oregon, and follow him to Rome, where he teaches at San Anselmo, to Paris and elsewhere. All is written with a sense of place, and love for community and its characters. Unforgettable is "Bonnie," his late Abbot, who loved to reenact ham scenes from the worst movies, and did so on his death bed, in a role of a sheriff who had been shot.

More intriguing still are visits to Driscoll's own inner thoughts—not didactic expositions, but subtle questioning, a mind puzzled with life: "Nothing that exists is necessary. But everything that exists, does. Tell me why, and I shall be much relieved."

While theology is a serious part of his life, Driscoll thinks in the context of prayer and speaks out of silence. His aim is "to think clearly and deeply and to do so with love." His willingness to write tentatively gives one a gentle nudge along in one's own hesitant search:

> There must be a way of being tentative that could be beautiful, helpful, that could move us closer to some greater grasp of things. So here is a goal for words proffered: humble speech in which the silence from which the speaker emerges and soon returns is also heard as a living, life-giving space.

These explorative, broadly diverse and sometimes whimsical *Pensees* are arranged alphabetically, so strive for no logical or chronological order. How could they? Here is a mind at play that often brings a smile, one salted with wisdom. In trying to shape thoughts about, for instance, the Risen Christ, he finds himself left with *nothing*: "...in that nothing I have this hope: that he is somewhere between the lines of it." The lines are open enough to be not a trap but web behind which one might sense a presence.

One carries away as well, a sense of what it is like to *be* a monk; one sees contemplative living from inside—or simply, what it is to be a human being in the midst of it all:

I am undone by the Mystery of it all: the mystery of our human living in the monastery, of our time in the world and in the Church.

Br. Paul Quenon

AU, Wilkie and Noreen Cannon Au, *The Discerning Heart: Exploring the Christian Path* (New York/Mahwah, N.J.: Paulist Press), pp. 248. ISBN 0-8091-4372-0 (paperback). $18.95.

The authors of *The Discerning Heart*, husband and wife team Wilkie and Noreen Cannon Au, aim in this study to present a holistic, adult vision of the practice of spiritual discernment. Before marriage both were longtime members of Catholic religious communities in which spiritual formation in the Ignatian mode was taken seriously. Presently Au teaches in the area of the pastoral ministry and spirituality at Loyola Marymount University while Noreen Cannon Au is in practice as a Jungian psychoanalyst. They pool their expertise to present a view of discernment that takes seriously the rich Ignatian heritage of Christianity while being cognizant of the wisdom of various schools of psychology as they relate to the development of an individually informed and inspired conscience. On occasion the complaint has been raised in Christian circles that the language of therapeutic psychology has invaded and even co-opted the traditional language of Christianity. These authors have managed to avoid this and give us instead a refreshing and wise guidebook in which the insights of psychology serve as important tools to facilitate inner freedom so that the Spirit has room to work.

The Discerning Heart reveals itself from the outset to be firmly planted in the theological tradition of Ignatian Christian humanism by asserting that the whole world can communicate divine guidance and that therefore discernment must take into account the many doorways through which God may pass in one's life. The opening chapter also affirms that finding and choosing God in all things is not simply a matter of passive assent to authority but that human beings are designed and called as loved sinners (to use the Ignatian phrase) to cooperate with grace in the process of detecting the movement of the divine Spirit in the world and in the human heart. An *adult* faith is thus required, one that proceeds from an "informed and inspired conscience," not from the remnant of childhood dependency.

Discernment for the Aus is not simply a technique for making a specific decision but a long, patient process of staying open to the dynamic prompting of the Spirit over the changing course of the life-cycle as well as growing in self-knowledge: the ways our distinctive personalities predispose us to grace, and the ways we are led astray or tempted to resist it. The wonderfully titled chapter, "Refining the Acoustics of the Heart," introduces the idea that the person is a psycho-somatic unity and that all aspects of that unity are rightly to be consulted in the discernment process. Mind, body, emotional states, imagination, feelings, intuition, and the senses all have their part to play. The goal is the integration of reason, affect and religious experience. Practical exercises such as a discernment process based on the Ignatian tradition and a template for discernment based on Friedrich von Hugel's theory of integrated development are included to suggest ways in which such integration might be encouraged.

Never losing sight of fundamental Christian humanist principles, the Aus counsel respect for individual differences and encourage their readers to take into account distinctive personal experiences of sensing God present and active. Here the psychological theory of multiple intelligences is brought to bear on the subject and case studies of individuals who have had deep insight into God's movements in their lives through various modes – linguistic, logical-mathematical, bodily-kinesthetic, spatial, musical, interpersonal and intra-personal – are included. A further chapter deals with the issue of images of God and how these affect discernment. Distorted images can impede true interior freedom. Thus the authors introduce the idea of "professed" and "operative" divine images and suggest methods for making implicit images explicit thus liberating the seeker to be available to the Spirit's prompting.

The chapter entitled Desires and Discernment seems particularly rich as it tackles the topic from multiple perspectives. The authors begin once again with an Ignatian (i.e. Christian humanist) assumption that discernment is more about *focusing our desires* than about any sort of technique, more about the quality of our relationships (with God, self and others) than any easy answer. At the center of the chapter is the classic affirmation that the desire for God is the plumb-line of the human heart as well as the classic themes of the mis-direction of desire and the freedom of the heart to choose with and for God. Thus the authors concern themselves with what psychologists call "introjects," (the "shoulds" we carry around with us) as well as unruly passions and untamed urges that inhibit our uncovering the deepest desires of our hearts And they make distinctions between wishful, instinctual, tentative and definitive desires as well as between root and branch desires. They provide some wise guidelines for determining the nature of authentic desires. In this dense chapter they also touch on the oft-misunderstood issue of "the will of God."

The chapter on dreams as messages from God is Jungian in orientation and includes a balanced discussion of the pitfalls of literal dream interpretation as well as instructions on fruitful dreamwork. *The Discerning Heart* closes with a plea for patience in the work of the spiritual life, the cultivation of a contemplative capacity for "not-knowing," and ongoing fidelity to the personal path that unfolds as one pays attention to the many varied ways that God is discovered in all things.

Each chapter in this book that is so rich in theory ends with a concrete exercise that a reader (or a group or spiritual guide) could use to further integrate the insights gleaned from reading. These include instructions for drawing a personal compass that allows one to visualize the competing energies that typically compel one; an imaginative meditation on one's inner wisdom circle designed to illuminate which parts of the self generally dominate; instructions for noticing experience based on the Gestalt Continuum of Awareness; a process to make implicit God images explicit; suggestions for sorting out secondary authentic desires including one based on the parable of the rich young man from the gospel of Mark; and a dream interpretation guide.

As suggested in this review, the theological framework of book is grounded in the Ignatian tradition. It is also attentive to Scripture: many of the stories used to illustrate the authors' ideas are drawn from the Old or New Testaments. There are nods to other traditions of Christian discernment throughout, for example the Quaker Clearness Committee or von Hugel's integrative approach. But these are few. As wonderful a book as this is it has some notable omissions, especially the wisdom of the Carmelite tradition: nowhere is there mention of the insights of John of the Cross or Teresa of Avila. Nor is there any inclusion of the important teachings of the desert fathers or Eastern Orthodoxy. Similarly, the Quaker tradition, which contains much that can be plumbed on the topic of discernment, especially communal discernment, is not much in evidence. But then, the book does not claim to be a study of the history of Christian discernment or to be inclusive of the wide variety of Christian approaches to the practice. Given what the Aus set out to do, and the framework in which they explicitly work, the achievement is a fine one. *The Discerning Heart* is written in an accessible manner but it is grounded in tested and tried spiritual and psychological wisdom so that, as clear a book as it is to read, the content conveyed is anything but simplistic or overly-simplified. It will be a valuable resource to individual seekers as well as to spiritual guides, teachers and students of spiritual formation.

Wendy M. Wright

RIZZETTO, Diane Eshin, *Waking Up to What You Do: A Zen Practice for Meeting Every Situation with Intelligence and Compassion* (Boston: Shambhala, 2006), pp. 197. ISBN 1-59030-342-3. $14.00.

Diane Eshin Rizzetto teaches at the Bay Zen Center in Oakland, California, and *Waking Up to What You Do* explores the ethical precepts of Zen Buddhism, and is written for a general audience. Like her teacher, Charlotte Joko Beck—author of *Everyday Zen* and Zen teacher at the Zen Center of San Diego—Rizzetto presents the teachings of Zen in a way that is clear, inviting, and practical. The precepts, Rizzetto says, are "keys to self-discovery, allowing us to see how our habitual patterns of thinking lead us to do things that are hurtful to ourselves and others." The precepts can serve as "a tool for waking up to our reactive thinking," and they can "reveal with crystal clarity the truth that our happiness and well-being are intricately connected to the happiness and well-being of others."

There have been many sets of precepts in the history of Buddhism. The set of sixteen precepts familiar to contemporary Zen practitioners dates back at least to Dogen Zenji,[1] the thirteenth-century founder of the Soto school of Zen in Japan. The first three precepts are the "three refuges," that is, taking refuge in the Three Treasures of Buddhism: the Buddha, the Dharma (the teachings of the Buddha), and the Sangha (the monastic community or, more broadly in the contemporary West, the community of practitioners). The next three precepts, the "pure precepts," are general ethical resolutions to refrain from evil, to do good, and to liberate all beings. And finally, the ten "grave precepts" are more specific ethical resolutions—and these are the subject of *Waking Up to What You Do.*

Traditionally, these precepts have been expressed negatively, as commitments to *refrain* from certain actions, and Rizzetto appreciates this formulation, which she says provides clear parameters for our behavior. But like many Western Zen teachers, Rizzetto prefers to express the precepts positively, as commitments to *aspire* to certain actions—"as pointers, directing us toward our natural propensity to take action out of love and concern for one another." So, for instance, the precept traditionally phrased as "not lying" becomes, in Rizzetto's formulation, "speaking truthfully," and "not killing" becomes "supporting life."

The first part of the book introduces the precepts, explores the Buddhist teaching of interconnectedness and the "dream of self," and explains a method for practicing with the precepts. The first step is "engaging the observer": patiently and nonjudgmentally observing our own behavior with regard to one of the precepts. The next step is "deepening the observation" to include our thoughts, emotions, and bodily sensations. Finally, we inquire even more deeply, exploring the "requirements" we place on ourselves and the world and engaging the precept as a stop sign for our reactionary behavior, and thereby opening up space for other possibilities. Practicing with the precepts, she says, enables us to move away from reactive patterns centered on the "self" and find the freedom to do *"what best serves life"* (emphasis hers).

The second part of the book explores the precepts one at a time. Because the book is aimed at a general audience, including people with no knowledge of or experience with Zen, Rizzetto skips two

396   The Merton Annual 20 (2007)

precepts that are more narrowly "Buddhist" than the others: "not withholding spiritual and material assets" and "not disparaging the Three Treasures." (In working with her Zen students, she includes them.) One chapter of her book is devoted to each of the other eight precepts: speaking truthfully; speaking of others with openness and possibility; meeting others on equal ground; cultivating a clear mind; taking only what is freely given and giving freely of all that I can; engaging in sexual intimacy respectfully and with an open heart; letting go of anger; and supporting life.

Rizzetto invites us to view the proscribed actions not as "moral defects" but as "the root or source of suffering." She observes that we often break the precepts because of our self-centered "requirements" about life—our deeply held beliefs about how we or others or the world ought to be. Rizzetto wants to help us see these "requirements" in action and let go of them.

This notion of "requirements" is the part of the book that I expect will stay with me. I particularly appreciated Rizzetto's reminders that we have self-centered requirements not only about the "outside" world, including other people, but also about ourselves. I am sometimes able to remember that I create suffering by "requiring" the world to be a certain way, but then I am apt to "require" that I not have those requirements about the world. Rizzetto reminded me that this is just another requirement—one about myself and my attitudes toward things—and that I can let go of that sort of requirement also.

The part of the book that I had the most trouble with was the chapter on "supporting life." It is interesting to consider, as Rizzetto does, that we inevitably take life, if only the lives of germs in a cut we disinfect or microorganisms in a glass of water we drink, and that even vegetarians take life in order to eat. It is also worth observing, as Rizzetto does, that decisions about issues such as using life-support technologies or engaging in war are often quite complicated and not black and white. Still, I wished Rizzetto had offered more specific suggestions about which sorts of actions tend to better "support life." For instance, I wished she had suggested that her readers would probably find that killing fewer animals and more plants for food would be more conducive, in a variety of ways, to "supporting life." And I wished she had said that what probably better supports life is to not have an abortion rather than to have one. I wonder, though, if Rizzetto might offer more specific ethical suggestions when dealing one-on-one with a particular student in a particular situation. Regarding the issue of abortion, she does suggest an interesting practice, for both mother and partner, of resting a hand on the mother's belly and patiently observing, without judgment, all the thoughts and feelings that arise. She also suggests listing the reasons that you would or would not continue the pregnancy and then noting how many of these "reflect your genuine concern for the unborn life and how many are concerned with how this unborn life serves or does not serve you."

Rizzetto has taken on a difficult project in this book—trying to help us change our way of being in the world—and bracketing our judgments about actions can make it much easier to observe our actions and thus to change how we act. Perhaps Rizzetto sometimes errs to the side of bracketing judgments too thoroughly, but *Waking Up to What You Do* does something valuable and all too rare: makes the practice of self-observation seem not only worthwhile but also interesting and even exciting.

Note

1. William M. Bodiford, *Soto Zen in Medieval Japan* (Honolulu, Hawaii: University of Hawaii Press, 1993),pp. 170–71.

Kim Boykin

BEHRENS, James. *Portraits of Grace, Images and Words from the Monastery of the Holy Spirit*, Preface by Patrick Hart (Skokie, IL: ACTA Publications, 2007), pp. 144. ISBN 0879463341. $19.95.

This color portfolio of good clear photographs is the work of writer / photographer James Behrens, a monk of the Conyers, Georgia Cistercian Monastery. Fr. James is known for his previous collections of meditations wherein he is best when focusing on the ordinary scenes or objects which he observes within his monastic world, or through memory, as he sparks his reader's imagination with stories of his past in relation to the sacred.

This book, sending messages both through photographs and texts, works like Fr. James earlier meditations collected in his earlier books. (He was asked to do this book after he sent a note-card with one of his photos to his editor—who then realized the keenness of eye and suggested Fr. James do such a gathering.)

The photographs are almost always carefully focused studies—pecan shells unfolding, preying mantis waiting—sometimes a tiny bit cute (Smiling Buddhas, words on a soda vending machine)—yet always arresting. Meant as a device for meditation this book is clearly a success because it is so modest in intent yet full of vision.

If one knows the way books of photographs which have been done of Gethsemani—the Motherhouse of Conyers—and they have ranged from the professional by Shirley Burden (with Merton's text) to the informal by Patrick Hart (photos made with Merton's camera)—it is possible to see what James Behrens so successfully seeks, does, accomplishes.

This book is of value for several reasons. It shows the viewer the beauty of the ordinary; it introduces the reader to the words of an insightful observer; it should help the user to pray and meditate.

Louis Scribbelarious

Contributors

David Belcastro is Professor of Religious Studies and Chair of the Department of Religion and Philosophy at Capital University in Bexley, Ohio. He published the Bibliographic Survey about Merton Scholarship, "An Obscure Theology Misread, 2003 Bibliographic Review," in *The Merton Annual*, Vol. 17.

Cynthia Bourgeault, Ph.D., is an Episcopal priest, writer, and retreat leader. She is the principal guest teacher for the Contemplative Society in Victoria, British Columbia, and a core faculty member of the Spiritual Paths Graduate Institute in Aspen, Colorado, and Santa Barbara, California. She is author of several books, including *Centering Prayer and Inner Awakening*, *The Wisdom Way of Knowing*, *Chanting the Psalms*, and *Love Is Stronger than Death*.

Kim Boykin, author of *Zen for Christians: A Beginner's Guide* (Jossey-Bass, 2003), is a Ph.D. candidate in religion at Emory University. She is Assistant Professor of Religious Studies at Carroll College in Waukesha, Wisconsin.

Ernest Daniel Carrere, O.C.S.O., is on leave from Gethsemani Abbey and currently serving on the faculty of Fresno Pacific University. He holds a J.D. and Ph.D. in psychological and religious anthropology.

Glenn Crider, production manager and editorial contributor for *The Merton Annual*, is a Th.M. candidate at Candler School of Theology, Emory University, where he studies modern philosophical theology. He has contributed to *The Merton Annual* since Vol. 14.

Catherine Crosby, a former Montessori Department Chair, heads *Pax Christi* Atlanta while serving as a spiritual director, retreat presenter, and twenty-five year catechist.

Robert Leigh Davis, Professor of English at Wittenberg University, teaches courses on American literature, the American Renaissance, the Beat Generation, and literature and medicine. Professor Davis' book on Walt Whitman's career as a Civil War nurse, *Whitman and the Romance of Medicine*, was published by the University of California Press. His current research focuses on issues of spirituality and grace in American poetry.

Paul R. Dekar is Niswonger Professor of Evangelism and Mission at Memphis Theological Seminary, where he has taught since January 1995. Recent publications include *Creating the Beloved Community. A History of the Fellowship of Reconciliation in the United States* (Telford: Cascadia, and Scottdale: Herald, 2005) and *Community of the Transfiguration. Journey of a New Monastic Community* (Eugene: Wipf and Stock, 2007). Member with his wife in a "new monastic" community, he is writing a book about Merton's witness on technology and simple living.

Mark DelCogliano is a Ph.D. student in the Graduate Division of Religion at Emory University, where he studies Patristics. His interests include ancient philosophy, the development of Christian theology, and early Christian monasticism. He has published articles as well as book reviews and translations in *Cistercian Studies Quarterly*, *The American Benedictine Review*, and *The Journal of Christian Studies*.

Keith J. Egan is the President of the Carmelite Institute, Washington, D.C., Aquinas Chair in Catholic Theology Emeritus, Saint Mary's College, and Adjunct Professor of Theology, the University of Notre Dame.

Emile Farge served as priest in the Galveston-Houston diocese from 1961 to 1970. After seeking laicization he received his doctorate from the University of Texas in 1974 in Public Health. He served twenty-four years in local, national and international public health concerns and since 1998 has pursued interests in business, meditation and yoga.

Donald Grayston retired in 2004 from fifteen years of teaching Religious Studies at Simon Fraser University, in Vancouver, British Columbia; he continues to teach part-time at SFU and elsewhere. He is past president of the Thomas Merton Society of Canada, current president of the International Thomas Merton Society, and co-director of the Pacific Jubilee Program in Spiritual Formation and Spiritual Direction.

Dana Greene, Dean Emerita, Oxford College of Emory University, served as the Acting Director of the Aquinas Center of Theology at Emory, 2006-2008. She has published books about Evelyn Underhill and Maisie Ward.

Martha Gross holds both an MTS and a Certificate in Spiritual Direction from Spring Hill College. She draws on Merton's insights and wisdom in giving spiritual direction and conducting retreats. Her first Merton book is still her favorite – a ragged and somewhat dog-eared, hardcover edition of *Contemplative Prayer* acquired in 1970.

Richard J. Hauser, S.J., teaches at Creighton University, Omaha, NE, where he is Professor of Theology and Director of the masters program in Christian Spirituality. His interest in Merton began in 1972 with his doctoral dissertation comparing the approaches to religious experience of Abraham Maslow and Thomas Merton. Hauser has written three books and numerous articles on contemporary Christian spirituality with particular focus on contemplation, discernment of spirits and suffering. He also regularly presents workshops on these topics.

E. Glenn Hinson is Professor Emeritus of Spirituality and John Loftis Professor of Church History at Baptist Theological Seminary at Richmond. In retirement he teaches at Baptist Seminary of Kentucky in Lexington, Bellarmine University, and Louisville Presbyterian Seminary. He and Merton developed a friendship when Hinson took students from the Southern Baptist Seminary in Louisville to the Abbey of Gethsemani in 1960.

Kathy Hoffman discovered Merton's writings during her studies at Spring Hill College, where she is currently pursuing an MA in biblical studies. She teaches Old & New Testament and World Religions at Blessed Trinity Catholic High School in Roswell, GA, but finds her greatest joy being with her family and traveling with her husband, Don.

Terrence Kardong is editor of the *American Benedictine Review.* He has written extensively about the *Rule* of St. Benedict.

Robert H. King, a retired professor of philosophy and religion and former academic dean at Millsaps College in Jackson, MS, now lives in Green Mountain Falls, Colorado. In 1998, King was a scholar-in-residence at the Institute for Ecumenical and Cultural Research in Collegeville, Minnesota. Recent publications include *Thomas Merton and Thich Nhat Hanh: Engaged Spirituality in an Age of Globalization* (Continuum, 2001) and, with his wife Elizabeth, *Autumn Years: Taking the Contemplative Path* (Continuum, 2004).

Dewey Weiss Kramer is Professor Emerita of German and Humanities. Her teaching and research have gravitated increasingly toward subjects with a spiritual dimension, with current focus on Hildegard of Bingen. She has had Benedictine connections for decades, going back to her grade-school years and recently gave the Community Retreat for the Benedictine Sisters of Holy Name Monastery in Florida. She is a founding editor of *The Merton Annual*; author of *Open to the Spirit*, the history of the Cistercian Monastery of the Holy Spirit in Georgia; Oblate of St. Benedict's Monastery in Minnesota; and an avid performer on the recorder. She also happily shares home, interests, and activities both scholarly and otherwise, with Victor A. Kramer.

Victor A. Kramer, founding editor of *The Merton Annual*, has seen some fifty books through the press. At present he gives days of recollection and retreats and is a spiritual director (CSD, 2006).

Kilian McDonnell is Professor Emeritus of Theology at St. John's University, Collegeville, MN. He is the founder of the St. John's Institute for Ecumenical and Cultural Research. He is also presently active as a published poet.

Paul Montello is Professor Emeritus in the School of Education at Georgia State University in Atlanta. One of his areas of expertise is Leadership. He is a member of the local International Thomas Merton (Book Club) Chapter in Decatur, GA.

Patrick F. O'Connell teaches English and Theology at Gannon University, Erie, PA. A founding member and former president of the International Thomas Merton Society, he serves as editor of *The Merton Seasonal*. He is co-author of *The Thomas Merton Encyclopedia* (2002), and editor of *The Vision of Thomas Merton* (2003), *Cassian and the Fathers* (2005), *Pre-Benedictine Monasticism* (2006), the first two volumes of Merton's novitiate conferences, and *Introduction to Christian Mysticism* (2007).

Raymond Pedrizetti served as Prior at St. John's Abbey, Collegeville, MN, until 2006. He has contributed articles to various theological and philosophical journals. He taught philosophy at St. John's for many years.

Malgorzata Poks holds a doctorate in American Literature from the University of Lublin, Poland. Her interests concern spirituality and modern American poetry, especially the poetry of Thomas Merton and Denise Levertov. She teaches courses and seminars in American Literature and Culture at the English Teacher Training College in Sosnowiec, Poland. Poks was a Shannon scholar in 2001/02 and has contributed articles to scholarly journals and publications, including *The Merton Annual*. She is a member of The Thomas Merton Society of Great Britain and Ireland and an International Advisor from Poland for The ITMS. Her book *Thomas Merton and Latin America: A Consonance of Voices* is about to be released in Poland.

Paul Quenon has been a monk at the Abbey of Gethsemani for nearly fifty years. He has published two books of poetry, and his various photography exhibits have appeared in the United States and Canada. He received his novitiate formation under Thomas Merton, has been a member of the Board of the ITMS and is a board member of The Thomas Merton Institute.

Louis Scribbelarious is a friend of several Cistercian monasteries. He usually resides in Dekalb County, Georgia.

Phillip Thompson, J.D. Ph.D., is the director of the Leadership Certificate Program in the School of Public Policy at the Georgia Institute of Technology. He is completing a book manuscript on Catholic intellectuals and their engagement with technology and science in the twentieth century that includes a chapter on Thomas Merton.

Bonnie Thurston is a founding member of the International Thomas Merton Society, and served as its third president. Professor Thurston has published many articles on Merton, particularly about the poetry and Merton's work in inter-religious dialogue. She edited *Merton and Buddhism* (Fons Vitae Press, 2007) and, having cheerfully abandoned academe, lives in solitude in West Virginia.

Harry Wells is Associate Dean of the College of Arts, Humanities, and Social Sciences and Professor of Religious Studies at Humboldt State University.

Wendy M. Wright is Professor of Theology and John C. Kenefick Faculty Chair in the Humanities at Creighton University. She often gives retreats and days of recollection.

Index

512